Economics of South African Townships

A WORLD BANK STUDY

Economics of South African Townships

Special Focus on Diepsloot

Sandeep Mahajan, Editor

WORLD BANK GROUP
Washington, D.C.

Contents

Boxes

Figures

Map

Photos

Tables

Acknowledgments

This report was prepared by a core team led by Sandeep Mahajan and that comprised Hans Binswanger, Catherine Cross, Rob Davies, Fernando Im, Taye Mengistae, Phindile Ngwenya, Kate Philip, Dirk van Seventer, Dorothe Singer, and Precious Zikhali (who was with the National Treasury at the time of her contribution). The team benefited from useful contributions of Evans Chinembiri (TIPS), Illana Melzer (Eighty20, consultant), Karuna Mohan (consultant), Subethri Naidoo (AFTU1), and Andrew Siddle (consultant). Mzolisi Mbikwana (consultant) was a tremendous resource in the township of Diepsloot, providing invaluable insights into the political and economic realities on the ground and accompanying the team on many interviews. Melanie Jaya (AFCS1) helped process the report at various stages. Mary Anderson edited the report.

The report was prepared under the guidance of Makhtar Diop (vice president, Africa Region), Marcelo Giugale (sector director, Africa Poverty Reduction and Economic Management), John Panzer (sector manager, Africa Poverty Reduction and Economic Management), Asad Alam (country director, South Africa), and Ruth Kagia (former country director, South Africa). The team is grateful to Shanta Devarajan (chief economist, Middle East and North Africa Region, and former chief economist, Africa region) for inspiring this report through several discussions.

The peer reviewers were Louise Fox (lead economist, AFRCE), Ravi Kanbur (Cornell University), William Maloney (lead economist, Development Economics Research Group, Macroeconomics and Growth), and Ingrid Woolard (University of Cape Town). We also gratefully acknowledge comments received from: Kwabena Amakwah-Ayeh, Deon Filmer, Michael Fuchs, Austin Kilroy, Gladys Lopez-Acevedo, Renosi Mokate (National Treasury), Patrick Osewe, Onur Ozlu, Laura Papi (International Monetary Fund), Kathrin Plangemann, Catriona Purfield, Ritva Reinikka, Jamal Saghir, Marco Scuriatti, David Sislen, Simi Siwisa, Roland White, and Chunlin Zhang.

The team greatly appreciates the solid support from its government counterparts: in particular, Fundi Tshazibana (deputy director general, National Treasury) and Neva Makgetla (deputy director general, Economic Development Department). National Treasury officials provided guidance at various stages and took the spirit of collaboration around the report to an admirable level in enabling one of their staff at the time (Precious Zikhali) coauthor one of the chapters of this report.

The field surveys in Diepsloot were carried out by Outsourced Insights, led by Stephen Rule and Serumula Siema. Craig Schwabe led a team at Africa Scope and provided excellent GIS support to the team.

Finally, this report could not have been written without the excellent survey work carried out by a team of remarkably talented young men and women from the township of Diepsloot: Thabang Progress Bodumele, Samkelo Buthelezi, Tinyiko Chauke, Ntombikayise Jondo, Lazarus Tebogo Lerumo, Miracle Majwe, Vhonani Makhado, Lettah Disebo Manamela, Minah Mashilo, Lerato Mathebula, Moyahabo Belinda Matlo, Evelyn Tebatso Matlou, Casius Mogano, Nancy Mohubedu, Rosina Mokhudu, Mphokoana Mokoena, Itumeleng Philia Morulane, Derick Ncube, Fhatuwani Netshidzati, Dimakatso Papale, Sello Aman Papale, Patrick Rabotapi, Mahlatse Fortunate Ramano, Mmantsopa Salphina Mangena, Zolani Saule, Matome Raymond Setaphala, Tiyani Hamphrey Simango, Vincent Vusumuzi Siroba, and Mahlaba Jacquoline Tlhako.

Vice President:	Makhtar Diop
Country Director:	Asad Alam
Sector Director:	Marcelo Giugale
Sector Manager:	John Panzer
Task Team Leader:	Sandeep Mahajan

About the Authors

Sandeep Mahajan is the World Bank's lead economist for Vietnam. At the time of the writing of this book, he was lead economist for Botswana, Lesotho, Namibia, South Africa, and Swaziland. With close to two decades of experience at the World Bank, he has led the Bank's policy dialogue in a number of client countries on a broad range of economic management issues. His research interests and publications cover the fields of macroeconomics, growth, political economy, and financial sector development. Born in New Delhi, India, Sandeep received his B.Com(Hons) from Delhi University and his Ph.D. in economics from Georgetown University.

Hans Binswanger is a development economist and a freelance consultant who currently is an extraordinary professor at the University of Pretoria in South Africa. He has done research on agricultural and rural development issues in India, Africa, and Latin America, covering a broad range of issues. During his 25 years at the World Bank, he has been a researcher, policy analyst, and designer of development programs. This involved assistance to countries in Latin America, Africa, and Asia in the development of agricultural and rural development strategies and in designing more effective agricultural and rural development programs. He has also coauthored the World Bank's rural development strategy of 1996. He is a fellow of the American Association for the Advancement of Sciences and of the American Association of Agricultural Economists, and has received the Elmherst medal of the International Association of Agricultural Economists.

Rob Davies is a Zimbabwean economist, living in Harare. He worked for many years at the University of Zimbabwe. He has also taught at a number of Universities in the United Kingdom, United States, and South Africa. He was a visiting research fellow at the Human Science Research Council in Pretoria. He currently provides capacity building advice to the National Treasury in South Africa, is a senior research fellow at TIPS, and is a director of *tralac* in Cape Town. He has published on a wide range of topics including the informal sector, trade, economywide modeling, and political economy.

Taye Mengistae is a senior economist with the Finance and Private Sector Development, Eastern and Southern Africa team of the World Bank's Africa region. Previously, he was with the World Bank's Development Research Group. He has published numerous articles in leading academic economic journals. His country work experience includes China, Ethiopia, India, Ghana, Kenya, Pakistan, and South Africa, and Zambia. His main areas of research interest include globalization, export competitiveness, capital flows, innovation, education, and labor markets. He holds a PhD in economics from Oxford University and an MA in economic statistics from the University of Leeds.

Dirk van Seventer lives in New Zealand. He studied economics at the Rijksuniversiteit in Groningen, Netherlands. He subsequently worked for 20 years as an economic analyst in South Africa—among others at the Development Bank of Southern Africa and as a research fellow at TIPS. After a 6-year stint as information analyst at the New Zealand Department of Labor, he rejoined TIPS in 2011 as a part-time research fellow combined with a role as economist at the New Zealand economic consulting firm Infometrics. His work focuses on regional, trade, and economywide data and policy analysis and capacity building thereof.

Precious Zikhali is an economist with the Poverty Reduction and Economic Management Unit at the World Bank. She currently supports the poverty and inequality work program of the World Bank covering Botswana, Lesotho, Namibia, South Africa, and Swaziland. Before joining the World Bank in 2013, she was a director of environmental economics in the Microeconomic Policy Unit within the Economic Policy Division, National Treasury of South Africa, where she was involved in interdepartmental efforts to incorporate green growth policies into the country's broader sustainable development agenda. She holds a PhD in economics from the University of Gothenburg, Sweden.

Phindile Ngwenya has been the World Bank's research analyst for Botswana, Lesotho, Namibia, South Africa, and Swaziland, where she has provided support for the macroeconomics and fiscal work for the past 6 years. Before joining the World Bank, she was senior economist with the National Treasury, where she focused on economic policy issues pertaining to the agriculture and mining sectors. Her research interests are in economic policy, natural resource economics, and poverty. She holds a MComm. in agriculture economics from the University of Pretoria.

Dorothe Singer is a consultant in the Finance and Private Sector Research Team of the Development Research Group at the World Bank. Her research interests include access to finance and the role of institutions in international finance. She holds a Ph.D. in economics from Tilburg University, The Netherlands.

Catherine Cross presently serves as the Human Sciences Research Council's lead consultant on the Department of Science and Technology/Council for Scientific and Industrial Research/Human Sciences Research Council partnership project

StepSA, previously IPDM, where her work has included important new research on spatial planning in the light of antipoverty impacts at household level. Catherine was born in the United States and received her MA in anthropology from University of Michigan, but has spent most of her adult life in South Africa. She has published extensively in the field of migration and settlement studies, and done consultancy work for South Africa's Presidency, the World Bank, USAID, GTZ, and the International Labour Organization in Geneva, as well as for the Development Bank of Southern Africa and the Human Sciences Research Council. Catherine conducted the baseline study of migration and rural densification commissioned for the Cabinet Investment Cluster work that became the National Spatial Development Perspective, and recently completed an Human Sciences Research Council/Financial and Fiscal Commission partnership study of self-financed housing in poor communities for the Financial and Fiscal Commission.

Fernando Im is an economist in the Poverty Reduction and Economic Management Unit at the World Bank, currently working on both South Africa and Swaziland. As a country economist, he has worked extensively in development issues in Southern Africa. Before his current appointment, he worked at the Development Economics, Operations and Strategy Unit of the World Bank. He holds a Ph.D. in economics from the University of Maryland at College Park (United States), an M.A. in economics from McGill University (Canada), and a B.A. in economics from the University of Buenos Aires (Argentina). His research interests are in economic growth, macroeconomics, and international finance.

Kate Philip has 25 years of experience as a development strategist, focusing on issues of inequality, employment creation and inclusive economic development. She has been an advisor to the South African Presidency, she lead a strategy process for the Presidency on inequality and economic marginalization, initiated and program-managed the pilot phase of the Community Work Programme, has consulted to the International Labour Organisation, and has run the employment creation programme of the National Union of Mineworkers for many years. Her PhD dissertation from the University of the Witwatersrand is titled, "Enterprise Development on the Mmargins: Making Markets Work for the Poor?"

Abbreviations

ANC	African National Congress
BEE	Black Economic Empowerment
CBD	central business district
CIPRO	Companies and Intellectual Property Registration office
CoGTA	Cooperation Governance and Traditional Affairs
CSP	Cities Support Program
CWP	Community Works Program
EAs	enumeration areas
EC	enterprise census (Diepsloot)
ES	enterprise survey (Diepsloot)
EU	European Union
FAE	formal advanced economy
FSC	financial sector charter
GDP	gross domestic product
GHS	General Household Survey
GNI	gross national income
GNP	gross national product
HS	household survey (Diepsloot)
IDP	Integrated Development Plan
IES	Income and Expenditure Survey
IME	informal modernizing economy
IS	urban informal settlements
ITE	informal traditional economy
LFS	Labor Force Survey
LSM	Living Standards Measure
MSMEs	micro, small, and medium enterprises
NEET	not in employment, education, or training
NPC	National Planning Commission
NPI	nonprofit institution

OECD	Organisation for Economic Co-operation and Development
OUA	other urban areas
PSU	primary sampling unit
QLFS	Quarterly Labor Force Survey
R	rand
RDP	Reconstruction and Development Program
SAM	Social Accounting Matrix
SAPS	South African Police Service
SASSA	South African Social Security Agency
SASSETA	South African Safety and Security Sector Education and Training Authority
SEZ	special economic zone
SMEs	small and medium enterprises
Stats SA	Statistics South Africa
TS	urban townships
T&IS	urban townships and informal settlements

All monetary amounts are in rand unless otherwise indicated.

Overview

> Development depends not so much on finding optimal combinations for given resources and factors of production as on calling forth and enlisting for development purposes resources and abilities that are hidden, scattered, or badly utilized.
>
> —Albert Hirschman, *The Strategy of Economic Development*, 1958

Introduction

Countries everywhere are divided into two distinct spatial realms: one urban, one rural. Classic models of development predict faster growth in the urban sector, causing rapid migration from rural areas to cities, lifting average incomes in both places. The process continues until the marginal productivity of labor is equalized across the two realms. The pattern of rising urbanization accompanying economic growth has become one of the most visible and self-evident empirical facts of development across the world, with almost 200,000 people making the rural-to-urban trek every day, according to the United Nations. Cities across the world are powering growth, development, and modernization.

The situation in South Africa throws up a trickier and more unconventional challenge. The country has symptoms of a spatial realm that is not fully connected with the urban systems (spatially, socially, or structurally) and is certainly disconnected from the rural economy. This is the realm of the country's townships and informal settlements (T&IS). Conceptually, they are relics of the country's special past, but the policies of postapartheid South Africa have inadvertently kept their contemporary reality alive.

In many ways, the townships and especially the informal settlements are similar to the slums in much of the developing world, although never was a slum formed with as much central planning and purpose as were some of the larger South African townships. Informal settlements in particular contain masses of people compactly huddled together in grim living conditions, evoking images of many a large urban slum. They are also a destination of choice for aspiring urban migrants wanting a foothold in the urban job market. Water, sanitation, electricity connections, and access to public health and education are still highly problematic in the South African T&IS, although not as much as in the urban slums of other countries.

And yet, there is something distinct about the T&IS. They are not rural, not fully urban, lying somewhat in limbo. For one thing, unlike most urban slums, most T&IS are geographically distant from urban economic centers. Widening the already vast spatial divide is the near absence of an affordable public transport system, making job seeking and other forms of economic integration prohibitively expensive. Consider the daily plight of a working woman in the township of Tembisa highlighted in South Africa's *National Development Plan 2030: Our Future: Make It Work* (NPC 2012): "A single mother of four children aged between 3 and 12 lives in Tembisa with her mother. She spends nearly five hours each day commuting to and from work in the Pretoria suburb of Brummeria, where she is an office cleaner. The journeys cost nearly 40 percent of her monthly salary of R 1,900. She leaves home at 05:00 … and may not get home until 19:00. She spends over R 700 a month on transport and nearly 100 hours on the road."

Even where the distances are more manageable, the structural and social barriers are imposing and can just as easily enclose the T&IS into isolation. Up against city bylaws that are enforced with exceptional vigor, even the most entrepreneurial T&IS resident has little chance of knocking on a door in a wealthy neighborhood or of finding a footing in a high-end commercial space to sell his wares. Such a cutoff of market access within national borders is rarely seen in the developing world. Moreover, economic activity in the city centers tends to be skills-intensive, generating a human capital divide that is too wide to allow any form of systematic transition out of the T&IS and into the formal economic structures in the near future. To be sure, formal sector banking and mass-production networks are spreading into the T&IS. But the latter is often at the expense of the local informal sector, and the banking sector's presence is felt more for transaction purposes than for expanding access to funding for local businesses.

Under apartheid, entrepreneurship was discouraged (even outlawed for certain trades), and it has yet to emerge in force in the wider consciousness of T&IS residents. Predictably, then, the economic landscape of T&IS is not teeming with the life and energy of a Dharavi in the middle of Mumbai or a Kibera in Nairobi. Dharavi is reported to have 15,000 single-room factories by one count (Economist 2007), unlike anything seen in any South African township or informal settlement. One can find spanking new shopping malls in South African townships, but it is hard to find the "bustling, informal labour market of street stalls, repair shops, barbers, ad hoc cinemas, and all manner of enterprise" discovered within minutes of entering many of the shantytowns of Africa, Asia, and Latin America. As a result, although South African T&IS account for 38 percent of the country's working-age population, they are home to almost 60 percent of its unemployed.

Motivated by the uniqueness of the South African T&IS and their special place in South African economic and social life, this study seeks to develop a systematic understanding of the structure of the township economy. The study first looks at a number of national datasets and groups them geographically (rural, urban townships, urban informal settlements, and other urban areas) to assess the role that T&IS play in the South African economy. What emerges is a rich information base on the migration patterns to T&IS, changes in their demographic profiles, their labor market characteristics, and their access to public and financial services.

The study then takes a close look at Diepsloot, a large township in the Johannesburg Metropolitan Area, to bring out more vividly the economic realities and choices of township residents. Although atypical in many ways—by the virtue of being newer, poorer, and more informal, with a bigger concentration of migrants (many of them foreign nationals)—than the historically established townships, Diepsloot also retains many of the economic characteristics of South African townships: Issues of joblessness, uneven access to basic public services, and overwhelming levels of crime and violence are almost as pervasive in Diepsloot as they are in other T&IS. At the same time, an emergent informal sector more visibly pervades the township than seen in the average township, which makes it a particularly useful place to study in order to develop an understanding of the kinds of economic activities that are feasible in townships.

It focuses particularly on the nature of business activity in the township, the key investment-climate constraints faced by its firms, income and expenditure patterns across households, and some aggregative social and human indicators. In a first attempt of its kind for a township, the report also develops a Social Accounting Matrix (SAM) of Diepsloot for a comprehensive and consistent picture of the place, including the circular flow of income within the township, the nature of its interaction with the rest of the South African economy, and a simple multiplier analysis of its economy.

It is important to emphasize that, being among the first attempts of its kind, the primary focus of this report is on compiling baseline information on the township economy, not to suggest a fleshed-out course of policy action. Some of the information compiled here tells a coherent story about development patterns in South Africa. But, being an early attempt, much of the information coming out of individual chapters would need to be deepened with further research and analysis before being translated into direct policy action.

A History of South African Townships

As chapter 1 relates, the history of South African townships is very much rooted in the country's apartheid past—their culture steeped in the richness of the struggle against it, their economic infrastructure left in tatters by its oppressive rules and regulations. For the decision makers at the time, the formation of townships reflected the tension between two needs: to keep black people close enough to provide cheap labor and to keep them far enough away to ensure a clear social distance. Of course, they also reserved the option of rolling out the blade wire to maintain that distance if it was ever at risk of being breached. From the start, the rationale was clear: black people—men and women alike—were in the cities as laborers. As far as possible, they were not to become permanent residents or "citizens" of the cities, nor were they to bring their families with them.

Townships under Apartheid

As the mining industry boomed in South Africa, other forms of enterprise and industry grew, too; thus the demand for labor broadened, and so did African urbanization and housing demand. This triggered an extensive national debate on urban policy—a debate that focused on the status of urban Africans, how best to limit their rights to be permanent urban residents, and how to control their movements. What emerged over time was a systematic framework of conditions under which townships could be developed, such as the following (CoGTA 2009, 41):

- The site should be an adequate distance from the white town.
- It should adjoin an existing African township so as to decrease the number of areas for Africans.
- It should be surrounded by open buffer areas.
- It should be separated from the white area by a buffer such as an industrial area.
- It should have land to expand away from white areas.
- It should be within easy distance of the town for transport purposes, by rail rather than road.
- It should have one road that connects it to the town.
- It should be a considerable distance from main and national roads.
- Housing with certain defined minimum standards should be built and allocated in areas for different ethnic groupings.

This, then, shaped the uniquely South African concept of a "township": a dormitory town built at a distance from economic activity as well as from white residential areas; with rows of uniform houses; and historically lacking services and infrastructure such as tarred roads, sanitation, water, or electricity. Even more so, it lacked economic infrastructure in a context in which—far from promoting local economic development—apartheid laws curtailed it.

Structuring a society in this way was possible only because it went hand in hand with the political subordination of nonwhite people—a complex exercise that started from the earliest days of colonialism and was later formalized as "apartheid" after the election of the National Party government in 1948.

A range of complementary policies and legislation further affected South Africa's urbanization process and township development. Among the most notable of these was the Group Areas Act of 1950, which made it compulsory for people to live in areas designated for the exclusive use of their racial group, with everyone classified as black, white, colored, or Indian.

Townships under Democracy

By the time South Africa made its transition to democracy, "the townships" had become a central locus of struggle, imbued with meaning and history unintended by the dry list of characteristics with which the apartheid government had created them. Once the dust had settled and the votes were counted, that dry list of characteristics still shapes the townships' spatial realities.

Perhaps most significantly, the spatial legacy of apartheid has proven tenacious, an outcome to which postapartheid urban development policies have inadvertently contributed. For the first 10 years of democracy, the free public housing program (the Reconstruction and Development Program, or RDP) became the de facto urban development strategy of South Africa, and the imperatives of public housing dominated urban development practice (Pieterse 2009). At one level, the pressure to roll out housing and services meant that this aspect of urban policy ran ahead of the complex processes of building new institutions able to imagine and deliver transformed outcomes at the city-region level. Municipalities were under intense pressure in this regard from above and below, but demand exceeded the limits of their capacities and budgets. Consequently, land-market logic determined the location of new settlements—and the cheapest land was typically the worst-located land.

On another level, a key feature of South Africa's negotiated constitution was the protection of private property and private assets, Pieterse (2009) contends. Therefore, as chapter 1 further discusses, city and local governments found it difficult to institute regulations that would be redistributive in effect, thus negatively affecting property rights in the name of social rights or public goods.

The result has been the massive development of postapartheid townships filled with RDP houses, typically as far—if not farther—from economic opportunities as the townships were under the original apartheid model. Often devoid of public spaces and access to social services, they have benefited from only limited spatial planning to enable local economic development—except to support the minibus taxi industry, which often provides the only form of transport linking these new-generation townships to city hubs and economic opportunities.

Over the same period, there has been massive growth of informal settlements and a new crop of urban townships (and often the two blended together) in and around the urban periphery—often closer to economic opportunities than even the apartheid-era townships. They are a manifestation of the pace of urbanization, acting as the first entry points into the cities for many rural migrants. This in turn reflects a gap in urban development policy that persists: the lack of a coherent strategy to address urbanization.

Among the larger and more dynamic postapartheid settlements is the township of Diepsloot, studied in depth for this report.

A Conceptual Framework for the Township Economy

Even in a very highly developed economy the tendency for capital to flow evenly through the economy is very weak; in a backward economy it hardly exists. Inevitably what one gets are very heavily developed patches of the economy, surrounded by economic darkness.

—Arthur Lewis, "Economic Development with Unlimited Supplies of Labour," 1954

South Africa's segmented spatial and economic structure poses important questions about the development trajectory of the country: How essential is the township economy to the country's desired objective of faster growth and job creation? Given its low development, its weak linkages with the formal sector, and the negligible industrial production within the township borders (features, highlighted throughout this report, that produce the decidedly low internal multipliers estimated in chapter 8), is it worthwhile for policy makers to focus on the prospects of the township economy? Or will it inevitably wither away and be absorbed by the expansion of the formal advanced economy?

A conceptual framework is needed to better understand the dynamics (past and potential) of South Africa's segmented, multilayered economy and the place of the township economy within it. The basis for such a framework lies in unifying two closely related analytical strands:

- First, theoretical and empirical analyses show that fast-paced growth in the urban informal economy (the township economy, in South Africa's case) is fully consistent with growth in the urban formal sector. There is nothing inevitable about the prospect, as some have advanced, that the township economy could wither away under the shadows of the formal advanced economy.
- Second, advanced economies don't grow fast; lagging economies do. Thus the township economy not only can chug alongside the urban formal economy but also can potentially become an important driver of near-term growth.

Strand 1: Role of the Urban Informal Economy in Relation to the Urban Formal Economy

A viable and dynamic urban informal sector is no longer just a theoretical possibility; it has become an empirical reality. Recent trends in the relative size of the informal economy show remarkably persistent, even rising, patterns in certain parts of the world, even during periods of high gross domestic product (GDP) growth. Parsing the experience of select Latin American and East Asian economies, a 2009 Organisation for Economic Co-operation and Development (OECD) study concludes, "Informality is increasingly becoming normal, not least in middle and even high-income countries …. The development in selected countries in Southeast Asia and Latin America is telling in this respect: over the last 30 years, growth in these countries was accompanied by increasing, not falling, informal employment" (Jütting and Laiglesia 2009).

An analytical framework that is particularly relevant for this report is the one developed by Ranis and Stewart (1999), which provides the basis for thinking about the potential role of the urban informal sector in relation to the urban formal sector. In a departure from the standard dual-economy models (notably, Lewis 1954) that typically encompassed a formal and an informal economy, Ranis and Stewart saw the urban informal sector as a dichotomous structure: a stagnant "traditional" part juxtaposed with a dynamic "modernizing" one. The *traditional* informal sector is associated with "very low capitalization, low labor productivity and low incomes, very small size (three or fewer workers), and static technology." (This mirrors the description of most firms in the township of Diepsloot as summarized in chapter 6.) The *modernizing* informal sector, on the other hand, is "more capital-intensive, usually larger in size (as many as 10 workers), more dynamic in technology, often linked to the urban formal or F-sector," an important category of firms that appears in short supply in South Africa.

The latter, if allowed to emerge under supporting conditions (especially those that strengthen its linkages with the formal urban sector), holds significant potential for expansion and participation in a country's growth process. Being largely anchored in the township space and township economy, it also holds promise for lifting the growth and job creation potential of the townships, especially the large urban ones that are relatively favorably situated. The modernizing informal sector can either compete with or complement the advanced formal economy. Competition is likely in markets for lower-end consumer goods, where both segments may operate. Complementarity would mainly take the form of production linkages as the informal modernizing sector produces and sells intermediate and low-end capital goods to the formal sector.

Fitting this framework to South Africa, it appears that the country is mired in a low-level, high-unemployment equilibrium that has a modestly performing formal urban sector with heavily concentrated ownership structures, a traditional informal sector that is predictably small with an extremely limited capability to expand, and only sporadic signs of an emerging modernizing informal sector that has strong supply-chain or market linkages with the urban formal sector. Breaking out of this low-equilibrium mold will require a coordinated policy push along multiple dimensions to (a) strengthen the economic and institutional linkages between the township economy and urban formal economy, (b) elevate the human capital and infrastructure base of the township economy, and (c) improve investment climate conditions, including access to credit, in townships.

Strand 2: Potential for Internal Integration and Economic Convergence

The phenomenon of economic convergence (whereby an economy, simply by the virtue of starting from a low base of income and productivity, is at an advantage in terms of its growth potential) has strong foundations in the literature.[1] Empirically, this has found validity in the experience of well-integrated economies: for example, in Europe as well as among the OECD countries, and even among the mainland U.S. states. It is important to note, however, that the theory and its empirical validation apply only to economies that, to begin with, are sufficiently similar in terms of their economic institutions and have porous borders for trade, technology, and capital flows.

South Africa's growth potential could be significantly enhanced if it can launch its own version of a convergence machine within—one that would enable rapid growth of the hitherto flailing township economy by unleashing its own internal economic dynamics (with a special focus on the informal modernizing sector) and by integrating it in meaningful ways with the modern urban economy. This catch-up strategy would involve building on the comparative advantages of the township economy: in particular, abundance of cheap, unskilled labor; adjoining land space that is more affordable than in city centers; and a potential consumer market that is still untapped.

While it seems crucial to understand and respond to the potential benefits of integrating the township economy into South Africa's growth process, we first need to recognize the challenging starting conditions of the T&IS.

Economic and Social Trends in Townships and Informal Settlements

The key household-level trends and characteristics of T&IS are presented in chapter 3 and contrasted against rural and other urban areas. Results show that the T&IS have seen by far the fastest population growth among the settlement types. For the first time, about half of South Africa's urban population lives in T&IS as a consequence of natural population growth and migration from rural areas and neighboring countries. Much of the recent migration has been concentrated in informal settlements, which have grown significantly faster than townships, being the first recipients of rural (and foreign) migrants in search of work. In 2011, about 3 million people lived in informal settlements and roughly 15 million in townships (Stats SA 2011).

T&IS, however, do not exist in isolation from rural and other urban areas; they are very much connected to the broader economy through the mobility of factors of production (labor and capital) as well as through the markets for goods and services. These interconnections, highly fragmented as they are in South Africa, are described throughout this report.

The labor market data suggest that T&IS contain poverty and unemployment traps for a large share of the urban labor force. Female-headed households and youth seem especially vulnerable. The people stuck in the poverty and unemployment traps are spatially and structurally isolated from the rest of the economy, failing to connect through the labor, capital, or goods markets. Moreover, the dismal employment trends in rural areas (see box O.1) has exacerbated the

---

Box O.1 Rural Causes for Some Urban Effects

The virtual collapse of rural employment over the past decade has, among other consequences, severely increased the employment pressures on urban areas. Rural employment fell by close to 1.5 million in the past decade because of losses in the commercial farm sector and the collapse of homeland agriculture, which sharply reduced self-employment opportunities there.

As a result, only one out of every four persons of working age in rural areas is currently employed, generating a growing reservoir of surplus labor that looks toward urban areas for job opportunities. Despite the widespread employment losses, rural areas have seen the highest growth rate in per capita consumption, likely reflecting their low initial levels and the widening of eligibility for social grants.

---

pressures on the T&IS, whose own economic structures are clearly not geared to bear the added burden.

Performance on social and service delivery indicators in T&IS has been mixed. Outcomes regarding education, hunger reduction, and nighttime security have all improved in T&IS, as they have in all other settlement types. At the same time, however, provision of housing, water, sewerage, and electricity, while increased in absolute terms, has had a hard time keeping up with the rapidly growing number of households. Finally, there has been little improvement in the health sector and deterioration in the proportion of the ill who receive treatment.

Access to finance is also problematic for township residents, including its entrepreneurs, which only adds to their vulnerability and economic exclusion. Although, on aggregate, South Africa exemplifies a fairly inclusive financial sector (World Bank 2013a), the aggregates mask great inequality in the use of financial services that mirrors the country's segmented economy. The analysis in chapter 4 shows that residents and businesses alike have lower access to financial services in townships than in nontownship urban areas. Moreover, adults in townships are twice as likely to be underbanked as adults in nontownship urban areas—and, in terms of credit, are two-thirds less likely to have a loan from a bank but one-third more likely to rely on one from family or friends.

Similarly, micro, small, and medium enterprises (MSMEs) in townships are 12 percentage points less likely to use a bank account than those in nontownship urban areas. Even those with an account are more likely to use a personal one than one in the business's name. Thus, while credit penetration is generally very low (with less than 5 percent of MSMEs in either townships or nontownship urban areas reporting any borrowing), most credit in townships originates from family and friends, whereas in nontownship urban areas it does so from banks. Moreover, as discussed in chapter 5, even the reliance on social networks for credit can be problematic because social networks among South Africans are not that strong.

Although townships and nontownship urban areas differ markedly in their residents' use of financial services, analysis suggests that these differences are not primarily the result of location alone but also of differences between the two groups' economic realities. When controlling for individual characteristics such as education, income, and employment status, rates of financial inclusion among adults do not differ by urban location. Similarly, differences in the use of credit and credit originating from banks among MSMEs do not relate to location but rather to firm size and whether a firm keeps financial records.

Expanding financial inclusion in townships is therefore not just a matter of advancing appropriate financial inclusion policies. It also must be understood in the larger context of an overall development strategy for townships and their linkages with the urban formal economy. As long as individuals in townships are less educated, more likely to be unemployed, and poorer than individuals in nontownship urban areas, and as long as township businesses are smaller and more likely to be informal, it would be unrealistic to expect similar rates of financial inclusion in township and nontownship areas.

Conditions for entrepreneurship in T&IS are otherwise formidable, too, as exemplified in the case study of Diepsloot in chapters 5–8 and discussed below. Foremost is the issue of low effective demand due to high joblessness and under-developed linkages between local supply chains and formal production networks. Often, even the limited purchasing power leaks out of the T&IS economy to the outside formal economy.

From the supply side, major supermarket chains (such as Spar, Pick n Pay, and Shoprite) and other formal mass-production networks have crowded out local production and street trading through price competition (Du Toit and Neves 2007), superior quality, and the convenience of purchasing a broader range of products in one location (Charman and Peterson 2008). Their appeal also lies in selling branded goods whose pull is enhanced by effective marketing. Somewhat surprisingly, there is little differentiation of products by quality, as is the case in other developing countries. Conspicuously missing from the township economy are the elements of an informal modernizing sector as described above.

The Township of Diepsloot: A Case Study

One of Johannesburg's newest large settlements is the township of Diepsloot. A wholly postapartheid development, it has, over time, emerged as a "dense for-est of shacks, crowds of unemployed people milling on the streets, and attempts by some at small-scale commerce in make-shift shops" (Harber 2011). Despite its burgeoning population[2] and relative proximity to wealthy suburbs and busy commercial areas,[3] Diepsloot finds but a rare mention in the mainstream media—and, when it does, the news mostly perpetuates its negative image as a place of crime, violence, and service delivery protests. Its bustling economic and social life, its daily grind of hardships, and its residents' (unmet) aspirations do not hold much interest for the outside world. But unleashing the energy latent in those aspirations may hold the key to the nation's objective of a faster, more inclusive growth path.

Its relatively close proximity to economic centers notwithstanding, Diepsloot is still only partially (and highly unevenly) integrated into the economic and social fabric of Johannesburg—a characteristic it shares with the other urban townships.[4] Township residents still have a good amount of hope, as revealed in the many personal interviews conducted for this report. However, disillusion-ment seems to be setting in. Much like the other large townships, Diepsloot ferments a brew of anger, suspicion, fear, and longing for opportunity—sentiments that are vividly captured in the personal accounts of its residents, featured in chapter 5.

Overall Profile
Like the rest of South Africa, Diepsloot has a young population. The average age of its residents is 25 years, virtually at par with the averages for the country as a whole and for all T&IS (as further discussed in chapter 7). Also in common with the other T&IS, virtually all of Diepsloot's population (97 percent) is black.

Almost one-fifth of its residents are foreign nationals, mostly from Zimbabwe and Mozambique.

Age

One of Diepsloot's most distinctive traits—its relative proximity to economic hubs—reflects an undeniable reality: it's a magnet for job seekers. Because it attracts so many people in desperate pursuit of work, the working-age component of its population (70 percent) is higher than elsewhere in the country. Correspondingly, its young and old dependency ratios are below the national and urban averages (for both township and nontownship areas).[5]

These age demographics also explain why Diepsloot's average household size of 3 persons is significantly smaller than the national average (3.7 persons). Males head most (60 percent) of Diepsloot's households, which is in line with the national average (60.6 percent). Being largely a migrant community, a significant proportion (almost one-third) of Diepsloot residents financially support nonhousehold members, almost 30 percent of whom live in other countries.

Housing

In Diepsloot's dense maze of housing arrangements, informal dwellings (shacks) make up almost half of all residential structures. Brick structures account for close to 30 percent of dwelling units. Foreign nationals seem more reluctant to own their residential property, likely reflecting their fears of potential dispossession at the hands of angry citizens: although two-thirds of households headed by a South African own their dwelling units, only half of the households headed by foreign nationals own theirs.

Contestation over land ownership lies at the core of Diepsloot's politics. Subsidized formal houses (built through the Reconstruction and Development Program, thus called "RDP houses"), reportedly selling for R 30,000–40,000 (US$3,000–4,000), are beyond the means of most incoming migrants, whether they are South Africans or foreign nationals. The process of renting or obtaining a residential lot with title therefore is considered enormously onerous by all but especially by newcomers, which contributes to a hovering distrust of township governance. Distrust, frustration, and perceived marginalization often seem to translate into perceptions of insecurity and vulnerability, with the potential to readily become toxins of cynicism and anger.

For now, the area occupied by Diepsloot appears to have filled up. The process of building new housing and assigning housing to people waiting in shacks appears to have stalled, leaving the different extensions[6] frozen in various stages of development—and entrenching a new class divide between the better-off households in RDP houses and the severely poor fraction left behind in the shack-housing sector.

Education

Formal education and training are lacking among Diepsloot's population. Although an estimated 62 percent of its residents attained some postprimary education, 13 percent have no formal education, 16 percent started but did not complete primary school, about 5 percent completed only primary school, about a third started but did not finish secondary school, and about a quarter completed secondary school. Only about 6 percent had some form of tertiary education or vocational training.

Educational outcomes are improving gradually but unevenly with the current school-age generation (aged 7–25). Only 2 percent of this cohort has not gone through any form of education, although a large additional share (26 percent) started but never completed primary education. Postprimary education comparisons between the overall and school-age populations are fairly similar.

Labor

Diepsloot's relative proximity to wealthier urban economic centers plays out in a number of ways. Compared with other T&IS, its labor market outcomes are somewhat more favorable, travel to work is less onerous, and its household purchases from outside the township are relatively high.

Still, finding a job is an elusive goal for many Diepsloot residents. The township's narrow unemployment rate (excluding discouraged workers) is an estimated 30 percent, which is in the same range as townships or informal settlements as separate groups (both at 33 percent).[7] The youth unemployment rate is noticeably lower: 43 percent in Diepsloot, compared with 50 percent nationwide in 2011 and an average of 60 percent in T&IS collectively. At 63 percent, Diepsloot's labor force participation rate is higher than the 55 percent national rate. It is, however, lower than the rates of both informal settlements (68 percent) and other urban settlements (65 percent) while being at par with townships as a group.

Because of its relative proximity to economic activity, people need less travel time to get to work than they do in most other townships: for almost 60 percent of the population, it takes 30 minutes or less to get to work. Even so, people who work outside Diepsloot must spend an average of 17 percent of their wages on work-related transport. In the bottom quintile of households (by income), those who must pay for some form of transport to work (as opposed to walking) spend almost half of their household income on transport to work; those in the second quintile spend 40 percent.

Income and Expenditures

Proximity to job opportunities (even if on a limited scale) also means that salaries and wages are by far the most important income source for Diepsloot residents, accounting for 80 percent of their income. The relative significance of income sources varies by income quintile, however. While salaries and wages make the greatest contribution to total income for those in the high income quintiles (roughly 85–87 percent), social grants and pensions constitute a relatively high share for those in the lower income quintiles (16–22 percent), accounting for more than a fifth of the bottom quintile's income.

Diepsloot households make a significant share of their total purchases (averaging 67 percent) inside the township—especially when it comes to groceries and other essentials (90 percent). Three-fourths of the in-township spending goes toward goods (as opposed to services) that are produced outside but retailed through a web of either formal or informal supply chains within the township. Of the share of household spending outside Diepsloot (about 33 percent), the bulk (40 percent) goes toward transfers and financial charges.

Economic Profile

The SAM for Diepsloot, presented in chapter 8, provides the big picture of Diepsloot's economy. It also addresses several questions that can yield important insights into the impact of current policies: How extensive are economic transactions within Diepsloot compared with those between Diepsloot and the rest of South Africa? Is there a Diepsloot multiplier that magnifies any initial income-creating impulse? Could such an internal economy provide an engine for driving growth there?

Size of the Economy

The SAM developed for Diepsloot tells us the following about the size of the township's economy:

- The equivalent of GDP at market prices for Diepsloot is around R 671 million, while its gross national product (GNP) is R 2.3 billion (close to US$230 million). The difference between the two represents the net factor payments to Diepsloot residents, estimated at R 1.6 billion.
  - *On the income side*, the GDP figure includes
    - R 275 million as factor payments to labor;
    - R 152 million as payments to capital;
    - R 227 million payments to capital in the form of housing rents;
    - R 2 million in activity taxes; and
    - R 14 million in sales taxes.
  - *On the production side*, the dominant activities by share of GDP are
    - Retail services (23 percent);
    - Education (19 percent);
    - Public administration (14 percent); and
    - Other services (33 percent), a category that combines wholesale, transport, financial, real estate, and other activities.
  - *On the expenditure side*, GDP at market prices includes
    - R 2.3 billion in household expenditure;
    - R 170 million in government expenditure;
    - R 189 million in expenditure by nonprofit institutions;
    - R 3 million in investment; and
    - A trade balance of nearly −R 2 billion, further discussed below, that is largely covered through net transfers (primarily grant transfers from government) from the rest of South Africa.[8]

- Predictably, most income—R 1.5 billion out of a total income of R 1.8 billion—to residents of Diepsloot is earned outside the township.
- The balance on current account is then R 52 million, or 8 percent of the township's GDP.

Multiplier Analysis

Estimation of the various income multipliers using the SAM model provides interesting results. The analysis captures the multiplier effects of exogenous income injections (increases in residents' income from causes completely external to Diepsloot), such as wage income earned outside Diepsloot, government transfers, and public works programs. Income injections first add to the incomes of the direct recipients, who then spend the additional income and thereby add to incomes for others in the next round, and so on. Multiplier analysis measures this impact by estimating the ratio of the overall rise in the income of the township to the initial rise in the injection.

The estimates of multipliers for most external income sources for Diepsloot are quite low—in absolute terms as well as relative to similar multipliers for the rest of the country. This finding reflects weak economic linkages within Diepsloot that result in large leaks to the wider economy outside. Diepsloot residents and firms use much of the additional income to make purchases outside Diepsloot; even the goods and higher-end services purchased within Diepsloot are ultimately sourced from outside. To enhance the multipliers will require the emergence and expansion of more growth-oriented, higher-value-added firms with relatively strong linkages within the townships. These firms would be part of the informal modernizing sector discussed in the conceptual framework (laid out in chapter 2), with a subset of these having strong value-chain linkages with formal sector firms in the modern economy part of South Africa.

Estimates of income elasticities of expenditures (measuring the percentage increase in spending on a particular expenditure item for each percentage increase in household income) in chapter 7 further show that as incomes rise within Diepsloot, the increases would largely leak out to the broader economy under current structures. In particular, demand for purchases made outside Diepsloot would grow at an increasing pace as income levels rise. A finer breakdown by the type of product, however, shows that the preference for nontradable services purchased within Diepsloot—such as personal care, training schools, and repairs—would increase with income levels. This finding sheds further light on the kinds of growth-oriented activity that can be expected to mushroom in Diepsloot and other similarly large townships.

The Business Enterprise Sector

Diepsloot is teeming with hundreds of microenterprises, as chapter 6 describes in detail. The township's business enterprises can be divided into two large categories: those embedded in the community within tight residential clusters and those operating in a more dynamic, open-space environment outside of the residential community, as described in the qualitative analysis of chapter 5. The dividing line is often thin, and many businesses traverse both sides.

Neighborhood Businesses

The dominant form of household business is the *spaza* shop: a micro-size grocery retail operation that serves as a local convenience shop. Other kinds of small household businesses include snack and other prepackaged food sellers as well as *shebeens* (taverns). Diepsloot's neighborhoods also host a number of small businesses in the services sector (hairstyling and beauty salons, in particular) as well as child care and a few informal computer training schools. Customers for these businesses are neighbors, relatives, or other connections of the business owner, while others may come from nearby localities or clusters. Few, if any, come from outside the neighborhood.

Household businesses are deeply embedded in their neighborhood communities. The owners often define their goals in terms of taking care of basic household needs and preserving community solidarity. Accepted social seniority and authority appear to dictate the level of financial success. Household businesses therefore tend to avoid the implicit radius of an existing business run by another established household. In this setup, markups tend to be high, pricing structures expensive, and customer bases thin. These fragile, tenuous compacts between the South African businesses and their customers do not hold up against the cheaper pricing often introduced by foreign migrants.

Noncommunity Businesses

Businesses not embedded at the community level flourish at certain strategic locations in Diepsloot. These entail more substantial fixed costs and are larger and more entrepreneurial on average than the neighborhood businesses and less constrained by the social equalization norms affecting household businesses. At the apex of the category is the Diepsloot Mall, which has a formal supermarket; large chain stores; and other formal outlets, including retail music, electronic, banking, and clothing businesses.

Apart from the mall, the noncommunity businesses cluster around high-traffic areas to access a wider customer base. The most profitable businesses in the category surround the taxi rank, Diepsloot's main transport hub. With a large customer base from the commuter trade, these enterprises include the larger *shebeens*, hair salons, metalworking and gold buying merchants, suppliers of construction materials and prefabricated shack-type structures, car wash and car repair businesses, used-furniture dealers, restaurants or street cafes, fashion clothing shops, cell phone dealers, and other specialized retail and service businesses. There are even signs that embryonic business clusters are emerging: for example, panel beating businesses and small workshops to recondition tires have sprung up near the taxi rank to cater to the taxi industry.

Residential Rental Activity

Residential rental activity—often combined with business use by the tenant—has also picked up significantly in Diepsloot. Rental activity is simultaneously a secure source of income, a vehicle for landlord social standing and authority, and a bulwark against house break-ins and other criminal residential attacks. Recorded household rental incomes vary from R 400 (US$40) to R 2,800 (US$280) monthly, depending on the number of tenants, the number of rooms, and the quality of accommodation. At the most basic level, no services are provided to the self-build tenant shacks, rented out at R 150–200 per month. More often, electricity and water are provided, and these rentals are in the R 300–350 range.

Entrepreneurial Outlook

Given the grim picture of Diepsloot often painted for the outside world—some of it based on facts, the rest on fear of the unknown and fear generated by mainstream media reports—many analysts and policy makers seem less than optimistic about the potential for enterprise development beyond "survivalist" activity in Diepsloot (or, for that matter, in any other large urban township). Their conventional picture is of the townships as dormitories, suppliers of cheap labor, and mills of perpetual urban discontent.

Pessimism runs the deepest regarding prospects for developing labor-intensive manufacturing (agro-processing, for example) in townships: the markets for such products are saturated with imports and formal mass production, against which township enterprises are deemed not competitive enough. These observers fear that even the traditional informal economy may be at risk, faced with growing competition from large formal retailers operating on scale and from cross-border traders operating on smaller margins and stronger business networks. The view gets even dimmer when it comes to South African entrepreneurs, arising from the worry that they lack the necessary business networks and skill sets to compete with the better-connected foreign traders.

Chapter 6 of this volume empirically examines this conventional view of business and its potential in Diepsloot by analyzing a firm-level survey for this work—conducted by a group of Diepsloot youth who, at the time of the survey, were armed with matric degrees but not jobs.[9]

General Findings. Based on a business census that documented 2,509 Diepsloot businesses and subsequent interviews with a sample of 450 business owners, the survey results confirm the following:

- *The vast majority of the township's self-employed indeed are "survivalists."* Most of the owners run their businesses from residential premises, not by active choice but because they don't have preferred employment in formal sector jobs.
- *Diepsloot firms are mostly informal, new, and micro-size.* Only 10 percent are registered for tax purposes, more than half started after 2006, almost half are run by only the owner with no employees, and over three-quarters needed R 5,000 or less in start-up capital.

- *Foreign nationals have an oversize presence.* Although foreign-born traders make up just 19 percent of the township's population, they own and run almost half of Diepsloot's businesses.
- *Diepsloot also harbors a rising class of* "active entrepreneurs." These owners, by choice, are profitably running growth-oriented, employment-generating businesses, with the potential of doing so on an even larger scale.

A high proportion of the "active entrepreneurs" are in processing activities or in construction, welding, and furniture making. These growth-oriented firms exhibit relatively high rates of return to fixed capital and attract more technically skilled entrepreneurs relative to retail trade and household services. This suggests that they have potential for future growth under more favorable conditions involving (a) lower risk perceptions of townships by outsiders, (b) otherwise stronger demand for their products, and (c) fewer and less-binding investment climate constraints.

Investment Climate Constraints. The constraints most widely reported by Diepsloot business owners include fear of crime, lack of access to Eskom's power grid,[10] shortage of space and serviced business sites, high transport costs, and lack of access to formal finance. Concerns around excessive licensing requirements and other regulatory burdens also preoccupy many township business owners, although the survey results here are within the conventional ranges. Membership in informal entrepreneurial networks is an important part of businesses' coping mechanisms against these constraints. The survey, however, found business connections among South Africans to be less dense than those among recent foreign migrants.

It is important to emphasize that this assessment of the investment climate constraints is based on existing business owners' perceptions. Perhaps more relevant are the issues that prevent people from successfully starting a business in the first place. That analysis, as important as it is, cannot be deduced from the results of this report and will require deeper research.

However, the survey did highlight factors that have supported successful business start-ups in Diepsloot. Indeed, a sizable number of township firms have managed to expand and thrive over the years. Forty percent of the surveyed businesses operated on a larger scale than they had started with, particularly if they engaged in processing or manufacturing (such as construction, welding, and furniture making) as opposed to retail trading and personal services. These and the other more viable Diepsloot enterprises generally had at least one thing in common at start-up: the proprietor-owner's prior experience, at least as a paid employee if not as a prior business owner.

Work experience seems to have provided not only business skills, but also (perhaps even more importantly) contacts and start-up capital. Therefore, one roadblock in the route to entrepreneurship is Diepsloot's (indeed, the country's) unusually high formal unemployment. To a limited extent, this deficit is offset by heavy reliance on recurrent temporary work, government grants, casual work, and small-business activity. The formal job market is difficult for Diepsloot residents to penetrate—as it is for residents of other townships—because of the lack of affordable public transport and the need for skills and contacts to be hired in a saturated labor market.

The current or aspiring entrepreneurs most severely affected by the barriers to business development in Diepsloot are women, youth, and foreign nationals. To expand economic opportunities in Diepsloot, the key challenges specific to these groups should be addressed:

- *Women entrepreneurs* are more deeply stuck than their male counterparts in the low-level equilibrium trap of the traditional household small-business sector, which has little room for expansion. They are 8 percent less likely than men to be "active entrepreneurs" (in business by active choice), according to the analysis in chapter 6. Although they want to break out of this trap to expand their businesses, they often feel effectively confined inside their neighborhoods because of well-founded concerns about poor public safety in the township. Their vulnerability to violence limits their entrepreneurial opportunities, suggesting the need for much more vigorous action on the part of the government and the community to ensure public safety in the township communities.

- *Youth* are keen to avoid not only the unemployment trap but also the household sector low-equilibrium trap. In fact, almost one-third of all businesses in Diepsloot are run by young people (aged 15–29), according to the business census carried out for this report. Faced with extremely limited formal employment opportunities (with national youth unemployment running at close to 50 percent), many would like to start larger semiformal businesses: computer schools, cell phone-related services, and construction work all are promising avenues for this in Diepsloot. Working against their ambitions are lack of support, red tape, and lack of access to capital. In addition, many of the business opportunities that the youth want to pursue require paper qualifications, permits, and bureaucratic approvals of technical qualifications, which can be slow and even prohibitively expensive in impoverished family situations. These aspects will require special policy attention to enable the entry of youth entrepreneurs.

- *Foreign-born entrepreneurs* face their own unique challenges. As reported in chapter 5, the fault line between the South African- and foreign-owned businesses has become deeply etched into the township's consciousness. Emotions around it are real, raw, and run high, and the political and social dynamics around the issue are going to shape the township's economic future to a large extent. Cross-border business persons seem increasingly well aware of the Diepsloot market's characteristics through their dense networks, and they usually arrive with a kit of resources well adapted to bottom-of-the-pyramid business models. For the most part, such businesses are embedded in legal and legitimate network associations—resources that are largely missing among the locals—and can often use high-turnover, low-margin strategies to grow to significant size, developing large client bases. The locals often view their growth as an encroachment into their own business space and an important reason for their own lack of business growth. A proactive public-citizen stance that allows the township to fully benefit from the entrepreneurial zeal of its diverse residents, while more broadly disseminating lessons for effectively running and growing small businesses in a competitive township environment, will prove crucial to Diepsloot's long-term economic viability.

Amid Formidable Conditions, Reasons for Hope. In sum, an unfavorable investment climate, lack of prior experience, weak business networks among South Africans, relatively low education levels, low effective demand, and weak linkages with the formal supply chains have weighed on Diepsloot's enterprise sector, preventing it from growing to its more dynamic potential. At the same time, however, a promising number of growth-oriented businesses have emerged, particularly in the areas of processing activities and making things. Because their marginal productivity of capital is reasonably high, diverting more capital toward these activities can help produce a more viable informal modernizing MSME sector in the township.

Toward a Dynamic Township Economy

A range of legacy issues dating back to the apartheid period continue to undermine economic efficiency and job creation in South Africa. Among the most significant of these historical distortions is the spatial and structural segmentation of the urban economy—broadly, into a formal advanced economy found mostly in South Africa's city centers (where living conditions often resemble those of OECD countries) and a traditional, largely informal economy of T&IS (whose living conditions are significantly worse).

Missing from the picture is a viable middle ground: a dynamic middle-income economic structure on a large scale that hosts a range of robust businesses (both labor-intensive and small enterprises) suited to absorb the limited skill levels available among the townships' unemployed masses. What is holding back the emergence of this more robust informal modernizing economy? This volume identifies some of the critical factors involved, on both the demand and supply sides.

Objective: A Virtuous Cycle of Growth

In the country's most vexing of development challenges—urban economic and spatial segmentation—also lies a major opportunity. The coexistence of the flailing township economy with a substantial (though modestly growing) modern urban economy that is much further along in terms of income and productivity points to the significant gains possible by enabling economic convergence between the two. If successfully ignited, this process would enable South Africa's growth engine to fire on two cylinders instead of one:

- First, the expansion of the modern urban sector—very much at the center of current policy.
- Second, and currently less appreciated, the creation of a modernizing informal sector, a push to increase its viability, and an integration over time with the formal urban sector.

At the moment, potential gains are limited by the marked segmentations in the urban economy that inhibit the free flow of goods, services, factors of production, and technologies between the modern formal and informal township economies. The policy challenge is to find ways to exploit the "arbitrage" between the two economies to ensure that capital flows into, not out of, the less-developed township economy—and that labor becomes more mobile toward the advanced economy while township entrepreneurs have greater access to its markets. The objective would be to start a virtuous cycle by first creating the conditions to make the informal modernizing sector viable, and then enabling it to grow rapidly.

Agenda: Mutually Reinforcing Reforms

Breaking out of South Africa's current low-level equilibrium will require a policy agenda that is comprehensive and holistic with important complementarities among the various policy reforms. In other words, a single, isolated policy change will not suffice: the efficacy of each policy reform will be determined by improvements on multiple fronts.

Policy action will first need to successfully integrate the township and urban formal economies by strengthening the economic and institutional linkages between the two economies and by elevating the township economy's human capital and infrastructure base. Targeted interventions to improve the investment climate in townships (including access to credit) will also be important. The policy agenda would, however, need to extend well beyond the T&IS to also tackle broader economic issues that directly affect the viability of the township economy.

To achieve tangible results, policy makers will need to focus on four broad areas: (a) improving economywide competitiveness, (b) strengthening urban management, (c) reversing the decline of the rural economy, and (d) targeting interventions specifically at the township level.

Improving South Africa's Economic Competitiveness

The economic fortunes of T&IS ultimately are tied to the broader policy and institutional environment within which they exist and must eventually adjust to thrive. The economic convergence discussed earlier can produce significant returns in the short-to-medium term, but both the task of enabling the convergence and the scale of its benefits are direct functions of the policy and institutional structures at the national and various subnational levels. T&IS are certainly not immune from the several competitiveness issues that ail the South African economy, keeping the national growth rate far lower than needed to address the country's exclusion and unemployment challenges.

National economic competitiveness continues to be held back by a number of well-identified constraints: crucial among them are a heavily concentrated industrial structure; skills shortages; labor market rigidities; and emerging gaps in critical infrastructure areas such as freight, telecommunications, and public transport. High industrial concentration and vertical integration within sectors are particularly pernicious (see, for example, Aghion et al. 2008; and Mncube, Khumalo, and Ngobese 2009). These supply-chain structures not only discourage private investment despite the relatively high returns to fixed capital (World Bank 2011), but also create an unfavorable environment for the informal modernizing economy in townships. Viability of the latter requires strong demand from the formal sector for cheaper sources of intermediate goods and service. That demand, in turn, depends on the size and structure of the formal sector: the larger, faster growing, more competitive, and less vertically integrated the formal sector is, the greater its demand for the informal modernizing sector's products and services will be (Ranis and Stewart 1999).

These critical issues and practical ways to tackle them—although beyond the scope of this work—are well documented in sources such as the government's *National Development Plan 2030* (NPC 2012).

Strengthening Urban Management
The future of South Africa's T&IS is also intimately linked to that of the cities and towns on whose peripheries the T&IS arose and to whose governance and public finance structures they belong. Hampered by the spatial impact of its apartheid legacy, South Africa has yet to find an appropriate model to unleash its cities' full potential to drive economic growth and job creation. Why? For one thing, the policy nexus that influences urban land development, transport management, and employment location has not been responsive enough.[11] For another, communities—especially T&IS communities—have become increasingly alienated and disconnected from decision-making processes and disempowered concerning municipal affairs (World Bank 2010).

South Africa's next generation of urban transformation would need to, and fortunately seems poised to, take on these complex challenges. Important lessons can be learned from the approaches of other urbanized middle-income countries. In countries that have already achieved the urban transition, such as Brazil and Mexico, cities as a third tier of government play an important role in supporting national priorities of economic growth and poverty reduction. China, considered a highly centralized country managed by a one-party state, decentralized power and resources into the hands of its mayors along with the accountability to ensure that cities respond to national goals. And India, as it consolidates its position as an urbanized middle-income society, has introduced the world's largest urban program: the Jawaharlal Nehru National Urban Renewal Mission, which is channeling US$30 billion into the modernization of 63 cities.

For its part, South Africa recently launched its US$5 billion Cities Support Program (CSP), which aims to support the 30 largest urban municipalities with investment and technical assistance.[12] Through the CSP, the government is reinforcing its policy commitment to support decentralization while holding city governments accountable for implementing policy around four key axes:

- Devolution of fiscal transfers to cities, especially in the areas of human settlement and transport subsidies.
- Introduction of new Urban Settlements Development Grants, which pass greater accountability to cities to improve the living and economic conditions in human settlement.
- Resolution of the regional electricity distribution debate about whether city governments should retain control of electricity distribution systems.
- Reform of land use management practices that will empower cities in line with the constitution.

Taken together, these policies will enable city governments to play a far larger role in faster and more inclusive urban economic growth and higher-quality service delivery, with significant implications for the betterment of the T&IS population.

Reversing Decline of the Rural Economy

Since the end of apartheid, agriculture sector employment has consistently declined. As many of these workers lost their jobs, they also lost housing and grazing or cultivation rights on the farm owners' land. Mechanization on the large commercial farms has driven much of the change, while agriculture in the former homelands has also fared poorly, virtually disappearing in many areas.[13] Without the linkages to a growing agriculture sector, the rural nonfarm sector has grown little and shed employment on a devastating scale. As a result, an estimated 1.5 million jobs were lost in rural areas between 2000 and 2010. This decline suggests that South Africa is no longer classic dual economy where a large majority of the rural population is either employed or self-employed in farming and nonfarm activities. Rather there is vast rural unemployment and a significant dependence on pensions and child support grants.

The analysis in this volume shows that the dire situation in rural areas has contributed to the difficult conditions in T&IS, particularly through a massive flow of rural-to-urban migrants who see T&IS (especially informal settlements) as their first point of entry to urban areas. The ultimate prize might be a job in the urban formal sector. However, in reality, several layers of spatial and structural disconnect between the township economy and the urban formal economy keep the migrants trapped in lives of very limited opportunities and mobility. It is hard to envision significant improvement in the livelihoods of T&IS residents without reversing, or at the very least stemming, the rapid decline of the rural economy.

The highly adverse rural sector developments have occurred despite legisla-tion to protect farmworkers and an ambitious land reform program that was not only about land transfers to redress the historical land dispossession of black farmers but also was intended to create rural employment. In particular, the impact of land reforms on the beneficiaries has been hindered by the program's past emphasis on creating group farms, rather than subdividing the land, and by extremely limited support for the acquisition of farm capital, inputs, and agricul-tural inputs (Lahiff 2009; van den Brink, Thomas, and Binswanger-Mkhize 2009). It is important to return these major reforms to their intended efficacy.

Improving the Investment Climate in Townships

The existing situation—of townships functioning largely as dormitories for urban laborers—cannot be an optimal one, especially where unemployment levels are so high. Policy makers would do well to address specific investment climate issues: focusing investments on the township's physical infrastructure, instituting a more business-friendly regulatory environment, improving governance more generally (with special focus on containing violent crime), and enhancing access to investment finance. Regarding the latter, the country's highly concentrated banking sector has contributed to high banking costs and a structure that is not conducive to extending financial inclusion to the poor and MSMEs, including those in the townships (World Bank 2013a). Therefore, any financial inclusion policies must also consider appropriate reforms to the structure of the banking sector.

Attention to improving educational outcomes is also likely to produce results: high school graduates were found to be 17 percent more likely than people with only primary-school education to be active entrepreneurs. A focus on educa-tion could also help ease tensions between South African nationals and foreign migrants. According to the report's analysis, a South African with a high school degree is just as likely to be actively involved in business as a foreign-born resi-dent of the same age.

However, the policy framework would need to extend beyond the immediate constraints to also tackle the following structural and image-related issues:

- The near absence of supply-chain links between the township firms and the formal-economy firms that operate on significantly larger scales.
- Low effective demand in the townships—a function partly of high unemploy-ment and relatively low income and partly of general demand preferences that are skewed toward goods produced and sold in the formal economy.
- Adverse perceptions of risks and security issues that seem to keep outsiders from viewing townships as places for commerce.

Opportunity: Pilot Programs

Turning the situation around is a tall order. It will require, among other things, a high level of coordination over a broad range of policies as well as a better under-standing of both consumer preferences and specific areas where strengthening of supply chains within the township would make economic sense. Given its complexity and the absence of clear-cut short-term solutions, the situation probably also calls for informed policy experiments.

Creation of special economic zones and clustering of industrial activity next to townships could be one policy experiment worth considering (as further discussed in Box O.2). The space for these kinds of clusters (currently conspicuous

---

Box O.2 Global Experience in Establishing Industrial Parks and Clusters

In the past couple of decades, a number of economies have successfully deployed special economic zones (SEZs) to attract foreign investment and boost their economic growth and job creation potential. They have done that by ensuring that the additional capital, integration with global supply chains, technology and skills transfers, and potential for SEZ-generated production links with local firms will eventually catalyze broader industrialization and better leverage opportunities of globalization. In circumstances where economywide reforms are deemed infeasible—because of either the costs or the political economy difficulties—the SEZs are often a viable second-best policy option. SEZs have also been viewed as a platform for experimenting with new and untested policies before their broader rollout in the rest of the country.

Although a suite of fiscal incentives and other short-term benefits such as subsidized access to land and credit may help establish an SEZ, its longer-term viability and profitability is not guaranteed and depends on the existence of certain context-specific complementary conditions:

• Close alignment of the SEZs with the country's comparative advantages (for example, in a country with surplus unskilled labor, a SEZ involved in low-wage, labor-intensive activity).
• The country's overall competitiveness and favorable investment climate.
• Ready access to markets, factors of production, and business services.
• A favorable business environment inside the SEZs—particularly, adequate infrastructure, access to credit, and trade facilitation (World Bank 2012).
• Ability of the SEZs to tackle the binding constraints to productive investment in the country (for instance, where infrastructure is the binding constraint across the economy, the SEZ provides firms with adequate infrastructure).

Given all these requisite complexities, it is not surprising that the global record on successful SEZs is rather patchy—with notable exceptions mostly in East Asia and Mauritius, in economies that largely got the enabling conditions right.

Countries can enhance the longer-term benefits of SEZs by clustering similar lines of business geographically. Clustering of industrial activity can generate increasing returns to scale from agglomeration, thus fueling high, sustained economic growth and job creation. Evidence is compelling that local clustering and global production networks are not only compatible but also mutually reinforcing. Agglomeration of similar firms generates local demand for their main inputs, gradually making input supply a profitable business in the

box continues next page

Box O.2 Global Experience in Establishing Industrial Parks and Clusters *(continued)*

clusters, whether through trade or local production. This has the potential to foster local entrepreneurship even where education or skill levels are low, as shown by studies for China, Ethiopia, and Vietnam.

Success with industrial clustering also depends on having complementary policies in place and remaining compatible with market incentives. The latter has been key to recent successes in China, where industrial parks and clusters have had major elements of a market economy— in particular, incentives and competition (World Bank 2013b).

---

by their absence in South Africa) may not be the most suitable immediately outside the urban centers because of both the real estate cost and the incongruence of such clusters with the existing urban economic structure. Townships, on the other hand, are surfeit with surplus labor and can also benefit from second- and third-round multiplier effects that downstream economic activity and employment stimulus that clustering will bring.

Any experiments along these lines would have to be conducted

- *Initially on a pilot basis*, involving a few large industrial parks (whose firms engage in labor-intensive production) located next to large, dense urban townships in the four big metro cities (Johannesburg, Tshwane, Cape Town, and Durban);
- *Incrementally*, with robust monitoring and evaluation systems in place to codify lessons from the experiment before considering whether to scale it up; and
- *Cautiously*, as the worldwide record on such activities is still quite patchy and highly conditioned by getting the enabling policy environment right.

Results: Townships as Economic Growth Engines

The chapters to follow illuminate some of the realities—and challenge some of the conventional perceptions—of the township economy in South Africa. The Diepsloot survey data gathered specifically for this work are benchmarked against nationwide household and business survey results and analyzed within a conceptual framework for understanding the unique dynamics of South Africa's segmented economy.

Currently those dynamics maintain a low-level, high-unemployment equilibrium comprising the three sectors previously discussed: a modestly performing formal urban sector; an informal traditional sector with extremely limited growth capability; and a virtually missing informal modernizing sector that, as this volume reveals, offers untapped potential for growth and job creation. Meanwhile, the relentless pace of urbanization continues, even though the closest these rural migrants and other desperate job seekers can get are the burgeoning T&IS on the urban peripheries—none of them more of a magnet than Diepsloot.

Could a thriving informal modernizing sector potentially develop in the townships, given the formidable conditions in these places and the low internal multipliers estimated in chapter 8? This volume's answer to this is a qualified yes. The low existent multipliers reflect the current economic structures of townships. Any single, isolated policy reform is unlikely to produce a game-changing shift in these multipliers.

The policy challenge, then, is to start a virtuous cycle by first creating the conditions to make the informal modernizing economy viable and then enabling it to grow. Yet a virtuous cycle can arise only from a major coordinated policy push on a wide and complex chain of mutually reinforcing events, highlighted above, to move to a higher equilibrium. Therefore, this by no means is a call to view the township economy as an autonomous, self-contained economic unit. It is a rather a call to envision a township economy whose linkages with the mainstream urban economy are first forged and then strengthened over time. The township economy, if jump-started, will not lead the growth process forever. As formal investment eventually chase down any excess returns, it will blend into the rest of the economy, whereupon growth patterns will not be spatially determined but affected by nationwide factors.

Failure to modernize the township economy, on the other hand, would make this an era of lost opportunities, not only for the townships but also for the nation. The stakes indeed are high. With unemployment concentrated in the townships, informal settlements, and formal homelands (whose residents also aspire for urban economic opportunity, seeing the townships as their first point of entry), the battle to reduce South Africa's staggeringly high unemployment rate will likely be won (or lost) in these places.

Such a policy approach—placing T&IS at its forefront—will require a radical break from the past, including a shift away from viewing these places as solely residential areas and toward viewing them as opportunities for economic growth and development. It will also require a fresh vision of the kinds of economic development that can take place in and near the T&IS, the ways to achieve that development, and the capacity to analyze how well those policies and programs work to bring about the required development.

Notes

1. The concept has its analytical foundations in the standard neoclassical growth models (Solow 1956; Cass 1965; Koopmans 1965).
2. Diepsloot is so densely occupied that sources' estimates vary widely, ranging between 150,000 and 350,000.
3. Diepsloot is located near several upmarket residential and commercial development centers, including Dainfern, Fourways, Midrand, Northgate, Sandton, and Sunninghill.
4. For example, the extensive network of minibus taxis connecting Diepsloot to the economic centers nearby remains too expensive and time-consuming a means of transport to bridge the geographical divide in a meaningful way. No train or bus service exists that would offer a less expensive alternative.

5. The dependency ratio is the age-population ratio of those typically not in the working age (therefore "dependent") to those typically of working age.

6. An extension is a type of spatial division, or neighborhood, that often represents an expansion from an area's original boundaries. The township of Diepsloot is divided into 13 extensions.

7. The broad unemployment rate includes discouraged workers. It is computed as (unemployed seeking + discouraged)/(unemployed seeking + discouraged workers + employed).

8. The trade balance essentially equals total imports of goods and services since there are no exports.

9. The matric degree is equivalent to a high school diploma.

10. Eskom, a South African electricity public utility, generates about 95 percent of the electricity used in South Africa and is the largest producer of electricity in Africa as a whole.

11. A number of other challenges at the urban level also remain largely unaddressed, including gaps in governance and accountability, weak financial management, high vacancies in critical senior management posts, and sometimes an inability to deliver even a core set of critical municipal services efficiently and effectively.

12. Over the course of the five-year program, the CSP seeks to achieve the following: (a) strengthen the capacity of cities to improve the delivery of human settlements and public transport functions; (b) strengthen their core spatial planning functions; (c) strength governance, including financial management and social management; and (d) improve environmental outcomes, including by mainstreaming climate resilience measures. This initiative addresses the need to drive a program of fiscal consolidation based on enhanced expenditure efficiencies and effectiveness and to respond to broader economic conditions. The program explicitly seeks to differentiate cities from other local municipalities to recognize their specific contexts and needs in changing the urban form. The approach aims to put important aspects of the responsibility for economic growth, urban poverty reduction, and improved built-environment outcomes squarely in the hands of municipalities (National Treasury 2012).

13. "Homelands" refers to the territories, often far from cities, to which South Africa's apartheid-era government forcibly moved nonwhite populations. The legal establishment of the homelands (previously called "reserves" and also widely known as "bantustans") formed the basis for the government to eventually regard the homelands as self-governing states, nominally independent of South Africa, and in 1970 to denaturalize the homelands' populations.

References

Aghion, P., M. Braun, and J. Fedderke. 2008. "Competition and Productivity Growth in South Africa." *Economics of Transition* 16 (4): 741–68.

Binswanger-Mkhize, H. P., C. Bourguignon, and R. J. E. van den Brink, eds. 2009. *Agricultural Land Redistribution: Toward Greater Consensus*. Agriculture and Rural Development Series. Washington, DC: World Bank.

Cass, D. 1965. "Optimum Growth in an Aggregative Model of Capital Accumulation." *The Review of Economic Studies* 32 (3): 233–40.

Charman, A., and L. Peterson. 2008. *Making Markets Work for the Poor—Understanding the Informal Economy in Limpopo*. Research report, Limpopo Centre for Local Economic Development, Limpopo, South Africa.

CoGTA (Department of Co-operative Governance and Traditional Affairs). 2009. *Township Transformation Timeline*. Pretoria, South Africa: COGTA and the European Union.

Du Toit, A., and D. Neves. 2007. "In Search of South Africa's Second Economy." *Africanus* 37 (2): 145–74.

Economist. 2007. "A Flourishing Slum: The Residents of Dharavi, Allegedly Asia's Biggest Slum, Are Thriving in Hardship." December 19.

Harber, A. 2011. *Diepsloot: A Place at the Side of the Road*. Cape Town, South Africa: Jonathan Ball Publishers.

Hirschman, A. O. 1958. *The Strategy of Economic Development*. New Haven, CT: Yale University Press.

Jütting, J. P., and J. R. de Laiglesia, eds. 2009. *Is Informal Normal? Towards More and Better Jobs in Developing Countries*. OECD (Organisation for Economic Co-operation and Development) Development Centre Study. Paris: OECD Publishing.

Koopmans, T. C. 1965. "On the Concept of Optimal Economic Growth." In *The Econometric Approach to Development Planning*, 225–87. Amsterdam, the Netherlands: North-Holland.

Lahiff, E. 2009. "Land Reform since the End of Apartheid." In *Agricultural Land Redistribution: Toward Greater Consensus*, edited by H. P. Binswanger-Mkhize, C. Bourguignon, and R. J. E. van den Brink, 169–78. Agriculture and Rural Development Series. Washington, DC: World Bank.

Lewis, W. A.. 1954. "Economic Development with Unlimited Supplies of Labour." *The Manchester School* 22 (2): 139–191.

Mncube, L., L. Khumalo, and M. Ngobese. 2009. "Do Vertical Mergers Facilitate Upstream Collusion: Evidence from Selected Cases in South Africa." Paper presented at the "Third Annual Competition Conference," South African Competition Commission, Pretoria, September 4.

National Treasury. 2012. "Cities Support Program: Framework Document—Final Draft (January 2012)." Department of the National Treasury, Republic of South Africa, Pretoria.

NPC (National Planning Commission). 2012. *National Development Plan 2030: Our Future: Make It Work*. Pretoria, South Africa: NPC.

Pieterse, E. 2009. "Post-Apartheid Geographies in South Africa: Why Are Urban Divides So Persistent?" Paper presented at the workshop, "Interdisciplinary Debates on Development and Cultures: Cities in Development—Spaces, Conflict and Agency," Leuven University, Belgium, December 13.

Ranis, G., and F. Stewart. 1999. "V-Goods and the Role of the Urban Informal Sector in Development." *Economic Development and Cultural Change* 47 (2): 259–88.

Solow, R. M. 1956. "A Contribution to the Theory of Economic Growth." *The Quarterly Journal of Economics* 70 (1): 65–94.

Stats SA (Statistics South Africa). 2011. "Quarterly Labor Force Survey 2011Q3." Stats SA, Pretoria, South Africa.

van den Brink, R. J. E., G. L. Thomas, and H. P. Binswanger-Mkhize. 2009. "Land Reform in South Africa: Additional Data and Comments." In *Agricultural Land Redistribution: Toward Greater Consensus*, edited by H. P. Binswanger-Mkhize, C. Bourguignon, and R. J. E. van den Brink, 201–14. Agriculture and Rural Development Series. Washington, DC: World Bank.

World Bank. 2010. *Accountability in Public Services in South Africa: Selected Issues.* Washington, DC: World Bank.

———. 2011. "South Africa Economic Update: Focus on Savings, Investment, and Inclusive Growth." *South Africa Economic Update*, Issue 1, World Bank, Washington, DC.

———. 2012. *Special Economic Zones in Africa: Comparing Performance and Learning from Global Experience.* Directions in Development. Washington, DC: World Bank.

———. 2013a. "South Africa Economic Update: Focus on Financial Inclusion." *South Africa Economic Update*, Issue 4, World Bank, Washington, DC.

———. 2013b. *Tales from the Development Frontier: How China and Other Countries Harness Light Manufacturing to Create Jobs and Prosperity.* Washington, DC: World Bank.

CHAPTER 1

A History of Townships in South Africa

Kate Philip

Introduction

Soweto, South Africa's most recognizable township, evokes a history of struggle—and, with it, not only the icons of struggle, such as Nelson Mandela and Desmond Tutu, but also the icons of culture such as singer Brenda Fassie, *shebeen* queens, *tsotsis*, and minibus taxis.[1] The name "Soweto" is in fact an acronym for "South Western Townships," a name derived from its spatial relationship to Johannesburg, the historical home of South Africa's mining industry, which is known locally as "eGoli" (from Zulu, "place of gold").

This spatial link to the "big city"—and to economic demand for labor—is at the root of the history of townships in South Africa. For those making the decisions at the time (from the late 19th century until 1994) townships reflected the tension between the need to keep black people close enough to provide a source of cheap labor but far enough away to ensure a clear social distance—with the option of rolling out the blade wire to maintain that distance if it was ever at risk of being breached.

Structuring a society in this way was possible only because it went hand in hand with the political and economic subordination of black people—a complex exercise that started from the earliest days of colonialism. It was later formalized as "apartheid" (from Afrikaans, "being apart") after the 1948 election of the Nationalist Government, which took socially engineered racial inequality and its associated capture of wealth to new levels.

Apartheid included the development of policies for urban planning and housing development that created the uniquely South African concept of a "township": a dormitory town built at a distance from economic activity as well as from white residential areas, with rows of uniform houses, historically lacking services and infrastructure such as tarred roads, sanitation, water, or electricity.

South Africa's first formal township, in Cape Town, was established in 1901 after bubonic plague hit the city—and black people were identified as a health hazard. A form of forced removal relocated many of them to a state farm called Uitvlugt.

Today, even after nearly two decades of democracy, South Africans still live in settlement patterns reminiscent of the apartheid era. The spatial legacy of apartheid has proven particularly tenacious. To compound matters, new urban development has reproduced some of the features of the old.

This chapter will explore the history of townships in South Africa, including post-apartheid developments, to understand what this history means for contemporary opportunities.

Townships, Labor Supply, and Apartheid

In the late 19th century, black people were still mainly engaged in agricultural activity, with little desire to settle in the towns. Instead, the conflict over resources focused primarily over rights, access, and ownership in relation to agricultural and pastoral land. The European settlers of the previous century entrenched their claims—mainly through conquest but also through localized truces and alliances with the relevant chiefs and tribes. The discovery of gold and diamonds changed all that because it introduced a need for labor on a new scale. At the same time, settlements started to expand on the outskirts of the towns, in an unplanned way. At this stage, racial segregation was not enforced.

Land for Whites, "Reserves" for Blacks

As the mining boom picked up pace, a labor shortage became one of the industry's main constraints and complaints. So much so that, in 1904, the government of the day entered into negotiations to secure indentured Chinese labor to work in the mines. By 1908, the Chamber of Mines had employed nearly 100,000 Chinese workers on the gold mines (Callinicos 1980).

This solution was only temporary, however. Policy makers' attention soon turned to more local supplies of labor—and to South Africa's black population, who showed no inclination to leave their traditional pastoral, land-based livelihoods to work in dark and dangerous conditions underground in the mines. Instead, black farmers were starting to supply the rapidly growing urban food markets, potentially posing a competitive threat to white farmers, who were trying to secure the same market opportunities (Callinicos 1980).

The consequence was the Natives Land Act of 1913, an unlikely convergence of two South African political interests: mining capital (mainly British) and agricultural capital (mainly Afrikaner) (Callinicos 1980).

Few pieces of legislation have had greater social and economic consequences for South Africa. The Natives Land Act of 1913 declared that black South Africans could not own or rent land in what was, from then on, defined as "white" South Africa. Instead, their access to land was limited to designated "reserves," which constituted a mere 7.6 percent of all land in South Africa (later expanded to 20 percent with the creation of *bantustans*).[2]

The Act was designed to force black South Africans off the land and into the labor market—and it worked. Part of the strategy to achieve this was to involve traditional leaders in governance of these areas and to pay them for their functions. Chiefs who resisted this process were replaced with more-compliant members of their tribes. Chief Albert Luthuli, the first president of the African National Congress (ANC) and winner of the 1960 Nobel Peace Prize, was removed from his position as chief for this reason in 1952.

Urban Influx—and "Influx Control"

So began the influx of African people to the cities: to the diamond fields in Kimberley and the gold mines in Johannesburg in particular. With this came a new policy imperative: "influx control," a term that became central to urbanization policy under apartheid.

From the start, however, the rationale was clear: black people—men and women alike—were in the cities as laborers. As far as possible, they were not to become permanent residents or "citizens" of the cities, nor were they to bring their families with them. Although pass laws had existed in various forms in South Africa for some time, they now became the critical instrument of influx control. To leave the reserves, black people had to get documentation in the form of a reference book (or pass) that stipulated their place of work and gave them permission to be in an urban area.

Different categories of permission applied: most common was short-term permission tied to a work contract, which required an individual to return to the reserves before a repeat contract could be issued. This practice became the backbone of South Africa's internal migrant-labor system. The most sought-after rights were under Section 10 of the Black (Native) Laws Amendment Act No 54 of 1952, which allowed permanent urban residence. Those with Section 10 rights could secure family accommodation in an urban township—in rented public housing.

Housing for black miners, however, was in single-sex hostels: large, barrack-like buildings housing thousands of men, with up to 20 men sharing a room, on bunk beds stacked three levels high. Hostels became the dominant form of accommodation for mine workers and a feature of the mining industry. In mining towns, hostels still house a significant number of men, with townships and informal settlements often developing contiguously. Municipalities also constructed and ran hostels for workers in other industries; some of these survive today, such as the Jeppe Hostel in Johannesburg.

As the mining industry boomed, other forms of enterprise and industry grew, too; thus the demand for labor broadened, and so did African urbanization and housing demand. Local authorities tried to address the problem by developing what were then called "locations," but they lacked the funding base to deal with the scale of the problem and turned to the national government for support. This triggered an extensive national debate on urban policy—a debate that focused on the status of urban Africans, how best to limit their rights to be permanent urban residents, and how to control their movements. This debate in turn led to a battery of new laws, starting in the 1920s, that laid the foundation for the racially segregated settlement patterns on which apartheid later built (COGTA 2009).

Townships under Institutionalized Apartheid

The National Party came to power in whites-only elections in 1948 and characterized its policies as a system of "apartheid." The period to 1960 saw the intensive consolidation of a range of policies and legislation governing urban development, some of the most important of which are further discussed in box 1.1. They included the following framework of conditions under which townships could be developed (COGTA 2009, 41):

- The site should be an adequate distance from the white town.
- It should adjoin an existing African township so as to decrease the number of areas for Africans.
- It should be separated from the white area by a buffer where industries exist or are being planned.
- It should have land to expand away from white areas.
- It should be within easy distance of the town or city for transport purposes, by rail rather than road.
- It should have one road that connects it to the town, preferably running through the industrial area.
- It should be surrounded by open buffer areas.
- It should be a considerable distance from main and national roads.
- Housing should be built and allocated in areas for different ethnic groupings.
- Although the standards and design of housing for Africans varied considerably before 1947, the central government thereafter specified the minimum standards for African and "Coloured"[3] housing. The four-room, 40.4-square-meter "51/6" prototype[4] was the most typical house built under this requirement.
- A mix of formal housing, site and service schemes, and hostels should be provided.
- Housing should be provided on a rental basis.

This, then, became the definition of a "township," and a concerted process of township development followed, shaping the spatial configuration of urban South Africa. Bonner and Segal (1998) characterized the process as "exerting control through form": "The key focus of the specifications set down for Townships was to enable the government to assert its control. Row upon row of identical dirt streets radiating from a central hub, line upon line of drab, cheap, uniform houses—a colourless mind-numbing monotony. Through regimentation and uniformity the government sought to establish a firm control that could not be challenged."

As important as the townships' physical form was, the key question was how they would be governed, administered—and funded. Initially, townships were managed by the white local authorities in adjacent areas, who were expected to raise funds for this purpose through payments for services (in particular, from rental income and from beer sales in the townships). The 1928 Liquor Act prohibited the production and distribution of traditional beer by the "nonwhite"

Box 1.1 Laws That Were Building Blocks for Apartheid

A range of complementary strands of policy and legislation also affected South Africa's urbanization process and township development throughout the apartheid era. Some of the most significant laws are summarized below.

The Group Areas Act of 1950

The Group Areas Act (amended several times)[a] made it compulsory for people to live in areas designated for the exclusive use of their racial group, with everyone classified as black, white, colored, or Indian. Despite a history of racial segregation policies, some areas in most cities were still multicultural—such as Sophiatown, in Johannesburg.

Sophiatown was close to the city center, famous in the 1950s for its jazz clubs and cosmopolitan atmosphere, where artists, authors, and political activists rubbed shoulders, shared the dance floor—and shared ideas. All "nonwhite" residents were forcibly removed from Sophiatown and spread out between the new Indian township of Lenasia, colored townships such as Eldorado Park, and African townships such as Soweto. The apartheid government then renamed Sophiatown "Triomf" (Triumph) just in case anyone had failed to get the point.

Such forced removals were also used to uproot established communities of color, including some whose long history in urban areas meant that, with the expansion of city centers, they were now living on prime urban land. This was the fate of District Six in Cape Town, on the slopes of Table Mountain. It had been a mixed community of freed Malay slaves, artisans, merchants, laborers, and immigrants since 1860. First, Africans were removed; then District Six was rezoned as a white area, and the remaining colored community was forcibly removed and dispersed within drab council housing on the Cape Flats. This pattern of destruction was repeated in communities around the country.

The Bantu Authorities Act of 1951 and the Black Homelands Citizenship Act of 1970

A major foundation for the policy of separate development, the Bantu Authorities Act of 1951, laid the basis for the "reserves" established by the Land Act of 1913 to become "homelands." This, however, was just a step in a somewhat bizarre direction, in which the government embarked on preparations for these homelands to become sovereign states, or "bantustans," independent of South Africa. This was where different ethnic groups within the black population were expected to exercise their citizenship.

In 1970, the Black Homelands Citizenship Act made black South Africans (irrespective of actual residence, even if living in "white South Africa") citizens of the homelands, thus canceling their South African citizenship. All political, social, and economic rights associated with citizenship were to be exercised in these *bantustans*, and black South Africans would officially be "foreigners" in the rest of South Africa.

The terms of such independence—and how it would be funded—required extensive negotiation with the traditional leaders recognized by the apartheid government in these areas. Some of the *bantustans*, such as Transkei and Bophuthatswana, took full "independence" and had their own border posts and passports, among other trappings. All kinds of incentives were put in place to attract industry to these areas, in the hope of stemming the tide to urban

box continues next page

Box 1.1 Laws that Were Building Blocks for Apartheid (continued)

areas. This effort did not work; it was expensive and it failed to dampen growing demands for political rights in South Africa.

In parallel with these processes of consolidating the *bantustans*, the government set about removing what were termed "black spots"—urban settlements of black people in "white" South Africa who were forced to move to within the borders of what were deemed to be their homelands, even if they had never lived there before.

The government also developed "townships in the veld": new rows of housing, just within a homeland's borders, that had no economic rationale. They were intended as commuter townships to service the nearest white towns despite the long distances often involved. This created a pattern of long daily commutes for employment.

a. Parliament later passed the Group Areas Act of 1957, which was repealed in 1966 and reenacted as the Group Areas Act of 1966.

population, giving local authorities a monopoly of these roles. By the 1940s, most municipalities were brewing beer and selling it in municipal beer halls in the townships. However, this major source of revenue required the destruction of a vibrant tradition of beer brewing, conducted mainly by women and rooted in customary practices. This informal enterprise was criminalized and heavily policed, which led the clandestine brewers to conceal their activity in increasingly creative ways. Tsoeu (2009) offers this example: "Shebeeners would dig a hole about a metre or two deep, place the beer inside the hole, cover it with a lid and wait for it to mature. The lid was covered with soil which had to be firmly plastered, avoiding any unevenness which might provoke curious eyes. This tricked police for a long time, but they caught up with the trend eventually. When police carried out their raids they came with poles to feel the ground for the tin lid under the soil."

In 1971 the central government took over township administration and set up Administration Boards for this purpose, albeit with no major change to local revenue collection strategy. These Boards had white members, appointed by the Minister of Native Affairs.

By the late 1970s, however, policy started to shift toward allowing limited and subordinate forms of black representation in township governance and recognizing the permanence of black urbanization. The Community Councils Act allowed for the establishment of elected Community Councils, under the jurisdiction of the Administration Boards; between 1977 and 1980, 224 such councils were elected in townships across the country. The Department of Cooperation and Development claimed an average voter turnout of 42 percent in contested wards (Seekings 1990).

Although many of these councils sought to implement development plans intended to address the needs of their constituents, the financial constraints imposed on them meant that the costs of such development had to be passed on to township residents in the form of rent increases—setting the scene for the resistance that followed (Seekings 1990).

Resistance, Reform, and the End of Apartheid

Resistance to apartheid took many forms—from individual livelihood strategies such as hiding traditional beer to more organized forms of protest and opposition. The latter escalated after 1948, as the agenda of "grand apartheid" gathered momentum. In the 1950s, such opposition included a range of forms of nonviolent protest and passive resistance, mainly under the leadership of the ANC as part of a wider Congress Alliance, a coalition representing different racial groups in a nascent form of nonracialism. This opposition took clearer shape in June 1955, when the Congress of the People adopted the Freedom Charter (ANC 1955), whose opening clauses declare "that South Africa belongs to all who live in it, black and white, and that no government can justly claim authority unless it is based on the will of all the people."

Underpinning the demand for political rights were a range of campaigns organized to oppose and resist specific forms of oppression and exploitation that affected people's lives. Many of these were rooted in the social and other conditions that influx control and life in the townships imposed. For example, the townships' distance from economic opportunity meant that the costs of public transport consumed a significant portion of workers' wages; increases in this cost became a flashpoint for protest. Among the early examples were the bus boycotts in Alexandra Township, in Johannesburg; in 1943, over 20,000 people refused to board the buses, and walked long distances to work instead. This highly visible form of protest was also an early example of the kind of township-wide mobilization that would become characteristic.

Heightened mobilization in the 1950s was met with heightened repression. This period reached a turning point with the Sharpeville massacre in 1960: the state's response to a campaign of defiance against the pass laws that included the burning of passes. The ANC and the Pan Africanist Congress were banned. Forced underground, the ANC turned to armed struggle. Nelson Mandela and other key leaders were arrested not long thereafter.

The scale of political repression in this period was devastating: its impacts dulled the edge of popular resistance throughout the 1960s while the institutions of apartheid consolidated. By the 1970s, however, resistance started to emerge once more, with trade union organization reemerging in the early part of the decade, and with the 1976 Soweto uprising opening a new chapter in South Africa's history. Although the clampdown was brutal, it could no longer contain resistance for long. Unclear as it was at the time, the balance of power started to shift.

A Second Wave of Turbulence

It was around this time that "reform" entered the vocabulary of South African politics. Repressive as it was, the apartheid regime was not without its internal contradictions, and within the ranks of its rulers was a growing recognition that the scope for a small minority to rule was limited without some measure of consent. This was compounded by an escalating economic crisis and increasing

international isolation. Prime Minister P. W. Botha launched what he called
South Africa's "total strategy": in essence, a strategy to retain power by appearing to share it, to grant greater representation to some disenfranchised groups
without ceding any real power.

This divide-and-rule approach included the extension of a limited form of
franchise to coloreds and Indians as well as the 1983 creation of the Tricameral
Parliament in which white, colored, and Indian people each had separate
chambers, with the white parliament still effectively in control. Political representation for black people was still to be exercised in the *bantustans*, but the
Black Local Authorities Act of 1982 granted greater powers to the Community
Councils.

This brazen social engineering helped to catalyze the most turbulent period
in South Africa's history, with waves of resistance met by increasingly brutal
repression—coupled with successive attempts at "reforming" apartheid.

Amid this turmoil, struggles took place in many different arenas: Workers,
students, youth, and women started to build constituency-based forms of
organization. In urban areas, civic organizations represented communitywide
issues. This development brought the new organizations into conflict with the
Community Councils, which were seen as local proxies for the apartheid government. Although the government had introduced the Community Councils
during a period of what Seekings (1990) calls "quiescence" in the late 1970s,
attitudes changed in the 1980s. As Seekings further states, "The Community
Councils Act provided for little genuine accountability by councilors to their
constituents. As councilors demanded bribes or favoured themselves in the
allocation of sites and licenses, and repeatedly increased rents despite their
constituent's protests, so they lost whatever legitimacy or support they had
earlier enjoyed."

The Rent Boycotts

The apartheid government's strategy was to create a buffer layer of black representatives to govern the townships—elected officials but with partial powers
and subordinate rights. Resistance to this practice, and to the appointed township
officials themselves, placed resistance to township governance at the heart of the
struggles of the period. For these councils, securing some measure of legitimacy
depended on their ability to improve living conditions. But, to do so, they had to
raise revenue—with the rentals on township houses an important part of their
revenue base. Attempts to increase rents were among the triggers for what was
called the "Vaal uprising," described by Franziska Rueedi as follows:

> On the 3rd of September 1984 violence erupted in the townships of the Vaal
> Triangle south of Johannesburg, following a protest march against rent increases,
> poor service delivery and an illegitimate and defunct local government. Within the
> first few days, four black local councilors were brutally killed by so-called mobs and
> dozens of people were shot dead and wounded by the police. Burning tyres, rocks
> and other objects were used to block the roads, hindering the police from moving

around the townships. Although the frequency of violent encounters subsided after the first days, the security forces and local authorities were neither able to quell protests nor break the rent boycotts that had started on that day. The Vaal Uprising heralded the beginning of a period of sustained popular protest that spread to large parts of South Africa, prompting the authorities to send in troops, to arrest the leadership and to declare a state of emergency. (Rueedi 2011)

Rent boycotts spread across the country and became a feature of township struggles for the next decade. The rallying call became make the townships "ungovernable" (Tambo 1984). There followed a seemingly unending cycle of repression and resistance, often catalyzed around the weekly funerals of victims of state violence, in a context in which all other public gatherings had been banned. Army troops were sent in to occupy townships, confirming that South Africa was a society at war with itself.

This repression and the ban on public meetings made communication and organization difficult, providing the context for alternative forms of organization and governance to emerge. In many townships, street committees created networks that enabled discussion and debate, as well as rapid communication and decision making across a whole township, without the risks of a public meeting. Street committee structures also hid activists on the run, including Umkhonto we Sizwe operatives.[5]

Attempts to break the rent boycotts through evictions of tenants were largely unsuccessful, as one ANC leader, Thami Mkhwanazi, described:

> After a Soweto eviction, the council rips the front and back doors off the house to prevent the tenants from moving back in. But within hours, the families are back in their houses, with their furniture re-installed—all courtesy of the local "comrades."

> The door strategy is not the only one a desperate Soweto council has adopted to break the two-year rent boycott.

> The local authority has been loading street committee members into vans and driving them to the rent offices for "negotiations" to end the boycott. But so far, street committee members have refused to negotiate.

> [This] was not the first time the "comrades" had been active in Mofolo South. In 1986, for example, the Soweto Council cut off electricity to the 1,000 houses in the area, but within 24 hours the township was lit again. Youths at a Soweto Youth Congress meeting resolved to reconnect the electricity, collected money to buy copper wire and asked residents to keep their yards unlocked to facilitate the re-electrification. (Mkhwanazi 1988)

By the time South Africa made its transition to democracy in 1994, "the townships" had become a central locus of struggle, imbued with meaning and history unintended by the dry list of characteristics with which the apartheid government had brought them into existence. At the same time, once the dust had settled and the votes were counted, that dry list of characteristics still shapes the spatial realities of townships.

Economics of South African Townships • http://dx.doi.org/10.1596/978-1-4648-0301-7

Postapartheid Policy and Practice

The heady early days of the postapartheid period saw massive processes of policy formulation. Edgar Pieterse (2009) describes how, between 1994 and 2002, "a plethora of Green Papers, White Papers, laws and policy frameworks were published" as Parliament and the new government tried to wipe apartheid away from every aspect of society. Urban policy was no exception, imbued also with a sense of urgency in the face of massive housing backlogs, the lack of access to basic services such as water and sanitation, and the need to craft new systems of governance as well as new systems to finance what was seen as a crucial part of a wider redistributive agenda.

Housing and Services: Priorities for a New Democracy

The Reconstruction and Development Program (RDP), South Africa's initial overarching postapartheid policy framework, set the goal, in its founding document, of "breaking down apartheid geography through land reform, more compact cities, decent public transport and the development of industries and services that use local resources and/or meet local need" (Section 4.3.3, quoted in NPC 2011).

In terms of urban development, this goal translated into the following main policy themes:

- Access to "housing, security, and comfort," with water, sanitation, and energy as the most critical areas for what is now termed "service delivery."
- Development of local governance systems to plan, consult on, and deliver these reimagined urban realities.
- Mechanisms to finance these resources, with a clear redistributive agenda, anticipated by the apartheid-era rallying cry of township civic organizations for "One City, One Tax Base."[6]

This set of policies was informed by a strong redistributive agenda, intended to address the basic needs of the poor. As Pieterse (2009) noted, "In the urban context, this takes the form of the public housing program, which in the first instance, seeks to provide a free asset for the poor if they can demonstrate incomes below a certain level."

Although early strategies for service delivery assumed a minimum level of cost recovery, the culture of nonpayment for services proved unyielding: by 2003, the housing policy was complemented by an explicit policy of providing "free basic services" to the poor, up to defined limits.

This should be a good-news postapartheid story. But the parts have not added up to an integrated whole or to integrated cities in which inequality and spatial and social distances have narrowed. Pillay, Tomlinson, and du Toit (2006) characterized the situation this way: "The urban policies were at the same time simplistic and complex. They were simplistic in setting targets for delivery whose realization required ignoring other development criteria; a million houses in five years being the notorious example of a numerical goal over-riding the need to build sustainable settlements. They were complex in the transformation of local government and the need to align boundary demarcation, institutional restructuring, financial and fiscal direction and resources, all with a view to building democratic and developmental institutions."

Inequality, Set in Concrete

For the first 10 years of democracy, the free public housing program became the de facto urban development strategy of South Africa, with the imperatives of public housing dominating urban development practice (Pieterse 2009). The result has been the massive development of postapartheid townships of RDP houses, which are typically as far—if not farther—from economic opportunities as the homelands under the original apartheid model. Often devoid of public spaces and access to social services, they have benefited from only limited spatial planning to enable local economic development—except to support the taxi industry, which often provides the only form of transport linking these new-generation townships to city hubs and economic opportunities.

A Persistent Spatial Divide

There has been much analysis of why and how this happened—and has continued to happen even in the face of policies attempting to reverse it. At one level, it is a case of competing priorities and trade-offs. The pressure to roll out housing and services meant that this aspect of urban policy ran ahead of the complex processes of building new institutions able to imagine and deliver transformed outcomes at the city-region level. Municipalities were under intense pressure in this regard from above and below, but demand exceeded the limits of their budgets. Consequently, land-market logic determined the location of new settlements—and the cheapest land was typically the worst-located land.

In addition, as Pieterse argues, a key feature of South Africa's negotiated constitution was the protection of private property and private assets.

> (W)hen South Africa embarked on its ambitious democratic transition in 1994, there was great anticipation that under the behest of a radical-democratic majority government, ways would be found to undo the paradigm of urban division—the apartheid city. This desire was both justified and misplaced. Justified in that the redistributive ambitions of the newly elected government invariably had to involve some form of urban justice and rebalancing because this was where the heart of economic apartheid resided; misplaced because the negotiated terms of the transition precluded radical interventions in either private property or the accumulated wealth of the white minority. (Pieterse 2009)

Pieterse further contends that these constitutional provisions have made it difficult for city and local governments to institute regulations that negatively affect property rights in the name of social rights or public goods. In addition, the introduction of "one city, one tax base" policies gave local governments a perverse incentive to avoid policies that might reduce middle- and upper-class property values, especially in a context without real scope to raise revenue for pro-poor policies from the poor themselves. In addition, not surprisingly, private sector investment has continued to focus on the areas of greatest opportunity, leaving the new ghettoes of the poor on the margins once more.

The short-term cost savings from locating new settlements on cheap but poorly located land are dwarfed by the longer-term social and economic costs to society:

- These dispersed settlement patterns significantly raise the costs of infrastructure development for service delivery.
- The long distances from economic opportunities in turn increase labor costs by raising the reserve wage and eroding workers' take-home pay.
- High transport costs can also make work seeking too expensive for people with little income.

Moreover, the time cost of distance has social costs, such as lost parenting time. South Africa's National Development Plan (NPC 2012) cited one example that is all too typical: "A single mother of four children aged between 3 and 12 lives in Tembisa with her mother. She spends nearly five hours each day commuting to and from work in the Pretoria suburb of Brummeria, where she is an office cleaner. The journeys cost nearly 40 percent of her monthly salary of R 1,900. She leaves home at 05:00 … and may not get home until 19:00. She spends over R 700 a month on transport and nearly 100 hours on the road."

Although RDP houses were intended to provide a massive redistributive boost to the assets of the poor, they have not always had this effect. Often, poor people cannot afford the recurrent costs of services in these households, or the transport costs to get to work or to seek work have been impoverishing. This has led some people with RDP houses to sell them—sometimes for a mere 10 percent of the cost of delivering them—and move to informal settlements[7] instead, closer to economic opportunities (Zack 2008).

Informal Settlements Proliferate

Over the same period, there has been massive growth of informal settlements in and around the urban periphery—often closer to economic opportunities than either the old or new townships. They are a manifestation of the pace of urbanization, acting as the first entry point into the cities for many rural migrants. This in turn reflects a gap in urban development policy that persists still: the lack of a coherent strategy to address urbanization. So, while influx control is a thing of the past, there has been no coherent strategy to enable entry to the cities for newcomers. Instead, urban development policy focuses its attention on the backlogs confronting its existing residents, in a form of policy denial at the rapid and relentless process of urbanization taking place.

By the time the South African government undertook a 10-year review of its policies in 2004, the negative implications of reinforced inequality in settlement patterns was already clear. In 2004, a new housing policy was launched by the

Department of Housing called Breaking New Ground (BNG),[8] which proposed "utilizing housing as an instrument for the development of sustainable settlements, in support of spatial restructuring." As the BNG plan states,

> After the 1994 elections, Government committed itself to developing more liveable, equitable and sustainable cities. Key elements of this framework include pursuing more compact urban form, facilitating higher densities, mixed land use development, and integrating land use and public transport planning, so as to ensure more diverse and responsive environments whilst reducing travelling distance. Despite all these well-intentioned measures, the inequalities and inefficiencies of the apartheid space economy have lingered on. (Department of Housing 2004)

Although early policy pronouncements on informal settlements included the call for their "eradication," BNG also envisioned a shift to support for informal settlement upgrading, where such settlements are well located, through the National Upgrading Support Program.

Despite ongoing policy efforts in this regard, spatial inequality has been set in concrete. In its National Development Plan, the National Planning Commission's vision for the future regarding human settlement issues provides a stark indictment of the present situation:

> By 2050, South Africa will no longer have: poverty traps in rural areas and urban townships; workers isolated on the periphery of cities; inner cities controlled by slumlords and crime; sterile suburbs with homes surrounded by high walls and electric fences; households spending 30 percent or more of their time, energy and money on daily commuting; decaying infrastructure with power blackouts, undrinkable water, potholes and blocked sewers; violent protests; gridlocked roads and unreliable public transport; new public housing in barren urban landscapes; new private investment creating exclusive enclaves for the rich; fearful immigrant communities living in confined spaces; or rural communities dying as local production collapses. (NPC 2011)

Impacts of Wider Policies and Social Dynamics on Human Settlements

In practice, one of the weaknesses of urban development policy has been a tendency to focus on strategies internal to township boundaries, losing sight of their spatial, social, and economic location within a wider context—as well as the impact that wider polices and trends have within their boundaries.

For a start, developments in rural areas profoundly affect urban townships and settlements. Although the "borders" of the *bantustans* no longer exist, these are still the areas where poverty is most concentrated. After decades of acting as labor reserves for migrant labor, these areas are significantly deagrarianized, and residents depend on a mix of wage remittances and the social grants that have become the backbone of South Africa's antipoverty strategies. However, remittances from urban areas are in decline, rural areas have been hard hit by the recession, and rural out-migration continues apace. In theory, a strong policy emphasis on rural development should slow rural out-migration, but in practice, there is little evidence of this effect. Although the largest overall flows are to the five big "metros," the secondary cities have seen the most rapid in-migration (Cross 2009). In urban areas, informal settlements act as the reception points for this in-migration, with rural migrants relying on networks from home to enable their first access to the city—in a context in which there is little in formal policy to enable that access (Cross 2009). Nevertheless, urban informal settlements are often closer to economic opportunities than formal housing in either traditional townships or RDP townships; they are turbulent and crowded but have some level of access to economic opportunity (Cross 2009).

There is also a trend of migration to small rural towns. This comes partly from the former *bantustans* as well as from displacement and evictions from commercial farms in what was formerly "white" South Africa. In the first decade after apartheid, an estimated 2.35 million people were displaced and almost 1 million people evicted from farms. The patterns of evictions suggest that a combination of drivers, including drought, political uncertainty, and a reaction to legislation aiming to protect farmworkers' land and labor rights (Social Surveys Africa and Nkuzi 2005). The combined effect of these two migration flows has been a proliferation of informal settlements on the periphery of rural towns.

In contrast to the relative dynamism of urban informal settlements, rural informal settlements represent "the people left behind" (Cross 2009). Conditions are poor, there is little access to work, and high percentages of households are either headed by women or have lost members to out-migration or illness. These are households that lack the resources to migrate to the cities and therefore migrate to rural towns instead (Cross 2009).

Although most urban inflows are from rural South Africa, there are also significant inflows of economic migrants, and refugees, from the rest of Africa. This increases the competition for jobs, for business opportunities, and for housing, which has fueled episodes of xenophobia—with disastrous consequences in the outbreaks of xenophobic violence in 2008 (Cross 2009). While such episodes have not yet recurred on the same scale, evidence suggests that xenophobia continues to simmer very close to the surface.

In addition to the pressures arising from in-migration, there has been a substantial shift in household composition since 1994. The decline in household size coupled with population growth has led to a significant increase in household numbers. In Johannesburg, the number of households increased by 8.05 percent per year to 2001, about double the national average (Pillay, Tomlinson, and du Toit 2006).

In turn, the increased number of households has caused housing and services backlogs to grow faster than the pace of delivery can address. For example, although the government delivered over 3 million subsidized housing units since 1994, the housing backlog is still bigger than it was when the housing delivery process began (NPC 2011). Backlogs in housing and service delivery are compounded by poor-quality outcomes and maintenance failures, in some instances reversing gains made in the provision of access. Frustration at these issues, compounded by high levels of unemployment, has fueled rising service delivery protests (Langa and von Holdt 2011). In the process, repertoires of organization and mobilization that had developed in the period of apartheid-era "ungovernability" find new expression.

South Africa has also been in the throes of a dual epidemic of tuberculosis and human immunodeficiency virus (HIV) and acquired immune deficiency syndrome (AIDS). Urban informal settlements have the highest overall HIV prevalence rate of 25.8 percent, which is nearly twice the prevalence in formal urban areas (Mahlangu, Vearey, and Thomas 2011). The disparity may reflect conditions in informal settlements that make residents more vulnerable to contracting HIV; certainly, it indicates higher vulnerability as a consequence of HIV. Access to services such as clean water, sanitation, and health care services become important determinants of health, yet often these are not available.

Townships within the Wider Economy

Townships were designed as dormitory towns for the labor required to serve the needs of mining and other industries. They had limited social services, and even less economic infrastructure, in a context in which—far from promoting local economic development—apartheid laws curtailed it. From 1952 to 1977, only the following categories of business activity were allowed in urban townships: general shops, butcheries, eating houses, the sale of milk and vegetables, and the hawking of goods. These restrictions were lifted after 1977, but to operate a business, a license was required from the Administration Boards, and these were restricted. Often, councilors and their families were believed to have preferential access to such licenses, as this account from the Duduza township on the East Rand illustrates (Seekings 1990): "My husband wanted to start a business [as] a funeral undertaker because there was none in the township. When he went to the offices to apply for a license, he was asked if he was a councillor. He was not a councillor, which then resulted in him not being issued with the license."

This perceived link between collaboration with the apartheid government and access to business opportunities in the townships did not augur well for businesspeople, and during the phase of "ungovernability" in the 1980s, township businesses were often considered legitimate targets of arson and attack. This did not, however, prevent the emergence of a range of informal activity—in particular, shebeens, spaza shops (informal convenience shops), street trading, and the taxi industry. However, as Luli Callinicos points out, where the informal sector in other countries was typically "extralegal," in the South African context, such activity was actually criminalized (Callinicos 1987, cited in Tsoeu 2009).

Post-1994, there was new scope to develop township economies, but many features of the townships' spatial design continued to militate against this. The biggest lost opportunity, however, was the failure to break the mold in the design of new RDP housing settlements, which typically reproduced the features of traditional townships that limit their scope to become sustainable human settlements—or to enable local economic development. This failure perpetuated the lack of effective public transport, lack of retail space, and lack of zoning for light industry or other business activity. It even extended to the shortsighted decision, motivated by cost-saving concerns, to limit households in some RDP housing developments to two-phase electricity instead of three-phase electricity. The use of two-phase electricity prevents the development of home-based enterprises reliant on the use of freezers, generators, sewing machines, welding equipment, and many other tools that require three phase electricity—in a context where most small enterprises in Gauteng Province are home-based, as the FinScope Small Business Pilot Survey in Gauteng found (African Response 2007).

While the development of vibrant local economies within townships face a range of internal constraints (the subject of chapters 4 and 7), the wider structure of the economy also affects the options and opportunities for local enterprise development. Nascent local economic development in townships and informal settlements takes place in the shadow of South Africa's developed core economy. For new entrepreneurs, one of the easiest entry points into markets is to make and sell the things your neighbors and community need. This can build on trust relationships, and the entrepreneurs are clear on the value proposition of their products in their own community contexts.

In poor communities, however, the basket of consumer goods that people buy is relatively small. And in South Africa, most of the items in that basket are already mass-produced in the core economy, whether they be bread, beer, canned goods, clothing, or less-regular purchases such as furniture. These are all readily available in branded stores in the nearby town center. The scale of such production makes it hard for new or small businesses to compete on price or on brand recognition. The dominance of the core production sector leaves few entry points into production or manufacturing of basic consumer goods. Instead, opportunities lie in niche products, in adding value to existing products, in services, and in retail. In practice, the retail sector heavily dominates South Africa's small business and informal sector, mainly by simply distributing branded products into areas (such as townships and informal settlements) that are not well served by retail networks.

Conclusions: Townships Today

The term "township" has become imbued with many meanings since the apartheid government first set out the criteria that were to define them. Postapartheid, the process of addressing ongoing urbanization and the housing crisis (and the gaps in doing so) must contend with emerging forms of urban settlement for new entrants to the city as well as for poor people.

Whether long-established or newly developed, formal or informal, most of these housing settlements still have these challenges in common:

- The lack of social and economic facilities required to build sustainable communities

- The continued distances—geographically and socioeconomically—from South Africa's economic heartlands
- The subordination of most of their internal economic activity to the economy outside their boundaries
- The limited extent to which money circulates internally before returning to the magnetic core
- The narrow range of business activities
- The marginality of the incomes earned

Or so, at least, it seems. The rest of the chapters in this volume will explore how accurate these perceived characteristics of township economies are—and how much they are changing.

Notes

1. "Shebeen queens" are black women who owned or operated *shebeens*, the illicit liquor outlets, often unlicensed and in the women's own homes, that the apartheid government tried "to shut down as a black person by law was not allowed to brew or drink beer, let alone spirits" (Mngadi 2012). "Tsotsis" (from Sesotho, loosely, "thug") is slang for someone, usually young or still a minor, who steals, lies, and is generally not to be trusted; sometimes used to lightly insult friends. The minibus taxis carry most of South Africa's commuters.

2. *Bantustans* (also known as Bantu homelands, black homelands, or simply homelands) were rural territories established by the government for South Africa's black population, the remaining land to be reserved for the white population.

3. The "Coloured" racial classification under the South African apartheid bureaucracy included people regarded as being of mixed-race descent. The other three legally defined racial groups were Black, White, and Indian.

4. The "51/6" house was so named after the date (1951) and the number (6) assigned to the prototype.

5. *Umkhonto we Sizwe* (commonly abbreviated as MK, translating to "Spear of the Nation") was the ANC's armed, or military, wing.

6. The call for "one city, one tax base" originated in a 1989 paper published by the Soweto People's Delegation (SPD), which concluded that the bulk of Johannesburg's income, coming from industry and commerce, was generated largely by the black workers from Soweto. Because Johannesburg provided rebates to its homeowners on their property taxes but returned no income to the township where its workers lived, the paper concluded, Soweto's black people were effectively subsidizing white Johannesburg. The SPD paper's call for "one city, one tax base" became a rallying cry for township activists—as well as a basis for negotiations to end Soweto's rent boycott.

7. Informal settlements are areas that are not surveyed and not designated for urban settlement, with informal governance arrangements. They exist inside and around townships and along roads and railroad tracks. Some are inside townships on areas not planned for urban settlement, and they are even in tribal areas.

8. The plan's full formal title is "Breaking New Ground: A Comprehensive Plan for the Creation of Sustainable Human Settlements" (Department of Housing 2004).

References

African Response. 2007. *FinScope Small Business Pilot Survey Report Gauteng 2006*. Report for FinMark Trust and Gauteng Enterprises Propeller by African Response, Bryanston, South Africa.

ANC (African National Congress). 1955. "The Freedom Charter." Statement of principles of the Congress Alliance, adopted at the Congress of the People, Kliptown, June 26. http://www.anc.org.za/show.php?id=72.

Bonner, P., and L. Segal. 1998. *Soweto: A History*. Cape Town, South Africa: Maskew Miller Longman (Pty) Ltd.

Callinicos, L. 1980. *Gold and Workers 1886–1924*, vol. 1 of *A People's History of South Africa*. Johannesburg, South Africa: Ravan Press.

———. 1987. *Working Life 1886–1940: Factories, Townships, and Popular Culture on the Rand*, vol. 2 of *A People's History of South Africa*. Johannesburg, South Africa: Ravan Press.

COGTA (Department of Co-operative Governance and Traditional Affairs). 2009. *Township Transformation Timeline*. Pretoria, South Africa: COGTA and the European Union.

Cross, C. 2009. "Migration Trends and Human Settlements: Some Implications for Service Centres." PowerPoint presentation, Human Sciences Research Council, Pretoria, October 27.

Department of Housing. 2004. "Breaking New Ground: A Comprehensive Plan for the Development of Sustainable Human Settlements." Department of Housing, Republic of South Africa, Pretoria.

Langa, M., and H. von Holdt. 2011. "Bokfontein: The Nations Are Amazed." In *New South African Review 2: New Paths, Old Compromises?* edited by J. Daniel, P. Naidoo, D. Pillay, and R. Southall, 258–75. Johannesburg, South Africa: Wits University Press.

Mahlangu, P., J. Vearey, and L. Thomas. 2011. "Addressing HIV in Informal Settlements and the Critical Role of Local Government in Achieving Targets set in the NSP 2012–2016: Submission to Zero Draft of the National Strategic Plan 2012–2016." Recommendations of the South African Medical Research Council and the African Centre for Migration, University of the Witwatersrand, Johannesburg.

Mkhwanazi, T. 1988. "Column on the Soweto Rent Boycotts." *Weekly Mail*, April 7.

Mngadi, S. 2012. "Shebeen Queens Nurture Communities." *City Press*, November 3. http://www.citypress.co.za/columnists/shebeen-queens-nurture-communities-20121103/.

NPC National Planning Commission. 2011. "National Development Plan." 11 November 2011. The Presidency, South Africa.

———. 2012. *National Development Plan 2030: Our Future—Make It Work*. Pretoria, South Africa: NPC. http://www.npconline.co.za/pebble.asp?relid=757.

Pieterse, E. 2009. "Post-Apartheid Geographies in South Africa: Why Are Urban Divides So Persistent?" Paper presented at the workshop, "Interdisciplinary Debates on Development and Cultures: Cities in Development—Spaces, Conflict and Agency," Leuven University, Belgium, December 13.

Pillay, U., R. Tomlinson, and J. du Toit. 2006. "Introduction." In *Democracy and Delivery: Urban Policy in South Africa*, edited by U. Pillay, R. Tomlinson, and J. du Toit, 1–21. Pretoria, South Africa: HRSC Press.

Rueedi, F. 2011. "When All Hell Broke Loose: The Vaal Uprising Revisited." Paper presented at the Nordic Africa Institute's 4th European Conference on African Studies (ECAS 2011), "African Engagements: On Whose Terms?" Uppsala, Sweden, June 15–18.

Seekings, J. 1990. "Broken Promises: Discontent, Protest, and the Transition to Confrontation in Duduza, 1978–1985." Paper presented at the History Workshop conference, "Structure and Experience in the Making of Apartheid," University of Witwatersrand, Johannesburg, February 6–10.

Social Surveys Africa and Nkuzi (Nkuzi Development Association). 2005. *Summary of Key Findings from the National Evictions Survey.* Joint study report, Social Surveys Africa, Johannesburg; and Nkuzi, Petersburg North, South Africa.

Stats SA (Statistics South Africa). 2004. *Census 2001 Concepts and Definitions.* Report 03-02-26 (2001), Pretoria, South Africa.

Tambo, O. 1984. "Address by Oliver Tambo to the Nation on Radio Freedom." Broadcast, Radio Freedom, October 10. http://www.anc.org.za/show.php?id=4470.

Tsoeu, M. 2009. "A Value Chain Analysis of the Formal and the Informal Economy: A Case Study of South African Breweries and Shebeens in Soweto." Master's thesis, University of the Witwatersrand, Johannesburg, South Africa.

Zack, T. 2008. "Development of the Urban Development Component for a Second Economy Strategy." Urban LandMark policy paper for the Second Economy Strategy Project of Trade and Industrial Policy Strategies (TIPS) for the Presidency's Accelerated Shared Growth Initiative of South Africa (AsgiSA) High Level Task Team, Republic of South Africa, Pretoria. http://www.tips.org.za/files/2E_Urban _LandMark_urbandevelopstrat_Sept08.pdf.

CHAPTER 2

A Conceptual Framework for the Township Economy

Sandeep Mahajan

An Integrated Analytical Approach

To better understand the dynamics (past and potential) of South Africa's segmented, multilayered economy and the place of the township economy within it, a conceptual framework is needed. The basis for the framework may be found in two closely related analytical strands:

- First, theoretical and empirical analyses show that fast-paced growth in the urban informal economy (the township economy, in South Africa's case) is fully consistent with growth in the urban formal sector. There is nothing inevitable about the prospect, as some have advanced, that the township economy could wither away under the shadows of the formal advanced economy (FAE).
- Second, advanced economies don't grow fast; lagging economies do. Thus the township economy not only can chug alongside the urban formal economy but also can potentially become an important driver of near-term growth.

Dual-Economy Literature and the Urban Informal Sector

South Africa's highly segmented economic structure poses important questions about its development trajectory: How essential is the township economy to the country's desired objective of faster growth and job creation? Given its low development, its weak linkages with the formal sector,[1] and the negligible industrial production within the township borders (features, highlighted throughout this report, that produce the decidedly low internal multipliers estimated in chapter 8), is it worthwhile for policy makers to focus on the township economy's prospects? Or will it inevitably wither away over time and get absorbed by the expansion of the formal, advanced economy?

Lewis's Dual-Sector Model

The starting point in pursuit of a conceptual framework is the dual-economy analysis developed by the economist Arthur Lewis in his seminal 1954 paper, "Economic Development with Unlimited Supplies of Labour." Lewis's dual-economy model included, on one hand, a "capitalist sector"—the modern, rapidly industrializing part of the economy with a narrow interest in capturing capital, knowledge, and new ideas. On the other hand, the Lewis model's "subsistence sector" represented a traditional, unproductive, static part of the economy so inundated with surplus unskilled labor that the marginal productivity of labor had been driven down to zero, or even negative levels in some situations—much lower, in any case, than in the modern economy. In this model, a virtually unlimited supply of unskilled labor in the traditional sector was waiting to be tapped by the growing modern sector that required the unskilled labor at the market-wage price.

Although Lewis was mainly motivated by the presence of large-scale "disguised" unemployment in rural areas, he saw his framework as just as applicable to the urban informal sector. For example, noting large redundancies in the numbers of porters on the shipping docks and of domestic workers, Lewis remarked, "These occupations usually have a multiple of the number they need, each of them earning very small sums from employment; frequently their numbers could be halved without reducing output in this sector." He similarly invoked petty urban retail trading by observing that "it is enormously expanded in overpopulated economies; each trader makes only a few sales; markets are crowded with stalls, and if the number of stalls were greatly reduced the consumers would be no whit worse off—they might even be better off, since retail margins might fall" (Lewis 1954).

The development process in the Lewis model therefore unambiguously viewed the modern sector as the dominant engine of economic growth; there was little scope for the traditional or informal sector to play a significant part. The binding constraint to the economic expansion process became the availability of capital and natural resources because labor was readily and cheaply available at any given wage price. The key, according to Lewis, was "the use which is make of the capitalist surplus. In so far as this is reinvested in creating new capital, the capitalist sector expands, taking more people into capitalist employment out of the subsistence sector. The surplus is then larger still, capital formation is still greater, and so the process continues until the labor surplus disappears" (Lewis 1954).

Taken at face value, Lewis's conclusions are significant for South Africa's dual-economy structure—and troubling. Its modern sector is at levels commensurate with the advanced economies, where the growth potential, almost by definition, is limited to the extent by which the economy operates at or near the frontiers of technology. If the fate of the country's employment generation and shared prosperity hangs mostly on the growth potential of its modern sector, then that by itself cannot be very encouraging news. It will surely be difficult to tackle unemployment in the range of 25 percent, most of it structural and involving unskilled workers, on the back of an economic sector that is incapable of growing faster than 3–4 percent a year on a sustained basis.

Dichotomy of the Urban Informal Sector

Lewis's influential analysis, however, was not the final word on the potential role of the traditional or informal sector. To be sure, a number of observers have remained skeptical about the prospects for the traditional economy. But others see the potential in the traditional economy to play a far more positive role—in part because they don't view the urban informal sector as monolithic.

Ranis and Stewart (1999) portray the urban informal sector as a dichotomous structure: a stagnant "traditional" part juxtaposed with a dynamic "modernizing" one. The *traditional* informal sector, these authors contend, is associated with "very low capitalization, low labor productivity and low incomes, very small size (three or fewer workers), and static technology." (This mirrors the definition of most firms in the township of Diepsloot as summarized in chapter 6.) The *modernizing* informal sector, on the other hand, is "more capital-intensive, usually larger in size (as many as 10 workers), more dynamic in technology, often linked to the urban formal or F-sector." Under the right conditions, therefore, the modernizing informal sector holds significant potential for expansion and participation in the growth process of a developing country.

The informal modernizing sector, in this setting, can either compete with or complement the advanced formal economy. Competition is likely in markets for lower-end consumer goods, where both segments may operate. Complementarity would mainly take the form of production linkages, with the informal modernizing sector producing and selling intermediate and low-end capital goods to the formal sector. Conversely, Ranis and Stewart (1999) also find that the formal sector's propensity to draw on these linkages would depend upon its own level of competition: the more competitive the formal sector, the greater the pressures to cut production costs and the higher the propensity to outsource orders for intermediate inputs or tasks to the informal modernizing economy (IME). The "Analytical Framework" section below explores the applicability of this framework to South Africa's dual economy.

Global Informality Trends

A viable and dynamic urban informal sector is not just a theoretical possibility; it has become an empirical reality. Recent trends in the relative size of the informal economy show remarkably persistent, even rising, patterns in certain parts of the world, even during periods of high gross domestic product (GDP) growth.[2] Figure 2.1, from a 2009 Organisation for Economic Co-operation and Development (OECD) study, shows the experience of selected Latin American and East Asian economies over the past two to three decades. These data led the report to conclude that "informality is increasingly becoming normal, not least in middle and even high-income countries. ... The development in selected countries in Southeast Asia and Latin America is telling in this respect: over the last

Figure 2.1 Informal Employment and GDP in Latin America (1990–2007) and Southeast Asia (1985–99)

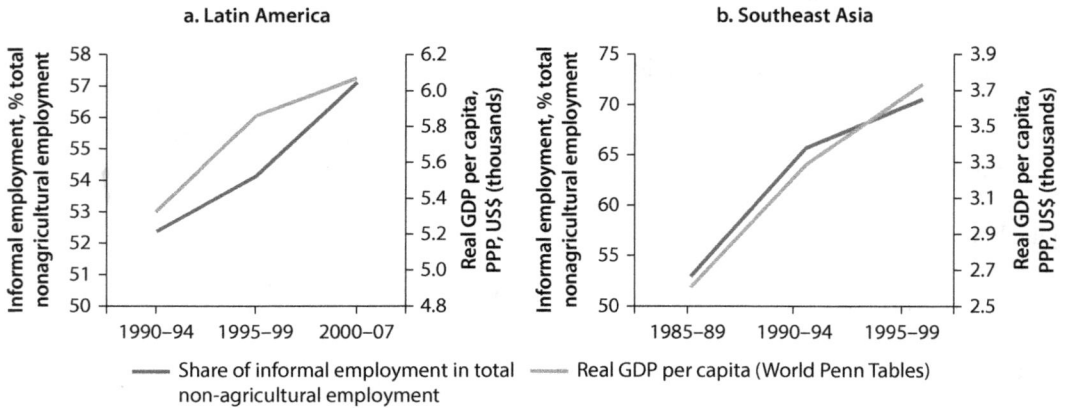

Sources: Jütting and Laiglesia 2009; GDP data from Penn World Table.
Note: GDP = gross domestic product; PPP = purchasing power parity.

30 years, growth in these countries was accompanied by increasing, not falling, informal employment" (Jütting and Laiglesia 2009).

These trends certainly go against the predictions of the dual-economy models of Lewis (1954) and others who saw rapid economic growth and relative decline of the informal sector as being commensurate. Kanbur (2011) attributes this positive relationship between growth and informality in the past quarter century to (a) weaker enforcement of regulations, (b) weaker regulations, and (c) trends in technology and trade that have tended to be skills- and capital-intensive and less employment generating. Based on the Ranis and Stewart (1999) dual-economy framework, it could also be because the informal sector has a significant modernizing component in addition to just the traditional component picked up by Lewis and others.

An Analytical Framework for South Africa's Urban Economy

The Ranis and Stewart (1999) framework described above opens up the possibility for a part of the urban informal sector (or the township economy) to become an important engine of growth under certain conditions. Drawing on that work, our analytical framework captures three parts of the South African urban economy:

- *A FAE* exists mostly in the urban city cores, representing high-end banking, capital-intensive manufacturing, and large-scale mining; operates with the latest available technologies; employs workers with at least a high school education or (likely) higher; creates an environment that is not highly competitive, limiting the sector's growth potential; provides easy access to formal finance plus significant surplus and savings in the sector; and has easy access to modern transport networks, though at relatively high costs.

- *An IME* exists mostly in large urban townships, using moderate levels of technology (perhaps an Internet connection and e-mail use); has its own transport (but not for shipment of goods) and a reliable electricity connection; requires a proper business premise (either owned or rented) on land with a title deed; has an owner or proprietor with at least a high school education; provides products and services that complement and do not compete with those of the FAE (with the IME supplying intermediate goods and contract services to the FAE); has motivated owners and proprietors who would prefer running a business over salaried employment; and has access to informal and some formal credit, albeit at relatively high cost.

- *An informal traditional economy (ITE)* exists almost entirely in townships and informal settlements, characterized by low productivity, very low capital intensity, and unreliable or no electricity connection; lacks its own transport, relying on expensive private commercial transport facilities; has limited use of technology (cell phone mostly); lacks bank accounts and access to formal credit, offering only membership in informal savings clubs; largely comprises household-sector enterprises (with not more than one or two paid workers); has proprietors likely to have less than a high school education who, if given a choice, would pick stable salaried employment in the formal sector; has a fair number of owners who are foreign nationals without formal documentation; lacks a downstream connection with the FAE while trading in products largely manufactured in the FAE; and predominantly features street vending and other small-scale retail sales operations, personal services (hair salons), and artisanal production. Vast majority of firms in South African townships appear to fall in the ITE category, as evidenced from the business census for Diepsloot reported in chapter 6.

Application to the Current Economy
Figure 2.2 formalizes the application of the Ranis and Stewart (1999) framework to South Africa's urban economy (we leave out the rural-urban dynamics for this part) along with further assumptions laid out below.

Assume that the labor markets clear in the ITE but not in the FAE (because of strong union influence) nor in the IME (because of a relatively high reservation wage). Labor mobility from the ITE to the IME, and further from the IME to the FAE, is mostly restricted not only by the different skill levels associated with each sector, but also by (a) the small levels of savings and limited access to finance for the two informal economies, and (b) the vast geographical distances between the informal economies and the FAE. The foreign nationals in the ITE are also hindered by lack of proper documentation.

So, what we have in this low-income-level, high-unemployment equilibrium is a modestly performing formal urban sector (FAE), a traditional informal sector (ITE) that is very small and has extremely limited capability to grow, and a virtually missing modernizing informal sector (IME) that has untapped potential for growth and job creation. The policy challenge, then, is to start a virtuous cycle by first creating the conditions to make the IME viable and then enabling it to grow.

Figure 2.2 Current Dual-Economy Representation of South Africa

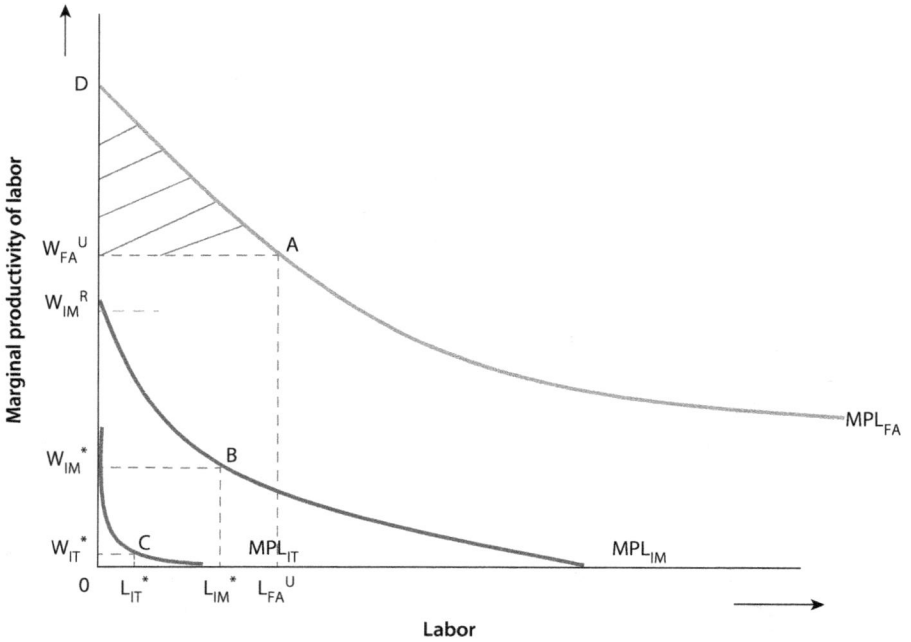

Note: FAE = formal advanced economy; ITE = informal traditional economy; IME = informal modernizing economy; MPL = marginal productivity of labor. Therefore, MPL_{FA}, MPL_{IT}, and MPL_{IM} are the marginal productivity of labor in the FAE, ITE, and IME, respectively. W_{FA}^U is the wage rate negotiated between unions and firms in the FAE. W_{IM}^R is the reservation wage of workers excluded from the FAE and who choose not to participate in the ITE. W_{IM}^* and W_{IT}^* are the market-clearing wages in the IME and ITE, respectively. The following assumptions also apply to the figure:

1. MPL_{FA} lies well above MPL_{IM} and the latter well above MPL_{IT} at all points because of higher capital stocks per worker, greater intensiveness of more advanced technology, and more sophisticated and efficient organizational structures.

2. L_{FA}^U and L_{IT}^* are the labor forces employed in the FAE and ITE, respectively, and L_{IM}^* would be the labor force employed in the IME at the market-clearing wage rate W_{IM}^*. W_{FA}^U is the wage rate negotiated between unions and firms in the FAE.

3. W_{IM}^R, the reservation wage of workers excluded from the FAE who choose not to participate in the ITE, is close to the highest point on the MPL_{IM}, so as to keep the size of the IME negligibly small. The high W_{IM}^R reflects the significant social transfers made to the less well off as well as the high entry barriers for black South Africans in the MSME (micro, small, and medium enterprise) sector because of a host of legacy issues.

4. The wage set in the FAE is above, and that set in the ITE is below, W_{IM}^R. Rural sector wages, not shown here, would lie somewhere between W_{IM}^R and W_{IT}^* per Ranis and Stewart (1999).

5. In the absence of a reservation wage, the market-clearing wage in the IME would have been W_{IM}^*, corresponding to an MPL represented at point B, which would have allowed OL_{IM}^* workers to be employed in the IME.

6. Assume that the actual employment level in the IME is close to zero, and that OL_{IM}^* is also the number of unemployed workers. Without a reservation wage and other structural barriers, there would not have been any unemployment (with the IME absorbing the surplus labor), although the labor market would clear at a very low wage rate. Similarly, there would also be no unemployment if wages were market-clearing in the FAE. Reflecting the current political economy, we don't consider the possibility of market-clearing wages in either the IME or the FAE.

7. Area ADW_{FA}^U is the producer's surplus in the FAE and gets reinvested there in the next period, leading to a dynamic process of growth in the FAE.

8. Because the IME has little output, it generates a negligible producer's surplus and thereby no investment and growth in that segment. With limited access to formal finance, it is trapped in a low-level equilibrium characterized by low-demand and adverse supply constraints.

Application with an IME Boost

To begin with, making the IME viable requires a big, coordinated policy push to move the IME's marginal productivity of labor outward in order to increase its profitability to a point that the sector as a whole generates employment and a sizable surplus that it can plow back into investment. Up to a point, the new marginal productivity of labor in the IME can even exceed the FAE wage level (as shown in figure 2.3)—implying that some people in the IME prefer it over opportunities in the FAE. As noted, wage flexibility in the IME and FAE would also boost employment growth (at lower wages), but we rule out this scenario to reflect the existing political economy.

Strengthening of the IME (based on a policy agenda mentioned below) would enable the growth engine to operate on two cylinders: first, the conventional one

Figure 2.3 Dual-Economy Representation of South Africa after Boosting the IME

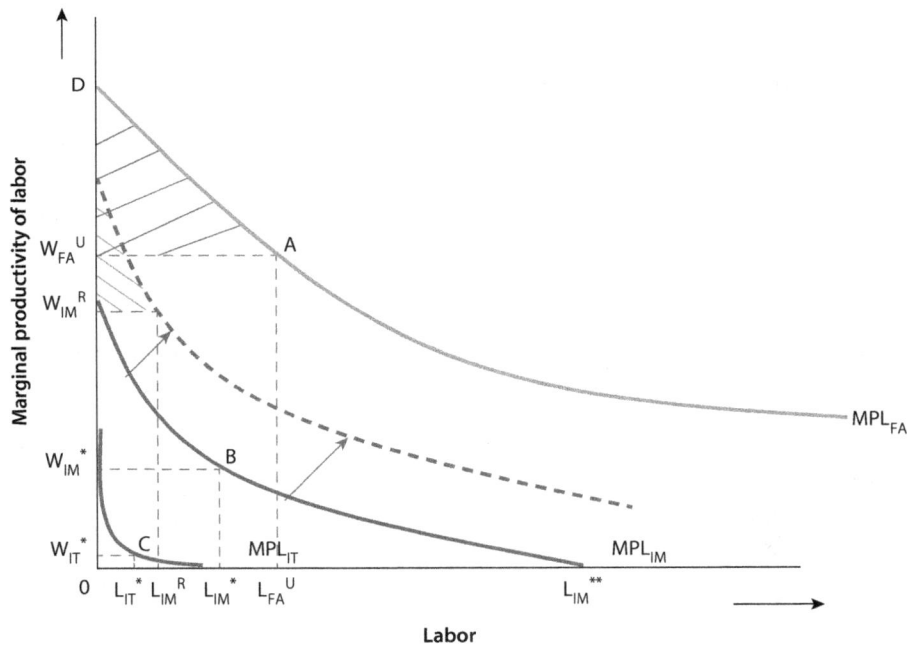

Note: FAE = formal advanced economy; ITE = informal traditional economy; IME = informal modernizing economy; MPL = marginal productivity of labor. Therefore, MPL_{FA}, MPL_{IT}, and MPL_{IM} are the marginal productivity of labor in the FAE, ITE, and IME, respectively. W_{FA}^U is the wage rate negotiated between unions and firms in the FAE. W_{IM}^R is the reservation wage of workers excluded from the FAE and who choose not to participate in the ITE. W_{IM}^* and W_{IT}^* are the market-clearing wages in the IME and ITE, respectively. MPL_{FA} lies well above MPL_{IM} and the latter well above MPL_{IT} at all points because of higher capital stocks per worker, greater intensiveness of more advanced technology, and more sophisticated and efficient organizational structures. L_{FA}^U, L_{IT}^*, and L_{IM}^R are the labor forces employed in the FAE, ITE, and IME respectively, and L_{IM}^* would be the labor force employed in the IME at the market-clearing wage rate W_{IM}^*. L_{IM}^R is necessarily smaller than L_{FA}^U and L_{IM}^*, and ($L_{IM}^* - L_{IM}^R$) is the new (and smaller) unemployment rate after the expansion of the IME. W_{FA}^U is the wage rate negotiated between unions and firms in the FAE. W_{IM}^R, the reservation wage of workers excluded from the FAE who choose not to participate in the ITE, is close to the highest point on the MPL_{IM}, so as to keep the size of the IME negligibly small in the absence of a productivity shock that pushes out the MPL_{IM} curve. The high W_{IM}^R reflects the significant social transfers made to the less well off as well as the high entry barriers for black South Africans in the MSME (micro, small, and medium enterprise) sector because of a host of legacy issues.

involving expansion of the formal urban sector, and second, an IME that becomes increasingly viable and also more deeply integrated over time with the FAE.

Policy Agenda for Boosting IME Growth

A broad range of policy reforms will be needed enable a takeoff of the hitherto flailing IME. Policies will need to tackle a range of supply- and demand-side issues:

- *Supply-side issues.* The relative size and growth potential of the IME depends partly on its own supply conditions, or its inherent ability to respond to increases in demand for its products. That, in turn, is a function of the amount of capital stock it has; its access to technology, infrastructure, and finance; and the skill and educational levels of its firm owners and workers. From the results of this report (chapter 6 on the investment climate and chapter 4 on access to finance), on most counts, the supply side is heavily constrained for the IME. Moreover, various historical legacy issues that have thwarted entre-preneurship (as discussed in chapter 1) also tie down the supply side. Supply-side conditions would therefore need to improve dramatically in a number of dimensions to get the desired magnitude of improvement in the marginal pro-ductivity of labor. The broad agenda here will involve strengthening education and skill-development programs, improving financial inclusion and access to basic infrastructural services, addressing crime and other business environment constraints identified in chapter 6, and developing affordable public transport links between townships and urban centers.

- *Limited FAE demand for IME goods and services.* Critical to strengthening the IME's viability is the level of demand from the FAE for its intermediate and capital goods. That demand, in turn, depends on the FAE's own size and struc-ture: the larger, the faster-growing, and the more competitive and less verti-cally integrated it is, the greater its demand will be for the IME's products and services (Ranis and Stewart 1999). Many consider the corporate formal sector in South Africa, while relatively large, to have highly concentrated ownership structures and thus limited competition. Its growth performance, too, has been modest at best. Large firms also tend to be more vertically integrated in South Africa relative to comparator countries (Mncube, Khumalo, and Ngobese 2009). Under these circumstances, the FAE's demand for the IME's goods and services is likely to be limited at best. Addressing the industrial concentration issues in the FAE will therefore be critical for growth and job creation not only in the FAE but also in the IME.

- *Low consumer demand.* Urban consumers are a second source of demand for the IME's goods and services. The strength of this demand will depend in par-ticular on the preferences and purchasing power of those in the middle- and low-income households: the more price elastic and the less brand-conscious their demand is, the stronger their purchases from the IME will be. This raises a particular concern in South Africa's case. As Philip (2010) and others have observed, consumer demand in South Africa is driven in large part by formal sector brand names. Chapters 7 and 8 further verify this, finding that a significant portion of consumer spending in the township of Diepsloot goes toward goods produced by large formal suppliers outside the township. Although more equal income distribution would enhance consumer demand for IME products (Ranis and Stewart 1999), South Africa's very high income-distribution inequality works further against the country's IME. Furthermore, unemployment rates in urban townships and informal settlements (T&IS) remain quite high (as detailed in chapter 3), keeping the purchasing power (and therefore the demand for IME products) in these locations quite low. An extensive network of extensive social grants (roughly 3.5 percent of GDP) to vulnerable groups and temporary public employment programs such as the Public Works Program and the Community Works Program do help the poor maintain a minimum threshold of expenditure levels. However, consumer demand, just like formal sector demand, under these conditions can be expected to remain low for the IME's products and services.

In Search of a South Africa "Convergence Machine"

Given the saturated growth potential of South Africa's formal advanced urban economy, faster economic growth must largely come from the less-developed township economy (together with a recovery of the rural sector), which could potentially take off just as the successful emerging-market economies of the world have. Therefore, South Africa's economic policy agenda will involve a big push to better integrate its township economy with its advanced economy, to allow it to catch up in terms of income and productivity levels and other measures of economic development.

There are important lessons to be learned from the catch-up experience known as "convergence" in other parts of the world, most notably Europe in recent times.[3] Europe successfully developed a powerful "convergence machine" that has greatly benefited all of the European Union (EU) member states, especially the economically weaker ones (World Bank 2012). Increasing integration of the EU's goods and services trade, as well as its financial and institutional integration, has enabled rapid income and productivity convergence on the continent. In the process, the member nations have become much more specialized in what they produce, leveraging their comparative advantages in trade with one another. At the same time, capital is flowing largely "downhill" in search of higher yield—that is, from richer to poorer countries.

It is important to note, however, that it is only groups of economies that are sufficiently similar in terms of their economic institutions and have porous borders for trade, technology, and capital flows that show clear tendencies for convergence. This is empirically true among similar economies—in Europe, for example, but also among the OECD countries (figure 2.4) or even among the mainland U.S. states (figure 2.5). Among the OECD countries, those that had

Figure 2.4 Unconditional Convergence in GDP Per Capita among OECD Countries, 1951–2010

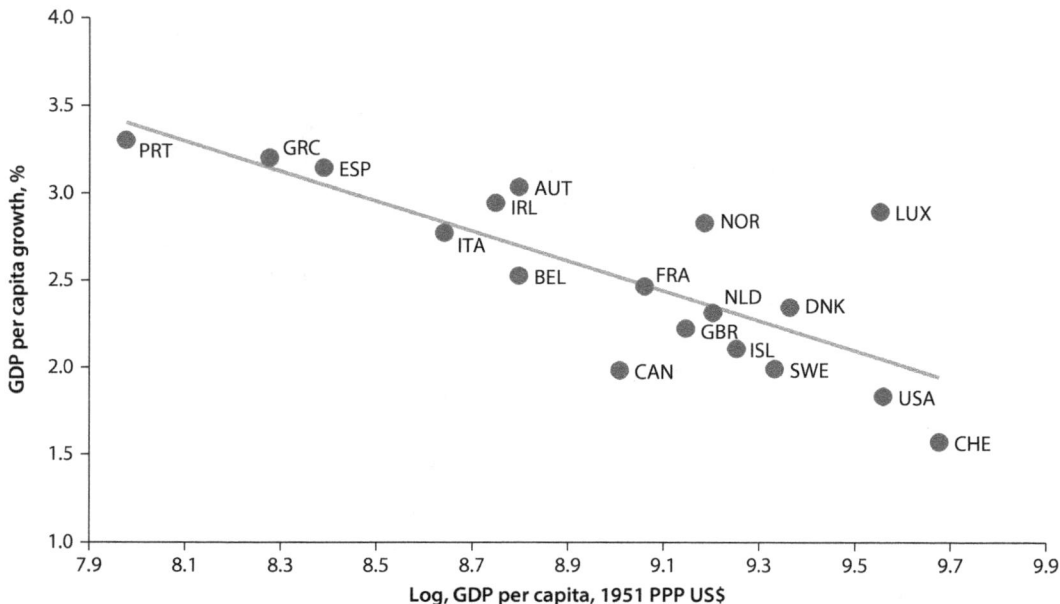

Source: GDP data from Penn World Tables.
Note: OECD = Organisation for Economic Co-operation and Development; GDP = gross domestic product; PPP = purchasing power parity.
Coefficient of correlation = −0.78.

Figure 2.5 Unconditional Convergence in Per Capita Personal Income among U.S. States, 1929–2010

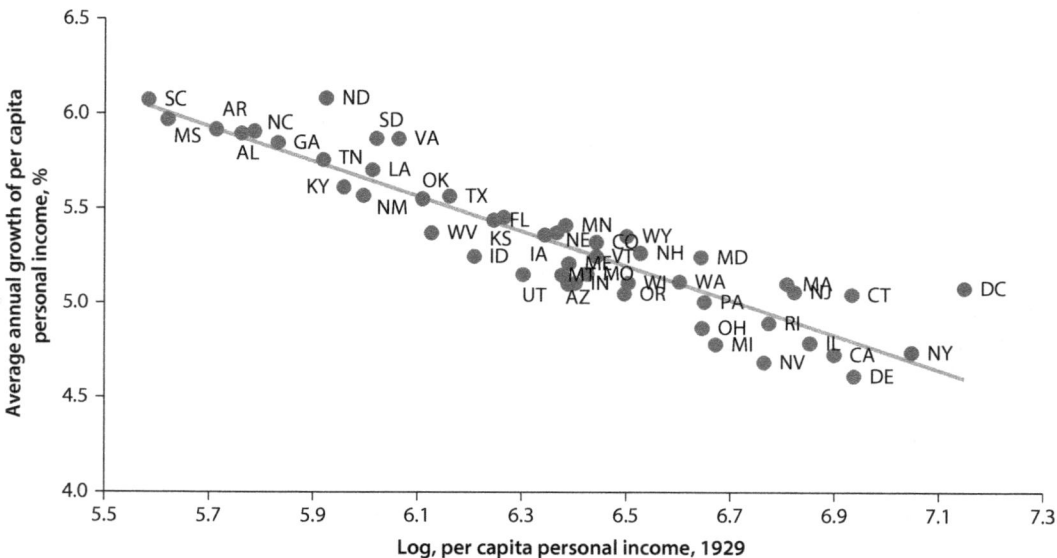

Source: Bureau of Economic Analysis, U.S. Department of Commerce.
Note: Coefficient of correlation = −0.91.

the lowest per capita GDP (in constant purchasing power parity [PPP] US$) in 1950—countries such as Greece, Portugal, and Spain—saw the fastest average GDP growth during 1951–2000. Similarly, U.S. states such as South Carolina, Mississippi, and Arkansas that had the lowest per capita personal income in 1929 saw among the fastest per capita income growth rates over the 1929–2010 period. On the other hand, a similar comparison for Sub-Saharan Africa—where barriers to labor, capital, and trade flows across borders are quite thick—does not show an inverse relationship between the initial incomes of countries and their subsequent long-term growth (figure 2.6).

That the township economy coexists with a substantial, modern urban economy that is far ahead in terms of income and productivity points to the significant gains possible by enabling economic convergence between the two. However, potential gains are limited by the marked segmentations that inhibit the free flow of goods, services, factors of production, and technologies between the two economies and thereby create major economic distortions. Policy makers must find ways to exploit the "arbitrage" between the two economies to ensure that capital flows into, not out of, the less-developed township economy—and that labor is more mobile toward the advanced economy while township entrepreneurs have greater access to its markets. Integrating the two economies will require a major focus on public transport infrastructure; commercially viable, low-income housing projects near urban centers; programs to boost the education and skills of the township youth; measures to enhance competition within the FAE; and efforts to loosen the constraints (identified in chapter 6) that impede progress in the townships' critical business environment.

Figure 2.6 No Signs of Convergence among Sub-Saharan Countries

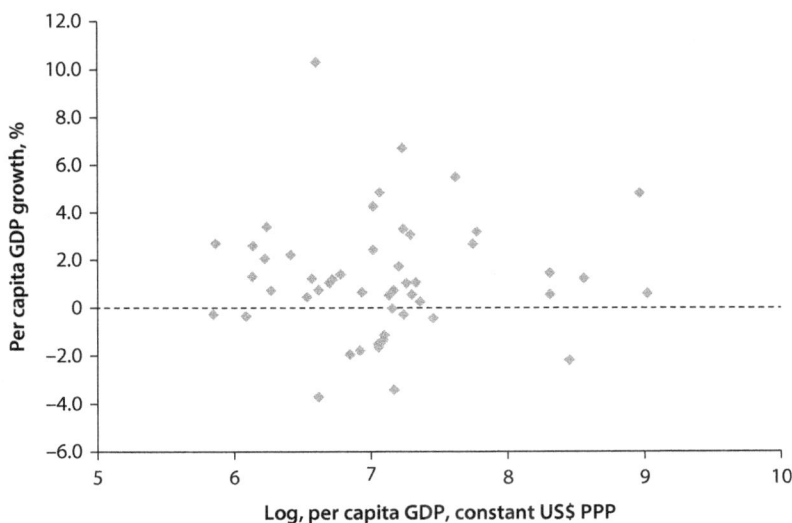

Source: World Development Indicators, World Bank.
Note: Coefficient of correlation = 0.02.

The oddity of the South African situation is that such stark geographic segmentations exist within common national borders. This very uniqueness, however, also highlights a major opportunity because bringing the segmentations down doesn't depend on complicated cross-border diplomacy: it is in South Africa's own hands. While still not a straightforward task, given the complex national history that has anchored much of the spatial divide, it is an achievable one. The needed transformations will require strong leadership, political will, and coordinated but resolute policy actions on the broad areas outlined here.

If South Africa can, indeed, launch its own version of a convergence machine—one enabling rapid growth of the township economy (with a particular focus on the IME) by unleashing its own internal economic dynamics and by integrating it in meaningful ways with the modern urban economy—the whole country's growth potential could be significantly enhanced. Such an effort would involve building on the township economy's comparative advantages: in particular, abundance of cheap, unskilled labor; adjoining, more affordable land space; and a potential, still-untapped consumer market.

While understanding and responding to the potential benefits of including the township economy into South Africa's growth process seems crucial, we also need to recognize the challenging starting conditions of the townships and informal settlements, as the following chapters describe in detail.

Notes

1. To be sure, both economies are products of the same inequality-breeding system (Philip 2010), which is feeding a growing presence of mass-production networks in townships. Nonetheless, major segmentations persist, as a result of which the labor flow from townships to urban formal areas remains prohibitively expensive, township entrepreneurs have virtually no access to the urban formal markets, and capital tends to flow "uphill"—from townships to the urban formal sector.

2. The relationship between countries' income levels and informality levels is strongly negative, indicating that informality declines with development over the very long run.

3. Convergence is a process by which an economy, simply by virtue of starting from a low base of income and productivity, is at an advantage in terms of its long-term growth potential. The concept has its analytical foundations in the standard neoclassical growth models (Solow 1956; Cass 1965; Koopmans 1965). Convergence is "unconditional" when poorer countries tend to grow faster over time irrespective of their policies, institutions, and level of integration with the group it is converging to. Convergence is "conditional" when the inverse relationship between initial income and subsequent growth holds only after accounting for difference in policies, institutions, and integration across countries.

References

Cass, D. 1965. "Optimum Growth in an Aggregative Model of Capital Accumulation." *The Review of Economic Studies* 32 (3): 233–40.

Jütting, J. P., and J. R. de Laiglesia, eds. 2009. *Is Informal Normal? Towards More and Better Jobs in Developing Countries*. OECD (Organisation for Economic Co-operation and Development) Development Centre Study. Paris: OECD Publishing.

Kanbur, R. 2011. "Avoiding Informality Traps." In *Reshaping Tomorrow: Is South Asia Ready for the Big Leap?* edited by E. Ghani, 260–78. New Delhi: Oxford University Press.

Koopmans, T. C. 1965. "On the Concept of Optimal Economic Growth." In *The Econometric Approach to Development Planning*, 225–87. Amsterdam, the Netherlands: North-Holland.

Lewis, W. A. 1954. "Economic Development with Unlimited Supplies of Labour." *The Manchester School* 22 (2): 139–91.

Mncube, L., L. Khumalo, and M. Ngobese. 2009. "Do Vertical Mergers Facilitate Upstream Collusion: Evidence from Selected Cases in South Africa." Paper presented at the "Third Annual Competition Conference," South African Competition Commission, Pretoria, September 4.

Philip, K. 2010. "Inequality and Economic Marginalization: How the Structure of the Economy Impacts on Opportunities on the Margins." *Law, Democracy & Development* 14 (2010): 105–32.

Ranis, G., and F. Stewart. 1999. "V-Goods and the Role of the Urban Informal Sector in Development." *Economic Development and Cultural Change* 47 (2): 259–88.

Solow, R. M. 1956. "A Contribution to the Theory of Economic Growth." *The Quarterly Journal of Economics* 70 (1): 65–94.

World Bank. 2012. *Golden Growth: Restoring the Lustre of the European Economic Model*. Washington, DC: World Bank.

CHAPTER 3

Economic and Social Trends in Townships and Informal Settlements

Hans Binswanger-Mkhize and Fernando Im

A Segmented Economic Terrain

This chapter analyzes the economic and social characteristics and trends across the four major settlement types in South Africa: rural areas, urban townships (TS), urban informal settlements (IS), and other urban areas (OUA). The analysis is based on a disaggregation of three types of national surveys[1] into these settlement types—the novelty of which is its differentiation between urban townships and informal settlements (T&IS) and the OUA category, which excludes T&IS.

First, the "Demographic Trends" section presents data that show that the T&IS had the highest population growth, by far, among the settlement types. For the first time, about half of South Africa's urban population lived in T&IS (Stats SA 2011a). This is the consequence of both natural population growth and migration from rural areas and neighboring countries. Much of this migration in the past decade has been concentrated in IS. In 2011, about 3 million people live in IS and roughly 15.3 million in TS.

Next, as the "Labor Market Trends" section discusses, T&IS do not exist in isolation from rural and OUA; they are connected to the broader economy through the mobility of factors of production (labor and capital) as well as through the markets for goods and services. Evidence suggests that households optimize their welfare by choosing where to live based on a combination of employment, housing opportunities, and access to public services. The IS typically are the first stops for migrants from rural areas and other foreign countries who are seeking employment opportunities. Subsequent movements from IS to TS and OUA occur as successful households improve their incomes over time. This interconnectivity between urban and rural areas will be a recurrent theme in this chapter. The interconnections, highly fragmented as they are in South Africa, are examined more deeply in the qualitative analysis of Diepsloot in chapter 5 and in the social accounting matrix for the same township in chapter 8.

Notably, T&IS are not a homogeneous group: systematic differences arise because employment opportunities are better near city centers, while housing is cheaper and more easily available farther away (Cross 2013). Households locate where the opportunities most closely match their needs. As a consequence, T&IS differ functionally across space to a significant degree: for example, the T&IS near urban centers function as entry points into the labor markets for young migrants who have limited housing needs, while the more-distant T&IS attract households that have greater housing needs and may have already found a job or have a stronger income cushion from family sources or government transfers.

The labor market data further suggest that T&IS contain poverty and unemployment traps for a large share of the urban labor force. Female-headed households and youth seem especially vulnerable, making them all the more susceptible to adverse income shocks, especially in the absence of systematic access by T&IS residents to formal finance (further discussed in chapter 4). Those stuck in these poverty and unemployment traps are spatially and structurally isolated from the rest of the economy, failing to connect through either the labor, capital, or goods markets.

In the rural areas, the poor employment trends in the past two decades have exacerbated the pressures on the T&IS, whose own economic structures are not geared to bear the added burden. According to national data sources, rural employment fell by 1.5 million in the past decade—from 4.4 million in 2000 to 2.9 million in 2011 (Stats SA 2000, 2011b). This was because of a fall in commercial farm employment, the virtual collapse of homeland agriculture that sharply reduced self-employment opportunities there, and job cuts in the mining sector. As a consequence, only one out of every four persons of working age in rural areas is currently employed. The broad unemployment rate has grown especially rapidly in rural South Africa, as job losses and lack of employment opportunities led to a sharp increase in the number of discouraged workers. The end result is that rural areas, despite out-migration in the past decade, still contain a reservoir of surplus labor.

In spite of the bleak overall employment situation, as the "Consumption and Poverty Trends" section discusses, per capita consumption improved and poverty rates decreased in all settlement types but the IS. The IS also have the lowest per capita consumption, followed by rural areas, TS, and OUA, whose share of national consumption is more than twice its population share. Despite the employment losses, rural areas have seen the highest growth rate in per capita consumption, albeit from a very low level. This growth appears to be associated with widening eligibility for social grants. That per capita income is lower in IS than in rural areas is consistent with the prediction of the Ranis and Stewart (1999) model (described in chapter 2) that the lowest wages are seen in the primary destination of rural-urban migration, where the traditional informal sector is prevalent.

The section also focuses on the multiple disadvantages of single-headed households.[2] In 2010, more than half of South African children lived in a single-headed household. Such a share was the highest in rural areas (with 61.1 percent of children living in single-headed households), followed by TS (51.3 percent), IS (45.4 percent) and OUA (35.1 percent) (Stats SA 2011a). The vast majority of single-headed households had a female head. This picture is explained by the fact that many men in urban areas have rural wives and children. Women face a far worse labor market situation than men in terms of unemployment and wages, making those living in female-headed households more likely to fall into poverty. As a consequence, consumption per capita for male-headed households remains almost two-thirds higher than consumption per capita of female-headed households.

The chapter's final theme is developed in the section on "Social Indicators and Access to Services." Survey data suggest noticeable (though highly uneven) improvements in educational outcomes, hunger reduction, and nighttime security across all settlement types. However, although the T&IS's access to housing, water, sewerage, and electricity all increased in terms of number of households, the proportion of households benefiting from them has stagnated. These services seem to have had a hard time keeping up with the rapidly growing number of households. Finally, improvement in health sector-related indicators has been limited, with the share of sick people receiving treatment deteriorating and health insurance coverage sparse in the T&IS.

Demographic Trends across Settlement Types

Over the past decade, T&IS have seen rapid population increases. Between 2000 and 2011, the urban population grew by 3 percent per year, while the rural population declined by 0.9 percent per year (as detailed in table 3B.1). As a result, in 2011 roughly 62.7 percent of the approximately 50 million South Africans lived in urban areas and 37.3 percent in rural areas (Stats SA 2011b). Further, the IS population, and to a lesser extent the TS population, grew faster than the population in OUA. Consequently, about 3 million people were living in IS (more than doubling in a decade) and about 15.3 million in TS (increasing by close to 40 percent) (Stats SA 2000, 2003, 2011a, 2011b). By 2010, for the first time, the combined T&IS population exceeded the OUA population (Stats SA 2011a).

Migration in response to economic opportunities and differences in population growth rates have strongly influenced the population patterns in the different settlement types. IS and newer, less-established TS such as Diepsloot have received a large influx of rural and foreign migrants in search of work, sometimes fulfilling a role of a transitional settlement between urbanism and rural life, as chapter 5 further discusses.

National household and labor force surveys also reveal the 2000–11 trends for each settlement type by race, age, household size, and gender, as described below (Stats SA 2000, 2003, 2011a, 2011b).

Townships and informal settlements are overwhelmingly black. While blacks made up about 79.5 percent of the total population in 2011, they were highly concentrated in T&IS, where they constituted over 95 percent of the population, as shown in table 3.1. They were only 42.6 percent of the population of OUA. Colored people represented 8.8 percent of the total population but only 4 percent or less of the T&IS population, and they were concentrated in OUA.[3] The situation for the Indian or Asian population was similar but more extreme, with only 0.1 percent in TS and none in IS. Whites were practically absent in T&IS. Instead, they were overwhelmingly concentrated in OUA.

Household sizes, age structures, and dependency ratios vary across settlement types. The average household size declined across all settlement types and stood at 3.7 persons in 2011, shown in table 3.2 (Stats SA 2011a, 2011b). As later sections of this chapter will discuss, this downward trend, together with the positive rate

Table 3.1 Population Distribution, by Settlement Type and Population Group in South Africa, 2000 and 2011

Percent

	Black		Colored		Indian or Asian		White	
	2000	2011	2000	2011	2000	2011	2000	2011
Total	78.6	79.5	8.8	8.8	2.5	2.6	10.1	9.0
Rural areas	94.4	97.2	3.7	1.4	0.1	0.1	1.8	1.3
Urban areas	64.7	69.0	13.3	13.2	4.7	4.1	17.5	13.6
Urban TS	95.7	95.7	4.1	4.0	0.1	0.1	0.1	0.2
Urban IS	97.7	97.1	1.9	2.2	0.5	0.0	0.0	0.0
Other urban areas (excluding T&IS)	36.9	42.6	21.5	22.2	8.7	8.0	33.0	27.0

Sources: Stats SA 2000, 2011b.
Note: TS = townships; IS = informal settlements; T&IS = townships and informal settlements. Population groups are determined by individual self-description and are undefined by Statistics South Africa. Computing the population group shares using General Household Surveys yields similar results (Stats SA 2003, 2011a).

Table 3.2 Household Size, Age Structure, and Dependency Ratios, by Settlement Type in South Africa, 2000 and 2011

	Average household size			Average age			Young dependency ratio[a]			Old dependency ratio[a]		
	2000	2011	Avg. growth[b] (%)	2000	2011	Avg. growth[b] (%)	2000	2011	Avg. growth[b] (%)	2000	2011	Avg. growth[b] (%)
Total	3.94	3.65	−0.66	25.9	27.4	0.54	54.8	47.4	−1.24	7.1	7.9	0.96
Rural areas	4.49	4.18	−0.62	24.2	25.3	0.42	72.1	61.0	−1.40	9.1	9.3	0.17
Urban areas	3.56	3.39	−0.41	27.4	28.7	0.44	42.4	40.3	−0.45	5.7	7.2	2.30
Urban TS	4.00	3.62	−0.87	26.0	26.5	0.21	45.7	44.5	−0.23	4.8	4.6	−0.33
Urban IS	3.31	3.13	−0.50	24.7	24.7	0.00	46.3	44.5	−0.34	2.3	1.8	−2.04
Other urban areas (excluding T&IS)	3.25	3.22	−0.09	28.6	30.9	0.71	39.7	36.2	−0.80	6.5	9.8	4.45

Sources: Stats SA 2000, 2011b.
Note: TS = townships; IS = informal settlements; T&IS = townships and informal settlements.
a. The young and old dependency ratios are the ratios of the "young" (aged 0–14) and "old" (aged 65 and older) populations, respectively, to the working-age population (aged 15–64).
b. "Average growth" is average annual growth.

of population growth, corresponded with a marked increase in the number of households—which also helps explain the difficulty of improving the household access rate to various public services. TS, rural, and IS populations were much younger, on average, than the OUA population, by between four and six years (table 3.2). The young and old dependency ratios also were lower in TS and IS than in the general population.[4] At the same time, there appears to be a concentration of children and old people in rural areas, where the total dependency ratio is about 70 percent.

The working-age growth rate far exceeded the general population growth rate. Between 2000 and 2011, the working-age population (aged 15–64) grew by 5 million, from 27.6 million to 32.6 million (Stats SA 2000, 2011b). The demographic dividend that resulted from the declining young dependency ratio (table 3.2) has increased national savings rates and GDP growth in other countries—gains that were not fully realized by South Africa (World Bank 2011). The growth (an average annual rate of 1.6 percent) was significantly higher in urban areas (the rural working-age population declined)—bumped up by the fast population growth in TS and IS (3.5 percent and 13.2 percent per year, respectively), as table 3B.2 details further. As a result, the working-age population increased by 38 percent in TS and more than doubled in IS during the 11-year period under analysis. Consequently, in 2011, the share of working-age population was higher in urban areas (68 percent) than in rural areas (59 percent), with similar ratios across the urban settlement types.

Gender ratios in the work force also vary considerably across settlement types. The ratio of males to females in the workforce[5] was the lowest in rural areas, at 87 percent in 2011 (Stats SA 2000, 2011b). This compared with 98.4 percent in urban areas, which saw intensive male migration from former homeland areas.[6] The male-to-female ratios were higher in TS (99.6 percent) than in the general population (94.4 percent), while in IS this ratio was significantly higher (109.7 percent), suggesting that the selectivity of migration by gender is highest for the IS (see table 3B.2 for details). Furthermore, as shown later in the chapter, the proportion of female single-headed households is significantly higher in rural areas, where a large share of children (50 percent) live either solely with their mothers or with neither of their biological parents (20.2 percent) (Stats SA 2003, 2011a). Overall, these characteristics support the fact that many urban migrant males have rural residences with wives and children.

Labor Market Trends across Settlement Types

Significant employment gains in urban areas have been largely offset by employment losses in the rural sector. Between 2000 and 2011, a net total of only 1.1 million jobs were created in South Africa (table 3.3), much lower than the working-age population increase of 5 million (Stats SA 2000, 2011b). Underlying the net job increase, urban areas generated an additional 2.6 million jobs, but this was largely offset by a decline of 1.5 million jobs in rural areas. Perhaps most troubling overall, labor force participation rates show a declining

Table 3.3 Labor Market Indicators, by Settlement Type in South Africa, 2000 and 2011

	Total		Rural		Urban		Urban TS		Urban IS		Other urban (excl. T&IS)	
	2000	2011	2000	2011	2000	2011	2000	2011	2000	2011	2000	2011
Working-age population	27,599,148	32,562,297	11,542,671	11,069,035	16,056,477	21,493,262	7,402,649	10,228,664	846,125	2,073,403	8,554,036	10,862,221
Labor force	16,681,296	17,767,525	5,914,693	3,957,661	10,766,603	13,809,865	4,797,284	6,466,934	613,421	1,400,677	5,892,193	7,082,793
Employed	12,184,076	13,325,182	4,373,894	2,882,465	7,810,183	10,442,717	2,923,059	4,305,521	391,668	944,477	4,832,677	5,946,042
Unemployed	4,497,220	4,442,343	1,540,800	1,075,196	2,956,420	3,367,148	1,874,225	2,161,414	221,753	456,200	1,059,517	1,136,751
Discouraged workers	1,597,166	2,203,553	886,736	1,366,857	710,431	836,696	437,239	502,611	47,805	90,731	270,285	313,869
Other noneconomically active	9,320,686	12,591,219	4,741,243	5,744,517	4,579,443	6,846,702	2,168,127	3,259,119	184,899	581,995	2,391,558	3,465,559
Unemployment rate, narrow (%)	27.0	25.0	26.1	27.2	27.5	24.4	39.1	33.4	36.2	32.6	18.0	16.0
Unemployment rate, broad (%)	33.3	33.3	35.7	45.9	31.9	28.7	44.2	38.2	40.8	36.7	21.6	19.6
Labor force participation (%)	60.4	54.6	51.2	35.8	67.1	64.3	64.8	63.2	72.5	67.6	68.9	65.2
Employment rate (%)	44.1	40.9	37.9	26.0	48.6	48.6	39.5	42.1	46.3	45.6	56.5	54.7

Sources: Stats SA 2000, 2011b.

Note: TS = townships; IS = informal settlements; T&IS = townships and informal settlements. "Working age" = aged 15–64 years. The "broad" unemployment rate includes "discouraged workers"; the "narrow" unemployment rate does not. "Discouraged workers," according to Statistics South Africa, are working-age individuals who were not employed during the reference period, wanted to work, and were available to work or start a business but did not take active steps to find work during the previous four weeks, provided that the main reason given for not seeking work was any of the following: no jobs available in the area; unable to find work requiring his or her skills; or lost hope of finding any kind of work.

trend across the board—among men and women alike and in all settlement types, albeit more so in rural areas than in urban areas, as shown in table 3B.9 (Stats SA 2000, 2011b).

Indicators by Settlement Type

Only 2.6 out of every 10 working-age people in rural areas were employed in 2011 (table 3.3), down from 3.8 out of 10 people in 2000. Over the 2000–11 period, the economywide employment rate (the ratio of employed people to the total working-age population) fell by 3.2 percentage points. The employment rate fell sharply in rural areas while remaining unchanged in urban areas. By 2011, employment levels in agriculture and mining were reduced to just 26 percent and 40 percent, respectively, of their 2000 levels (table 3B.3).

The dismal performance of rural labor markets had a major consequence: the continuous strain exerted on urban labor markets in several ways.

Urban informal settlements have borne the brunt of labor market pressures. Employment growth for IS residents was 12.8 percent per year, although even this was not enough to keep pace with the fast working-age population growth (Stats SA 2000, 2011b). As a result, the employment rate in IS fell from 46.3 percent in 2000 to 45.6 percent in 2011 (table 3.3). In TS, however, average annual employment growth outpaced working-age population growth, raising the employment rate from 39.5 percent in 2000 to 42.1 percent in 2011. In OUA, average annual employment growth was 2.1 percent, slightly slower than working-age population growth, leading to a slight decline in the employment rate over the 11-year period. About 5.5 out of 10 members of the working-age population were employed in OUA, compared with just 4.2 and 4.6 persons in TS and IS, respectively (figure 3.1). Regardless of the direction of change, South Africa's overall employment rates remain among the lowest in the world.

Labor market indicators have not improved overall. The narrow unemployment rate fell nationally as well as in all urban settlement types (figure 3.2) while increasing in rural areas. The decline in the narrow unemployment rate was overshadowed by the much larger increase in the number of discouraged workers, driven mostly by events in the rural sector. As a consequence, the broad unemployment rate[7] stayed constant at 33.3 percent nationally, with significant variation among the different settlement types: it rose sharply in rural areas from 35.7 percent to 45.9 percent, while declining from 31.9 percent to 28.7 percent in urban areas, with large declines in T&IS (Stats SA 2000, 2011b). Mirroring the increase in discouraged workers, labor force participation rates plummeted in rural areas between 2000 and 2011 (from 51.2 percent to just 35.8 percent), leading to a sharp decline in the national labor force participation rate, from 60.4 percent to 54.6 percent.

Despite the net job creation in urban areas, the urban unemployment situation remains worrisome. Urban areas saw the number of unemployed and discouraged workers rise by roughly 537,000, of whom the great majority—about 420,000— were T&IS residents (Stats SA 2000, 2011b).[8] Given the high starting levels of unemployment in both TS and IS, the broad unemployment rate remained

Figure 3.1 Employment and Labor Force Participation Rates, by Settlement Type in South Africa, 2000 and 2011

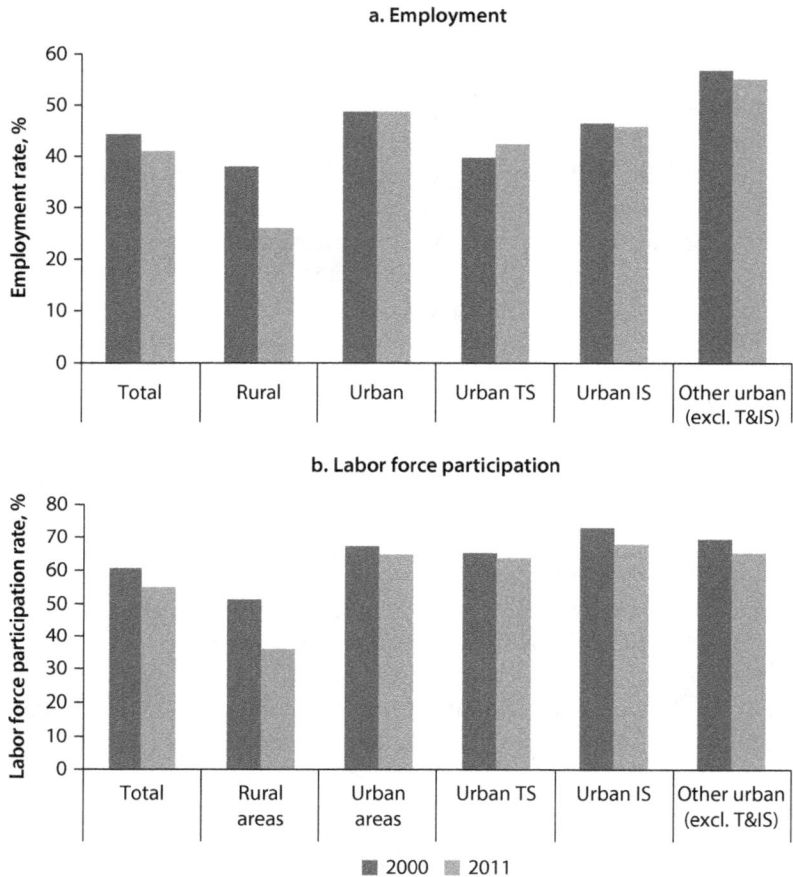

a. Employment

b. Labor force participation

■ 2000 ■ 2011

Sources: Stats SA 2000, 2011b.
Note: TS = townships; IS = informal settlements; T&IS = townships and informal settlements.

unacceptably high (at 38.2 percent and 36.7 percent, respectively) in 2011 despite the improvement in the previous decade.

The imbalances in employment patterns across settlement types in 2011 can be summarized as follows (Stats SA 2011b):

- Rural areas represented about 34 percent of the total working-age population, 24 percent of all unemployed workers, and 62 percent of discouraged workers.
- TS accounted for 31 percent of the total working-age population, 49 percent of all unemployed workers, and 23 percent of all discouraged workers.
- IS represented 6 percent of the total working-age population, 10 percent of all unemployed, and 4 percent of all discouraged workers.
- OUA accounted for 33 percent of the total working-age population, just 26 percent of unemployed workers, and 14 percent of discouraged workers.

Figure 3.2 Narrow and Broad Unemployment Rates, by Settlement Type in South Africa, 2000 and 2011

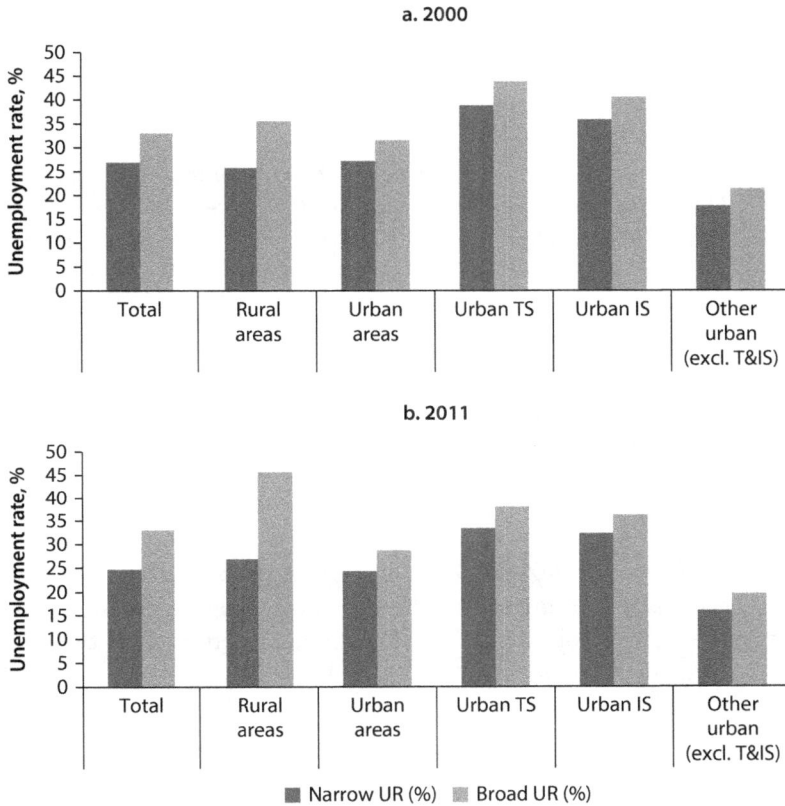

a. 2000

b. 2011

■ Narrow UR (%)   ▨ Broad UR (%)

Sources: Stats SA 2000, 2011b.

Note: TS = townships; IS = informal settlements; T&IS = townships and informal settlements; UR = unemployment rate. The "broad" unemployment rate includes "discouraged workers"; the "narrow" unemployment rate does not. "Discouraged workers," as defined by Statistics South Africa, are working-age individuals who were not employed during the reference period, wanted to work, and were available to work or start a business but did not take active steps to find work during the previous four weeks, provided that the main reason given for not seeking work was any of the following: no jobs available in the area; unable to find work requiring his or her skills; or lost hope of finding any kind of work.

Indicators by Gender and Age Group

Turning to gender- and age-specific labor market indicators, we see further imbalances—and, reflecting employment losses especially in rural areas, an alarming proportion of working-age South African youth who neither work nor attend school. The remaining labor market trends described below reflect not only the lack of job opportunities in rural areas, but also the pressures that build as a stagnant South African economy—where millions of job seekers face a bleak outlook—leaves more and more people behind.

The employment situation for women is significantly worse than for men. Although the urban labor market for females has improved, key labor market indicators remain behind those for males (table 3B.9). The overall female employment rate was only 34.7 percent in 2011 compared with 47.5 percent for men, and female unemployment rates were significantly higher in every category (nationwide unemployment rates were 28 percent for women and 22.5 percent for men) (Stats SA 2000, 2011b). As further discussed later in this chapter, female-headed households are also more likely to fall into poverty when faced with adverse shocks.

Among the different age groups, employment losses have been most keenly felt by the youth. The number of working-age youth (15–24 years old) grew by more than 1 million, to 10.3 million, between 2000 and 2011. However, total youth employment declined from 1.6 million to 1.3 million over the same period. The fall in the number of unemployed youth was fully offset by an increase in the number of discouraged workers. As shown in table 3B.4, this trend was again driven by rural areas, where about 381,000 youth jobs were lost between 2000 and 2011. By 2011, fewer than 1 out of 10 young persons were employed in rural areas. Urban areas did not fare much better, posting a positive but negligible youth employment growth: just 110,000 youth jobs were created in 11 years, whereas the urban youth population increased by almost 1.2 million over the same period.

In a particularly worrying sign, a rising proportion of youth neither works nor attends school. As a consequence of the employment losses and the relatively slow expansion of school attendance (further discussed later in the chapter), figure 3.3 shows that, between 2000 and 2011, the percentage of the youth not working, attending school, or in training rose from 28.4 percent to 30.3 percent in 2011 for the country as a whole (Stats SA 2000, 2011b).[9] In rural areas, this percentage rose even more steeply, from 27 percent to 31.2 percent, whereas it fell marginally by 0.2 percentage points in urban areas.[10]

Figure 3.3 Youth Not in Employment, Education, or Training, by Settlement Type in South Africa, 2000 and 2011

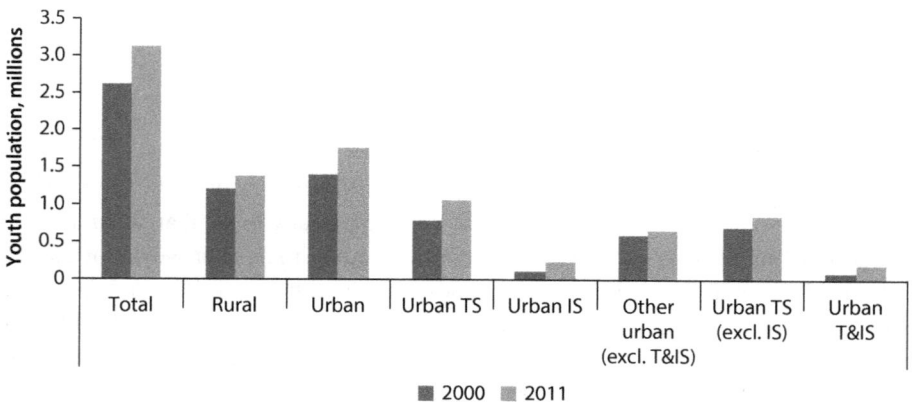

Sources: Stats SA 2000, 2011b.
Note: TS = townships; IS = informal settlements; T&IS = townships and informal settlements. "Youth" = 15–24 years old.

Economics of South African Townships • http://dx.doi.org/10.1596/978-1-4648-0301-7

Consumption, Poverty, and Household Trends across Settlement Types

Despite the poor labor market outcomes, per capita consumption has increased and poverty rates have declined in all settlement types except the IS. The following subsections examine these trends and their underlying factors.

Improvements in Consumption and Poverty

Increased consumption notwithstanding, the degree of improvement varied among settlement types. Alone among the settlement types, IS saw a drop in consumption per capita over the five-year period measured. And despite dismal rural employment trends, rural areas saw the fastest consumption rate increase, likely due to a marked increase in social-grant coverage. Although South Africa's national poverty headcount fell over the same five-year period—including drops in TS, OUA, and rural areas—it changed only marginally in IS. The lack of progress in IS again mirrors the enormous pressures of rural urban migration and of out-migration of the more successful IS inhabitants.

Consumption per Capita

The distribution of consumption across settlement types is extremely skewed relative to population distribution. Annual consumption per capita in the OUA was by far the highest at R 66,397, followed by TS (R 18,419), rural areas (R 15,069), and IS (R 11,839) (Stats SA 2012).[11] That the average consumption per capita was higher in rural areas than IS aligns with the Ranis and Stewart (1999) model: the lowest wages are seen in the primary destination of rural-urban migration, where the traditional informal sector is prevalent. Rural households represented about 39 percent of total population in 2010/11 but accounted for just 16 percent of total consumption, as shown in figure 3.4. About 29 percent of South Africans lived in T&IS, but their share of aggregate consumption was just 17 percent.

Figure 3.4 Shares of Consumption and Population, by Settlement Type in South Africa, 2010/11

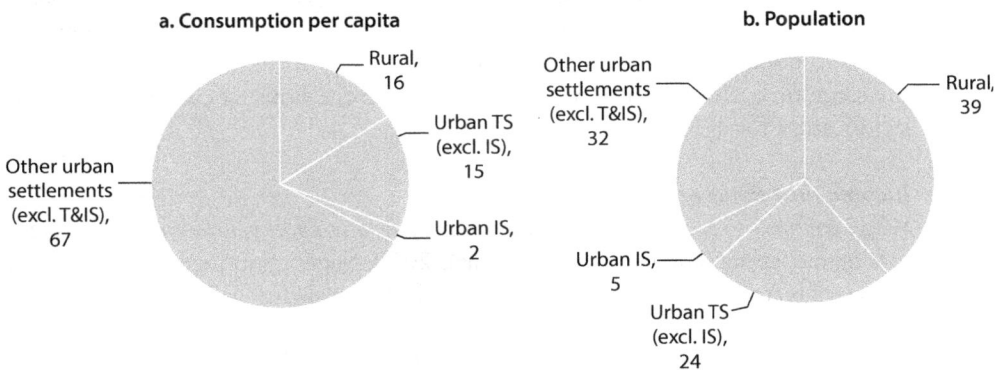

a. Consumption per capita

- Rural, 16
- Urban TS (excl. IS), 15
- Urban IS, 2
- Other urban settlements (excl. T&IS), 67

b. Population

- Other urban settlements (excl. T&IS), 32
- Rural, 39
- Urban IS, 5
- Urban TS (excl. IS), 24

Source: Stats SA 2012.
Note: TS = townships (excl. IS); IS = informal settlements; T&IS = townships and informal settlements.

Economics of South African Townships • http://dx.doi.org/10.1596/978-1-4648-0301-7

OUA households accounted for most of the consumption (about 67 percent in 2010/11), more than twice their population share.

Improvements in consumption also varied significantly across settlement types. Nationally, between 2005/06 and 2010/11, average consumption per capita rose 3.6 percent, to R 34,897 (table 3B.6). Consumption in OUA and TS grew similarly: by 2.1 percent and 2.5 percent per year, respectively. However, consumption per capita in the IS fell at an annual rate of 0.8 percent—a decline that likely reflected persistent migration pressures from rural areas and selective out-migration to other urban settlement types (TS and OUA) of persons who succeeded in the labor market. The relatively low level of real consumption per capita further correlates with socioeconomic characteristics of the IS such as lower average age (negatively correlated with income because of factors such as lower experience and education), lower average educational attainment relative to other urban settlements, and a lower employment rate.

During the five-year period studied, rural per capita consumption grew the fastest. In view of the rural areas' dismal rural employment trends, this requires some explanation. Social grants likely played a significant role because of a sharp increase in the number of eligible recipients. For example, in 1998, the Child Support Grant covered only children aged 0–6 years. It was later extended to cover children under 15 years old in 2009, and currently children up to 18 years old are eligible. Since real increases in the value of social grants were small, it is the expanded social grants' coverage over time that appears to have been a major contributor here.[12] According to the General Household Survey 2010 (Stats SA 2011a), remittances were reported as the main source of income by 15.6 percent of rural households in 2010, and together with pensions and grants (at 39 percent), they are well above the national averages for those categories (9.8 percent and 23.8 percent, respectively).[13]

The composition of consumption varies widely by settlement type. Households in rural areas and T&IS spent relatively higher percentages of total consumption on food and nonalcoholic beverages, probably because of their relatively lower levels of income (table 3B.7) (Stats SA 2012). Expenditures on transport and housing for households were below the national averages in T&IS but higher in OUA.[14] Because of income and consumption growth, the percentages of income spent on food and nonalcoholic beverages fell over time in both rural and urban areas. At the same time, the proportion of expenditures in the housing category increased significantly for all urban settlements.

Income and Poverty

Wages continue to account for the major share of income, while pensions and grants provide an increasing share. Between 2002 and 2010, wages continued to be the main source of income in South Africa, although declining slightly from 59.3 percent to 57.4 percent of total household income (figure 3C.1) (Stats SA 2003, 2011a). In OUA and IS, the proportion was the highest, with around 70 percent of households reporting wages as the main source of household income. In TS, wages represented the main source of income to about 64 percent of households.

Strikingly, the proportion of households having no income at all—4.1 and 5.7 percent in TS and IS, respectively, in 2002—fell sharply in both urban settlement types to 1.6 percent or less by 2010.

Poverty headcounts have fallen significantly. Except in IS, the poverty headcount has decreased significantly in both urban and rural areas (table 3.4).[15] The main explanation again relates to the expansion of social-grant recipients. According to Statistics South Africa's Income and Expenditure Survey (IES) 2005/06, 14.7 percent of South Africa's population lived on less than the US$1.25 a day in PPP 2005 prices (Stats SA 2008). This figure fell to 9.2 percent in the IES for 2010/11 (Stats SA 2012). Rural areas showed the largest improvement, seemingly helped by extended coverage of social grants and remittances. While the poverty headcount (measured as US$2.50 a day in PPP 2005 prices) also fell in both TS and OUA, it marginally rose in IS, from 42.5 percent in 2005/06 to 42.7 percent in 2010/11—consistent with the decline in average consumption per capita in IS (Stats SA 2008, 2012). The lack of progress in IS again mirrors the enormous pressures of rural urban migration and of out-migration of the more-successful inhabitants of the IS.

Disadvantages of Single-Headed Households

In 2010/11, female-headed households accounted for 39 percent of all households and about 43 percent of total population in South Africa (Stats SA 2012). Roughly 59 percent of all female-headed households were living in urban areas. The ratio of female-headed households to total households rose in South Africa between 2005/06 and 2010/11, and this change was more pronounced in T&IS (table 3B.10).

Single-headed households are more highly concentrated in rural areas than in urban areas. In South Africa, there were about 3.9 million single-headed households[16] with children in 2010, equally distributed between rural and urban areas, as shown in table 3.5 (Stats SA 2011a). However, 61 percent of rural households are single-headed, relative to 42 percent of urban households. Within the urban areas, single-headed households are most concentrated in T&IS. About 1.2 million single-headed households live in T&IS (representing more than 90 percent of all T&IS households). Overall, the vast majority (86 percent) of single-headed households had a female head.

More than half of South African children now live in single-headed households. The percentage of children in single-headed households rose in rural areas as well as in all urban settlements (table 3.6). As a result, more than half of all children (51.7 percent) nationwide lived in single-headed households in 2010, predominantly in female single-headed households (Stats SA 2011a). The proportion of children living in female single-headed households was the highest in rural areas (54.5 percent), followed by TS (44.5 percent) and IS (40.6 percent). Only 6.4 percent of children lived in male single-headed households in 2010—reflecting not only the tendency of many urban men to maintain a rural wife and children but also the fact that most orphans are paternal orphans.

Table 3.4 Poverty Headcount, by Consumption Level and Settlement Type in South Africa, 2005/06 and 2010/11

Percent

Consumption

	Households						Persons					
	Food poverty line[a]		$1.25 a day (PPP)		$2.50 a day (PPP)		Food poverty line		$1.25 a day (PPP)		$2.50 a day (PPP)	
	2005/06	2010/11	2005/06	2010/11	2005/06	2010/11	2005/06	2010/11	2005/06	2010/11	2005/06	2010/11
Total	12.2	9.9	10.0	6.7	31.2	23.6	20.4	15.9	17.0	11.1	44.7	34.6
Rural areas	24.0	19.2	19.9	13.4	52.4	41.7	35.3	27.2	30.0	19.5	66.6	54.9
Urban areas	5.9	5.4	4.6	3.4	19.9	14.8	10.0	8.9	8.0	5.8	29.4	21.9
Urban townships	8.4	7.8	6.5	4.9	28.1	21.2	12.8	11.8	10.0	7.6	39.1	29.3
Urban informal settlements	10.7	14.6	8.9	9.8	33.9	34.4	17.4	21.9	15.1	15.2	46.0	46.2
Urban areas (excl. T&IS)	3.5	3.1	2.8	2.1	12.0	8.9	6.9	5.6	5.6	3.8	19.2	14.4

In kind consumption

	Households						Persons					
	Food poverty line		$1.25 a day (PPP)		$2.50 a day (PPP)		Food poverty line		$1.25 a day (PPP)		$2.50 a day (PPP)	
	2005/06	2010/11	2005/06	2010/11	2005/06	2010/11	2005/06	2010/11	2005/06	2010/11	2005/06	2010/11
Total	12.0	9.7	9.7	6.6	30.8	23.3	20.1	15.6	16.7	10.9	44.3	34.3
Rural areas	23.9	19.0	19.8	13.3	52.1	41.5	35.1	26.9	29.8	19.3	66.3	54.7
Urban areas	5.7	5.1	4.4	3.3	19.4	14.4	9.7	8.5	7.6	5.6	28.9	21.5
Urban townships	8.0	7.5	6.1	4.6	27.5	20.7	12.4	11.3	9.6	7.2	38.3	28.7
Urban informal settlements	10.3	14.4	8.3	9.6	33.4	34.3	16.6	21.6	14.1	15.0	45.4	46.1
Urban areas (excl. T&IS)	3.4	3.0	2.7	2.0	11.7	8.7	6.8	5.4	5.4	3.7	18.9	14.1

Sources: Stats SA 2008, 2012.

Note: TS = townships; IS = informal settlements; T&IS = townships and informal settlements; PPP = purchasing power parity.

a. The South African "food poverty line" is R 305 per person per month in March 2009 prices (based on a daily per capita energy requirement).

Table 3.5 Single-Headed Households, by Settlement Type in South Africa, 2002 and 2010

	Single-headed HH		Male single-headed HH		Female single-headed HH		Dual-headed HH	
	2002	2010	2002	2010	2002	2010	2002	2010
Total	3,027,563	3,877,579	412,525	553,915	2,615,038	3,323,664	3,319,445	3,946,830
Rural areas	1,636,897	1,942,696	209,693	256,054	1,427,203	1,686,642	1,166,491	1,242,062
Urban areas	1,390,667	1,934,883	202,832	297,861	1,187,835	1,637,022	2,152,954	2,704,768
Urban TS	797,431	1,141,338	121,331	169,991	676,100	971,347	846,568	1,155,423
Urban IS	87,105	169,168	10,490	18,272	76,615	150,896	114,614	215,601
Other urban (excl. T&IS)	584,895	754,013	80,758	125,481	504,137	628,532	1,296,102	1,496,564

Sources: Stats SA 2003, 2011a.

Note: HH = households; TS = townships; IS = informal settlements; T&IS = townships and informal settlements. Single-headed households are those with head (or acting head), no partners, and at least one child under 18 years old. If these conditions are satisfied, the following definitions apply: (a) In a "female single-headed household," the head or acting head is female. (b) In a "male single-headed household," the head or acting head is male.

A child is more likely to be living with his or her mother than with both biological parents. Nationwide, only 37.1 percent of children were living with both biological parents (table 3B.8) (Stats SA 2003, 2011a). This percentage was the highest in OUA (55.2 percent) and the lowest in rural areas (26 percent). In fact, rural children were more than twice as likely as urban children to be living with neither of their biological parents. Moreover, rural children were the likeliest to be orphans. In 2010, 20 percent of children nationwide were orphans, but 23.2 percent of rural children were orphans (table 3B.8). Among the rural orphans, most (57.1 percent) were paternal orphans, followed by double orphans (22.7 percent) and maternal orphans (20.2 percent).

Consumption per capita is two-thirds higher in male-headed households than in female-headed ones.[17] The gender gap seems wider in rural areas than in urban ones, as figure 3.5 shows. Between 2005/06 and 2010/11, this gap narrowed in OUA while increasing in rural areas (Stats SA 2008, 2012). Consumption declined in only one category: those living in female-headed households in IS, where average consumption per capita fell by about 2.4 percent per year.

Female single-headed households and IS residents are particularly disadvantaged in terms of per capita consumption. Factors influencing per capita consumption have been analyzed using a multivariate regression (shown in table 3B.11) as follows: To measure the correlations of per capita consumption with the various factors discussed above, we run an ordinary least squares (OLS) regression with the logarithm of consumption per capita as the dependent variable on several household characteristics (household size, number of workers in the household, number of social-grant recipients, and a dummy variable for single-headed households); head-of-household characteristics (age, gender, and race of the head, and education attainment dummy variables); and settlement-types dummy variables. OLS regressions have been weighted by the sample weights, and standard errors are clustered by primary sampling units (PSUs). Overall, the regression results are in line with descriptive statistics.[18]

Table 3.6 Children in Single-Headed Households, by Settlement Type in South Africa, 2002 and 2010

	Children < 18 years			Single-headed HH (% of all children)		Male single-headed HH (% of all children)		Female single-headed HH (% of all children)		Dual-headed HH (% of all children)	
	2002	2010	Annual avg. growth (%)	2002	2010	2002	2010	2002	2010	2002	2010
Total	18,620,325	18,523,917	-0.1	48.5	51.7	5.8	6.4	42.8	45.3	51.5	48.3
Rural areas	9,871,664	8,778,226	-1.4	56.9	61.1	6.2	6.6	50.6	54.5	43.1	38.9
Urban areas	8,748,661	9,745,691	1.4	39.2	43.3	5.3	6.3	33.9	37.0	60.8	56.7
Urban TS	4,401,564	4,876,215	1.3	47.7	51.3	6.4	6.8	41.2	44.5	52.3	48.7
Urban IS	521,379	717,039	4.7	43.0	45.4	3.8	4.9	39.2	40.6	57.0	54.6
Other urban (excl. T&IS)	4,296,458	4,693,498	1.2	30.4	35.1	4.2	5.9	26.2	29.2	69.6	64.9

Sources: Stats SA 2003, 2011a.

Note: HH = households; TS = townships; IS = informal settlements; T&IS = townships and informal settlements. Single-headed households are those with head (or acting head), no partners, and at least one child under 18 years old. If these conditions are satisfied, the following definitions apply: (a) In a "female single-headed household," the head or acting head is female. (b) In a "male single-headed household," the head or acting head is male.

Figure 3.5 Consumption Per Capita of Male- and Female-Headed Households, by Settlement Type in South Africa, 2005/06 and 2010/11

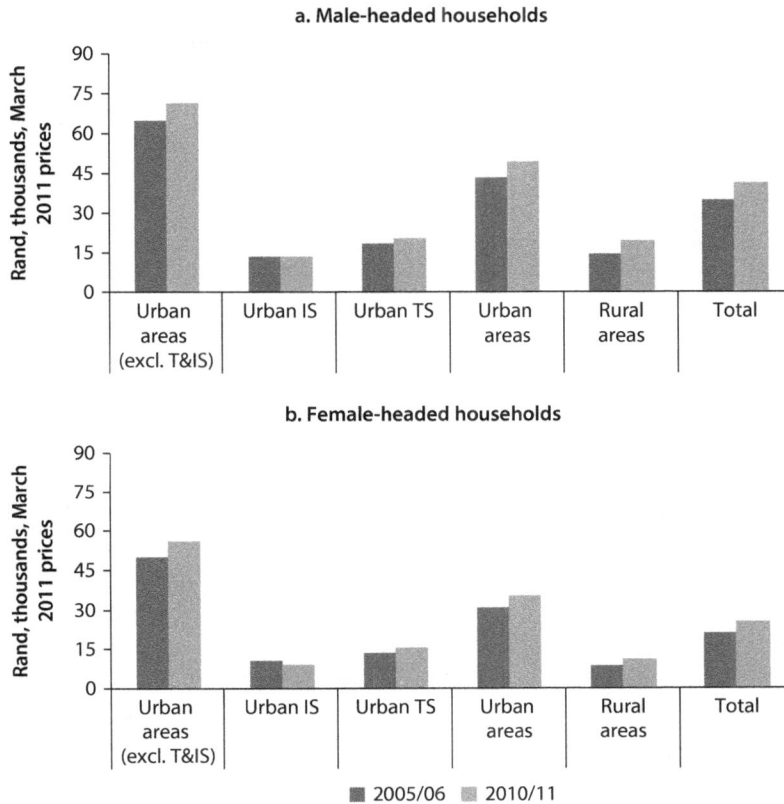

a. Male-headed households

b. Female-headed households

■ 2005/06 ■ 2010/11

Sources: Stats SA 2008, 2012.

Note: TS = townships; IS = informal settlements; T&IS = townships and informal settlements. These data include all male- and all female-headed households regardless of whether they are single-headed or dual-headed. The Income and Expenditure Survey of 2005/06 (Stats SA 2008) did not include a question to determine whether a household was single-headed.

Keeping in mind that we are not implying causality, columns (1) and (3) of table 3B.11 suggest that, compared with rural areas, consumption per capita is lower in IS than in rural areas, but higher in TS and OUA, respectively, which is consistent with the predictions of the Ranis and Stewart (1999) model. Population group dummies have the expected signs and are statistically significant. Regression results further suggest the following:

- A larger household size is associated with lower consumption.
- Consumption increases with the educational level of the head of the household (that is, a household headed by an individual of lower educational attainment is more likely to have lower consumption per capita).
- A female-headed household is associated with lower per capita consumption.

- Consumption per capita increases with the age of the head of the household (perhaps on account of the high levels of youth unemployment and also on a positive sloping earnings curve).
- The larger the number of employed persons in the household, the larger the consumption per capita.
- Consumption per capita declines with the number of social-grant recipients in the households.[19]

Columns (2) and (4) of table 3B.11 show that interaction effects between matric (high school education) and TS and IS have a negative sign and are statistically significant at the 5 percent and 1 percent confidence levels, suggesting a lower return to secondary education for those residing in these settlements. The same seems to hold for those with some tertiary education who live in IS.

Social Indicators and Access to Services

Progress on social indicators and access to services has been mixed. There have been noticeable (though highly uneven) improvements across settlement types in educational outcomes, hunger reduction, feeling safe at night, and housing. In T&IS, an increasing *number* of households have access to housing, water, sewerage, and electricity, but the *proportion* of households benefiting from them has stagnated. These services have had a hard time keeping up with the rapidly growing number of households. Finally, improvement in the health sector has been limited, with deterioration seen in the proportion of the ill who receive treatment. In the following subsections, we first describe those social indicators and access to services that have improved, followed by those with mixed outcomes and finally those with deteriorating outcomes. In each case we analyze what has happened across the different settlements.

Improved Indicators and Services
School Enrollment and Outcomes
The percentage of the population under the age of 25 attending any type of educational institution rose slightly between 2002 and 2010, from 58.2 percent to 59.6 percent for the country as a whole, driven by the increase observed in rural areas (figure 3C.3) (Stats SA 2003, 2011a). The data also suggest that school attendance across gender is similar for each geographical settlement.

The educational achievement of the population 25 years and older has also improved. For example, between 2002 and 2010, the proportion of persons with less than matric education (equivalent to a high school diploma) declined by 6.2 percentage points, to 63.1 percent, and the decline was uniformly seen across all settlement types, as shown in figure 3.6. In a complementary finding, the proportion of those who completed matric or have some tertiary education rose in both urban and rural areas. Predictably, educational attainment was the lowest in IS, followed by TS. OUA display the largest percentages of persons over 25 who have completed matric or have some tertiary education.

Figure 3.6 Educational Levels of Adults 25 and Older, by Settlement Type in South Africa, 2002 and 2010

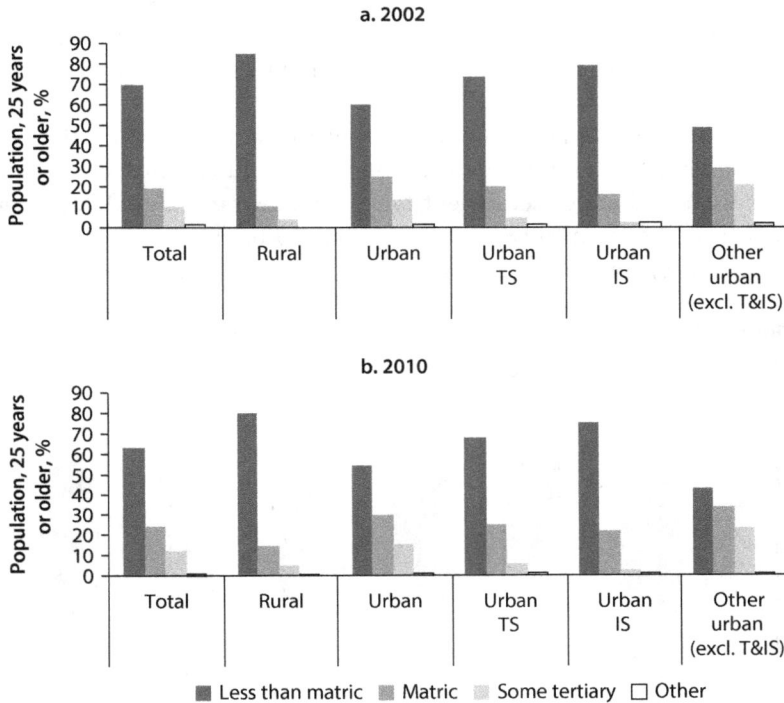

a. 2002

b. 2010

■ Less than matric ■ Matric ▨ Some tertiary □ Other

Sources: Stats SA 2003, 2011a.
Note: TS = townships; IS = informal settlements; T&IS = townships and informal settlements. "Matric" is equivalent to a high school diploma.

Progress has been made in terms of time taken to reach schools. OUA recorded little change between 2002 and 2010, with almost 50 percent of students being able to reach their schools in less than 15 minutes, and close to 90 percent in less than 30 minutes (table 3B.12) (Stats SA 2003, 2011a). For students in TS, the situation improved slightly: a smaller share of students reported needing more than 30 minutes to reach their respective schools. The students in IS continue to be significantly disadvantaged, taking much longer to reach their respective schools. But the situation has improved significantly between 2002 and 2010 for them, especially by reducing the proportion of children who spend more than 30 minutes going to school to just 17.4 percent.

Food, Safety, Housing, and Services

Hunger in both adults and children has declined significantly. A much larger proportion of households reported they never or seldom experience hunger (87.2 percent of adults and 86.1 percent of children in 2010), representing increases of about 10 percentage points in both cases (figure 3C.4) (Stats SA 2003, 2011a). These improvements occurred across all settlement types, but the proportion of households affected by hunger was relatively higher in rural areas and IS and the lowest in OUA. About 3.8 percent of adults and children in T&IS are often or always hungry. Government assistance, especially through social grants, may have been a significant factor in this positive trend—consistent with the significant decline in households reporting no income at all, especially in IS.

The security situation has also improved over time. For instance, the proportion of households who agree with a statement about feeling safe walking at night has improved across settlement types, as shown in figure 3.7. Nationally, the proportion rose from 50.8 percent in 2002 to 65.9 percent in 2010 (Stats SA 2003, 2011a). In OUA this improvement is even more striking, reaching

Figure 3.7 Perception of Nighttime Safety, by Settlement Type in South Africa, 2002 and 2010

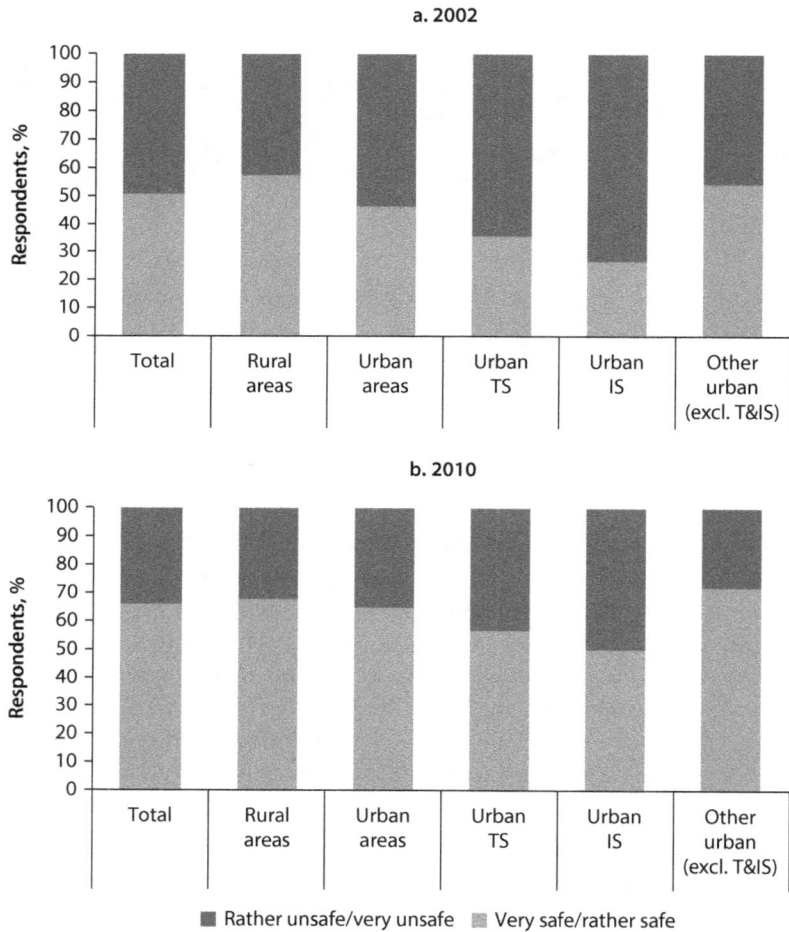

a. 2002

b. 2010

■ Rather unsafe/very unsafe   ▨ Very safe/rather safe

Sources: Stats SA 2003, 2011a.
Note: TS = townships; IS = informal settlements; T&IS = townships and informal settlements. Survey respondents were asked whether they felt safe walking in their areas at night.

71.8 percent in 2010. Improvements have also been striking in TS, IS, and rural areas. However, the large gap in safety perceptions between T&IS on one hand, and OUA on the other, still remained in 2010.

Housing access shows mixed results. The proportion of households living in Reconstruction and Development Program (RDP) houses increased from 5.5 percent in 2002 to 9.6 percent in 2010 (Stats SA 2003, 2011a). Increases were recorded across all geographical settlements, as seen in figure 3.8. Urban areas, especially TS (17.3 percent) and IS (11.4 percent), have been the major beneficiaries of the program.[20] In contrast, about 59 percent and 27.5 percent of households in TS and IS, respectively, reported a shack as the main dwelling. About 1.4 million households were living in RDP houses by 2010. Another 1.9 million households were living in shacks, up from 1.4 million in 2002, which has left the proportion of households living in shacks constant over time at 13 percent.

Figure 3.8 Households Dwelling in RDP and Shack Housing, by Settlement Type in South Africa, 2002 and 2010

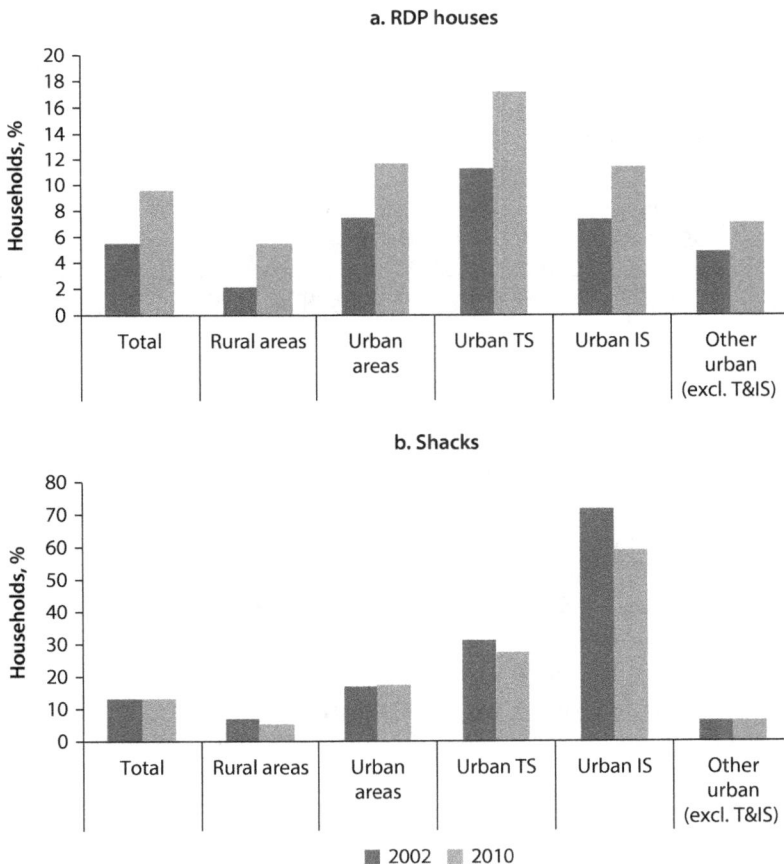

a. RDP houses

b. Shacks

Sources: Stats SA 2003, 2011a.
Note: TS = townships; IS = informal settlements; T&IS = townships and informal settlements.
RDP = Reconstruction and Development Program (public housing).

Access to water has improved slightly. The percentage of households having water sources in their dwellings went up from 70.1 percent in 2002 to 72.3 percent in 2010 (figure 3C.5), and those having access to water outside the house rose from 19.7 percent to 21.5 percent (Stats SA 2003, 2011a).[21] Predictably, the situation for OUA residents is much better, with around 93.3 percent of households having water sources in their dwellings in 2010; TS were a close second with 86.3 percent. In IS, however, where the population and number of houses have grown the fastest, water supply has not even stabilized the percentage of households with a water source in their dwellings, which declined from 57.5 percent to 52.7 percent. The outside-dwelling water supply in IS improved by 5.2 percentage points—now almost equaling the percentage with in-dwelling or in-yard water supply. Unsafe water from streams, ponds, and open wells has been all but eliminated in urban areas, remaining a problem only in rural areas, where household use fell from 20.2 percent to 11.2 percent over the period.

Mixed Results
Access to Sanitation
Results on improving access to sanitation have been mixed. Nationally, the proportion of households with an indoor toilet connected to a sewage system has barely risen between 2002 and 2010, suggesting that it has just about kept pace with the growth of dwellings (figure 3C.6) (Stats SA 2003, 2011a). TS are catching up with OUA, but in IS the situation is much worse and has not improved. The use of septic tanks for indoor toilets has increased across the country, rising from 2 percent in 2002 to 3.3 percent in 2010. This increase occurred across all urban settlement types. The use of bucket toilets has fallen to less than 1 percent nationally, but it still stood at 1.9 percent in TS and 4.4 percent in IS.

Access to Electricity, Telephones, Television
Connection to electricity also shows mixed results. Nationally, the proportion of households with an electricity connection has increased from 76.7 percent in 2002 to about 82 percent in 2010, mainly because of improvements in rural areas (figure 3C.7) (Stats SA 2003, 2011a). In urban areas, the proportion of households connected to electricity mains fell slightly over the period. A further disaggregation suggests that although the situation improved marginally in OUA, this proportion dropped by 0.6 percentage points in TS, with 80.6 percent of households connected in 2010. In IS, the situation improved by 0.8 percentage points, with electricity reaching 51.7 percent of households by 2010.

More positively, the cellular phone revolution has substantially reduced inequality: in 2010, the proportion of households owning them ranged between 83.5 percent in the rural areas to 89.7 percent in OUA. Television ownership has also risen, but inequalities across rural areas, OUA, TS, and IS persist (Stats SA 2003, 2011a).

Unimproved or Worsening Results

Health Outcomes

Health sector outcomes show little improvement, even worsening in some areas. In the month preceding the 2010 household survey, 11.2 percent of people had been ill—almost the same proportion as in 2002 (figure 3C.8) (Stats SA 2003, 2011a). The illness rate ranged between 11.2 percent and 12.8 percent across different settlements, with the highest percentage in OUA, probably because this population is older (by four to five years) than in TS and IS. The percentage of people with illness increased marginally in rural areas (to 9.7 percent) and in IS (to 11.5 percent) between 2002 and 2010. The upward trend in IS may be explained by increasing overcrowding or aging of the population. Regrettably, the proportion of those who were ill and received treatment declined significantly across all settlement types between 2002 and 2010 (Stats SA 2003, 2011a).

In urban areas, access to medication for some illnesses show marked differences by settlement type. The proportion of people receiving medication for certain illnesses after diagnosis is shown in figure 3C.9 (Stats SA 2011a).[22] The medication rate was highest for diabetes (92.3 percent), followed by hypertension (87.5 percent). It was significantly lower (76.3 percent) for the human immunodeficiency virus (HIV) and acquired immune deficiency syndrome (AIDS), either because patients with high CD4 counts[23] had not yet been put on treatment or because the treatment rollout was incomplete by 2010. Diabetes medication rates are almost the same across settlement types. However, the hypertension medication rate was best in OUA and lower in TS and IS, with almost a 6.3 percentage point difference between IS and OUA. On the other hand, it is noteworthy that medication coverage of those diagnosed with HIV and AIDS is lower in OUA than in TS and IS. Such a stark and counterintuitive difference will require some special investigation.

Access to Health Insurance

Health insurance coverage remains sparse in townships and informal settlements. In 2010, only 17.5 percent of South Africans had access to health insurance, a figure that increased only slowly since 2002 (figure 3.9) (Stats SA 2003, 2011a). Medical insurance is concentrated in OUA, where coverage has reached 38.7 percent. Access is much worse in T&IS. It is just a little bit of comfort that coverage is growing fastest in the IS, where it has nearly doubled, albeit from a very low base.

Summary and Conclusions

The results presented in this chapter showed overall improvements in income, consumption, and poverty; a mixed picture for social indicators and access to services; and a worrisome employment outlook that has hit rural areas and youth especially hard. Some of these disappointing trends reflect the following key factors:

- Continuing population growth, even more so in the working-age population
- Urban economic growth at far lower rates than targeted

Figure 3.9 Access to Health Insurance, by Settlement Type in South Africa, 2002 and 2010

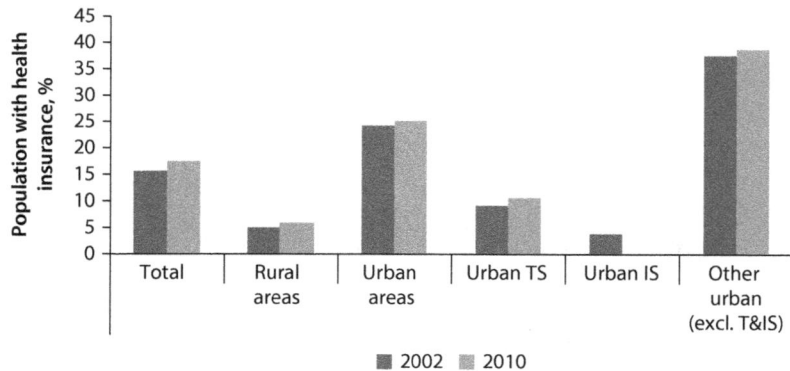

Sources: Stats SA 2003, 2011a.

Note: TS = townships; IS = informal settlements; T&IS = townships and informal settlements.

- Struggles of public services to keep pace with the rapid growth in household numbers
- The collapse of jobs and self-employment opportunities in rural areas
- Lack of a modernizing informal sector in urban areas and limited factor-market and product-market links with the formal urban sector

The chapter has also highlighted the great plight of South African youth. Although the number of working-age youth grew by more than 1 million between 2000 and 2011, rising to 10.3 million, total employment for youth declined, from 1.6 million in 2000 to 1.3 million in 2011. Rural areas bore the brunt of the changes, losing about 381,000 youth jobs. By 2011, fewer than 1 out of 10 young persons were employed in rural areas. Urban areas posted slightly positive but negligible youth employment growth: just 110,000 youth jobs were created in 11 years, whereas the urban youth population increased by almost 1.2 million persons over the same period, highlighting South Africa's youth employment crisis.

The other disadvantaged social group—female single-headed households—exist everywhere but are more concentrated in rural areas, where single women who take care of a disproportionate number of children have been adversely affected by the employment losses. As heads of households, single women have sharply lower labor participation rates, employment rates, and incomes than their male counterparts. These features have also been recognized and pose a huge challenge for gender policy.

Overall, this chapter illustrates that the concentration of surplus labor in rural areas that has resulted from a virtual collapse in rural employment puts immense pressure on labor markets in all urban settlement types, but especially in the IS. Because of labor mobility, rapid urban job creation would eventually benefit rural workers, too, but it is hard to envision significant improvement in the livelihoods of T&IS residents without new sources of both rural employment growth and the development of small and medium enterprises, which represent a significant source of employment in many countries.

Among the major policy implications, these stand out: The quest for employment and enterprise creation must encompass all parts of the economy and all settlement types. In addition, building economic linkages between the informal modernizing sector and the formal modern sector is imperative in addition to enabling labor mobility out of the traps in which many populations find themselves.

Annex 3A: The Data Sources and Their Limitations

It is important to bring forward a few caveats regarding the scope of the chapter as well as some of the limitations inherent to the relevant datasets. First, none of the Statistics South Africa (Stats SA) surveys we drew upon (the General Household Surveys [GHS], Labor Force Surveys [LFS], or Income and Expenditure Surveys [IES]) are dynamic panels, and as such, only a small proportion of the households are represented in the initial and end year of each type of survey. One drawback of this is the ability to observe migration flows across settlements. Second, the occurrence of the global financial crisis of 2009 between our initial and end points may have also weakened some of the linkages that we may observe in the data, especially those related to economic outcomes that may differ across settlement types. Finally, some of these datasets may not be fully comparable. We have made several adjustments to address some of the above concerns.

We are analyzing the households and individuals residing in the Enumeration Areas (EAs) and PSUs that formed the master sample for Stats SA based on the 2001 Census. This unified sampling frame was in effect during the entire past decade for all three surveys. During that decade, new settlements were built whose populations are not captured in these data. Therefore, the samples have over time diverged somewhat from the entire population. However, for each survey, new samples were drawn up in the EAs and PSUs, so the samples remain representative of the master sample frame of EAs and PSUs.

The labor market section explores the different labor market outcomes across rural and urban areas, TS, informal settlements, and other urban settlements (excluding TS and informal settlements) using the LFS of September 2000 and the QLFS of 2011Q3 (Stats SA 2000 and 2011b, respectively), which minimizes the impact of seasonal fluctuations. Because the LFS and QLFS are not fully comparable, efforts were made to reconstruct variables based on the survey instruments that reflect some of these changes and could make comparisons across different years more meaningful. Most notably, "discouraged workers" are not reported separately in the September 2000 LFS (Stats SA 2000)—a category that is important in explaining some of the dynamics in the labor market, especially in an environment of high unemployment that characterizes South African labor markets.

The section on consumption, income patterns, and poverty estimation relies mainly on data from the IES of 2005/06 and 2010/11 (Stats SA 2008, 2012). Although a longer time span may convey additional information, the main advantage of using the 2005/06 IES over the 2000 IES is comparability. The 2000 IES was based on a recall method, whereas both the 2005/06 IES and the 2010/11 IES were based on a combination of a diary and recall methods, thus the decision to use the 2005/06 IES instead of the 2000 IES. The recall method is generally associated with overreporting, while the diary method is often associated with underreporting, especially of frequently bought household items such as food. We also analyze other social and service indicators using the 2002 and 2010 GHS (Stats SA 2003, 2011a), such as type of dwelling, source of water, educational attainment, and connection to electricity.

Annex 3B: Tables with Detailed Data

This annex contains tables reported in the text but that are too detailed to include in the text.

Table 3B.1 Rural and Urban Population, by Settlement Type in South Africa, 2000–11

		Total	Rural areas	Urban areas	Urban TS	Urban IS	Other urban areas (excluding T&IS)
LFS2000H2–							
QLFS2011Q3	2000	44,874,226	20,943,715	23,930,511	11,167,025	1,259,951	12,624,357
	2011	50,556,305	18,848,076	31,708,229	15,259,337	3,034,165	15,855,411
	Growth (%)	1.15	−0.91	2.95	3.33	12.80	2.33
GHS2002–							
GHS2010	2002	45,533,300	20,572,025	24,961,275	11,669,047	1,394,031	13,145,914
	2010	49,858,295	19,803,675	30,054,620	13,945,700	2,188,467	15,577,214
	Growth (%)	1.19	−0.47	2.55	2.44	7.12	2.31
IES2000–							
ES2010/11	2000	43,287,467	19,572,102	23,715,365	11,160,457	1,203,031	12,425,448
	2010/11	50,423,022	19,438,169	30,984,853	14,157,602	2,524,331	16,197,942
	Growth (%)	1.65	−0.07	3.07	2.69	10.98	3.04
IES2000–							
IES2005/06	2000	43,287,467	19,572,102	23,715,365	11,160,457	1,203,031	12,425,448
	2005/06	47,371,442	19,419,727	27,951,715	13,624,181	2,599,852	13,915,374
	Growth (%)	1.89	−0.16	3.57	4.42	23.22	2.40
IES2005/06–							
IES2010/11	2005	47,371,442	19,419,727	27,951,715	13,624,181	2,599,852	13,915,374
	2010/11	50,423,022	19,438,169	30,984,853	14,157,602	2,524,331	16,197,942
	Growth (%)	1.29	0.02	2.17	0.78	−0.58	3.28

Sources: Stats SA 2000, 2002, 2003, 2008, 2011a, 2011b, 2012.

Note: TS = townships; IS = informal settlements; T&IS = townships and informal settlements; LFS = Labor Force Survey; QLFS = Quarterly Labor Force Survey; GHS = General Household Survey; IES = Income and Employment Survey. Average growth rates computed using the following formula: (Y_end/Y-initial − 1)/Number of Years. For the 2005/06 and 2010/11 IES (Stats SA 2008, 2012), we assume that population figures correspond to the initial year. All figures are reported for reference purposes; the text refers to the longest available time span, which is covered by the LFS.

Table 3B.2 Total and Working-Age Populations, by Gender and Settlement Type in South Africa, 2000 and 2011

	2000			2011			Average annual growth (%)		
	Total	Males	Females	Total	Males	Females	Total	Males	Females
a. All ages									
Total	44,874,226	22,069,497	22,799,948	50,556,305	24,639,109	25,917,196	1.2	1.1	1.2
Rural areas	20,943,715	10,114,160	10,826,728	18,848,076	8,986,018	9,862,057	−0.9	−1.0	−0.8
Urban areas	23,930,511	11,955,337	11,973,219	31,708,229	15,653,091	16,055,138	3.0	2.8	3.1
Urban TS	11,167,025	5,541,666	5,624,282	15,259,337	7,608,594	7,650,744	3.3	3.4	3.3
Urban IS	1,259,951	679,828	580,123	3,034,165	1,580,517	1,453,648	12.8	12.0	13.7
Other urban settlements (excl. T&IS)	12,624,357	6,333,312	6,290,167	15,855,411	7,768,339	8,087,072	2.3	2.1	2.6
b. Working age									
Total	27,599,148	13,385,020	14,210,784	32,562,297	15,812,576	16,749,721	1.6	1.6	1.6
Rural areas	11,542,671	5,385,296	6,155,357	11,069,035	5,151,259	5,917,776	−0.4	−0.4	−0.4
Urban areas	16,056,477	7,999,725	8,055,427	21,493,262	10,661,317	10,831,945	3.1	3.0	3.1
Urban TS	7,402,649	3,679,919	3,721,653	10,228,664	5,103,337	5,125,327	3.5	3.5	3.4
Urban IS	846,125	449,783	396,341	2,073,403	1,084,794	988,609	13.2	12.8	13.6
Other urban settlements (excl. T&IS)	8,554,036	4,263,785	4,290,003	10,862,221	5,363,489	5,498,733	2.5	2.3	2.6

Sources: Stats SA 2000, 2011b.

Note: TS = townships; IS = informal settlements; T&IS = townships and informal settlements.

Table 3B.3 Employment, by Industry and Settlement Type in South Africa, 2000 and 2011

	Agriculture	Mining	Primary	Manufacturing	Electricity	Construction	Secondary	Trade	Transport	Finance, real estate, and business services	Community and personal services	Tertiary	Private households	Total
a. 2000														
Total	1,895,001	601,718	2,496,719	1,572,438	93,890	679,848	2,346,176	2,468,666	579,993	974,199	2,078,409	6,101,267	1,136,935	12,081,097
Rural	1,688,325	318,531	2,006,856	309,697	28,960	270,913	609,570	664,031	105,589	82,606	446,140	1,298,366	434,587	4,349,379
Urban	206,676	283,188	489,863	1,262,740	64,930	408,936	1,736,606	1,804,635	474,405	891,593	1,632,269	4,802,901	702,348	7,731,718
Urban TS	79,485	76,181	155,666	535,068	13,757	198,276	747,102	781,152	192,354	194,846	469,187	1,637,538	362,973	2,903,279
Urban IS	7,777	12,112	19,889	63,309	1,587	43,913	108,809	94,065	24,285	31,733	45,603	195,686	65,607	389,991
Other urban (excl. T&IS)	124,750	206,143	330,893	722,381	50,748	203,724	976,853	1,010,849	280,203	690,785	1,150,582	3,132,418	333,829	4,773,992
Total (%)	15.7	5.0	20.7	13.0	0.8	5.6	19.4	20.4	4.8	8.1	17.2	50.5	9.4	100.0
Rural (%)	38.8	7.3	46.1	7.1	0.7	6.2	14.0	15.3	2.4	1.9	10.3	29.9	10.0	100.0
Urban (%)	2.7	3.7	6.3	16.3	0.8	5.3	22.5	23.3	6.1	11.5	21.1	62.1	9.1	100.0
Urban TS (%)	2.7	2.6	5.4	18.4	0.5	6.8	25.7	26.9	6.6	6.7	16.2	56.4	12.5	100.0
Urban IS (%)	2.0	3.1	5.1	16.2	0.4	11.3	27.9	24.1	6.2	8.1	11.7	50.2	16.8	100.0
Other urban (excl. T&IS) (%)	2.6	4.3	6.9	15.1	1.1	4.3	20.5	21.2	5.9	14.5	24.1	65.6	7.0	100.0

(table continues next page)

Table 3B.3 Employment, by Industry and Settlement Type in South Africa, 2000 and 2011 (continued)

	Agriculture	Mining	Primary	Manufacturing	Electricity	Construction	Secondary	Trade	Transport	Finance, real estate, and business services	Community and personal services	Tertiary	Private households	Total
b. 2011														
Total	623,918	323,636	947,554	1,739,492	73,405	1,086,453	2,899,349	3,013,440	758,170	1,768,049	2,836,374	8,376,032	1,098,298	13,321,233
Rural	443,492	125,656	569,148	227,230	11,563	277,745	516,538	630,171	126,117	165,368	587,738	1,509,393	287,386	2,882,465
Urban	180,425	197,980	378,406	1,512,262	61,842	808,708	2,382,811	2,383,269	632,053	1,602,681	2,248,636	6,866,639	810,912	10,438,768
Urban TS	53,007	67,784	120,791	642,314	17,566	402,835	1,062,716	1,027,114	278,261	520,201	785,550	2,611,126	510,427	4,305,060
Urban IS	14,101	4,523	18,624	149,249	3,879	99,916	253,044	231,591	42,299	137,113	108,107	519,109	153,700	944,477
Other urban (excl. T&IS)	122,111	130,196	252,307	845,888	44,275	382,543	1,272,706	1,311,737	346,866	1,053,585	1,440,067	4,152,255	265,286	5,942,554
Total (%)	4.7	2.4	7.1	13.1	0.6	8.2	21.8	22.6	5.7	13.3	21.3	62.9	8.2	100.0
Rural (%)	15.4	4.4	19.7	7.9	0.4	9.6	17.9	21.9	4.4	5.7	20.4	52.4	10.0	100.0
Urban (%)	1.7	1.9	3.6	14.5	0.6	7.7	22.8	22.8	6.1	15.4	21.5	65.8	7.8	100.0
Urban TS (%)	1.2	1.6	2.8	14.9	0.4	9.4	24.7	23.9	6.5	12.1	18.2	60.7	11.9	100.0
Urban IS (%)	1.5	0.5	2.0	15.8	0.4	10.6	26.8	24.5	4.5	14.5	11.4	55.0	16.3	100.0
Other urban (excl. T&IS) (%)	2.1	2.2	4.2	14.2	0.7	6.4	21.4	22.1	5.8	17.7	24.2	69.9	4.5	100.0

Sources: Stats SA 2000, 2011b.
Note: TS = townships. IS = informal settlements. T&IS = townships and informal settlements.

Table 3B.4 Labor Market Indicators, by Age Group and Settlement Type in South Africa, 2000 and 2011

	Total 2000	Total 2011	Rural 2000	Rural 2011	Urban 2000	Urban 2011	Urban TS 2000	Urban TS 2011	Urban IS 2000	Urban IS 2011	Other urban (excl. T&IS) 2000	Other urban (excl. T&IS) 2011
a. Youth (aged 15–24)												
Working-age population	9,206,096	10,326,977	4,483,053	4,411,051	4,723,043	5,915,926	2,355,228	3,028,182	246,059	617,403	2,334,994	2,771,827
Labor force	3,057,707	2,616,203	1,226,588	657,033	1,831,119	1,959,170	831,414	1,016,576	106,660	224,989	983,515	906,211
Employed	1,568,892	1,297,455	699,469	318,427	869,422	979,027	285,216	393,451	30,356	88,695	577,891	566,811
Unemployed	1,488,816	1,318,748	527,119	338,605	961,697	980,143	546,198	623,124	76,304	136,294	405,624	339,400
Discouraged workers	566,802	728,914	329,625	457,933	237,177	270,981	148,143	160,232	14,883	33,809	88,065	101,358
Other noneconomically active	5,581,586	6,981,860	2,926,840	3,296,084	2,654,746	3,685,775	1,375,671	1,851,375	124,516	358,605	1,263,415	1,764,259
Unemployment rate, narrow (%)	48.7	50.4	43.0	51.5	52.5	50.0	65.7	61.3	71.5	60.6	41.2	37.5
Unemployment rate, broad (%)	56.7	61.2	55.1	71.4	58.0	56.1	70.9	66.6	75.0	65.7	46.1	43.7
Labor force participation (%)	33.2	25.3	27.4	14.9	38.8	33.1	35.3	33.6	43.3	36.4	42.1	32.7
Employment rate (%)	17.0	12.6	15.6	7.2	18.4	16.5	12.1	13.0	12.3	14.4	24.7	20.4
b. Adults (aged 25–64)												
Working-age population	18,393,052	22,235,321	7,059,619	6,657,984	11,333,434	15,577,336	5,047,422	7,200,483	600,065	1,455,999	6,219,041	8,090,394
Labor force	13,623,589	15,151,323	4,688,105	3,300,628	8,935,483	11,850,695	3,965,870	5,450,358	506,761	1,175,688	4,908,678	6,176,582
Employed	10,615,185	12,027,728	3,674,424	2,564,038	6,940,760	9,463,690	2,637,843	3,912,069	361,312	855,781	4,254,786	5,379,231
Unemployed	3,008,404	3,123,595	1,013,681	736,590	1,994,723	2,387,005	1,328,027	1,538,289	145,449	319,906	653,892	797,351
Discouraged workers	1,030,364	1,474,638	557,111	908,923	473,253	565,715	289,096	342,380	32,922	56,922	182,220	212,511
Other noneconomically active	3,739,100	5,609,359	1,814,402	2,448,433	1,924,698	3,160,926	792,456	1,407,744	60,382	223,389	1,128,143	1,701,301
Unemployment rate, narrow (%)	22.1	20.6	21.6	22.3	22.3	20.1	33.5	28.2	28.7	27.2	13.3	12.9
Unemployment rate, broad (%)	27.6	27.7	29.9	39.1	26.2	23.8	38.0	32.5	33.1	30.6	16.4	15.8
Labor force participation (%)	74.1	68.1	66.4	49.6	78.8	76.1	78.6	75.7	84.5	80.7	78.9	76.3
Employment rate (%)	57.7	54.1	52.0	38.5	61.2	60.8	52.3	54.3	60.2	58.8	68.4	66.5

Sources: Stats SA 2000, 2011b.

Note: TS = townships; IS = informal settlements; T&IS = townships and informal settlements. "Working-age population" denotes the total youth population in panel a and the total adult population in panel b. The "broad" unemployment rate includes "discouraged workers"; the "narrow" unemployment rate does not. "Discouraged workers," as defined by Statistics South Africa, are working-age individuals who were not employed during the reference period, wanted to work, and were available to work or start a business but did not take active steps to find work during the previous four weeks, provided that the main reason given for not seeking work was any of the following: no jobs available in the area; unable to find work requiring his or her skills; or lost hope of finding any kind of work.

Table 3B.5 Youth Employment, School Attendance, and NEET Rates, by Settlement Type in South Africa, 2002 and 2010

	Youth population (aged 15–24 years)			Attending school (%)		Working (%)		NEET (%)	
	2002	2010	Annual avg. growth (%)	2002	2010	2002	2010	2002	2010
Total	9,233,009	10,280,992	1.4	53.2	51.6	13.5	15.2	34.6	34.4
Rural areas	4,312,093	4,482,850	0.5	55.7	56.7	9.4	8.1	35.8	35.5
Urban areas	4,920,916	5,798,142	2.2	51.1	47.5	17.0	20.7	33.5	33.5
Urban TS	2,434,539	2,840,078	2.1	51.1	46.1	10.3	15.6	39.1	39.0
Urban IS	279,281	448,397	7.6	47.2	42.4	11.6	17.4	41.9	41.0
Other urban (excl. T&IS)	2,457,085	2,861,907	2.1	51.3	49.1	23.6	26.0	27.9	27.8

Sources: Stats SA 2003, 2011a.
Note: NEET = not employed, in education, or in training; TS = townships; IS = informal settlements; T&IS = townships and informal settlements.

Table 3B.6 Consumption Per Capita, by Settlement Type in South Africa, 2005/06 and 2010/11

		Total	Rural areas	Urban areas	Urban IS	Urban TS	Urban areas (excl. T&IS)
Number of households	2005/06	12,453,858	4,341,365	8,112,493	791,570	3,686,327	4,294,489
	2010/11	13,112,216	4,289,538	8,822,678	715,409	3,832,554	4,826,040
Avg. consumption per capita (R)	2005/06	29,635	11,440	39,372	12,352	16,362	60,064
	2010/11	34,897	15,069	44,538	11,839	18,419	66,397
	Avg. growth (%)	3.6	6.3	2.6	−0.8	2.5	2.1
Avg. consumption per capita (R) (excl. imputed and actual rents)	2005/06	24,484	10,144	32,159	11,512	14,735	47,840
	2010/11	25,615	12,024	32,222	10,560	14,809	46,784
	Avg. growth (%)	0.9	3.7	0.0	−1.7	0.1	−0.4
Avg. consumption per capita (R) (incl. in kind)	2005/06	30,469	11,722	40,502	12,526	16,750	61,865
	2010/11	35,900	15,348	45,892	12,014	18,955	68,443
	Avg. growth (%)	3.6	6.2	2.7	−0.8	2.6	2.1

Sources: Stats SA 2008, 2012.
Note: TS = townships; IS = informal settlements; T&IS = townships and informal settlements; R = rand. 2005/06 data were in March 2006 prices. These have been deflated to March 2011 prices using the headline consumer price index to make comparisons meaningful.

Table 3B.7 Expenditures on Major Consumption Categories, by Settlement Type in South Africa, 2005/06 and 2010/11

	2005/06						2010/11					
	Total	Rural areas	Urban areas	Urban TS	Urban IS	Urban areas (excl. T&IS)	Total	Rural areas	Urban areas	Urban TS	Urban IS	Urban areas (excl. T&IS)
a. Expenditures (% of total income)												
Alcohol and tobacco	1.2	1.2	1.1	1.5	2.1	1.0	1.1	1.0	1.1	1.8	2.3	0.9
Clothing and footwear	5.0	7.1	4.6	7.8	8.6	3.7	4.5	6.4	4.1	7.4	8.8	3.3
Communication	3.5	3.2	3.6	3.6	4.0	3.6	2.8	2.6	2.9	3.2	4.0	2.8
Education	2.4	3.1	2.3	2.4	1.7	2.3	2.7	1.5	2.9	2.4	2.0	3.0
Food and NAB	14.3	24.4	12.5	20.9	27.0	10.2	12.8	23.7	10.7	18.9	25.7	8.5
Furniture	6.9	8.8	6.5	7.5	7.5	6.3	5.1	6.5	4.9	5.1	4.9	4.8
Health	1.7	1.8	1.6	1.4	1.6	1.7	1.4	1.2	1.5	1.4	1.4	1.5
Housing	23.6	16.4	25.0	17.8	14.2	26.9	32.1	24.8	33.5	26.2	17.4	35.4
Miscellaneous	14.4	13.4	14.6	12.5	11.2	15.2	14.7	12.2	15.2	12.3	9.9	16.0
Recreation	4.6	3.1	4.9	3.9	4.0	5.1	3.0	2.4	3.2	2.3	2.0	3.4
Restaurants	2.2	1.9	2.3	2.4	3.2	2.2	2.4	2.0	2.5	2.5	4.7	2.5
Trasnport	19.9	15.4	20.8	18.0	14.7	21.5	17.2	15.4	17.5	16.5	16.9	17.7
Unclassified	0.3	0.2	0.3	0.2	0.2	0.3	0.1	0.4	0.1	0.1	0.1	0.1

(table continues next page)

Table 3B.7 Expenditures on Major Consumption Categories, by Settlement Type in South Africa, 2005/06 and 2010/11 *(continued)*

	2005/06						2010/11					
	Total	Rural areas	Urban areas	Urban TS	Urban IS	Urban areas (excl. T&IS)	Total	Rural areas	Urban areas	Urban TS	Urban IS	Urban areas (excl. T&IS)
b. Expenditures (R, millions)												
Alcohol and tobacco	11,056	1,851	9,205	2,512	489	6,576	13,697	2,106	11,591	3,715	526	7,717
Clothing and footwear	47,481	10,766	36,715	13,021	2,030	23,381	56,169	12,954	43,214	15,206	2,048	27,559
Communication	33,629	4,836	28,793	6,071	953	22,599	35,288	5,228	30,061	6,523	929	23,349
Education	23,158	4,628	18,530	4,015	408	14,477	33,355	2,942	30,413	4,941	463	25,394
Food and NAB	137,397	36,898	100,499	35,020	6,400	64,583	159,572	47,925	111,647	38,910	5,957	71,254
Furniture	66,037	13,359	52,677	12,525	1,774	39,887	63,944	13,021	50,923	10,495	1,133	40,178
Health	15,927	2,673	13,255	2,343	368	10,885	17,794	2,340	15,454	2,793	323	12,580
Housing	226,174	24,851	201,324	29,834	3,371	171,236	399,992	49,966	350,026	53,926	4,040	295,207
Miscellaneous	137,995	20,314	117,681	20,967	2,646	96,391	183,756	24,568	159,187	25,240	2,309	133,469
Recreation	44,084	4,745	39,339	6,527	943	32,702	38,015	4,907	33,108	4,711	453	28,304
Restaurants	21,047	2,898	18,149	4,031	762	14,032	30,332	4,017	26,315	5,147	1,100	20,625
Transport	190,920	23,265	167,655	30,209	3,479	137,054	213,977	31,072	182,905	34,035	3,912	148,065
Unclassified	2,939	361	2,577	384	57	2,190	1,760	766	993	261	20	729
Total consumption	957,844	151,446	806,399	167,461	23,680	635,995	1,247,650	201,812	1,045,838	205,903	23,213	834,430

Sources: Stats SA 2008, 2012.

Note: TS = townships; IS = informal settlements; T&IS = townships and informal settlements; R = rand; NAB = nonalcoholic beverages. Domestic currency monetary values for 2005/06 are expressed in March 2011 prices using the headline consumer price index.

Table 3B.8 Orphans and Living Arrangements, by Settlement Type in South Africa, 2002 and 2010
Percent

	Not orphan		Paternal orphan		Maternal orphan		Double orphan	
	2002	2010	2002	2010	2002	2010	2002	2010
Total	85.2	80.0	10.2	11.6	2.9	3.9	1.7	4.4
Rural areas	84.2	76.8	10.8	13.3	3.1	4.7	2.0	5.3
Urban areas	86.4	83.0	9.6	10.1	2.6	3.3	1.4	3.6
Urban TS	82.7	79.3	12.0	12.6	3.3	3.6	2.0	4.6
Urban IS	86.7	79.5	10.0	12.8	1.7	3.5	1.6	4.2
Other urban (excl. T&IS)	90.2	86.9	7.0	7.5	1.9	3.0	0.9	2.6

	Living with both parents		Living with father only		Living with mother only		Living with none	
	2002	2010	2002	2010	2002	2010	2002	2010
Total	41.5	37.1	3.3	4.2	41.3	44.7	13.9	14.1
Rural areas	32.2	26.0	3.2	3.8	45.8	50.0	18.8	20.2
Urban areas	51.7	46.4	3.4	4.5	36.3	40.2	8.5	8.9
Urban TS	42.2	37.6	3.5	4.3	44.3	48.4	10.0	9.7
Urban IS	49.7	44.4	3.3	3.6	40.1	44.6	6.9	7.5
Other urban (excl. T&IS)	61.1	55.2	3.3	4.8	28.5	31.9	7.0	8.1

Sources: Stats SA 2003, 2011a.
Note: TS = townships; IS = informal settlements; T&IS = townships and informal settlements. "Orphan" is defined as a child up to 17 years of age who has lost one or both parents.

Table 3B.9 Labor Market Indicators, by Gender and Settlement Type in South Africa, 2000 and 2011

	Total		Rural		Urban		Urban TS		Urban IS		Other urban (excl. T&IS)	
	2000	2011	2000	2011	2000	2011	2000	2011	2000	2011	2000	2011
a. Males												
Working-age population	13,385,020	15,812,576	5,385,296	5,151,259	7,999,725	10,661,317	3,679,919	5,103,337	449,783	1,084,794	4,263,785	5,363,489
Labor force	9,038,547	9,701,411	3,159,592	2,110,535	5,878,955	7,590,876	2,596,844	3,575,393	353,210	817,192	3,236,593	3,875,995
Employed	6,912,550	7,515,756	2,413,624	1,584,875	4,498,926	5,930,881	1,707,359	2,525,390	258,381	591,557	2,755,835	3,301,643
Unemployed	2,125,998	2,185,654	745,969	525,659	1,380,029	1,659,995	889,485	1,050,004	94,829	225,635	480,758	574,352
Discouraged workers	590,638	963,248	334,598	624,756	256,041	338,492	161,520	189,356	17,507	36,046	92,975	138,088
Other noneconomically active	3,755,835	5,147,918	1,891,106	2,415,969	1,864,729	2,731,949	921,555	1,338,588	79,067	231,556	934,217	1,349,406
Unemployment rate, narrow (%)	23.5	22.5	23.6	24.9	23.5	21.9	34.3	29.4	26.8	27.6	14.9	14.8
Unemployment rate, broad (%)	28.2	29.5	30.9	42.1	26.7	25.2	38.1	32.9	30.3	30.7	17.2	17.7
Labor force participation (%)	67.5	61.4	58.7	41.0	73.5	71.2	70.6	70.1	78.5	75.3	75.9	72.3
Employment rate (%)	51.6	47.5	44.8	30.8	56.2	55.6	46.4	49.5	57.4	54.5	64.6	61.6
b. Females												
Working-age population	14,210,784	16,749,721	6,155,357	5,917,776	8,055,427	10,831,945	3,721,653	5,125,327	396,341	988,609	4,290,003	5,498,733
Labor force	7,641,693	8,066,115	2,754,293	1,847,126	4,887,400	6,218,989	2,200,440	2,891,541	260,211	583,485	2,655,353	3,206,799
Employed	5,270,875	5,809,426	1,959,866	1,297,590	3,311,009	4,511,836	1,215,700	1,780,131	133,287	352,920	2,076,594	2,644,399
Unemployed	2,370,818	2,256,689	794,427	549,536	1,576,391	1,707,153	984,739	1,111,410	126,924	230,565	578,759	562,400
Discouraged workers	1,005,451	1,240,305	552,138	742,101	453,313	498,204	274,642	313,255	30,299	54,686	177,310	175,781
Other noneconomically active	5,563,640	7,443,301	2,848,926	3,328,549	2,714,714	4,114,753	1,246,572	1,920,531	105,832	350,439	1,457,340	2,116,153
Unemployment rate, narrow (%)	31.0	28.0	28.8	29.8	32.3	27.5	44.8	38.4	48.8	39.5	21.8	17.5
Unemployment rate, broad (%)	39.0	37.6	40.7	49.9	38.0	32.8	50.9	44.5	54.1	44.7	26.7	21.8
Labor force participation (%)	53.8	48.2	44.7	31.2	60.7	57.4	59.1	56.4	65.7	59.0	61.9	58.3
Employment rate (%)	37.1	34.7	31.8	21.9	41.1	41.7	32.7	34.7	33.6	35.7	48.4	48.1

Sources: Stats SA 2000, 2011b.

Note: TS = townships; IS = informal settlements; T&IS = townships and informal settlements. "Working-age population" denotes the total male or female population aged 15–64 years. The "broad" unemployment rate includes "discouraged workers"; the "narrow" unemployment rate does not. "Discouraged workers," as defined by Statistics South Africa, are working-age individuals who were not employed during the reference period, wanted to work, and were available to work or start a business but did not take active steps to find work during the previous four weeks, provided that the main reason given for not seeking work was any of the following: no jobs available in the area; unable to find work requiring his or her skills; or lost hope of finding any kind of work.

Table 3B.10 Female- and Male-Headed Households, by Settlement Type in South Africa, 2005/06 and 2010/11

		Total	Rural	Urban	Urban TS	Urban IS	Other urban (excl. T&IS)
2005/06	Number of male-headed households	7,606,019	2,223,226	5,382,793	2,324,726	555,910	2,956,728
	Number of female-headed households	4,839,140	2,113,129	2,726,011	1,361,495	235,535	1,334,303
	Total population in male-headed households	26,767,826	9,133,930	17,633,896	7,828,819	1,620,470	9,517,112
	Total population in female-headed households	20,569,866	10,264,424	10,305,442	5,795,044	979,008	4,386,576
2010/11	Number of male-headed households	7,948,556	2,162,476	5,786,081	2,358,832	475,383	3,323,976
	Number of female-headed households	5,163,659	2,127,062	3,036,597	1,473,721	240,026	1,502,065
	Total population in male-headed households	28,748,439	9,010,777	19,737,662	8,087,119	1,540,826	11,302,268
	Total population in female-headed households	21,674,583	10,427,392	11,247,191	6,070,483	983,505	4,895,674

Sources: Stats SA 2008, 2012.
Note: TS = townships; IS = informal settlements; T&IS = townships and informal settlements.

Table 3B.11 Regression of Consumption Correlates from IES2010/11

	(1) ln_pccons	(2) ln_pccons	(3) ln_pcconskind	(4) ln_pcconskind
ln (HH size)	-0.5824*** (0.0131)	-0.5835*** (0.0131)	-0.5808*** (0.0131)	-0.5819*** (0.0131)
ln (age head of HH)	0.3441*** (0.0210)	0.3463*** (0.0210)	0.3495*** (0.0211)	0.3517*** (0.0211)
female (1 if head female, 0 o/w)	-0.0791*** (0.0156)	-0.0795*** (0.0157)	-0.0788*** (0.0158)	-0.0792*** (0.0159)
color (1 if color, 0 o/w)	0.1744*** (0.0367)	0.1729*** (0.0369)	0.1787*** (0.0371)	0.1771*** (0.0373)
indian (1 if indian/asian, 0 o/w)	0.7390*** (0.0562)	0.7354*** (0.0561)	0.7401*** (0.0571)	0.7364*** (0.0569)
white (1 if white, o/w)	1.2124*** (0.0466)	1.2084*** (0.0466)	1.2118*** (0.0468)	1.2081*** (0.0468)
single-headed HH (1 if single headed, 0 o/w)	-0.0327** (0.0164)	-0.0322** (0.0164)	-0.0313* (0.0165)	-0.0308* (0.0165)
matric (1 if matric completed, 0 o/w)	0.4509*** (0.0201)	0.5334*** (0.0389)	0.4635*** (0.0203)	0.5465*** (0.0393)
tertiary (1 i f tertiary completed, 0 o/w)	0.9412*** (0.0268)	1.0095*** (0.0683)	0.9659*** (0.0271)	1.0345*** (0.0675)
other education (1 if other, 0 o/w)	0.0656 (0.0802)	-0.0802 (0.1092)	0.0645 (0.0801)	-0.0795 (0.1088)
number of workers in HH	0.1792*** (0.0085)	0.1785*** (0.0086)	0.1818*** (0.0086)	0.1810*** (0.0086)
number of social grant recipients	-0.0691*** (0.0056)	-0.0679*** (0.0056)	-0.0710*** (0.0057)	-0.0698*** (0.0056)
tsnis (urban townships excl. is)	0.2351*** (0.0233)	0.2530*** (0.0240)	0.2449*** (0.0235)	0.2624*** (0.0241)
is (urban is)	-0.1708*** (0.0422)	-0.1097** (0.0444)	-0.1702*** (0.0423)	-0.1093** (0.0445)
urb_other (other urban excl. T&IS)	0.4066*** (0.0395)	0.4134*** (0.0416)	0.4155*** (0.0398)	0.4230*** (0.0420)
matric_x_tsnis		-0.1229** (0.0481)		-0.1245** (0.0488)
matric_x_is		-0.3596*** (0.0748)		-0.3609*** (0.0756)
matric_x_urb_other		-0.0620 (0.0512)		-0.0625 (0.0517)
tertiary_x_tsnis		-0.0570 (0.0842)		-0.0492 (0.0838)
tertiary_x_is		-0.3429** (0.1485)		-0.3274** (0.1588)
tertiary_x_urb_other		-0.0729 (0.0791)		-0.0758 (0.0785)
other_x_tsnis		-0.0255 (0.1480)		-0.0268 (0.1484)
other_x_is		-0.2234 (0.2168)		-0.2307 (0.2174)
other_x_urb_other		0.4876*** (0.1888)		0.4846*** (0.1880)
constant	8.3454*** (0.0811)	8.3275*** (0.0810)	8.3292*** (0.0815)	8.3111*** (0.0813)
N	25,327	25,327	25,327	25,327
adj. R-sq	0.644	0.644	0.645	0.646

Source: Based on data from Stats SA 2012.

Note: The settlement categories are as follows: is = informal settlements; T&IS = townships and informal settlements; tsnis = urban townships (excluding is); urb_other = other urban areas (excluding tsnis and is). Standard errors are in parentheses. The dependent variable is the natural log of consumption per capita and consumption per capita (plus in kind). Standard errors are clustered in primary sampling units. Number of workers per household (HH) denotes the number employed per HH. Ordinary least squares (OLS) regressions have been weighted by sample weights.

Significance level: * = 10 percent; ** = 5 percent; *** = 1 percent.

Table 3B.12 Transportation Time to School, by Settlement Type in South Africa, 2002 and 2010

Percent

	<15 min		15–30 min		>30 min	
	2002	*2010*	*2002*	*2010*	*2002*	*2010*
Total	39.3	38.8	40.3	41.9	20.4	19.2
Rural areas	33.0	30.6	41.5	44.0	25.5	25.4
Urban areas	45.8	46.5	39.1	40.0	15.1	13.5
Urban TS	41.8	44.1	40.0	41.6	18.2	14.3
Urban IS	29.2	37.2	42.7	45.3	28.1	17.4
Other urban (excl. T&IS)	49.9	49.4	38.1	38.2	12.0	12.5

Sources: Stats SA 2003, 2011a.

Note: TS = townships; IS = informal settlements; T&IS = townships and informal settlements. The denominator is the sum of all those attending school who opted for one of the choices depicted in the columns.

Annex 3C: Figures with Detailed Data

This annex contains figures and charts on which we report in the text but that are too detailed to include in the text.

Figure 3C.1 Main Household Income Sources, by Settlement Type in South Africa, 2002 and 2010

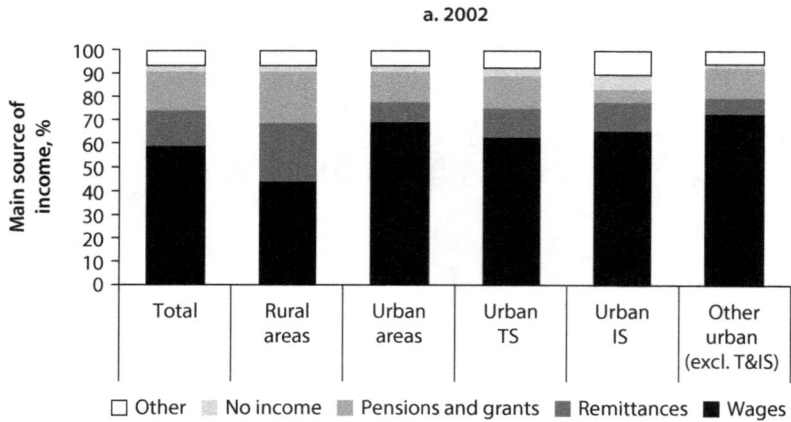

a. 2002

figure continues next page

Figure 3C.1 Main Household Income Sources, by Settlement Type in South Africa, 2002 and 2010 *(continued)*

b. 2010

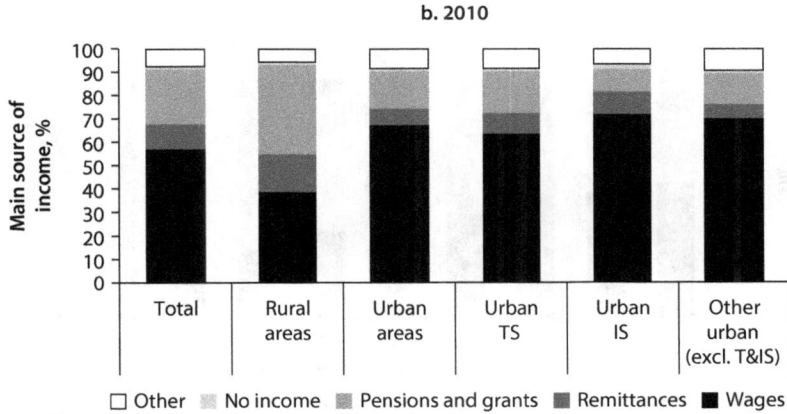

Sources: Stats SA 2003, 2011a.

Note: TS = townships; IS = informal settlements; T&IS = townships and informal settlements.

Figure 3C.2 Distribution of Household Consumption and Income Deciles, by Settlement Type in South Africa, 2005/06 and 2010/11

Percent

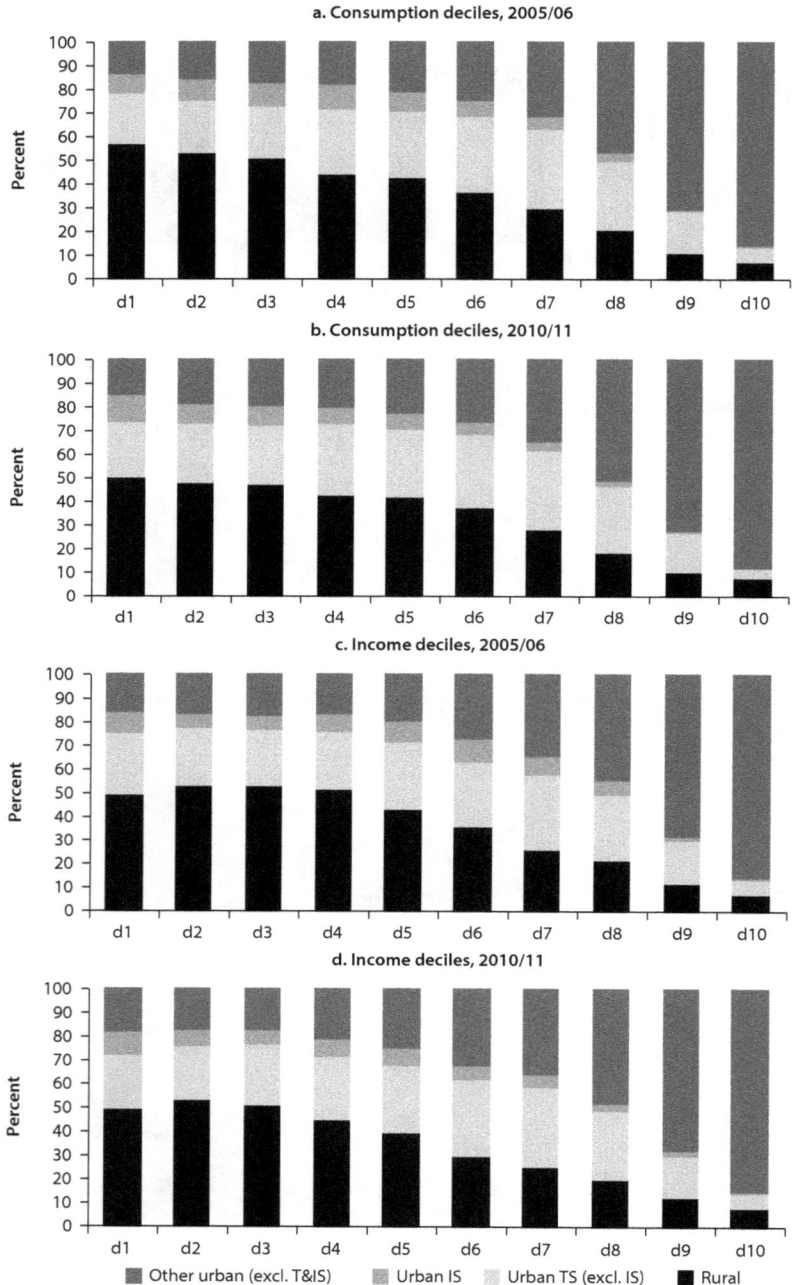

a. Consumption deciles, 2005/06

b. Consumption deciles, 2010/11

c. Income deciles, 2005/06

d. Income deciles, 2010/11

Other urban (excl. T&IS)   Urban IS   Urban TS (excl. IS)   Rural

Sources: Stats SA 2008, 2012.
Note: TS = townships (excluding IS); IS = informal settlements; Other urban (excl. T&IS) = other urban areas (excluding townships and informal settlements); T&IS = townships and informal settlements; d = decile (1–10 being lowest to highest).

Figure 3C.3 Proportion of Population Younger Than 25 Years Attending School, by Settlement Type in South Africa, 2002 and 2010
Percent

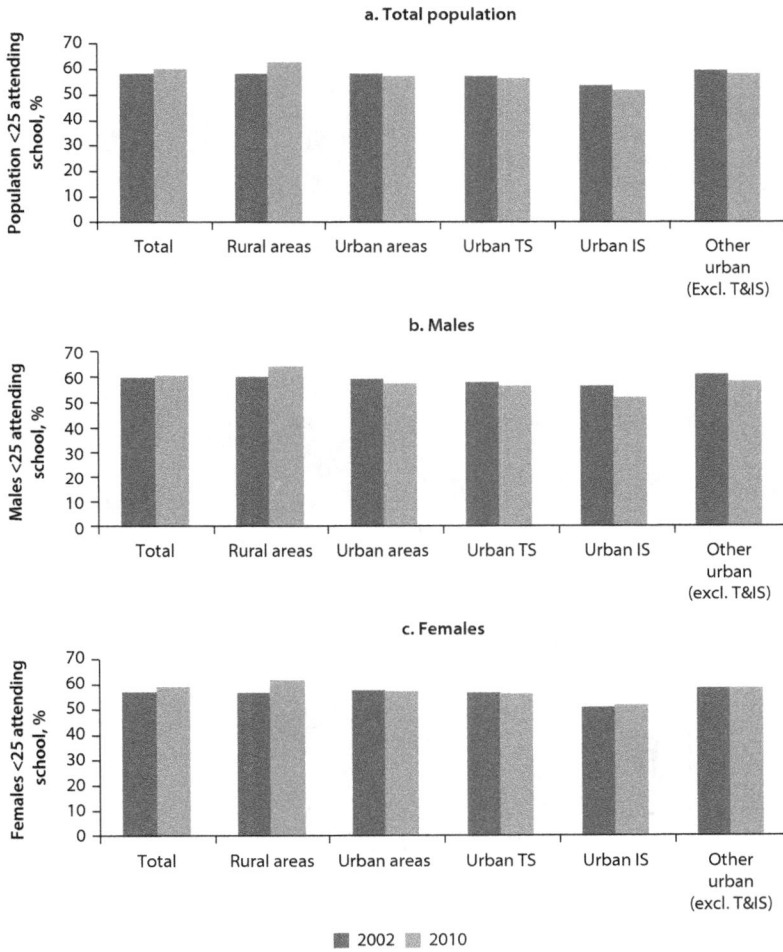

a. Total population

b. Males

c. Females

■ 2002   ▨ 2010

Sources: Stats SA 2003, 2011a.
Note: TS = townships; IS = informal settlements; T&IS = townships and informal settlements.

Figure 3C.4 Frequency of Adult and Child Hunger, by Settlement Type in South Africa, 2002 and 2010

Percent

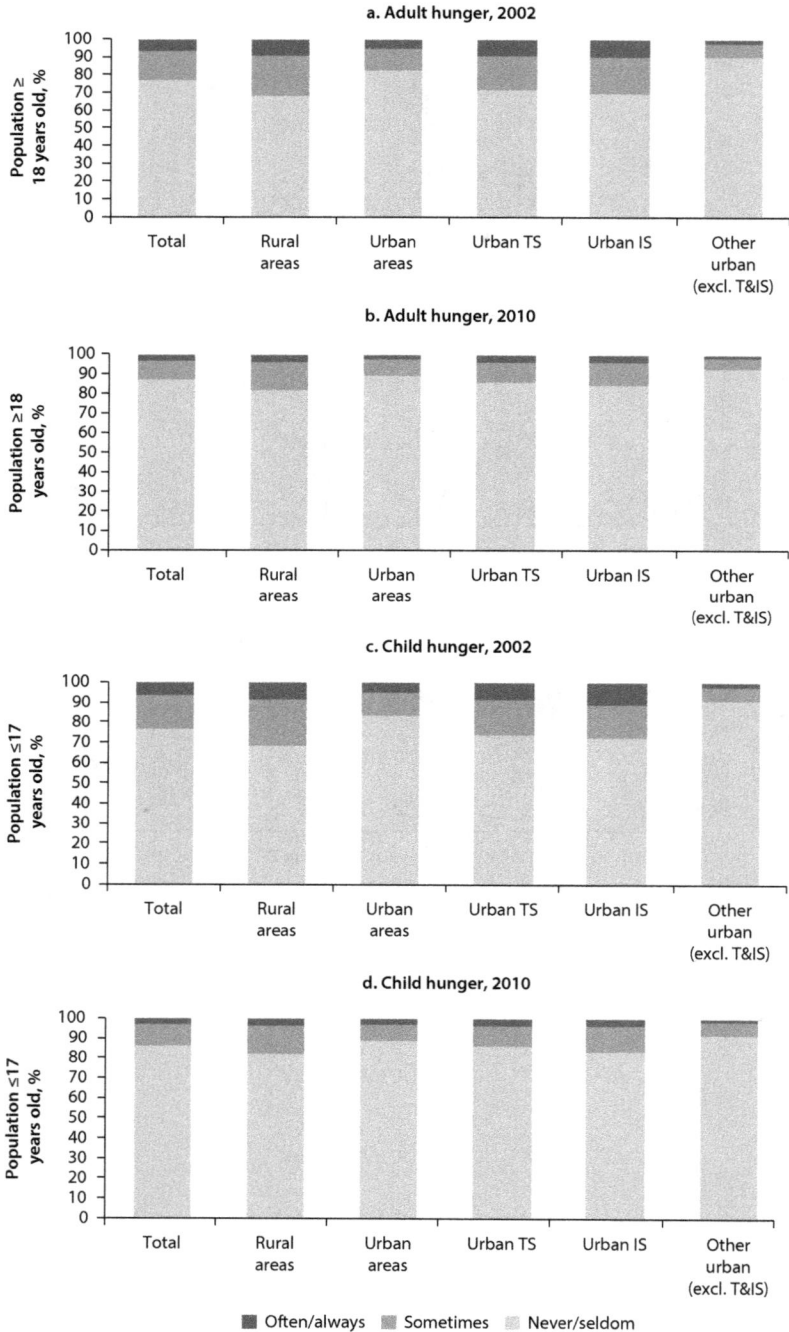

a. Adult hunger, 2002

b. Adult hunger, 2010

c. Child hunger, 2002

d. Child hunger, 2010

■ Often/always   ▨ Sometimes   ▦ Never/seldom

Sources: Stats SA 2003, 2011a.

Note: TS = townships; IS = informal settlements; T&IS = townships and informal settlements.

Figure 3C.5 Household Water Source, by Settlement Type in South Africa, 2002 and 2010

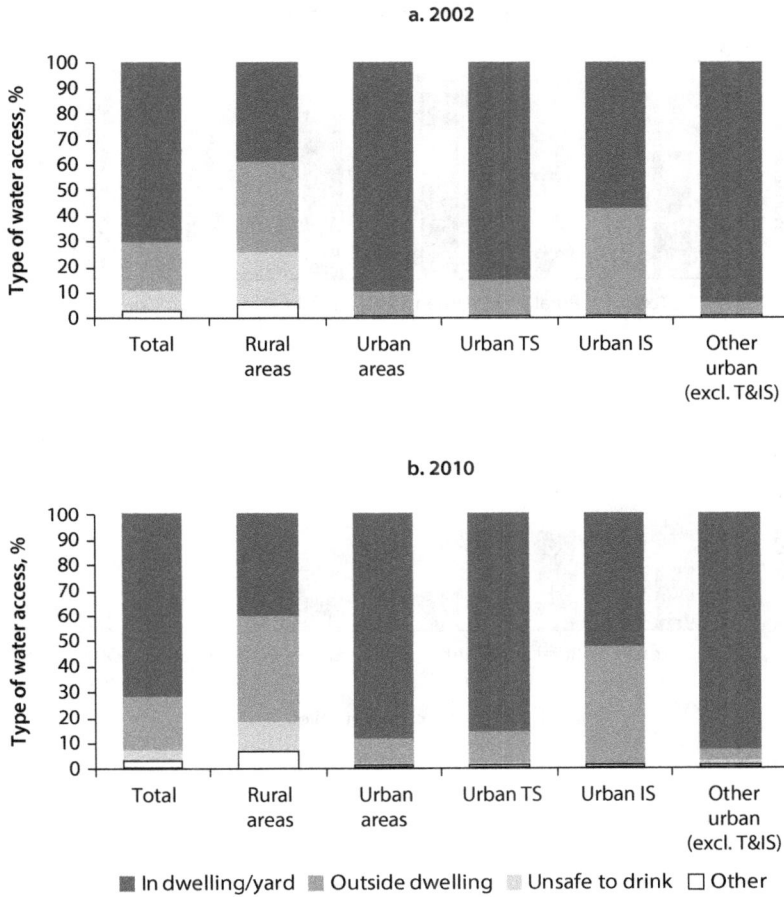

a. 2002

b. 2010

■ In dwelling/yard ■ Outside dwelling ▨ Unsafe to drink ☐ Other

Sources: Stats SA 2003, 2011a.
Note: TS = townships; IS = informal settlements; T&IS = townships and informal settlements.

Figure 3C.6 Distribution of Toilets, by Settlement Type in South Africa, 2002 and 2010

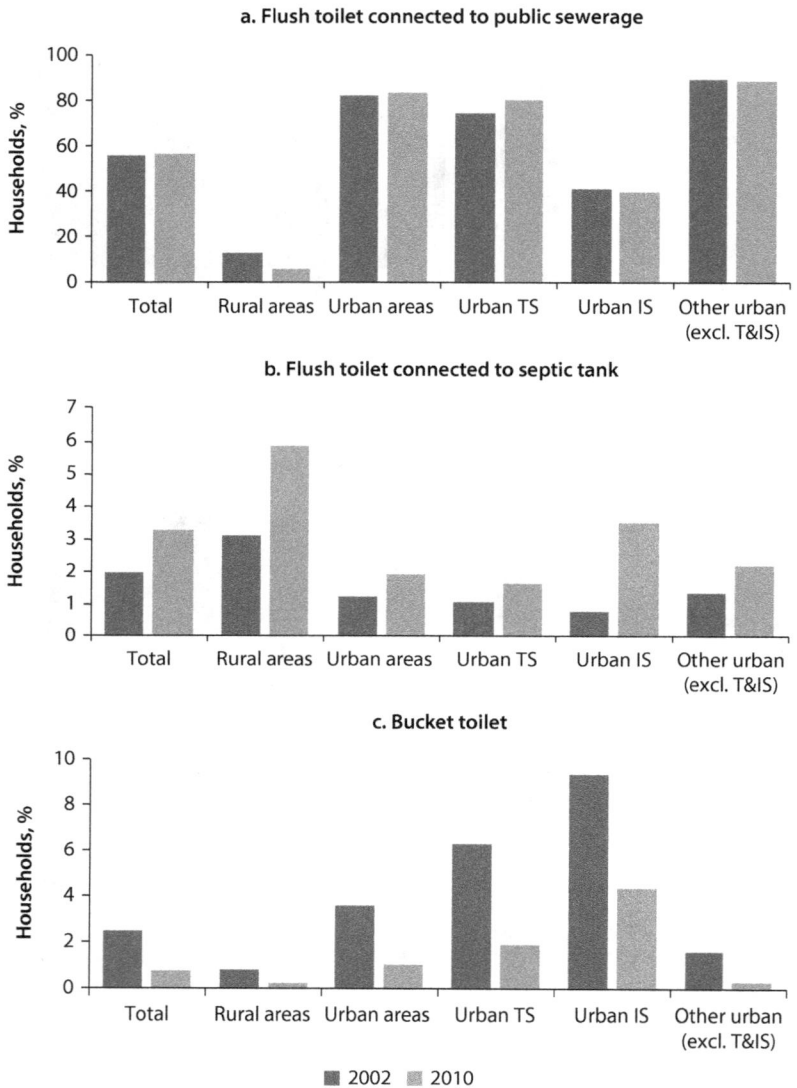

a. Flush toilet connected to public sewerage

b. Flush toilet connected to septic tank

c. Bucket toilet

■ 2002   ■ 2010

Sources: Stats SA 2003, 2011a.
Note: TS = townships; IS = informal settlements; T&IS = townships and informal settlements.

Figure 3C.7 Access to Electricity, Cell Phones, and Television, by Settlement Type in South Africa, 2002 and 2010

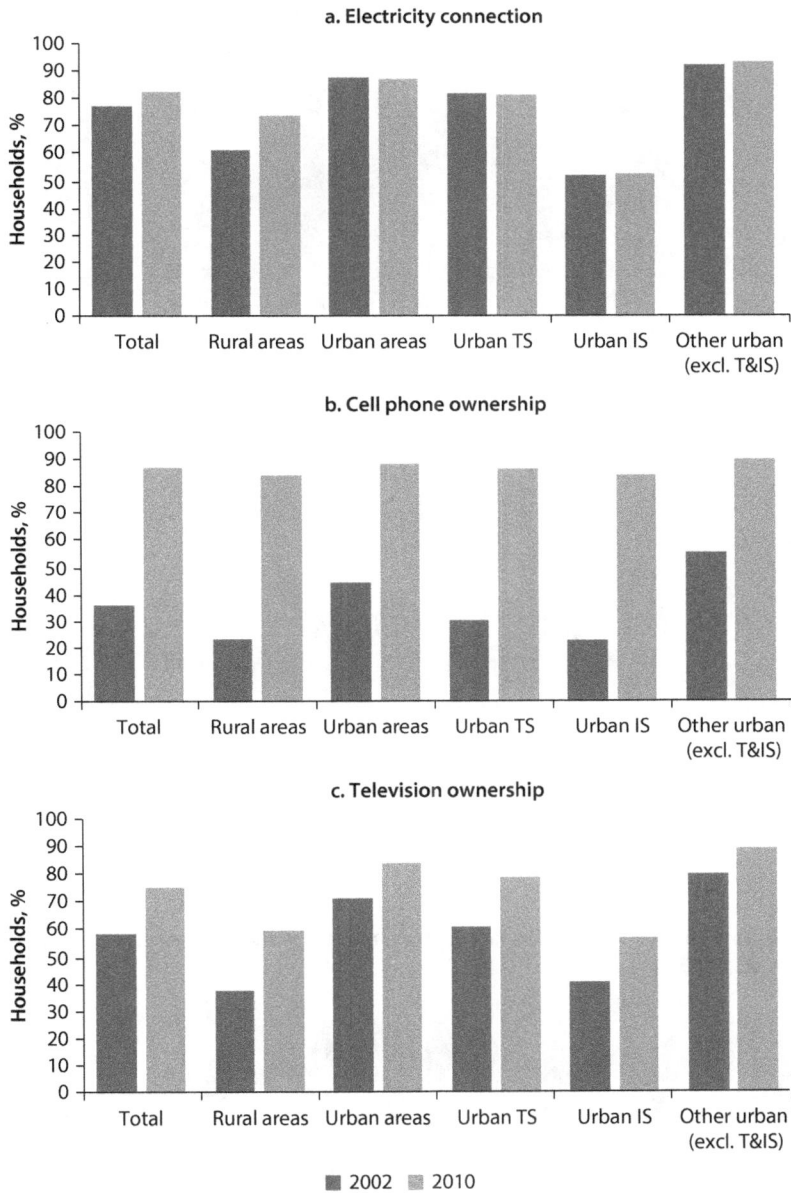

a. Electricity connection

b. Cell phone ownership

c. Television ownership

2002   2010

Sources: Stats SA 2003, 2011a.
Note: TS = townships; IS = informal settlements; T&IS = townships and informal settlements.

Figure 3C.8 Illness and Health Care, by Settlement Type in South Africa, 2002 and 2010

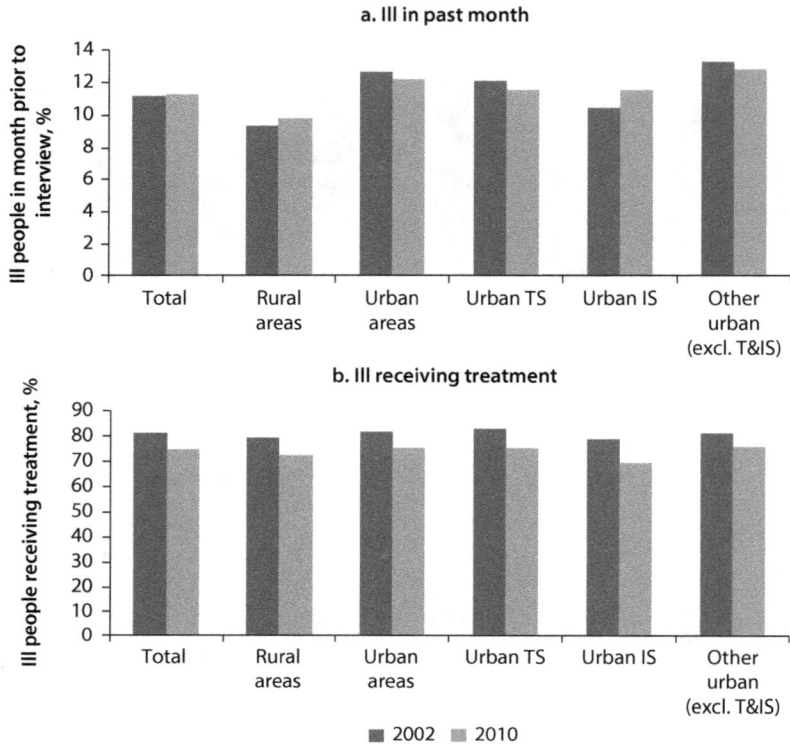

a. Ill in past month

b. Ill receiving treatment

■ 2002 ■ 2010

Sources: Stats SA 2003, 2011a.
Note: TS = townships; IS = informal settlements; T&IS = townships and informal settlements.

Figure 3C.9 Access to Medication for Selected Diagnoses, by Settlement Type in South Africa, 2010

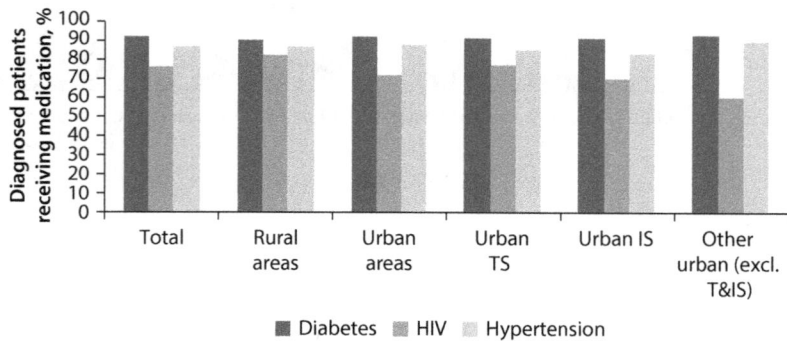

■ Diabetes ■ HIV ■ Hypertension

Source: Stats SA 2011a.
Note: TS = townships; IS = informal settlements; T&IS = townships and informal settlements; HIV = human immunodeficiency virus.

Notes

1. Income and Expenditure of Households (various rounds), General Household Survey (various rounds) and Labor Force Survey (various rounds).

2. Single-headed households are defined here as households comprising a head (or acting head), no partners, and at least one child under 18 years old. If the above conditions are satisfied, the following definitions apply: (a) In a "female single-headed household," the head or acting head is female. (b) In a "male single-headed household," the head or acting head is male.

3. The former apartheid government decided an individual's race based on appearance—regarding "Coloured" people as being of mixed-race descent. The other three legally defined racial groups at the time were Black, White, and Indian. Today, Statistics South Africa (Stats SA) asks people to self-identify as one of five "population groups": "black African," "white," "coloured," "Indian or Asian," or "unspecified/other." Stats SA does not define these terms. At the same time, those who describe themselves as "coloureds" have viewed themselves as distinct from other groups (Economist 2012).

4. The dependency ratio is the age-population ratio of those typically not of working age (therefore "dependent") to those typically of working age (aged 15–64).

5. This ratio is defined as the ratio of the working-age male population to the working-age female population.

6. "Homeland areas" refers to the territories, often far from cities, to which South Africa's apartheid-era government forcibly moved nonwhite populations. The legal establishment of the homelands (previously called "reserves" and also widely known as "bantustans") formed the basis for the government to eventually regard the homelands as self-governing states, nominally independent of South Africa, and in 1970 to denaturalize the homelands' populations.

7. The broad unemployment rate includes discouraged workers. It is computed as (unemployed seeking + discouraged)/(unemployed seeking + discouraged workers + employed).

8. It should be noted that the data may also mask some of the adverse consequences of the global financial crisis as well as individual characteristics that may have an impact on labor market outcomes, such as educational attainment, past job experiences, and duration of unemployment. A further examination may shed some light on these issues by examining whether the global financial crisis had heterogeneous effects across settlements. However, this is beyond the scope of this chapter.

9. Stats SA has computed the numbers of youth "not in employment, education, or training" (NEET) since the release of the Quarterly Labor Force Survey (QLFS) 2012Q3. Before then, this measure was not computed, and the question of whether a person was currently attending an educational institution was not asked. We compute the NEET for the Labor Force Surveys of September 2000 and Quarter 3, 2011 (Stats SA 2000, 2011b) using questions in the survey instruments that convey similar information. The correlation between our proxy measure of the NEET and the ones reported by Stats SA for QLFS2012Q3–QLFS2012Q4 is above 0.9, which is reassuring.

10. These results should be taken with care because the NEET was computed using different questions for the LFS2000H2 (Stats SA 2000) and the QLFS2011Q3 (Stats SA 2011b). Using the General Household Survey (GHS) 2002 and the GHS2010 (Stats SA 2003 and 2011a, respectively) for the computations (as shown in annex table 3B.5) shows contrasting results—suggesting little change between

initial- and end-year figures across all settlements. For the nation as a whole, the NEET stood at 34.4 percent in 2010.

11. All average income and consumption per capita figures are in rand (March 2011 prices). The nominal average rand-US$ exchange rate in March 2011 was 6.91, according to the South Africa Reserve Bank (http://www.resbank.co.za/Research /Rates/Pages/Rates-Home.aspx).

12. In April 2006, 7,044,901 children received the Child Support Grant (R 190 per month in nominal terms), and 2,093,440 people received the Old Age Grant (R 820 per month in nominal terms). By 2011, both the numbers of recipients and their grants increased to 10,154,000 children (R 260 per month) and 2,647,000 elders (R 1,150 per month), respectively (Budget Review, various years, National Treasury, South Africa, http://www.treasury.gov.za/documents/national%20budget/default .aspx).

13. The proportion of rural households reporting remittances as the main source of income fell between 2002 and 2010 (from 23.6 percent to 15.6 percent). This fall was countered by a large increase in rural households reporting pension and grants as the main source of income. If remittances were relatively small, the larger amount of children and old people per household in rural areas, together with the expansion in eligibility of children up to 18 years old in 2010, may partly explain the downward trend in the share of households reporting remittances as the main source of income between 2002 and 2010.

14. The higher transport expenditure by residents of OUA relative to residents of TS and IS likely reflects significantly higher automobile ownership.

15. We compute the number of households and persons below several poverty lines. We calculate the number of poor households and persons on the basis of the poverty lines derived from US$1.25 a day in purchasing power parity [PPP] in 2005 prices and US$2.50 a day PPP in 2005 prices. These thresholds yield annual poverty lines in March 2006 prices of R 2,118 and R 4,235, and in March 2011 prices of R 2,901 and R 5,802.

16. Single-headed households are defined here as households comprising a head (or acting head), no partners, and at least one child under 18 years old. If these conditions are satisfied, the following definitions apply: (a) In a "female single-headed household," the head or acting head is female. (b) In a "male single-headed household," the head or acting head is male.

17. These data include all male- and all female-headed households regardless of whether they are single-headed or dual-headed. The Income and Expenditure Survey of 2005/06 (Stats SA 2008) did not include a question to determine whether a household was single-headed.

18. Results should be interpreted keeping in mind that the excluded variable is a dual-headed household living in rural areas, with a black male head who has less than secondary education (less than matric [high school] completed).

19. The negative correlation of consumption with number of grant recipients in the household suggests that the grants go to households with low consumption to start with.

20. RDP is the South African socioeconomic policy framework first implemented in 1994 to address a range of problems that had resulted from apartheid-era policies. Among the RDP's central urban priorities has been the development of public housing in postapartheid townships.

21. We classify water sources into three categories: First, water in the house or yard (piped water in house or yard, borehole in yard, or rainwater tank) that normally are safe. Second, water outside the house (water from neighbors or a public tap, a public borehole, or a water tanker) that is also safe if the systems are properly maintained. Third, intrinsically unsafe sources such as water flowing in a stream or river, stagnant water in a dam or pool, and wells (that are not boreholes).

22. The General Household Survey 2010 (Stats SA 2011a) also reports data for other diseases that are not reported here.

23. CD4 (cluster of differentiation 4) cells—often called T-helper cells or T4 cells—are a type of white blood cell that fights infection. Depletion of CD4 cells leaves the body vulnerable to a wide range of infections that it would otherwise have been able to fight.

References

Cross, C. 2013. "Migration and the Access Dynamics for Jobs and Informal Business in South Africa." Background paper, World Bank, Washington, DC.

Economist. 2012. "Race in South Africa: Still an Issue." February 4. http://www.economist .com/node/21546062.

Ranis, G., and F. Stewart. 1999. "V-Goods and the Role of the Urban Informal Sector in Development." Economic Development and Cultural Change 47 (2): 259–88.

Stats SA (Statistics South Africa). 2000. Labor Force Survey 2000, September. Data file release, Pretoria. http://catalog.ihsn.org/index.php/catalog/2269#page=overview &tab=study-desc.

———. 2002. Income and Expenditure of Households 2000. Statistical Release P0111, Pretoria.

———. 2003. General Household Survey 2002. Statistical Release P0318, Pretoria.

———. 2008. Income and Expenditure of Households 2005/2006. Statistical Release P0100, Pretoria.

———. 2011a. General Household Survey 2010 (Revised version). Statistical Release P0318, Pretoria.

———. 2011b. "Quarterly Labour Force Survey." Quarter 3. Statistical Release P0211 Pretoria.

———. 2012. "Income and Expenditure of Households 2010/2011." Statistical Release P0100, Pretoria.

World Bank. 2011. "South Africa Economic Update: Focus on Savings, Investment, and Inclusive Growth." South Africa Economic Update, Issue 1, World Bank, Washington, DC.

CHAPTER 4

Access to Finance in Townships and Informal Settlements

Dorothe Singer

An Unequal Access to Finance

The South African economy is often described as a dual economy with a developed, high-end economy resembling Organisation for Economic Co-operation and Development (OECD) countries in sophistication coexisting with a less-developed, low-end economy found mostly in townships and informal settlements in urban areas and in former homelands in the rural areas. The high income inequality generated by this dual economy is reflected in, among other things, unequal access to finance.[1]

Although South Africa exemplifies a fairly inclusive financial sector relative to other African and developing countries (World Bank 2013), the overall numbers mask great inequality in the use of financial services that mirrors the country's dual economy. For example, while overall 60 percent of adults residing in urban areas report using a formal bank account, 66 percent of adults in nontownship urban areas do so compared with 54 percent of adults in townships.[2] Moreover, adults in townships are twice as likely to be underbanked as adults in nontownship urban areas—and, in terms of credit, are two-thirds less likely to have received a loan from a bank but one-third more likely to have relied on one from family or friends (FinMark Trust 2013).

When it comes to businesses, micro, small, and medium enterprises (MSMEs) in townships are 12 percentage points less likely to use a bank account than MSMEs in nontownship urban areas. Even if they do have an account, they are more likely to use a personal one than one in the business's name. And while credit penetration is generally very low (less than 5 percent of MSMEs in either townships or nontownship urban areas report any borrowing), most credit in townships originates from family and friends, whereas in nontownship urban areas it does so from banks.

Financial exclusion and uneven access to finance for the poor and small businesses—to the degree that they are involuntary and the results of market imperfections—are thus a major concern in South Africa.[3] Importantly, though, this chapter, shows that this inequality is not directly due to the spatial location of townships but rather is an indirect consequence of a whole set of different economic realities that township residents face such as lower income, lower education, and higher unemployment.

Well-functioning financial systems serve the vital purpose of offering savings, credit, payment, and risk-management products to wide-ranging classes of individuals. A growing body of research using field experiments shows that financial inclusion can have significant beneficial effects such as increasing savings (Aportela 1999) and consumption as well as productive investment of entrepreneurs (Dupas and Robinson 2009).[4] Financial inclusion is especially likely to benefit the poor. Without inclusive financial systems, the poor must rely on their own limited resources to invest in education, become entrepreneurs, and withstand income shocks; small enterprises must rely on their limited earnings to pursue growth opportunities. These constraints can contribute to persistent income inequality and slower economic growth (Beck, Demirgüç-Kunt, and Levine 2007; Beck, Levine, and Loayza 2000; Demirguc-Kunt and Levine 2009; Klapper, Laeven, and Rajan 2006; World Bank 2008).

The objective of this chapter is to characterize patterns of financial service usage in townships relative to the rest of South Africa to provide clarity on the need for specific financial inclusion policies. While financial institutions offer an array of financial services, the chapter will focus on the use of accounts, formal payments, savings, and credit.[5]

Because numbers without a benchmark provide little insight, the chapter will contrast the use of financial services in townships with that in urban nontownship areas. The following two sections explore access to finance for households and MSMEs, primarily using data from the "FinScope South Africa 2012" household survey and the "FinScope South Africa Small Business Survey 2010" for small and medium enterprises (SMEs) (FinMark Trust 2011, 2013). It then briefly discusses how the structure of South Africa's banking sector further complicates access to finance for both the poor and MSMEs. The concluding section addresses the policy implications arising from the observed usage patterns.

Note on Data and Methodology

FinScope surveys are nationally representative studies of demand, usage, and access to financial services conducted in a number of African countries by the FinMark Trust, an independent trust financed by the United Kingdom's Department for International Development (DFID).[6] Unlike other access-to-finance surveys in South Africa such as the Global Financial Inclusion Database (Global Findex)[7]—a comparable dataset of financial inclusion indicators across 148 economies collected by the World Bank—FinScope surveys are uniquely suited for this study because they contain geographic identifiers that can be used to determine not only whether a respondent resides in a rural area or urban area, but also whether, within urban areas, respondents live in townships.[8] All reported statistics use individual weights to ensure a representative sample, and all reported differences in the text are statistically significant unless indicated otherwise.

Household Access to Finance[9]

Access to Financial Services and Accounts

Overall, 67 percent of South African adults are considered to be formally banked, that is, they use some kind of formal financial product such as a bank account, including just using a bank card to receive social grants, or having a personal loan from a bank (FinMark Trust 2013). FinScope's definition of the banked population is rather generous. A narrower, more commonly used definition in the literature that considers only account ownership reveals that only 53 percent of South African adults have access to an account that offers transactional and savings functions. Regardless of the definition used, however, these averages mask a large variation in access to finance across individuals living in different geographical areas (figure 4.1).

Both formal financial inclusion and account ownership is 20 percentage points higher among the urban population (74 percent banked, 60 percent account ownership) than the rural population (54 percent banked, 40 percent account ownership)—a finding in line with the literature on financial inclusion that documents a general urban-rural divide (Allen et al. 2013). Among those not "formally banked," that is, adults who have or use financial products or services provided by a commercial bank, the FinScope study distinguishes between those who are (a) *formally served*, a nonbank category including those who own a store

Figure 4.1 Access to Financial Services, by Location, 2012

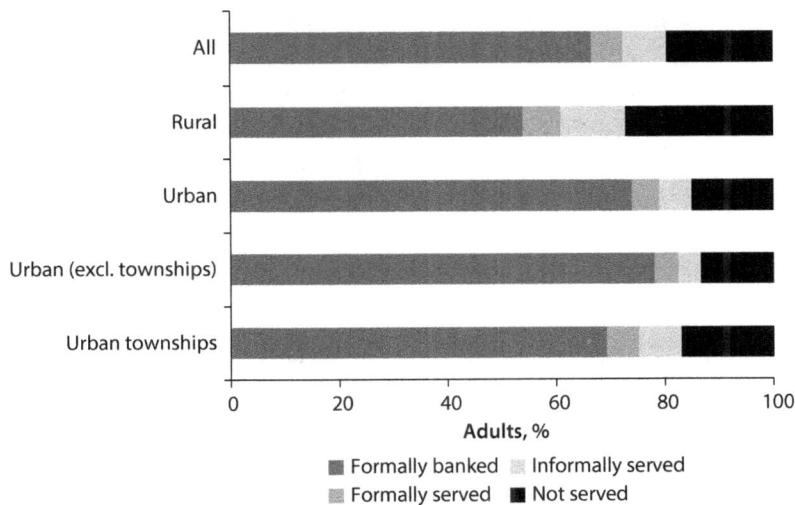

Source: FinMark Trust 2013.
Note: "Formally banked" = adults who have or use financial products or services provided by a commercial bank regulated by the central bank. "Formally served" = adults who have or use financial products or services provided by a financial institution (bank or nonbank). "Informally served" = adults who have or use financial products or services that are not regulated such as cooperatives, farmers associations, savings clubs or groups, and private money lenders. "Not served" (also termed "financially excluded") = adults who do not have or use any financial products or services; if borrowing, they rely only on friends and family, and if saving, they save at home.

card or can buy on credit from a store; (b) *informally served*, including those who have access to informal financial institutions such as saving clubs, *stokvels* (rotating savings and credit associations, or ROSCAs),[10] or burial societies;[11] and (c) *not served*, including those who neither have nor use any financial products or services at all; if borrowing, they rely only on friends and family, and if saving, they save at home. While many respondents use financial services from more than one category (for example, 24 percent of adults are both banked and use informal financial services), the survey assigns them to the category of highest financial formalization.

In contrast to formal financial inclusion, the use of nonbank financial services is higher in rural areas than in urban ones, compensating partially for the lower rates of being formally banked. While around 6 percent of both rural and urban residents use nonbank formal financial services, the use of only informal financial services is twice as high in rural areas (12 percent) than in urban areas (6 percent). Nevertheless, even when counting those using informal financial services as financially included, rates of financial exclusion are nearly twice as high in rural areas (27 percent) than in urban areas (15 percent).

There are also significant differences in the use of financial services within the urban population, reflecting the fact that townships are part of South Africa's second economy while the rest of urban South Africa resembles an advanced-market economy. In townships, 69 percent of adults use formal financial services (54 percent have an account) compared with 78 percent in nontownship areas (66 percent have an account). While there is again no significant difference in the use of nonbank formal services, the exclusive use of informal financial services is twice as high in townships (8 percent) than in nontownship urban areas (4 percent), echoing the rural-urban divide.

On average, financial inclusion rates in townships fall between those in rural areas and those in nontownship urban areas. The subsequent analysis will benchmark the use of financial services in townships against that in nontownship urban areas to highlight areas for potential policy interventions.

The uneven access to finance across the two economies in South Africa and the importance of informal financial services such as *stokvels*, saving clubs, and burial societies in providing township residents with access to finance becomes even clearer when we consider their use regardless of the use of formal financial services. As figure 4.2 shows, one-third of adults in townships use at least one of the three informal financial services, with nearly 29 percent being member of a burial society and 11 percent being a member of either a *stokvel* or savings club. While adults in nontownship urban areas also make significant use of informal financial institutions in similar proportions, their overall use of informal financial services is about one-third lower than that of township residents.

Use of Financial Services and Individual Characteristics

The differences in the use of financial service between individuals residing in urban township and those in nontownship areas are manifestations of the differences between the two groups' economic realities. Almost 85 percent of the

Figure 4.2 Use of Informal Financial Services, by Location, 2012

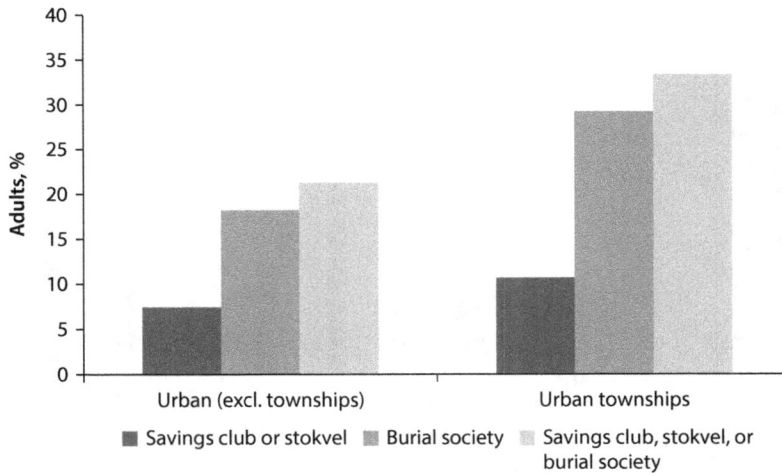

Source: FinMark Trust 2013.
Note: A *stokvel* is a rotating savings and credit association (ROSCA) whereby people contribute at defined intervals to a group fund that distributes the contributions to members on a rotating basis.

township population falls into Living Standards Measure (LSM) category 6 or below (the lower- to middle-income category). In contrast, over 45 percent of the nontownship urban population falls into LSM category 7 or above (the middle- or high-income category), as shown in figure 4.3 and table 4.1.[12] The literature has shown that financial inclusion varies significantly by individual characteristics such as gender, age, education level, employment status, and income: women, youth, the elderly, the less educated and unemployed, and the poor are less likely to own an account (Allen et al. 2013). Given the skewed distribution of LSM classifications or income groups between township and nontownship residents, the differences in their use of financial services are hardly surprising.[13]

Besides income, differences in financial inclusion also reflect differences in individual characteristics such as gender, age, education, and employment between residents of township and nontownship urban areas (table 4.1). The proportion of women living in township areas is about 5 percentage points higher than in nontownship urban areas, and township residents are, on average, three years younger than nontownship urban residents. Most township residents have not completed secondary education, whereas most residents of urban nontownship areas have done so, and 7 percent of nontownship residents moreover hold a university degree. Finally, just 16 percent of adults in townships work for a formal employer while almost twice as many are unemployed. In nontownship urban areas, in contrast, 27 percent of adults work for a formal employer while 12 percent are unemployed.

Regression analysis shows that after controlling for individual characteristics, location is not significant in explaining the difference in formal account penetration between township and nontownship urban residents (table 4A.1).

Figure 4.3 Distribution of Urban Population, by LSM and Location, 2012

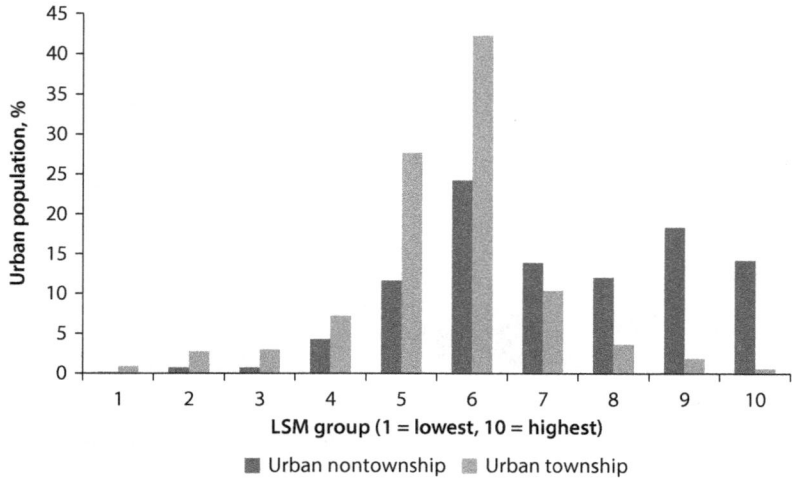

Source: FinMark Trust 2013.
Note: LSM = Living Standards Measure. An LSM level of 1 or 2 would indicate extreme poverty; 3, poverty; 4–6, lower to lower-middle income; 7–9, middle to upper-middle income; and 10, upper income.

Table 4.1 Individual Characteristics of Urban Residents, by Location, 2012

	Urban nontownship	Urban township	
	Mean	Mean	Sig. diff.
Female	0.5067	0.5559	*
Age (years)	39.2822	36.2549	***
Education: less than secondary degree	0.3906	0.5259	***
Education: secondary degree	0.5402	0.4608	**
Education: tertiary degree	0.0692	0.0133	***
Employment: formal	0.2681	0.1564	***
Employment: self-employed	0.2326	0.1824	*
Employment: informal	0.0376	0.0491	
Employment: for individual	0.0249	0.0373	
Employment: unemployed	0.1166	0.2988	***
Employment: out of labor force	0.3185	0.2759	
LSM low (1–4)	0.0580	0.1372	***
LSM middle (5–6)	0.3580	0.6988	***
LSM high (7–10)	0.5840	0.1639	***

Source: FinMark Trust 2013.
Note: LSM = Living Standards Measure. An LSM level of 1–4 would indicate poverty to low income; 5–6, lower to middle income; and 7–10, upper-middle to high income.
$*p < 0.1$, $**p < 0.05$, $***p < 0.01$

In line with the general finding of financial inclusion and individual characteristics being correlated, a nationally representative study on financial literacy by the Financial Services Board (FSB 2011) finds that financial literacy is largely dependent on educational attainment and income levels. For example, the presence of a household budget, typically indicative of higher financial literacy, is strongly related with income levels. Seventy-nine percent of households in the richest income quintile report having household budgets, compared with 36 percent in the poorest income quintile.

Banking Behavior

The FinScope estimate of account ownership of 53 percent is in line with data from the World Bank's Global Findex database, which estimates that 54 percent of adults in South Africa use a formal account. Financial inclusion, as measured by account ownership, is higher in South Africa than in the rest of Africa (33 percent) and the developing world overall (42 percent) (Demirguc-Kunt and Klapper, 2013; World Bank 2013).

However, among those who are banked, a substantial number of adults report that they make little use of their account and use it primarily for "cash management" purposes—that is, withdrawing and depositing cash rather than using payment or saving services. This behavior is more prevalent in townships than in nontownship areas, exacerbating the effective financial inclusion gap between township and nontownship areas. For instance, 40 percent of adults living in townships report that they withdraw money from their accounts as soon as it is deposited, almost twice the rate of adults living in nontownship areas (figure 4.4).

Figure 4.4 Banking Behavior of Currently Banked, by Location, 2012

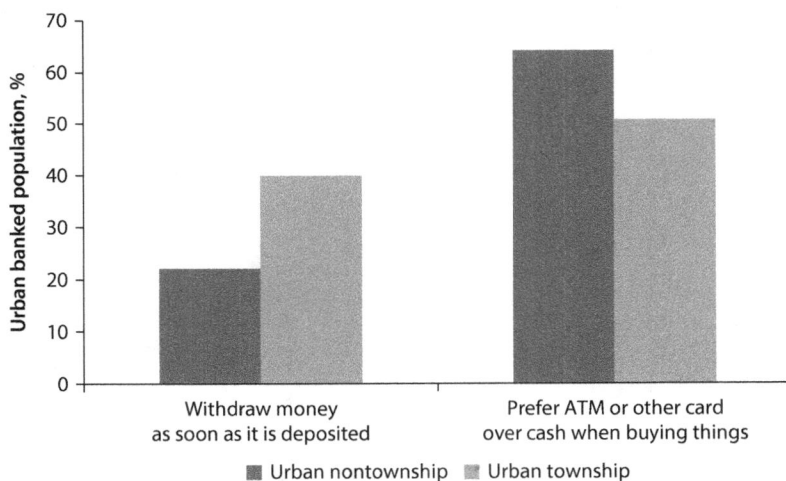

Source: FinMark Trust 2013.
Note: "Banked" = adults who have or use financial products or services provided by a commercial bank regulated by the central bank. ATM = automated teller machine.

Moreover, in townships, only 42 percent of adults use their accounts for purposes other than immediate withdrawal (such as to save or make payments), compared with 61 percent of adults in urban nontownship areas. Similarly, only about half of those banked in townships indicate that they prefer to pay for things electronically by card over cash. In comparison, 64 percent of adults in nontownship areas prefer electronic payment by card over cash.

Especially in townships, the challenge with regard to financial inclusion is therefore twofold: First, expand access to financial services to currently excluded parts of the population. Second, decrease the percentage of the "underbanked," that is, those who are financially included but with very low usage of formal payments and savings.

Distance to Financial Service Outlets

Unequal access to formal financial services also manifests itself in the travel time it takes to access a bank branch or automated teller machine (ATM). Among township residents, 19 percent live within 14 minutes of travel time to a bank, and an additional 37 percent live within 29 minutes (figure 4.5). Yet another 37 percent can access a bank within 59 minutes. For the remaining 7 percent of township residents, reaching a bank takes 60 minutes or more. ATMs are relatively more readily accessible in townships where 35 percent of adults live within 14 minutes of an ATM and another 37 percent within 29 minutes.

By comparison, among individuals living in nontownship urban areas, 47 percent can access banks within 14 minutes, and 65 percent can access an ATM within that time period. Travel distances to financial service outlets broadly

Figure 4.5 Travel Time to Financial and Other Services, by Location, 2012

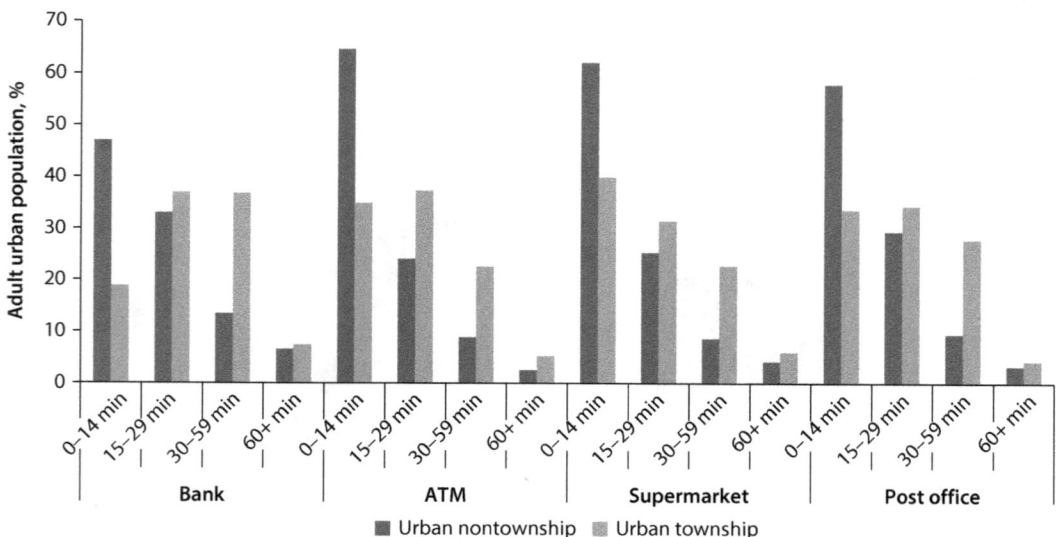

Source: FinMark Trust 2013.

reflect differences in access to other services as well: whereas most of the urban nontownship population lives within 14 minutes' travel time of a supermarket or post office, less than 40 percent of urban township residents do.

The FinScope survey does not ask directly about barriers to financial inclusion, but Global Findex data show that the unbanked in South Africa are significantly more likely than those in other African countries to cite distance as a barrier to account ownership (Demirguc-Kunt and Klapper, 2013; World Bank 2013). However, distance is only the third most frequently mentioned barrier (35 percent; multiple responses permitted). As in other countries, by far the largest self-reported barrier to account use is the lack of money—cited by more than 70 percent, twice the proportion who report distance as barrier—followed by high cost (40 percent). Lack of necessary documentation comes in fourth, with just over 20 percent reporting it as a perceived barrier. Lack of trust is the last-ranked factor, with less than 20 percent of the unbanked citing it as a barrier to account ownership.

Trust in Financial Institutions

Global Findex data suggest that lack of trust is the least widely perceived barrier to financial inclusion. However, the FinScope survey found significant differences between township and nontownship residents in their levels of trust in financial service providers—differences that correlate broadly with the two groups' relative use of formal and informal financial services.

Although banks are the most trusted financial services providers for both groups of residents, 51 percent of adults living in nontownship urban areas indicate that they trust banks, compared with only 43 percent of adults living in townships (figure 4.6).

In townships, the second-most trusted financial services providers (trusted by 26 percent) are informal providers such as savings clubs, *stokvels*, and burial societies. In nontownship areas, however, only 14 percent of adults indicated that they trust in informal financial services providers—ranking them fourth.

Notably, the differences in trust are restricted to financial institutions. There are no statistically significant differences in the level of trust in other common service providers such as supermarkets, post offices, cell phone stores, and supermarket counters for sending remittances.

Financial Inclusion Efforts

Financial inclusion has been a policy concern in South Africa for over a decade, with the financial sector agreeing to commit to industrywide targets regarding key areas of economic development as part of the first Financial Sector Charter (FSC) in 2003.

One major initiative coming out of the FSC was the 2004 introduction of Mzansi accounts, which are basic, low-cost accounts for the poor. Uptake of the product has been significant: an estimated 6 million accounts opened in the first four years, and a 10 percent penetration rate among adults highlights the strong demand for this simple, no-frills account (BFA 2009; World Bank 2012b).

Figure 4.6 Trust in Financial Service Providers, by Location, 2012

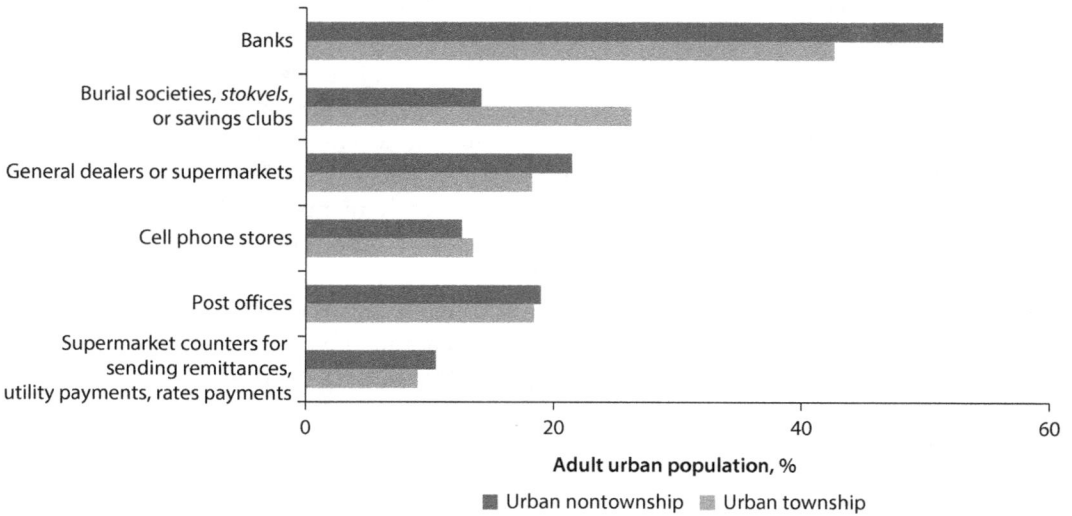

Source: FinMark Trust 2013.

Note: A *stokvel* is a rotating savings and credit association (ROSCA) whereby people contribute at defined intervals to a group fund that distributes the contributions to members on a rotating basis.

Currently, 6 percent of adults report using a Mzansi account. Although some individuals have since transitioned to traditional accounts, and others may have decided they do not need an account, Mzansi accounts remain an important avenue of financial inclusion, especially for the poor: 7 percent of township residents use a Mzansi account, compared with 4 percent of adults in nontownship urban areas (FinMark Trusts 2013). Against the background of 70 percent of South Africans who identify lack of money as barrier to formal account ownership, ensuring the provision of low-cost financial products such as the Mzansi account will be key to increasing financial inclusion for poor households.

Another way in which South Africa has been trying to promote financial inclusion is through the electronic payment of social grants. South Africa makes over 15 million grant payments per month to approximately 9.2 million beneficiaries, totaling more than R 105 billion per year (MasterCard 2012). In early 2012, the South African Social Security Agency (SASSA) awarded the disbursement contract to Cash Paymaster Services, which offers biometric identification and disperses payments to recipients through MasterCard-branded interoperable debit cards. A significantly larger fraction of the adult population in townships (32 percent) receives SASSA grants relative to adults in nontownship urban areas (19 percent). Moreover, a larger fraction of SASSA recipients in townships receive their grants by SASSA card than do other urban recipients (figure 4.7).[14]

Grant payments provide a unique opportunity to promote financial inclusion of the poor. Even though promoting financial inclusion is one of the stated goals of transitioning from a combination of cash payments and direct bank deposits to the electronic payments through the SASSA debit cards, the primary objective

Figure 4.7 SASSA Recipients and Disbursement Channels to SASSA Recipients, by Location, 2012

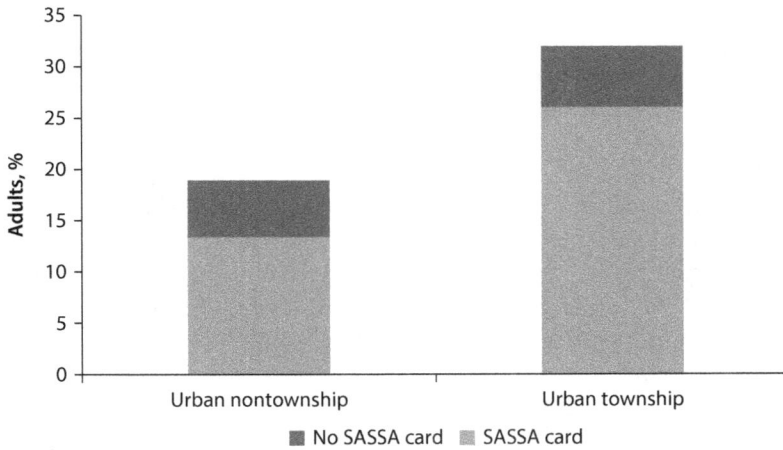

Source: FinMark Trust 2013.
Note: SASSA = South African Social Security Agency. "No SASSA card" designates recipients who opt to receive grant payments by other means such as direct bank deposit or cash.

of the new disbursement process is to minimize fraud and significantly reduce disbursement costs (CGAP 2011).[15] As such, SASSA understandably imposes restrictions on the disbursement of social grants to keep them completely separate from other forms of financial intermediation such as credit.

Yet those restrictions also constitute a missed opportunity for promoting more meaningful financial inclusion among the unbanked and the underbanked. Currently, SASSA recipients in both township and nontownship urban areas are 50 percent more likely than non-SASSA recipients to withdraw money from their accounts as soon as it is deposited. Similarly, they are one-third less likely than non-SASSA recipients to prefer bank cards over cash. This finding is in line with results from countries such as Brazil, Colombia, and Mexico showing that social-grant recipients are unlikely to automatically use bank accounts for more than withdrawing benefits (CGAP 2012). Realizing the full potential benefits of electronic social-grant payments through increased usage of payments and savings depends not only on products that enable those uses but also, critically, on clear communication regarding such features.

Finally, new technologies such as mobile financial services offer new opportunities for expanding financial inclusion in a more cost effective manner than traditional banks can. Mobile banking has been taking hold in South Africa, but penetration remains low, with just 11 percent of South Africans reporting that they use their cell phones for financial transactions, compared with 16 percent penetration among adults in Sub-Saharan Africa overall and as high as 68 percent in Kenya (Demirguc-Kunt and Klapper, 2013).

Moreover, while cell phone ownership is virtually universal across all urban areas in South Africa, mobile financial services so far have achieved the broadest success among nontownship urban adults, of whom 15 percent report having used a mobile phone for a financial transaction, compared with 10 percent of adults in townships. Although adoption of new technologies often starts among the more affluent population before spreading to poorer segments, South Africa's low penetration that still skews toward the wealthy highlights the yet unrealized potential to advance financial inclusion through this channel.

Savings

The urban township and nontownship populations also exhibit differences in savings behavior. While just over half of adults living in urban nontownship areas say they save each month, only 43 percent of adults in the townships report doing so (figure 4.8). When asked whether they are saving regularly, however, only 36 percent and 25 percent, respectively, "agree" or "agree completely" that they do so. This likely more realistic, lower average is in line overall with the global average among developing countries in Global Findex database (Demirguc-Kunt and Klapper, 2013). In contrast with the previous analysis of formal bank account penetration, regression analysis shows that location remains a statistically significant determinant of savings behavior after controlling for individual characteristics such as gender, age, education, employment, and income group (table 4A.1).

Credit

About 20 percent of adults in South Africa have borrowed in the past 12 months. In urban areas, the rate is slightly higher, with 22 percent of adults having borrowed, compared with 14 percent in rural areas. Unlike in the case of formal account ownership and savings, there is no difference in the proportion of adults who have borrowed in nontownship and township urban areas. However, there

Figure 4.8 Savings Behavior, by Location, 2012

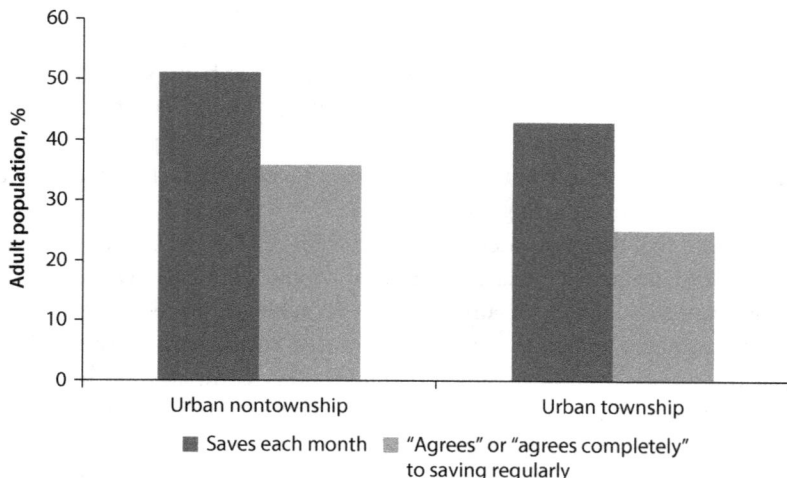

Source: FinMark Trust 2013.

are differences regarding the source of credit. Family and friends are by far the most common source of credit, both in township and nontownship areas, as is common in developing countries (Demirguc-Kunt and Klapper, 2013). In townships, two-thirds of adults who have borrowed in the previous 12 months have done so from family and friends (figure 4.9). The next most common credit sources are informal financial services such as *stokvels*, saving clubs, and burial societies (13 percent), followed closely by banks (11 percent) and *mashonisas*, or money lenders (6 percent).

In comparison, just over 50 percent of loans in nontownship areas originate from friends and family, followed by banks (32 percent) and *stokvels*, savings clubs, or burial societies (14 percent). Virtually no loans are reported to have originated from money lenders.

In both urban areas, a significant proportion of loans also originated from "other sources," a category including (but not limited to) loans from insurance companies, loans from retail stores, in-kind store credit, and educational loans.

Overall, among those who have borrowed within the previous 12 months, adults in townships are thus two-thirds less likely than adults in nontownship urban areas to have credit from formal sources such as a bank or in the form of a salary advance. The gap in credit from formal sources is made up primarily by credit originating from family and friends. Although informal financial services such as *stokvels*, savings clubs, and burial societies at least partially compensate for the relative lack of formal financial services in townships with regard to account

Figure 4.9 Credit Sources for Urban Adults, by Location, 2012

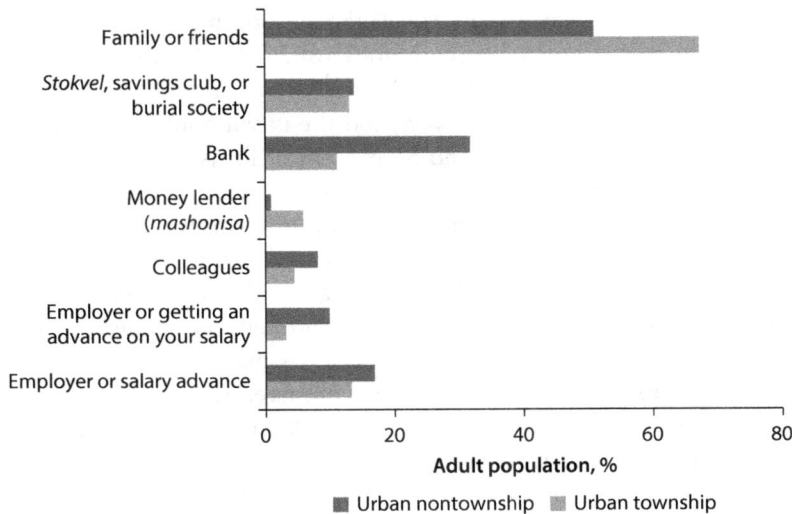

Source: FinMark Trust 2013.
Note: The figure shows responses from adults who have borrowed within the previous 12 months. Multiple responses are permitted. A *stokvel* is a rotating savings and credit association (ROSCA) whereby people contribute at defined intervals to a group fund that distributes the contributions to members on a rotating basis. "Other" includes (but is not limited to) loans from insurance companies, loans from retail stores, in-kind store credit, and educational loans.

and savings options, informal financial services originate credit at roughly the same rate to all urban residents.

However, the differences in access to credit sources are not due to location, but can be explained once again by real economy manifestations of South Africa's dual economy. Regression analysis shows that after controlling for individual characteristics such as gender, age, education, employment status, and income group, location is not a statistically significant determinant of whether individuals borrow from a bank (table 4A.1).

Household debt has been a large and growing problem over the past decade. According to the South African Reserve Bank, debt amounted to 76 percent of disposable household income in the second quarter of 2012 (SARB 2012). In June 2012, the National Credit Regulator reported that 9.22 million, or 47 percent, of the 19.6 million credit-active consumers covered by credit bureaus have impaired records. The percentage of consumers with impaired records has been above 45 percent since December 2009. Although no direct breakdown by location is available, the FinScope survey data suggest that consistent household indebtedness might be relatively more prevalent among township residents. Asked whether they often have to spend more money than they have available, 29 percent of adults in townships say they "agree" or "agree completely" with the statement, compared with 20 percent of adults in non-township urban areas.

Access to Finance for Micro, Small, and Medium-Size Enterprises[16]

Firm Characteristics

Most of the businesses covered by the FinScope South Africa Small Business Survey 2010 are microenterprises (FinMark Trust 2011). Relative to the national average of 1.08 employees per firm, the surveyed firms in urban townships employed an average of 0.77 employees, and the urban nontownship firms, 2.1. Broken down by size, 64 percent and 57 percent of firms surveyed in township and nontownship urban areas, respectively, have no employees aside from the owner (figure 4.10). Overall, 97 percent of firms in townships and 87 percent of firms in nontownship urban areas have fewer than five employees.

Informality among the surveyed firms is high, with only 17 percent of firms being formally registered. The high rate of informality is primarily due to the large presence of microenterprises: on average, 14 percent of firms with fewer than five employees are formally registered compared with 82 percent of firms with five employees or more. Given that virtually all firms in townships have fewer than five employees, it is not surprising that only 15 percent of MSMEs are registered in townships compared with 30 percent of MSMEs in nontownship urban areas. However, even after controlling for size category, township-based MSMEs are about one-third less likely than their nontownship-based urban equivalents to be formally registered.

In terms of sectoral distribution, MSMEs in urban townships and nontownship areas are broadly similar. Most of them are retailers, followed by other

Figure 4.10 Urban Firm Size, by Location, 2010

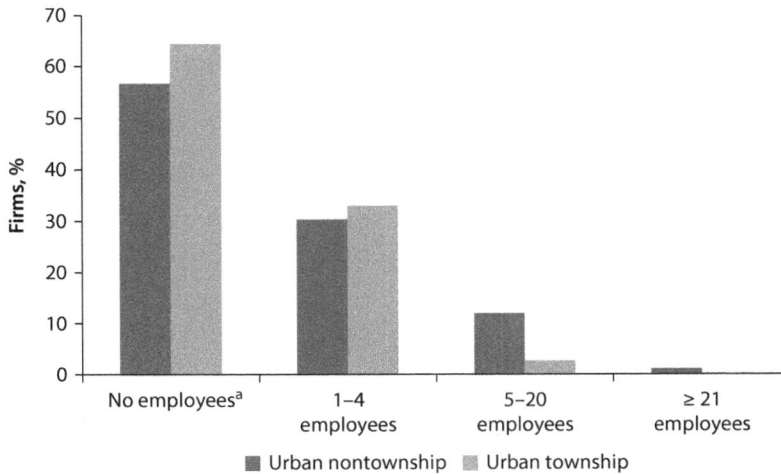

Source: FinMark Trust 2011.
a. No employees in addition to the business owner.

service providers, with a slightly larger proportion of firms in townships involved in retail than in other services (figure 4.11).

Obstacles to Growth

Only 8 percent of MSMEs in South Africa perceive access to finance to be the single biggest obstacle to growing their business. After space to operate (16 percent) and competition (13 percent), it is the third-most identified single biggest obstacle. Nineteen percent of firms claim to face no obstacles at all. Notably, township-based businesses do not differ in their perception of access to finance as single biggest obstacle from businesses located in other areas.

Although access to finance might not be the single biggest obstacle to growth, money-related matters such as sourcing money and cash flow are the most frequently cited (39 percent) problem South African business owners said they faced when starting their businesses (figure 4.12). Unlike other commonly cited obstacles, it also disproportionately affects businesses in townships. Forty-two percent of businesses there cite it as an obstacle they faced, compared with 34 percent of businesses in nontownship urban areas.

The fraction of businesses that identify access to finance as obstacle may appear low, but it is in line with data for generally larger, formal SMEs in South Africa. Surveying formal firms with five employees or more, the World Bank's Enterprise Surveys find that formal SMEs in South Africa are relatively less likely to report being credit-constrained than they are elsewhere in Sub-Saharan Africa and in other developing countries.[17] Only 16 percent of South African firms report access to finance as a constraint compared with 45 percent of firms in Sub-Saharan Africa and 33 percent globally. This is in part explained by South Africa's relatively highly vertically integrated firm structure, resulting in high

Figure 4.11 Sectoral Distribution of Urban Firms, by Location, 2010

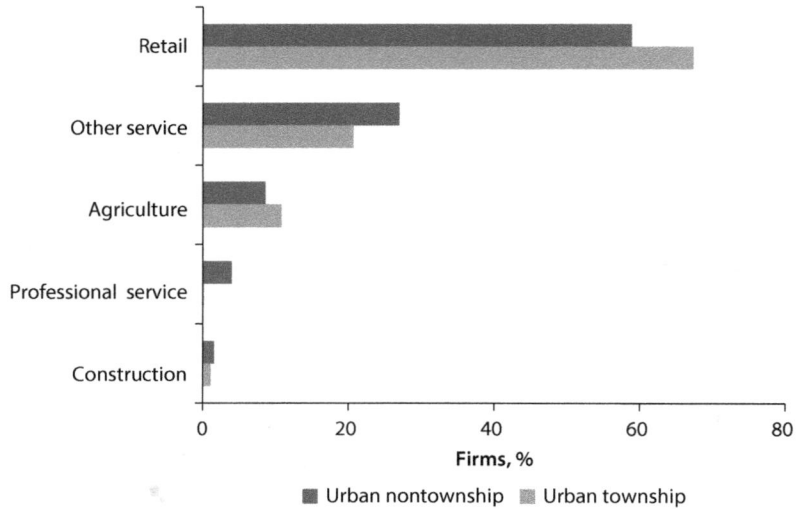

Source: FinMark Trust 2011.

Figure 4.12 Obstacles Faced by Urban Firms during Start-Up, by Location, 2010

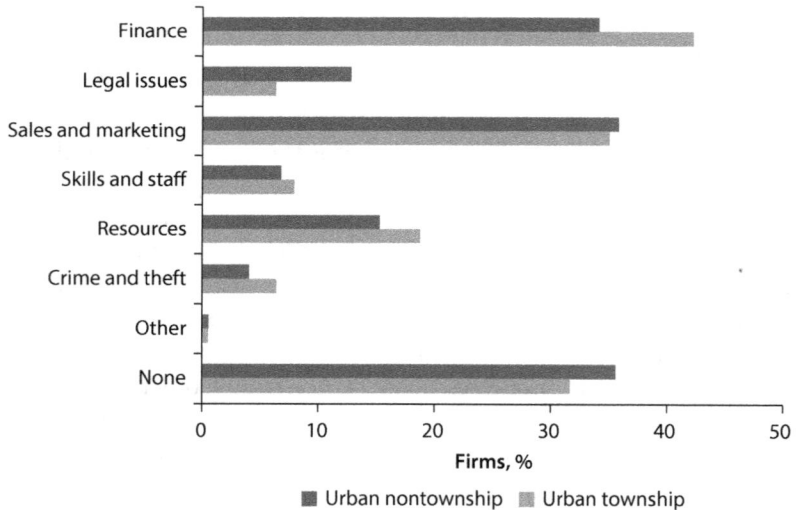

Source: FinMark Trust 2011.

levels of supplier credit and buyer credit. For example, the portion of working capital financed by supplier credit (22 percent) is almost twice as high as it is both in Sub-Saharan Africa and globally (12 percent).

The finding is also broadly in line with evidence from the business survey carried out in the township of Diepsloot (see chapter 6), where 24 percent of business owners report credit as one of the three biggest constraints to business growth.

Before analyzing the use of credit in more detail, the next subsections will first document the degree of financial inclusion observed through urban firms' account use and savings behavior.

Accounts

As for households, account penetration is lower among firms in townships than in nontownship urban areas (table 4.2). This may in part be driven by the lower proportion of registered township businesses, which in turn may have more difficulty in opening an account. When the sample of surveyed firms is split by registration status and location, registered firms are twice as likely as unregistered firms in either area to use an account. Among unregistered firms that do use an account, more than 90 percent of business owners use their personal account rather than an account in the business's name. In contrast, among registered firms, most firms use an account in their business's name. Townships are an exception, where only a third of registered firms use such accounts. Interestingly, though, business account ownership rates for *unregistered* businesses are twice as high in township areas than elsewhere.

As is the case for individuals, regression analysis shows that characteristics other than location explain the differences in account ownership rates: for MSMEs, firm size and registration status matter (see table 4A.2).

By far the most frequent reason township-based firms cite for not having a business account is their small business size and lack of sufficient income generated by the business (54 percent), followed by irregular income (21 percent) (multiple answers permitted). Bank charges and minimum balance requirements, on the other hand, are cited by only 9 percent and 4 percent, respectively, of township-based business owners. Eleven percent of business owners state that they do not need a business account.

One of the reasons why account use is higher among registered firms than unregistered firms may be that 75 percent of registered firms perceive banks to offer products and services designed for their needs, compared with only 44 percent of unregistered businesses across both township and nontownship urban areas. Another reason may be that a higher proportion of MSMEs in

Table 4.2 Firms' Account Use, by Location, 2010

Percent

Location	All firms		Unregistered firms		Registered firms	
	Use account	Of which use account in business's name	Use account	Of which use account in business's name	Use account	Of which use account in business's name
All	45.6	21.7	38.0	6.3	81.5	56.1
Rural	36.6	11.8	33.8	4.2	62.1	49.1
Urban	52.4	27.0	41.8	7.8	88.0	57.7
Nontownship	58.0	34.4	43.7	4.3	90.9	67.6
Township	46.3	17.1	40.2	11.2	81.7	33.4

Source: FinMark Trust 2011.

townships are involved in businesses requiring lower financial sophistication, and thus believe they could manage without an account (49 percent versus 41 percent of nontownship MSMEs). Trust in banks does not appear to play a role, because both township and nontownship firms and registered and unregistered businesses alike exhibit similar levels of trust.

In both townships and nontownship urban areas, the use of accounts is dominated by cash deposits and withdrawals. Just over 50 percent of banked business owners in both locations report having deposited money, and 45 percent report having withdrawn cash, in the previous month. In nontownship urban areas, 35 percent of banked MSMEs pay their utility bills and 25 percent their suppliers by electronic transfer. In townships, however, the use of noncash transactions by businesses remains rather limited, with only 11 percent using electronic transfers. Finally, one in five banked MSMEs in both townships and nontownship urban areas report that they have not conducted any banking transaction at all in the previous month.

Again, as for households, the challenge for financial inclusion of MSMEs is thus twofold: not only expanding access to financial services to currently excluded firms—the first step to financial inclusion—but also decreasing the percentage of the underbanked businesses, that is, those businesses with very low usage of formal payments.

Savings

In the FinScope survey, around 45 percent of MSMEs in both townships and nontownship urban areas report saving or investing for business purposes. As is the case for account use, however, there is a stark difference in savings behavior between registered and unregistered firms (table 4.3). Registered firms are twice as likely to save or invest as their unregistered counterparts in both areas. And whereas most of the firms in both areas save at banks, 90 percent of firms in urban nontownship areas do so compared with 72 percent in townships.[18]

Informal financial institutions such as *stokvels*, savings clubs, and burial societies play an important role in filling the gap, with 15 percent of township-based businesses that save indicating they so do at informal financial institutions. Such institutions are important not only for unregistered firms but also for registered firms, which save at a comparable rate at these institutions despite the fact that 92 percent of them also indicate that they save at a bank (multiple responses permitted).

Credit

The use of credit by businesses is very low. Less than 5 percent of MSMEs in both township and nontownship urban areas report having borrowed in the previous 12 months or currently owing or repaying money (table 4.4). Of those businesses that have borrowed, one in two businesses in townships has borrowed exclusively from family or friends, and 29 percent report having borrowed from a bank. In nontownship urban areas, the reverse holds, with 53 percent of borrowers having borrowed from banks compared with 28 percent having borrowed from family and friends only.[19] These numbers suggest a dearth of financial

Table 4.3 Firms' Savings Behavior, by Location, 2010
Percent

	Urban nontownship			Urban township		
	Save	Of which save at		Save	Of which save at	
		Bank	Stokvel, savings club, or burial society		Bank	Stokvel, savings club, or burial society
All firms	44.8	90.7	2.8	42.6	72.4	15.3
Unregistered firms	29.9	82.5	3.9	37.5	65.9	15.4
Registered firms	78.8	97.9	1.1	72.0	91.9	17.9

Source: FinMark Trust 2011.
Note: Multiple responses were permitted regarding where firms save. A *stokvel* is a rotating savings and credit association (ROSCA) whereby people contribute at defined intervals to a group fund that distributes the contributions to members on a rotating basis.

Table 4.4 Firms' Use of Credit, by Location, 2010
Percent

	All firms			Unregistered firms	Registered firms
			Of which from		
Location	Any credit	Bank	Family and friends only	Any credit	Any credit
Nontownship	4.9	52.7	28.3	2.5	10.5
Township	3.9	28.7	51.3	3.8	4.7

Source: FinMark Trust 2011.

institutions that cater to the lower end of the SME market, particularly institutions targeting microenterprises and those in townships that have to rely instead on family and friends for credit.

Borrowing behavior also varies by registration status, with registered firms in nontownship areas being four times more likely to have borrowed than unregistered firms. In townships, however, there is no statistically significant difference between the fraction of registered and unregistered businesses that have borrowed. Given the small number of businesses that borrow, there are unfortunately not enough observations to split the sample both by registration status and source of credit.[20]

The low credit penetration is in line with the observation that commercial banks are generally reluctant to lend to the MSME sector because of the high perceived risk (Fuchs et al. 2011). In most instances, these enterprises are unable to provide comprehensive information to assess their creditworthiness, lack appropriate accounting records, and have little or no collateral.

However, when asked why they did not borrow in the previous 12 months, business owners most frequently claim that they do not believe in borrowing (figure 4.13). This reason is given by around 35 percent of business owners in townships and nontownship urban areas, closely followed by 30 percent in each group that indicated that they have no need to borrow. The next most commonly cited reasons are slow business, variable earnings, and general risk aversion ("scared"), with slow business being the only reason that is significantly

Figure 4.13 Firms' Reasons for Not Borrowing Money, by Location, 2010

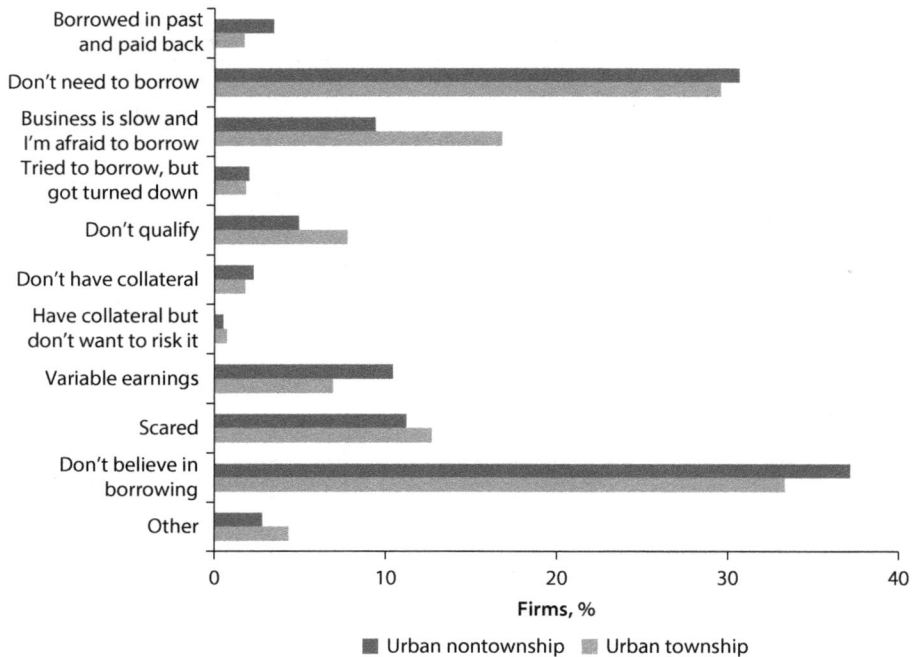

Source: FinMark Trust 2011.
Note: Multiple responses were permitted.

more often cited by township-based businesses compared to nontownship ones. Contrary to evidence from other studies, lack of collateral does not appear to be a significant barrier to credit—at least from the business owners' perspective.

When asked about the financial and accounting information they keep that may help banks evaluate the riskiness of extending credit, only half of the businesses in both townships and nontownship areas state that they keep financial records. In both cases, registered firms are twice as likely as unregistered firms to do so (figure 4.14). But even when businesses keep records, they are likely to be incomplete given that less than 4 percent of businesses in townships keep their financial records up to date. The percentage of businesses that have a written business plan, a written business strategy, or a budget is similarly low. Businesses in nontownship urban areas are two to three times as likely to keep such records as businesses in townships. Nevertheless, the numbers remain very low and do not exceed 10 percent.

Support for the SME sector has been a long-standing policy priority in South Africa, and an extensive program for SME financing has been established, which includes wholesale and retail financing, credit guarantee schemes, and ancillary services such as business development services.[21] Nonetheless, the evidence suggests that more effort needs to go into ensuring that programs support access to formal financial services and development of lending to the lower end of the SME market—the microenterprises—that dominate the SME segment in townships.

Figure 4.14 Presence of Business Records, by Location, 2012

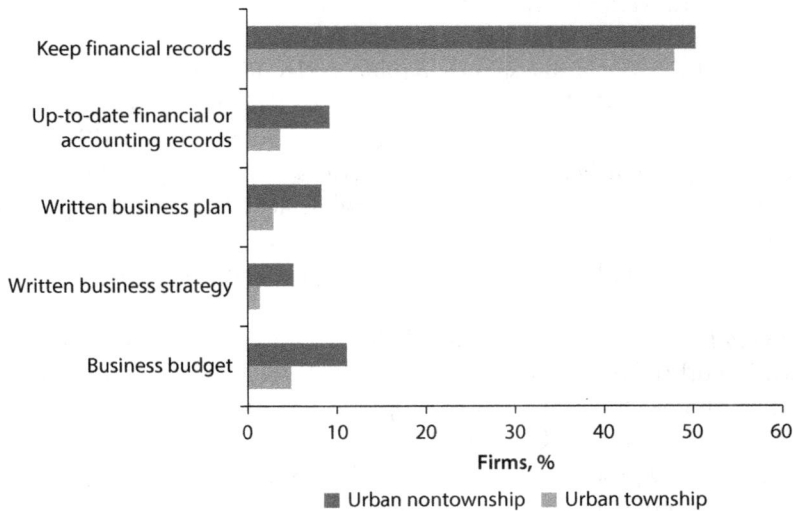

Source: FinMark Trust 2013.

Access to Finance and Banking Structure in South Africa

As the previous two sections have already touched upon, access to finance for the poor and MSMEs in South Africa is further complicated by a very concentrated formal banking sector that focuses primarily on serving the advanced economy. The four largest banks[22] account for 84 percent of banking sector assets and have developed sophisticated organizational structures and products aligned with serving South Africa's advanced economy but at odds with serving the more basic needs of the second economy in a viable manner. This has resulted in high costs of providing financial services, making them unaffordable for many in the second economy.

Moreover, the concentrated ownership structure has distorted the incentives of banks to migrate down-market and offer products tailored to the needs of those who are part of South Africa's low-end economy. The situation is further exacerbated by (a) a lack of microfinance or cooperative institutions that might be especially suitable for serving the poor and MSMEs and might bridge the financial service space between informal service providers such saving clubs, *stokvels*, and burial societies, on one hand, and formal banks, on the other hand; as well as (b) gaps in the regulatory environment that limit contestability, competition, and product innovation in the market and thus perpetuate the current market structure.[23]

Conclusions

Using data from the FinScope 2012 household and 2010 small business surveys, this chapter has characterized patterns of usage of financial services in townships and contrasted them with the use of financial services in nontownship urban areas. Three observations stand out:

- *Both households and businesses in townships are less likely to own an account, and, if they do, are more likely to be underbanked than their nontownship counterparts.* The financial inclusion challenge for both poor households and MSMEs is thus twofold: expanding access to financial services to currently excluded parts of the population and business community while also decreasing the percentage of "underbanked" in the system—that is, those who are technically financial included but make low use, if any, of formal payment and savings products.

- *Access to financial services is uneven.* While individuals and businesses in non-township urban areas are primarily served by formal financial institutions such as banks, those in townships rely disproportionally on informal financial services such as savings clubs, *stokvels*, and burial societies as well as friends and family to access saving products and credit. The lack of greater uptake of formal sector financial products among township residents might in part be explained by the lack of financial products tailored to their needs, such as low-cost accounts.

- *The marked differences in the use of financial services between urban townships and nontownship areas are not primarily the result of location alone.* Rather, they are manifestations of South Africa's dual economy, which has resulted in very real economic differences that can explain differences in financial inclusion and usage patterns.

Expanding financial inclusion for both individuals and business owners in townships is therefore not just a matter of advancing appropriate financial inclusion policies. It also must be understood in the larger context of an overall economic development strategy for townships and interlinking South Africa's two economies. As long as individuals in townships are less educated, more likely to be unemployed, and poorer than individuals in nontownship urban areas and township businesses smaller and more likely to be informal, it is unrealistic to expect equal rates of financial inclusion for individuals and businesses in township and nontownship areas.

At the same time, South Africa's highly concentrated banking sector has resulted in high banking costs and a structure that, at the moment, is not conducive to extending financial inclusion to the poor and MSMEs in townships. Therefore, any financial inclusion policies must also consider appropriate reforms to the structure of the banking sector. And although access to finance for MSMEs does not appear to be the most important binding constraint to their growth, access to finance at a competitive cost will become imperative if growth-oriented firms in the informal modernizing economy are to successfully continue growing. Building the foundation for a competitive financial sector that is able to serve the needs of MSMEs at the lower end of the spectrum as well as poorer individuals will therefore be critical.

Annex 4A: Regression Analyses

Table 4A.1 Regression Analysis of Financial Inclusion and Individual Characteristics

	Banked	Savings	Any credit	Credit from bank	Credit from bank if credit
Female	0.176** (0.027)	0.021 (0.770)	0.036 (0.671)	−0.064 (0.510)	−0.146 (0.404)
Age (in years)	0.054*** (0.000)	0.050*** (0.001)	0.040*** (0.002)	0.097*** (0.005)	0.101** (0.020)
Age (in years) squared	−0.000** (0.014)	−0.000** (0.013)	−0.000*** (0.005)	−0.001*** (0.009)	−0.001** (0.048)
Education: less than secondary degree	−1.414*** (0.000)	−0.932*** (0.000)	−0.243 (0.111)	−0.839*** (0.000)	−0.890** (0.014)
Education: secondary degree	−0.643** (0.033)	−0.445*** (0.005)	−0.284** (0.045)	−0.686*** (0.000)	−0.574** (0.036)
Employment: self	−0.860*** (0.000)	0.010 (0.928)	−0.176 (0.172)	−0.093 (0.509)	−0.106 (0.605)
Employment: informal	−1.271*** (0.000)	−0.603*** (0.002)	−0.757*** (0.001)	−1.080*** (0.001)	−0.824* (0.082)
Employment: for individual	−1.104*** (0.000)	−0.253 (0.192)	−0.422** (0.022)	−0.403 (0.125)	−0.339 (0.383)
Employment: unemployed	−1.484*** (0.000)	−0.874*** (0.000)	−0.463*** (0.001)	−0.468 (0.101)	−0.384 (0.314)
Employment: out of labor force	−1.506*** (0.000)	−0.791*** (0.000)	−0.465*** (0.001)	−0.830*** (0.000)	−0.875*** (0.006)
LSM[a] low (1–4)	−0.871*** (0.000)	−0.738*** (0.000)	−0.201 (0.237)	−0.190 (0.484)	−0.234 (0.571)
LSM[a] middle (5–6)	−0.469*** (0.000)	−0.395*** (0.000)	0.036 (0.731)	−0.343** (0.047)	−0.589** (0.010)
Township	0.029 (0.735)	0.245** (0.021)	0.050 (0.658)	−0.154 (0.367)	−0.355 (0.124)
Constant	1.654*** (0.000)	0.005 (0.989)	−1.058*** (0.000)	−2.527*** (0.001)	−1.746* (0.084)
Observations	2,976	2,976	2,976	2,976	575

Source: Data from FinMark Trust 2013.

Note: All dependent variables are dummy variables, and regressions are estimated with probit, taking survey design parameters into account. P-values reported in parentheses.

a. LSM = Living Standards Measure (1–4 indicates poverty to low income; 5–6, lower-middle to middle income.

$*p < 0.1, **p < 0.05, ***p < 0.01.$

Table 4A.2 Regression Analysis of Financial Inclusion and Firm Characteristics

	Personal account	Business account	Save at bank	Borrowed in past 12 months	Borrowed in past 12 months from bank
Employees: 0	0.639 (0.145)	−1.745*** (0.000)	−1.417*** (0.000)	−0.356 (0.438)	−1.208*** (0.004)
Employees: 1–4	1.033** (0.016)	−1.172*** (0.006)	−0.760** (0.014)	−0.269 (0.555)	−0.605 (0.151)
Employees: 5–20	0.023 (0.961)	0.083 (0.858)	−0.224 (0.527)	0.063 (0.899)	−0.189 (0.697)
Registered	0.024 (0.859)	1.352*** (0.000)	0.935*** (0.000)	0.059 (0.680)	0.541*** (0.001)
Township	−0.062 (0.593)	−0.088 (0.496)	−0.030 (0.725)	0.227 (0.232)	−0.036 (0.837)
Constant	−1.030** (0.018)	−0.343 (0.433)	0.522* (0.089)	−1.791*** (0.000)	−1.564*** (0.000)
Observations	3,861	3,861	3,861	3,861	3,861

Source: Data from FinMark Trust 2011.
Note: All dependent variables are dummy variables, and regressions are estimated with probit, taking survey design parameters into account.
P-values reported in parentheses.
$*p < 0.1, **p < 0.05, ***p < 0.01$.

Notes

1. With an income Gini index of 0.70, South Africa has one the highest recorded levels of inequality in the world (World Bank 2012a).

2. Overall formal account penetration is 67 percent in South Africa, and in rural areas, 54 percent of respondents indicate using a formal account (FinMark Trust 2013). Informal settlements are included in the township category if they are urban.

3. For a recent overview on financial inclusion in South Africa overall from both the demand (household and business) and supply (financial institutions) side, see World Bank (2013).

4. For a review of the literature, see Karlan and Morduch (2009).

5. Insurance and saving for retirement are beyond the scope of this chapter.

6. For more information or for other research initiated by the FinMark Trust, see its website at http://www.finmark.org.za.

7. For more information, see the Global Findex website at http://www.worldbank.org /globalfindex.

8. Informal settlements are included in the township category if they are urban.

9. The key results of this section are based on the FinScope South Africa 2012 survey (FinMark Trust 2013). It surveyed 3,900 South African residents age 16 or older, and the data are weighted to Statistics South Africa's 2011 mid-year population estimates. Of the 3,900 individuals surveyed, 876 lived in townships and 2,994 in nontownship urban areas. Fieldwork was conducted in May to July 2012.

10. *Stokvels* (originating from the term "stock fairs") are a local name (more generally known as rotating credit and savings associations, or ROSCAs) for a traditional form of banking whereby a group of people agree to contribute at defined intervals to a fund that distributes the contributions to group members on a rotating basis.

11. Burial societies are informal self-insurance schemes that cover the costs associated with burying a deceased family member and provide both material and nonmaterial relief to the family. Based on monthly contributions, they are distinct, historically important mutual aid groups that ensure that the family has the financial resources to observe the cultural requirements associated with predominantly black funerals (ECIAfrica Consulting 2003).

12. The South African Audience Research Foundation (SAARF) LSM (Living Standards Measure) is the most widely used marketing research tool in Southern Africa. It divides the population into 10 LSM groups, from 1 (lowest) to 10 (highest). Instead of directly eliciting income levels, LSM groups individuals according to their living standards using criteria such as degree of urbanization and ownership of cars and major appliances. For more information, see the SAARF website at http://saarf.co.za/.

13. Although the FinScope survey collects data on income, only two-thirds of respondents chose to provide such data.

14. SASSA recipients can currently opt out of the receiving the payment by card and instead opt for direct bank deposit or a cash payment. A breakdown of those options is unfortunately not available.

15. Fifty-eight percent of SASSA grants had been made via bank deposit before the switch to the new MasterCard-branded disbursement system (CGAP 2011).

16. The analysis in this section is based on the 2010 SME round of the FinScope South Africa survey, the most recent one available (FinMark Trust 2011). It surveyed 5,676 South African business owners age 16 and older with less than 200 employees and is nationally representative. Out of the 5,676 business owners surveyed 1,585 reside in townships and 2,276 in nontownship urban areas. The data are weighted to the population, as in the household survey.

17. The South Africa data reported here are for 2007. For more information about World Bank Enterprise Surveys, see the website at http://www.enterprisesurveys.org.

18. The regression analysis in table 4A.2 shows that after controlling for firm size and registration status, township location is not a significant determinant of whether a firm saves at a bank.

19. Other potential sources of credit include informal financial institutions such as *stokvels*, saving clubs, and burial societies; microfinance institutions; money lenders; goods on credit; employers; and government agencies. Although businesses in townships appear to rely disproportionally on informal financial institutions and money lenders for credit relative to businesses in non-township urban areas, there are too few observations to draw any meaningful statistical interference.

20. Again, regression analysis confirms this general finding (see table 4A.2). However, given the small fraction of firms that have access to credit—and, especially, access to credit from banks in townships—the results have low statistical power.

21. For a comprehensive overview, see Fuchs et al. (2011).

22. The four largest banks are Absa Bank, Standard Bank, First National Bank, and Nedbank.

23. For a more in-depth overview of how the structure of the banking sector affects access to finance in South Africa, see World Bank (2013).

References

Allen, Franklin, Asli Demirgüç-Kunt, Leora Klapper, and Maria Soledad Martinez Peria. 2013. "The Foundations of Financial Inclusion: Understanding Ownership and Use of Formal Accounts." Working Paper 6290, World Bank, Washington, DC.

Aportela, Fernando. 1999. "Effects of Financial Access on Savings by Low-Income People." Dissertation, Department of Economics, Massachusetts Institute of Technology, Cambridge, MA.

Beck, Thorsten, Ross Levine, and Norman Loayza. 2000. "Finance and the Sources of Growth." *Journal of Financial Economics* 58 (1): 261–300.

Beck, Thorsten, Asli Demirgüç-Kunt, and Ross Levine. 2007. "Finance, Inequality, and the Poor." *Journal of Economic Growth* 12 (1): 27–49.

BFA (Bankable Frontier Associates). 2009. *The Mzansi Bank Account Initiative in South Africa*. Report prepared for the FinMark Trust by BFA, Somerville, MA.

CGAP (Consultative Group to Assist the Poor). 2011. *CGAP G2P Research Project: South Africa Country Report*. Study report, Washington, DC.

———. 2012. "Social Cash Transfers and Financial Inclusion: Evidence from Four Countries." Focus Note 77, CGAP, Washington, DC.

Demirguc-Kunt, Asli, and Leora Klapper. 2013. "Measuring Financial Inclusion: Explaining Variation Across and Within Countries." Brookings Papers on Economic Activity. Spring: 279–321.

Demirguc-Kunt, Asli, and Ross Levine. 2009. "Finance and Inequality: Theory and Evidence." *Annual Review of Financial Economics* 1 (1): 287–318.

Dupas, Pascaline, and Jonathan Robinson. 2009. "Savings Constraints and Microenterprise Development: Evidence from a Field Experiment in Kenya." Working Paper 14693, National Bureau of Economic Research, Cambridge, MA.

ECIAfrica Consulting. 2003. "Burial Societies in South Africa: History, Function and Scope." Working Paper 2, Deutscher Genossenschafts- und Raiffeisenverband e.V. (DGRV SA), Pretoria. http://www.dgrvsa.co.za/Publications/Burial%20societies%20in%20South%20Africa.pdf.

FinMark Trust. 2011. *FinScope South Africa Small Business Survey 2010*. Survey report, FinMark Trust, Johannesburg. http://www.finmark.org.za/publication/finscope-south-africa-small-business-survey-2010-report.

———. 2013. *FinScope South Africa 2012*. Household survey report, FinMark Trust, Johannesburg. http://www.finmark.org.za/wp-content/uploads/pubs/FinScope_SA_Booklet_2012.pdf.

FSB (Financial Services Board). 2011. "Financial Literacy in South Africa: Results of an OECD/INFE Pilot Study." Research report, FSB, Pretoria.

Fuchs, Michael, Leonardo Iacovone, Thomas Jaeggi, Mark Napier, Roland Pearson, Giulia Pelligrini, and Carolina Villegas Sanchez. 2011. "Financing Small and Medium Enterprises in the Republic of South Africa: Will Trouble Blow across the Sahara?" Financial Sector Policy Note, World Bank, Washington, DC.

Karlan, Dean, and Jonathan Morduch. 2009. "Access to Finance." In *Handbook of Development Economics*, vol. 5, edited by D. Rodrik and M. Rosenzweig, 4704–84. Amsterdam, the Netherlands: Elsevier.

Klapper, Leora, Luc Laeven, and Raghuram Rajan. 2006. "Entry Regulation as a Barrier to Entrepreneurship." *Journal of Financial Economics* 82 (3): 591–629.

MasterCard. 2012. "More Than 2.5 Million MasterCard Debit Cards Issued to Social Welfare Beneficiaries in South Africa." Press Release, July 30. http://newsroom.mastercard.com/press-releases/more-than-2-5-million-mastercard-debitcards-issued-to-social-welfare-beneficiariesin-south-africa.

SARB (South African Reserve Bank). 2012. *Quarterly Bulletin*. 265 (September). SARB, Pretoria, South Africa.

World Bank. 2008. *Finance for All? Policies and Pitfalls in Expanding Access.* A World Bank Policy Research Report. Washington, DC: World Bank.

———. 2012a. "South Africa Economic Update: Focus on Inequality of Opportunity." South Africa Economic Update, Issue 3, World Bank, Washington, DC.

———. 2012b. *South Africa—Report on the Observance of Standards and Codes (ROSC): Insolvency and Creditor Rights.* ROSC assessment report, World Bank, Washington, DC.

———. 2013. "South Africa Economic Update: Focus on Financial Inclusion." South Africa Economic Update, Issue 4, World Bank, Washington, DC.

CHAPTER 5

Qualitative Assessment of the Diepsloot Economy

Catherine Cross

All the rubbish from Africa comes here, to spoil South Africa.

Diepsloot is hell.

The police don't take South African-born business people seriously—for instance, if they raid a foreign national's shop, they don't expatriate them, send them home. Instead they take bribery to let them go on living here.

It's risky—it's corrupt. I was robbed. It was a burglary. I had to go to the police; they need to be beefed up to handle these things better here.

What I do to live, I look after people's babies. There are no jobs here—sometimes we go to sleep hungry.

Where I come from, in Polokwane in Limpopo, it's better there, but we are far from the firms that offer jobs, so we come here regardless.

There are a lot of businesses needed here, to cater for everyone—yes, it's a good place, the place is overpopulated, so that means opportunities.

—Diepsloot residents, interviewed in 2012

Diepsloot Township: A Potent Brew of Anger, Disillusionment, Suspicion, Fear—and Hope

The settlement of Diepsloot (now a township) came about after the end of apartheid. It has, since emerging as a "dense forest of shacks, crowds of unemployed people milling on the streets, and attempts by some at small-scale commerce in make-shift shops" (Harber 2011). Despite its burgeoning population of close to 200,000, it finds only a rare mention in the mainstream media—and that for the occasional report of a violent crime resolved through mob vigilante justice, an outburst of service delivery protests, a flare-up of xenophobic attacks, or the escape of a dangerous criminal who eluded police by melting into Diepsloot's density after a crime spree. Its bustling economic and social life, its daily grind of hardships, and its residents' (unmet) aspirations do not hold much interest for the outside world. But unleashing the energy latent in those very aspirations holds the key to the nation's objective of a faster, more inclusive growth path.

Based on a series of interviews with residents and local entrepreneurs and focus group discussions in Diepsloot, this chapter provides a qualitative assessment of the various facets of life in the township. Quantitative assessments of the business environment and the economic decisions of the households of Diepsloot will follow in chapters 6 and 7.

An Overview of Diepsloot

Geographical Advantages, Economic Distances

Diepsloot is situated in the north of the Johannesburg Metropolitan Municipality, within its peripheral Region A (bordering the Tshwane Municipality)—placing it in the heart of Guateng, South Africa's wealthiest province, as shown in map 5.1. Ideally located along the nation's economic powerhouse—the

Map 5.1 Location of Diepsloot, in the City of Johannesburg, Guateng Province

Source: ©Johannesburg Development Agency (JDA). Reproduced, with permission, from JDA; further permission required for reuse.
Note: CoJ = City of Johannesburg.

Johannesburg-Midrand-Tshwane corridor—it is less than 50 kilometers south of the Pretoria central business district (CBD) and 40 kilometers north of the Johannesburg CBD. Three well-developed highways facilitate access to and from Diepsloot to the rest of the corridor.[1]

The township is also uniquely located close to the significant economic opportunities provided by upmarket residential and commercial development centers, including Dainfern, Fourways, Midrand, Northgate, Sandton, and Sunninghill. Yet, despite its prime location, Diepsloot is far from being integrated into the urban economic or social map.[2]

Brief History

Established in 1995 after the end of apartheid, Diepsloot is one of Johannesburg's newest settlements. It was originally designated as a transit camp for evictees from informal settlements in Alexandra, Honeydew, and Zevenfontein. No public services (for example, water and sanitation services) were provided initially because the relocations were intended to be temporary. Since then, Diepsloot has grown into an economically and socially vibrant neighborhood stretching over 5 square kilometers, (about 2 square miles) divided into a total of 13 extensions,[3] and home to around 200,000 residents (a fourfold increase since 2001).[4]

The large influx of migrants (from as far away as Pakistan) adds another layer of distinction to Diepsloot. It is then, in many ways, an atypical township: newer, poorer, more informal, and hosting a bigger concentration of migrants (many of them foreign nationals) than the historically established townships set up during apartheid.

Johannesburg's Joburg 2040 Growth and Development Strategy, its Growth Management Strategy, and its Upgrading of Marginalized Areas Program recognize Diepsloot as a priority development area. The city's 2010 Urban Development Framework highlights its commitment to foster Diepsloot's social, economic, and environmental viability as a human settlement while at the same time improving the settlement's spatial integration into the City of Johannesburg.

Services and Infrastructure
Housing
On its establishment, Diepsloot was only an informal housing area. Today, a maze of formal and informal housing developments prevails in Diepsloot, featuring four main types of houses:

- Informal dwellings or shacks made mainly of corrugated iron sheets.
- Government-subsidized housing, built through the Reconstruction and Development Program (RDP), that are made of brick walls and iron-sheet roofing and found mainly in extensions 4–11.
- Bank-financed or credit-linked houses made of brick walls and tiled roofing and found mainly in Tanganani (extension 3). These houses are bonded by financial institutions and range from affordable to upmarket units.
- Self-built houses on serviced stands.

In terms of home ownership, beneficiaries of RDP houses and residents of self-built houses on serviced stands have titles to their houses. Although shacks in reception or temporary housing sites have no title, residents in these areas consider themselves to be the owners, emboldened by the fact no one legally challenges their claim. Yet, lack of legal titles to their residence hampers them in many ways, from accessing formal finance to selling their property or accessing public infrastructure. In addition, Diepsloot hosts a range of informal rental housing options, including shack rental in homeowners' yards, rental of ready-built shacks, and purchase or rental of RDP houses outside the formal system.

This maze of arrangements is influenced, in part, by the significant inflow of migrants, which has raised the demand for housing—a demand met in large part by a surge in backyard shacks and informal dwellings rather than a planned urban development response. Consequently, 47 percent of Diepsloot residents (according to the findings in chapter 7) live in shacks. While shacks are a common feature in all the areas, extensions 1, 12, and 13 comprise only shacks.

Education

We counted 13 schools in Diepsloot: four high schools and nine primary schools. Three schools are in extension 5, and two each are in extensions 6, 10, 2, 9, and Riversands (across the road from Diepsloot). Of these, two are private schools, which are the main absorber of undocumented foreign-nationality students (children of illegal immigrants) because public schools demand South African identification or proof of legal residence. Complementing the schools are many (close to 50, by our count) early learning development (ECD) centres, commonly referred to as preschools or crèches.

Health

Only two public clinics service Diepsloot's entire population. One was upgraded from 8 to 18 consulting rooms in 2010 to meet increasing demand. Demand naturally remains overwhelmingly high, often pushing out people to travel as much as 20 kilometers to the Witkopen public clinic for medical services. However, several private medical doctors (at least 15 by our count, but likely many more in reality) run their own practices in Diepsloot. The township has no ambulance service.

Transport

In general, Diepsloot residents rely heavily on public transport, mainly on minibus taxi services. But those services have long been meager and still are costly. Diepsloot was established without formal infrastructure or public transport by way of bus or train services. In July 2012, a brand new minibus taxi rank was opened in extension 2 and now serves as the township's main transport hub. The rank—on Ingonyama Road, the main arterial into the settlement—also boasts intelligent power supply grids, security (there is a police station nearby), and 28 fixed stalls for informal traders. In addition, a number of informal taxi ranks support the transport infrastructure of Diepsloot.

Most roads in about half of the extensions are tarred roads, an important improvement of recent years. However, most of the roads in the other half are still not tarred. In some cases, tarred roads have potholes, and there are ongoing efforts to repair and upgrade these through the national government's Community Works Program (CWP).

Other Public and Private Services

Formal dwellings have access to water and sanitation services (tap water, flush or chemical toilets) provided by the City of Johannesburg through Johannesburg Water. Waste is removed weekly through Pikitup. Informal dwellings, on the other hand, are serviced through communal taps and toilets. Illegal electricity connections are common and have been increasing over the years.

Recreation services are extremely limited. Only one park (Serafina Park in Diepsloot West) serves all of Diepsloot. There is a Youth Development Center and the Social Development Control Center. The former offers short-term training in computers, dressmaking, and other skills. Limited information and communication technology services are available but very expensive. A post office and two pension pay points are also available. There is ample land on the outskirts of Diepsloot for the youth to organize an occasional pickup soccer game. There are no cinema theaters, at least none visible from the street.

Infrastructure for emergency services includes one South African Police Service (SAPS), one metro police station, an Emergency Management Center, and a fire department.

A shopping mall was opened in extension 9 in 2007 and is currently the only formal retail destination in Diepsloot. The on-site taxi rank facilitates access to and from the mall. The mall hosts some major South African brands, indicating Diepsloot's potential as a market for big businesses. In addition to the mall, some informal trading and small-scale businesses characterize and support the township's economy.

Financial services comprise the six main banks, all located in the mall: ABSA, African Bank, Capitec Bank, First National Bank, Nedbank, and Standard Bank. Numerous automated teller machines (ATMs) are scattered across the township.

The Politics of Housing and Land Ownership

Squatter camps keep increasing here because corruption in housing allocation is rife.

Almost every year there are people taking our details and promising RDP houses, but we don't get those houses.

Government officials just earmark RDP houses for their own families. We just vote, but we get nothing.

—Diepsloot residents, 2012

Arriving and settling in Diepsloot is not a planned event. Newcomers are registered as they arrive. If they do not rent spaces from registered owners of lots, they get assigned to building spaces by street committees and the local administrative bodies, a process frequently seen as inequitable, unreliable, and corrupt by those involved.

Obtaining either a subsidized house or a residential stand with title is similarly considered difficult and contributes to a hovering distrust of township governance, as several residents expressed in interviews with the authors for this assessment:

> You need to speak to the street committees—you pay R 150–200 to come in and be written down and allocated a stand. Some of them are taking bribery to ensure that you get a place.

> You can get a place in a nice settlement cluster as if you're buying a house, but right after that you can end up renting all the same—your serviced stand, that you thought you had for a house, just becomes your shack on a rented plot and nothing else.

> People can jump the waiting list to get an RDP house even though they came and registered after those who registered earlier and who should have had those houses.

> Foreign nationals receive RDP houses if they pay bribery.

> I have been here for 11 years, since the Red Ants removed us and brought us here, and I still don't have a subsidy house.

> —Diepsloot residents, 2012

The belief that administrative structures use a corrupt or informalized process to collect money from the relatively helpless township inhabitants was a recurring theme in the interviews and focus group discussions conducted for this report. Distrust, frustration, and perceived marginalization seemed to translate into uncertainty and perceptions of insecurity and vulnerability, with the potential to readily become toxins of cynicism and anger. Foreign migrants were more guarded in their statements, reflecting similar feelings only in sporadic moments of candor when they admitted their own cynical views that officials were readily accommodating them only as potential sources of income.

Contestation over land ownership lies at the core of Diepsloot's politics. Subsidized formal houses, reportedly selling for R 30,000–40,000 (US$3,000–4,000), are beyond the means of most South African migrants and shack residents. On the other hand, foreign migrants often appear too frightened to even want to become property owners, as confirmed by Congolese trader Jethro A., who continues to rent the premises for his large, spaza-type (informal convenience shop) business. He is acutely aware that this is an inflammatory issue, knowing as he does foreign nationals who were killed or whose houses were burned down by angry citizens. However, other foreign-born traders have not hesitated to buy housing units for their businesses.

For now, the area occupied by Diepsloot appears to have filled up. The process of building new housing and assigning housing to people now waiting in shacks appears to have stalled, leaving the different extensions frozen in various stages of development—and entrenching a new class divide between the better-off households in RDP houses and the severely poor fraction left behind in the shack-housing sector. It is not clear what chance the remaining shack residents now have of new houses being built.

The rest of this chapter peeks into the township's economic life through a series of interviews and focus group discussions with Diepsloot residents (discussed further in box 5.1). It will particularly emphasize its vibrant small business sector, which has the potential to do much better; its precarious labor market situation; and the tense fault lines between the South African citizen- and foreigner-owned business communities.

Box 5.1 Methods and Sample Description

The methodology adopted for the qualitative study described here is based on anthropological qualitative approaches, using open-ended interview questions and discussion groups to enable respondents to develop their own stories and their own perceptions in as much depth as time and resources allowed. The main interview study took place in two stages: initial household interviews and in-depth, life history interviews of selected respondents. Some 30 baseline household interviews with South African respondents and 7 with foreign traders were conducted, together with 15 life history interviews. In addition, 6 brief sociometric interviews about client bases, 5 business interviews with owners of larger semiformal businesses, and 2 institutional key informant interviews were carried out, for a total of 62 qualitative interviews and 5 focus group discussion workshops.

Qualitative Interviews

The inquiry was not conceived as a study comparing different types of informal enterprise but rather as a study of households that do and do not operate informal businesses, with a view to exploring underlying factors.

The qualitative sampling was carried out nonstatistically, on a quota sample basis, with the specification that the sample quota should adequately cover both informal areas and formalized settlements with subsidized housing. Table B5.1.1 shows the sample distribution of South African citizens across 5 of Diepsloot's 13 extensions. Using the approach of nonprobability data collection based on personal recollection by individuals, the study makes no claim to statistical representativeness. The different Diepsloot residential extensions have different characters depending on their age, level of development and amenities, and the standard of housing and public services. Both formal housing and shack-type housing are found in most of the extensions.

Among the respondents, 10 were in households living in their own shacks on public land without title to their temporary housing site; 3 rented rooms in subsidized houses; 3 either rented sites for their own shacks in the yards of subsidized-housing owners or rented ready-built shacks; 3 lived in owner-built houses on stands with title; and 10 had received RDP-type subsidized houses, all with title. These different modes of housing and accommodation are

box continues next page

Box 5.1 **Methods and Sample Description** *(continued)*

Table B5.1.1 Descriptive Summary of Interview Sample for Qualitative Assessment of Diepsloot

Extension no.	Formal/informal/upgrading	No. of cases	% of total cases	% formally housed
1	Informal, designated temporary	5	17	0
2	Formal, township appearance	7	23	43
6	Formal w/informal renting	6	20	100
7	Formal w/informal renting	6	20	83
12	Informal, upgrading	6	20	0

Note: "Formal" = formal subsidy housing only or almost only type. "Informal" = informal self-build housing only or almost only. "Designated temporary" replacement formal housing promised, not being actively supplied to current population. "Township appearance" = looks like a formal township, which Diepsloot as a whole does not. "Formal w/ informal renting" = formal housing with informal rentals on stands of formal houses. "Upgrading" = undergoing informal settlement upgrading process (government service/housing delivery intervention).

closely tied into the kinds of economic support activity found in the occupying family, through the role of permanent and semipermanent housing in determining how the household is inserted into the local and regional economies.

The seven interviews with foreign traders were carried out, on a key informant basis, in Extensions 1 and 2. Five of the 15 in-depth interviews and 3 of the semiformal business interviews were done in Extension 2, where informal economic activity is often concentrated, but the follow-up interviews included respondents from households in the other listed extensions.

Focus Groups

Focus groups included three group workshops with South African citizens, bringing together men and women of all ages, with emphasis on youth, from different Diepsloot extensions. Another two focus groups brought in the foreign trading community: one for the mainly Muslim grouping of Somalis and Pakistanis (according to their preferred associational alignment) and the other comprising Zimbabweans, Congolese, and Ethiopians.

The Small-Business Sector

Diepsloot is a very good place to run a business, because it has a reliable market, and because it allows multiple businesses.

There are people who are successful in business, who have raised their children through that.

People make enough to make a living—that's all. Even if it's from hand to mouth, only enough to get through the day, that's what it is—nothing left for savings.

If you are poor then you have no option but to run a business, even if you are not skilled and it does not fit well into your household.

Mostly, businesses are in people's yards. There are a lot of shops here in the yards, or on people's own stands—there's another one every 20 meters.

Having your own business is better than working, because then there's no one who's complaining to you. Business gives cash every day, but a job needs you to wait till the end of the month.

Security for small businesses is not good enough here—it's the police that are taking people's stock, and they accept bribes from the robbers.

—Diepsloot residents, 2012

Business enterprises in Diepsloot may be divided into those embedded in the community within tight residential clusters and those operating in a more dynamic, open-space environment outside of the residential community. The dividing line is often thin, and many businesses often traverse both sides. As in the other townships, formal commercial outlets in Diepsloot have penetrated deeply into communities that historically had been served only by scattered small businesses and occasional trading stores.

Local Neighborhood Businesses

Narratives at the local neighborhood level suggest that business operations are largely merged into the household structure and embedded in the community social norms in ways that limit outright market competition and business expansion. Most businesses are highly localized, with small client bases built through social connections.

Local neighborhood businesses in Diepsloot appear to be aligned in a territorial hierarchy, in several tiers of the distribution systems tied to the larger formal economy: household businesses, general dealers, and informal supermarkets.

Household Businesses

At the local neighborhood level, the most prevalent businesses are the spaza shops: mostly grocery retailers that operate as the local convenience shops. These are mostly micro-size, such as the one run by Callista N. (see box 5.2). However, larger operations such as the one run by Joshua K. may also be found (see box 5.3). Their products are bought largely from the formal economy through small specialist suppliers in the metropolitan cities. Run from shacks and houses, they are found inside all local neighborhoods.

Other kinds of prevalent small retail businesses include snack and other prepackaged-food sellers as well as *shebeens* or taverns. Diepsloot's neighborhoods also host a number of small businesses in the services sector, including hairstyling and beauty salons in particular, as well as child care and a few informal computer training schools.

Household businesses are deeply embedded in their neighborhoods, with social values and norms that seem to make the establishment of a customer base a quasi-social resource allocation exercise. Goals are often defined in terms of taking care of basic household needs and avoiding rocking any neighborhood boats or disrupting community solidarity. To take up too large a share of existing local cash flow and to do more than what is needed to support a household

---

Box 5.2 A Medium-Size, Shack-Based Spaza

Callista N. describes the shop in her shack as a household grocery operation, but she also sells paraffin as a separate line of enterprise since her area has no electricity, and she runs a phone kiosk. As a committed entrepreneur, she moved in 2011 from Extension 1 to Extension 12 to be able to buy her own stand, though her property is extremely small and can only accommodate her own shack and one tenant.

She is now 33, and her current operation is probably a little larger than most spazas run from shacks. She evaluates her business as doing very well, and she has definite plans to expand once her area receives electricity delivery and she can buy equipment. She sells to customers through a shuttered window in her shack, and though her fiancé has now come to live with her, she still has serious concerns about security because business owners in her neighborhood have recently been killed in robberies.

She drew her start-up capital partly out of savings from previous business activity and partly from her relatives at home in Venda. She came to Diepsloot of her own accord looking for business opportunities. To make connections and buy her stand, she used the good offices of her classificatory brother, who was already living at Diepsloot. Her child is still at her family home in the rural sector, together with her younger brothers and sisters, whom she partly supports. She goes to Marabastad market in Pretoria by public transport to fetch supplies once every two weeks, and it costs her about R 300 per trip, which is easily met from her turnover. Her fiancé assists when she is away from home, and she expresses satisfaction that she has no employees, which maintains her control and keeps her costs down.

---

would then violate an implicit social norm. Women in particular fear resentment from their local settlement groupings. Cristabel H., whose household was conspicuously well off because of her fast-food business, repeatedly noted that she wished everyone in her neighborhood could have what she had.

Household businesses therefore appear to avoid the implicit radius of an existing business run by an established household. Before starting a business, residents canvass their neighbors to obtain their consent, who after that are expected to trade with them. Customers are likely to be close neighbors and connections or relatives of the business owner, while others may come from other nearby localities or clusters. Few if any, come from outside the neighborhood. The outcome resembles in some ways a cooperative in that the customer base is an active part of the structure.[5]

Customer bases in this setting are usually thin, probably fragile, compacts that do not hold against cheaper pricing. Sociometric interviews recorded 6–10 households each among the client base of the 6–10 canvassed household businesses. Accordingly, Diepsloot pricing structures tend to be expensive, and one focus group (the Somalis and Pakistanis) observed that the indigenous South African businesses charged excessively high markups that made them vulnerable to lower-priced competition.

Box 5.3 A Larger, Home-Based Spaza

Joshua K. operates one of the larger spaza shops, selling groceries and household items from his RDP house in Extension 7, and has invested more than R 4,000 each in an attached structure for his home-business premises and in his facilities for his three tenants. His business operation and his tenants provide the household's only regular sources of income, averaging about R 4,000 per month, and he estimates he has around R 1,200 in hand at the end of a good week.

Household income fluctuates. Joshua K. reports that he has enough customers to consider expansion, but he has had several periods of shortage in the past year, especially when he had to pay for new school uniforms and school fees for four children. His working daughter in Bronkhorstspruit remits R 800 to the parents every now and then, and the family of eight currently eats two meals per day to save money.

The business is about 17 years old. Joshua K. was unemployed when he first arrived at Diepsloot in 1995 at the age of 30, but he had some savings from his previous job as a security guard. He began a small business selling fruits and vegetables at Extension 1, eventually receiving his RDP house so that he could slowly expand the business. He hires a *bakkie*[6] as his transport when going to Marabastad market in Pretoria for supplies, at R 350 per trip; he brings back supplies twice a month, and he estimates the supplies cost R 5,000 monthly, though this figure may be high in the light of his reported present turnover. Electricity costs him R 300 monthly for the family, the business, and the tenants, and water costs R 150. Family members assist in the business without being paid, and there are no hired employees.

Joshua K. says he is considering registering the business and is collecting information on the requirements. Although he does not specifically mention problems with crime or competition, he does indicates problems with budgeting and told the interview team that running the business is becoming more difficult. He reported that he might take out a bank loan to deal with the household's current consumption shortfalls.

General Dealers

On the next tier up from the local neighborhood household businesses are general dealers whose larger shops are farther from residential clusters, although still within walking distance. These shops sell bulkier goods (such as hardware) that are not daily needs, and they need to draw customers from a larger feeder area. As one resident stated,

> General dealers are not that far from here, it's maybe 20 minutes walking. They are located close by in these localities, and we are their customers in buying cement and other building materials. We also have spaza shops around here, which don't sell those lines, but we go there more often. The main thing is it doesn't cost us money to get there, and the spaza shops are very much closer to our dwellings than the general dealers, so that's all right with us.

—Diepsloot resident, 2012

Informal Supermarkets

Informal supermarkets are a third tier—the largest community-level businesses, on average, and also more sparsely distributed in Diepsloot's commercial space. Often they appear to overlap the size range of the general dealers and, like the general dealers, are usually developed from RDP houses.

These community-level supermarkets stock a wider range of goods than the spaza shops or general dealers. In the cases recorded, they were cash businesses that rarely gave customer credit. The supermarkets require significant capital to establish, and perhaps for this reason they were reportedly owned for the most part by South Asian nationals, as their business networks seemed more powerful in mobilizing financial resources. However, some of the supermarket businesses were owned by South African members of the Diepsloot Chamber of Business, creating a potential business fault line. One resident described the situation this way:

> In many businesses here we are dealing with foreign people, most of the bigger shops here are run by foreigners now—there are very few South Africans who are running these types of businesses. These bigger shops sell more than just household things, they also sell building materials, and they are located right here in our neighborhood now. It doesn't cost us a cent to get there because those businesses are right around here. All the same, the foreign owners are not providing their customers with credit; they expect us to pay in cash. These dealerships are owned by Pakistani people who say that South Africans are not trustworthy enough to be given credit.
>
> —Diepsloot resident, 2012

Noncommunity Businesses

Businesses not embedded at the community or residential-cluster level ("noncommunity businesses" from here on) are flourishing at certain strategic locations in Diepsloot. These entail more substantial fixed costs and are larger and more entrepreneurial on average than the neighborhood businesses and less constrained by the social equalization norms previously mentioned.[7] The apex position in the category is held by the Diepsloot Mall in Extension 9, at the edge of the settlement. It has a formal supermarket; large chain stores; and other formal outlets, including retail music, electronic, banking, and clothing businesses. To reach the mall, most Diepsloot residents must pay R 5 per trip for minibus taxi transport.

Apart from the mall, noncommunity businesses cluster around high-traffic areas to access a wider customer base. Many are concentrated along the busy Main Street in Extension 2, in a bustling area past the Civic Center and the police station long under construction. These enterprises include *shebeens* (taverns), hair salons, metalworking and gold buying merchants, suppliers of construction materials and prefabricated shack-type structures, car wash and car repair businesses, used furniture dealers, restaurants or street cafes, fashion clothing dealers, cell phone dealers, and other specialized retail and services businesses. The large majority of the Main Street (or "Government Road") and mall businesses are owned by foreigners, occupying leased premises for the most part: Nokuthemba J., the Zimbabwean pavement cafe operator on Main Street, said her informally leased premises, owned by a taxi owner and businessman, cost R 2,000 per month.

The most profitable businesses in the category are around the taxi rank with the commuter trade as their customer base. (This category would include the taxi industry itself, not addressed in this chapter.) Among the business owners is Christabel H., a 57-year-old, rural-born, single female head of household with no previous business experience. She supports a three-generation family of nine on her business earnings. She reported no inclination to expand or move up the formality chain, and her main goal is to keep her large household intact by enticing her children and grandchildren to remain at home. She does not bring family members into the business, where she is solely in charge. If her figures are reliable, her total business turnover may be close to R 90,000 per year, comfortably above the average annual income of R 60,613 for a black South African household (Stats SA 2012), although she has a larger-than-average household.

We never have any problem with having food in our household, because I'm selling fast food myself. I started this business in 2007. My family eats three meals a day, and I can afford that—our household income per month is about R 12,000 altogether. I'm paying all the household expenses myself, so that the two child support grants remain with my younger grandchildren and their mothers, and the earned wages of my son and daughter are for their own use.

I have three lines of business. I'm selling food—a plate of meat and maize meal stiff porridge at R 10—and I'm also selling airtime and operating a kiosk phone. The food business is located at the taxi rank, in the morning and the evening rush times, but I use my house for selling airtime and for the public phone business. That's because during the day I only cook, and I'm at home. So those businesses are mostly for the neighborhood—the fast-food business is for commuters and travelers, but mostly for the taxi people.

I buy airtime twice in two weeks for R 500, and I buy R 200 worth of red meat that will last for a week. And I also buy 25 kilos of maize meal for one week, and that costs R 60. Then I also pay R 50 for electricity. For transport, I pay R 300 per month, because it costs me R 150 for two weeks' supplies. We are five women selling at the taxi rank, so we normally hire a *bakkie* to get to Marabastad market in Pretoria to buy our supplies. That has become R 150 per return trip for each of us—however, that only happens once every two weeks. No, I don't have employees in this business, I'm working alone. I can count on my income from selling, it's reliable—in a day I go home with a minimum of R 350–400, and I count R 1,800 in a week, including transport. I have many customers in a day, hard to count—maybe 40. It's promising.

—Christabel H.

For deeper insights, supplementary interviews of five entrepreneurial businesses were conducted. Three were owned by men: a taxi owner also operating a snacks business, a panel beater (auto body mechanic), and a custom furniture manufacturer (see boxes 5.4, 5.5, and 5.6). All three were actively expanding their businesses, and two managed to get bank business financing. The two women business owners sold cooked food at the taxi rank: Lissa D. was considering registering her business to be able to compete for government tenders. Melanie H. anticipated expanding with a branch in the Diepsloot Mall area, though without plans to formally register it.

Three of the five entrepreneurial businesses (all located at strategic points on the Main Street) belonged to emerging, small-scale business clusters. Ike R.'s panel beating business catered to the nearby taxi rank and was adjacent to a small workshop that reconditioned tires, creating a nucleus for an embryonic business cluster in, or downstream of, the automotive subsector. The women selling cooked food occupied stalls provided by the municipality, about half a kilometer from the taxi stand, where they were part of a food business cluster that catered to the large number of taxi drivers.

All five businesses were in contact with the Diepsloot Chamber of Business, which has significant control over the allocation of business sites. The chamber does not recognize any informal radius rules protecting existing businesses, and together with the officials in charge of allocating formal housing and stands, is committed to promoting free-market competition. Lissa D., who was motivated

---

Box 5.4 A Semiformal Manufacturing Business

Arthur B., who runs a furniture manufacturing business in an upgraded extension but also trades extensively in formal areas outside of Diepsloot, began by leaving school early in rural KwaZulu-Natal because of his parental household's need for additional income. He started in the domestic sector as a gardener at age 15, then went into construction as soon as he could work legally. After striving to learn carpentry skills, he moved to Gauteng Province to work for a number of years in a formal enterprise that manufactured furniture and installed kitchens. There he made contacts and learned enough management and finance skills to strike out on his own at age 42.

He obtained a bank loan for R 50,000 in 2008, with the help of a cousin who worked for the government and who became a partner. They decided on Diepsloot to open their registered furniture business because of the high demand, large potential customer base, and lack of competition. He has gone out of his way to establish friendly relations with Diepsloot's officials.

To establish themselves, they first rented and then later bought an RDP house to develop as a factory and showroom. Arthur B. now has a large client base both in Diepsloot and in the surrounding towns, and he says business is booming. His clients are mainly civil servants, but he also manufactures a low-priced line to sell to poor households as well as to supermarket owners for retail sale.

Box 5.5 A Plan to Diversify Business, Expand Client Base

Ike R., owner of the panel beating business, has given notice to his Zimbabwean business tenant, indicating that he will be taking over the street foods area to establish a restaurant and tavern directly linked to his panel beating operation. To do this, he is negotiating for formal bank financing of more than R 250,000 and has obtained consultant assistance in preparing an in-depth business plan.

Ike R.'s business plan in support of his loan application describes his aims to attract a larger customer base but perhaps also refers back to the household sector diversification approach: it projects future investment in his existing panel beating operation to make it a more sophisticated client experience but centers the capital aspects on adding a restaurant and tavern as a linked enterprise, with an explicit cross-selling rationale. Rather than working to induce a static client base to spend more money at his present enterprise on additional products, Ike R. anticipates growing his total customer base by adding the attraction of food and drink to the present panel beating clientele, so as to become a neighborhood social hub. He expects to increase employment from three staff members to six.

Ike R. bases his plan on the successful introduction of similar combined enterprises in Soweto and other townships, which may reflect the risk-reduction attractions of diversified business models to many South African citizen entrepreneurs at the township level.

Box 5.6 Café Operator Balances Location and Costs

As operator of a pavement cafe that she took over from the previous owner, Nokuthemba J. told the interview team that she was planning to give up her informal lease on her restaurant space on the main street in Extension 2. Nokuthemba J. sells a plate of food with a sandwich, fried chips, and a vienna sausage for R 15, with mineral drinks or beer extra, and spends R 600 per month on travels to Pretoria to fetch supplies. On her covered open-air premises is a small kitchen with a refrigerator, washing and cooking facilities, and enough space for four tables that seat four or five people each.

Her space presently rents to her for R 2,000 per month from the owner, a taxi operator. With customer numbers dropping at the end of the year to around five per day, she would be taking in only R 1,500–2,000 per month, and therefore intends to find another location. For small to medium-size, foreign-owned businesses, rentals in the R 1,000–2,000 range may not be easily sustainable.

to start her business by a free training workshop in Diepsloot after she lost her job as a domestic worker, said she favored the free-market philosophy:

> We were told that the government could not help people who are not helping themselves, and the speakers encouraged people to start small businesses so that the government could meet them halfway. After hearing that, it was then that I decided to start my own initiative, to undertake my cooking business. Now I can say that

there are new people who have just started their business next to us—and we do not have problems with that, it just gives us a challenge to expand our own business.

It soon became apparent, however, that her support for the free market was conditional: she leaned toward managed competition rather than hard, head-to-head competition in the same product line:

My business specializes in a unique food product—I am selling cooked chicken intestines and feet, and also cattle tripe and head meat. My neighbor in this business sells chicken stew and beef stew, but I am selling only intestines, and that gives good business competition.

The five women selling food at the taxi rank covered in this chapter appear to have deliberately avoided direct competition. In effect, they act as a business association, dealing together with the administration, pooling transport costs, and dividing their market so that each fast-food business has a segment of it. Consultations over price setting were not reported but are likely.

Specialized Businesses
Renting to Tenants
Residential rentals are often combined with business use by the tenant. Rental activity is simultaneously a secure source of income, a vehicle for landlord social standing and authority, and a bulwark against house break-ins and other criminal residential attacks. Several residents described the benefits:

It's better to get tenants than to run a business—the rental business in Diepsloot is booming.

What you can earn from renting to tenants is very reliable—the rent money comes to you every month, and when one tenant moves out another one comes right away. With a business, it's up and down, you never know.

Having tenants is better than running a business—businesses risk people's lives, because they are always being robbed.

There are a lot of people needing a place.... Foreign nationals are most of the people who are paying rent.

In the 30-case qualitative sample, 13 of the 16 households that had secured formal title to their land (either an RDP house with a backyard or self-built formal house on titled land) rented out either a room or space for self-built shacks. The option of renting out also exists for shack households: Regina O., a Zimbabwean trader, rents a room in a shack with her husband.

Rental as Income Source. Recorded household rental incomes varied from R 400 to R 2,800 monthly (about US$40–280), depending on the number of tenants, number of rooms, and the quality of accommodation. At the most basic level, no services were provided to the self-built tenant shacks, rented out at R 150–200 per month. More often, electricity and water were provided, and rentals varied in the R 300–350 range. Buhle Z., a single mother not receiving social grants, relied entirely on her tenant income to support her family of seven. She said that she put in electricity for tenants to boost rental income after receiving an RDP house:

> To start renting to tenants, I spent only R 600 to extend the electricity connection from my house to my tenants, because they brought their own materials and built their own shacks in my yard. Since it's done like this, they are paying R 300 each per month. But if a person wants to rent a room instead of building his own shack, he will pay R 350–400 a month, and that's how we operate here.

Depending on accommodation standards, rents may run at R 350–500 per room: Richard S., a teacher, paid R 950 monthly for two good-quality rooms in cement construction. At the top end of the scale, Joanna P.'s family rents out their RDP house for R 500 per month while living in another house they built using hired contractors. According to Mustafa B., renting of entire houses from their owners, as opposed to renting rooms or substructures, was common among the foreign community.

Rental as Social Status and Defense. The rental system also delivers social stature and leadership status: renting out space in a private residential yard gives the landlord the status and authority of cluster head. Under the rural principle that giving the right to build within a landholding establishes the relationship of authority between the giver and recipient, the tenants consider themselves to be social subordinates or followers within the landlord's territorial cluster. Their identities as tenants of a house owner who has title and full residential rights then provides them with affiliation in the larger Diepsloot community.

Given a spatial and social basis for cohesion, the collective rental group is also able to secure shared defense against criminal attacks (a major risk in Diepsloot), often carried out by stoning or burning the intruders. As one tenant described it,

> Criminals are always around in this place, but they don't usually attack people living in a cluster. We in our cluster have killed two when they were attacking us, we burned them, and now they've learned not to come back here again.

As a landlord, Lily M. commented,

> The rental business is considered a very good support option by people here in Diepsloot if they have a yard of their own.... It's true that crime is very high and unpreventable in Diepsloot, but running a rental business is very private—criminals are failing to target rental enterprises. Compared to a shop or tavern, it is safe—you cannot be robbed by criminals, as is always happening to the businesses around here.

A cooperative, social-flocking type of cluster defense can represent an important though uncertain form of security for small businesses in particular. However, once a business becomes larger, accounts suggest it is considered advisable—especially for foreign nationals—to hire security guards. Apparently, foreign business tenants who have developed RDP houses as relatively large supermarket-type businesses are largely responsible for their own defense in case of criminal attack.

Only three of the 30 interviewed householders—Bongiwe R., John H., and Sipho D.—had enough title-protected yard space to sustain tenant housing but chose not to. The first two are relatively well-off, with household income levels estimated above R 4,000 per month; they kept the yard space for their families. Sipho D.'s family had never taken on tenants while the parents were alive and employed; once orphaned, the four unemployed and unmarried adult children no longer qualified for housing rights under conservative indigenous land tenure principles, and thus their de facto ownership standing might be seen as weak or risky. Even financial privation did not persuade them to rent out space. Sipho D. notes the risk that tenants would bring in strangers, and the sibling household might be pushed off their inherited stand by well-connected tenants and become dispossessed, as sometimes happens to weak orphan households in the rural sector.

Local Contractors and Informal House Construction

Home construction (of both shacks and formal-quality structures) is an important industry. Diepsloot contains a significant share of formal-quality, owner-built houses on serviced stands as well as self-built or contractor-built shacks in corrugated iron or zinc. People drawn to Diepsloot in hope of employment aspire to RDP-quality housing or better, in brick construction or comparable durable materials. Catering to aspirational housing in brick or cinderblocks is a specialty that creates its own informal industry, as one resident described:

> When building our houses, due to their experience and construction knowledge we normally hire the builders who have lost their jobs at the big construction companies. They are charging cheaper prices—they charge people according to their standard of living, since they know that many people are unemployed here. Recently one informal contractor built a double-story house for my cousin in Extension 6, and just charged him R 1,800 for the work.

Another respondent noted a usual construction price of R 1,200 (US$120) for a two-room shack. By comparison, buying a finished 1.5-room shack on a stand with title cost Mangaliso C. a total of R 3,750 (US$375), wiping out his savings and causing his small jobless household an income crisis lasting months; he considered the expenditure well worth it though, and commented,

> As for our situation here, I'm generally proud, because I have my own place in Gauteng, and I own it. But I'm looking forward to my house-building beyond this, because finally, in the end, I must have a properly built house with rented rooms outside.

As an alternative to hiring informal builders, a prefabricated corrugated iron shack bought from a Main Street dealer would cost about R 3,700 for the prefab structure alone.

Constraints to Doing Business in Diepsloot
Starting a Business

> To run a small business you need to have capital, your own stand, business skills, and good security.

> Those who open businesses here and run them successfully have been running businesses before—they are the ones who come here with capital to start up.

> —Diepsloot business owners, 2012

For Diepsloot residents, the most immediately evident constraints to starting a new business are management and financial skills, business contacts, and especially start-up capital. In the qualitative sample, two women and one man on the lower rungs of the income distribution (Thandiwe M., Camellia D., and Thomas K.) said they had not tried their hand at business and identified lack of start-up capital as the factor holding them back.

Lily M.'s experience suggests, however, that start-up capital for a modest household enterprise may be quite low:

> The start-up capital for my last retail business operation was from my savings from my latest employer: I had about R 2,800 saved that I could use to start out in business. It meant that the financial demands of getting started were not serious for me, as I had the resources. There in Erasmia I spent about R 1,200 to buy cigarettes, sweets, fruits, and vegetables, to start out selling on a street corner.

A larger spaza-type, home-based retail enterprise would need significantly more capital. Dingiswa T. mentioned that starting up his substantial tuck shop operation (small food retailer) used up his savings from seven years of formal sector work as a security guard: perhaps more than R 3,000. His also hinted at extralegal payments to obtain an RDP house almost as soon as he moved to Diepsloot: such payments would increase total start-up costs, but the record does not indicate the going rate at the time he may have made the payment.

In the foreign trading community, Regina O. used her wages to start a hair-styling salon that needed a stock of artificial hair extensions. It cost her close to R 1,000 to stock initially, and her salon now generates weekly turnover of more than R 500 on top of her formal job and in addition to the share taken out by her unemployed younger sister as the weekday operator.

At least six potential options are available in Diepsloot for generating start-up capital and other forms of informal business support:

- *Social network credit.* Diepsloot appears to lack the social-capital networks seen in the older settlements, although networks among its foreign- national communities are strong. Narratives like Callista N.'s do show networks in rural home areas that assist in capitalizing business start-ups; however, her home region of Venda is known for the strength of its social capital. Moreover, her family there is conspicuously well-off and successful in their own businesses, where Callista N. was formerly an unpaid helper. Few of the other households have similar home-area resources.

- *Trade associations.* The foreign trading community reported powerful trade associations that connected them to supply chains all the way up to wholesalers, and as individuals, connections to overseas businesses run by relatives. These networks are exclusive to their member communities, with the largest and best resourced appearing among South Asians, followed by the Somalis. Among South Africans, the taxi industry stands out for its network strength.

- Stokvel *credit.* Diepsloot is well provided with indigenous *stokvel* savings groups.[8] In particular, the residential yard clusters that residents use for mutual support and collective defense often reported having their own *stokvels* to provide a lending function as social insurance against economic shocks such as deaths in their member families. However, the usual short repayment cycle and high interest rates make it difficult to use *stokvel* credit for business capital in a start-up context. Although longer and cheaper loans are sometimes negotiated in rural areas for purposes such as housing construction, there were no such cases in the qualitative sample.

- *Formal banking capital.* Access to formal financing has opened up at a remarkable pace in recent years in South Africa. Bank loans, however, have been salary-based and not made to microenterprises (World Bank 2013). In the cases of Fikile V. and Joanna P., formal bank credit was obtained by wage-earning family members to cover funeral costs at R 10,000 each. Joshua K., whose spaza operation may be in trouble, is considering taking out a bank loan for household consumption purposes but not for capital investment. Lily M. is negotiating a formal business development loan to upgrade the quality of the rooms she wants to put up for rent—most likely an "unsecured" credit drawn up against her husband's formal sector paycheck.

- *Government welfare transfers.* Social grants, in contrast to wage income, were not reported to be used in capitalizing new business in Diepsloot. Old-age grants may possibly arrive just at the stage when people are likely to start seeing themselves as outside the entrepreneurial window for new economic enterprises. John H., a pensioner with rental income, remarked that he considered himself too old to run around undertaking a business start-up.

- *Savings from wage income.* As the business focus groups noted, the few people in the qualitative sample who had successfully established substantial business start-ups had used their own savings from previous employment. Dingiswa T., Lily M., and Joshua K. are cases in point. Jethro A. from the Democratic Republic of Congo and Mustafa B. from Pakistan brought capital with them when they came to South Africa intent on commerce, and were able to set up businesses immediately. Regina O., a Zimbabwean, used savings from wage income to set up her beauty salon staffed during the week by an unemployed relative. However, Christabel H., whose main fast-foods business line is one of the most profitable recorded, was assisted by a gift of R 20,000 from her employer when the employer moved to Nelspruit. In a closely related business, Lissa D. appears to have been assisted by her husband's wage savings.

Past employment (especially in the formal sector) therefore appears to be an important determinant of a Diepsloot household's ability to start, sustain, and grow a business. Prior informal business experience did not seem as critical: in fact, the most successful ones did not have any, but they each had formal sector work experience and savings. With South Africa's exceptionally high chronic unemployment rates and weak network support systems, the lack of such experience and savings throws up a formidable challenge for aspiring small-business entrepreneurs.

Expanding an Existing Business

As noted earlier, local social norms often act as a barrier to the growth of the household business sector. Accordingly, the business model becomes more about risk minimization than profit maximization, yielding a focus on diversification strategies for reducing and dispersing risk. Philip (2010) and others have also noted that small household businesses of the kind found in Diepsloot tend not to grow. Expansion and investment in this setting typically involves adding more business lines to the same small neighborhood client base, as Callista N. and Cristabel H. have been doing, rather than developing areas of core competence and actively scaling these up.

Owners of more substantial businesses—such as Joshua P. or Arthur B.—who discussed developing their existing single lines of business often tended to see expansion in terms of opening new, similar small branches in other localities, rather than through investing further in their existing operations to compete for more customers locally, as the foreign-owned informal supermarkets have done. Furniture manufacturer Arthur B., however, did not discuss how he would staff and manage the additional branches, where he intended to locate them, or whether his family members would help him in running the business.

> Yes, we're planning to establish branches, because our business is unique, there is demand for our product, and we're not competing with anyone around here. So in order to expand, we've developed friendly relations with the Diepsloot Chamber of Business, who can help us to identify any suitable place that is for sale, especially RDP houses being sold by the owners. This is so that we can have a number of branches around Diepsloot. We've also contributed to the ward committee members, by installing bookshelves in their offices, so that they too could be of help to us in order to find additional premises for our expansion.

> Our business is vibrant, it's booming, and today it is providing its product even in places beyond Diepsloot. We have advertising photographs posted at our suppliers' premises in Cosmo City, and at other places as well. We're also expecting to obtain a contract for installing bookshelves and wall-wardrobes in the classrooms at the school here in Diepsloot. So far, our business employs four people from around this area, and we plan to employ some others after we've expanded.

> —Arthur B.

The aversion to expansion of single business lines was stronger among the women. For the most part, they expressed stronger risk aversion than men, reported no plans to expand their businesses, and when offered the choice, took the alternative of lower steady business returns over higher but fluctuating business earning, a more frequent choice of the men. In their accounts of their business histories, women respondents situated their lives and their businesses in the context of family and children, and they would rather spread risk through diversification than move toward profit maximization. In considering adding a new branch, Melanie N. therefore was an exception.[9]

The Labor Market

Small business is rarely a first choice for South Africans, who strongly prefer holding a job, which, in their estimate, offers greater returns and more security with less exposure to risks from crime and competition. Finding a formal, permanent job was also the overriding objective cited by the respondents for coming to Diepsloot.

However, finding a job has proven elusive for Diepsloot residents, as it has for their compatriots in other townships and informal settlements. The obstacles to succeeding in the job market include Diepsloot's peripheral location (even though it is better situated than most other townships and informal settlements) and the associated cost of transport; the lack of skills and prior experience among its residents; and, because of Diepsloot's equivocal reputation, the need for personal referrals to be accepted for a job. The labor market has proven especially difficult to penetrate for migrants from rural districts whose social networks in Gauteng are weak. Unless family members with surplus income are prepared to continue contributing, job searches can often be broken off because of the accumulating costs. If so, aspiring rural-born youth risk being trapped in lifelong unemployment in the middle of one of South Africa's main metro labor markets.

As noted earlier, an extensive private minibus taxi network connects the township to the big-metro peripheries. But it is expensive, and affordable only for the working residents, while trapping in the unemployed, whose job searches can last months or even years. Funded by his working sister, Sipho R. searched for two years before finding a low-paid, unregistered job at a vegetable market. Few unemployed Diepsloot residents seem to try the Johannesburg or Pretoria city centers because of the R 30 (US$3) cost for a single trip and because the central city labor markets favor those who are skilled and more educated. Even a round trip to the nearby (about 10 kilometers) Dainfern suburb or Fourways commercial center costs in excess of R 20, as one resident described:

> Places where jobs can be found by people who live in Diepsloot are Fourways, Northgate, and the Kya Sands factories. But we lack transport to these places because we have no bus or train service here.

At the same time, job hunting becomes difficult because low-skill jobs are thinly distributed, often oversupplied with candidates, and frequently not listed in the media, as several residents remarked:

Because of my lack of education, most of the jobs I can get are not advertised.

Security and domestic work are the most prevalent kind of jobs for us here in Diepsloot, but there are a lot of people looking for those jobs.

Those who do domestic work or work at the Indaba Hotel get employed through recruitment agents—it costs R 60 to list with them.

I look up opportunities in the newspaper, the Job Mail.

To do an online search on the Internet, it costs R 25 per hour, and it's R 5 for a single trip to the mall to do that.

Most of us rely on connections.

Facing formidable barriers, Diepsloot residents see the Gauteng Province labor market as being skewed and one that gives preferential access to insiders, urban-core citizens with urban networks, and foreigners willing to pay. The focus groups repeatedly brought up the need for referrals, contacts, or even bribes:

In security jobs, it's word of mouth and referrals.

Construction work is dominant around here—though there are jobs, there is also nepotism and corruption around who is employed.

I was asked for an [African National Congress] card to work at Pikitup [rubbish collection agency], but I could not get one because I'm not an ANC member.

Job interviews are supposed to be 50/50—fair and equal, but unfortunately there is bribery involved in who actually gets the job.

The same also reportedly applied to technical and training institutions, some respondents said:

I'm running a computer school business, and business people like me have to pay bribery to the people who have government assessor certificates, just to get our qualification recognized so we can operate.

With driving schools, you have to bribe the school principal to get your license after you have completed the training. I once went for a driver's test in Strydom Park–I was told I passed, but I couldn't get my license card because I didn't pay the bribery. So I paid R 2,500 just to get the card, so I could have a better chance of finding a job.

There were several cases like that of Lily M. (owner of an informal business in Erasmia before moving to Diepsloot), who searched extensively before giving up:

Since coming here I don't have any informal business, and I'm totally unemployed. Since I arrived in Diepsloot I've searched for jobs in all the surrounding suburbs, all over the northwestern part of Johannesburg, but I haven't been able to find a suitable position. And it costs R 15 to go to Rosebank, and R 11 to Randburg and to Halfway House. In all the different stops that we have made as we moved around, I always made successful attempts at finding work. But since we've been in Diepsloot, jobs are just too scarce—the population here is growing all the time, with so many young people coming from the rural areas to Diepsloot in search of employment in the nearby factories. For jobs it's very competitive here. My husband and I are held back because we don't have qualifications, or even matric, and nowadays matric is the minimum requirement for employment.[10]

The focus group discussions made it clear that jobs were closely related to out-migration: Diepsloot residents tended to move up and out to better-serviced residential areas when they obtain reliable, decently paid jobs, which leaves Diepsloot with an even stronger sense of being a poverty and unemployment trap.

Serial Temporary Work

Among the options for some without permanent jobs are serial temporary jobs, or "piece work." These are based on verbal agreements or short-term written contracts, and they represent unregistered and often clandestine or illegal jobs. Jobs in this category are unpredictable for incidence and duration, and usually carry no formal benefits or labor protection; where there is protection under a written contract, wages are not always paid according to the agreement. Income levels therefore are highly unpredictable. Sipho D. comments,

> Our household income is not always the same, because the other household members who are not employed permanently are contributing through doing temporary piece work or odd jobs during the year.

Sipho D. defines his own unregistered job at a vegetable market as "formal" because the verbal contract is for monthly paid, full-time work to continue indefinitely with no prefixed termination date. This type of employment exists in extralegal space and is entirely at the discretion of the employer. It falls outside the net of labor legislation and counts in official statistics as part of the informal economy, but it is more stable than the day work and short-term temporary jobs that make up the rest of the complement of serial temporary employment.

Because these individual employment-access points are sensitive to location and transport costs, a move over any distance tends to cut off access. Nellie F. remarks,

> For making a living, our arrival here ended up worse than before, because my husband's piece jobs were cut off. He had been obtaining those jobs in Erasmia, where he would be called in to work. But the Diepsloot-to-Erasmia return trip costs too much for what he could earn there, so he couldn't continue with that work.

Several other households—particularly evictees from other townships—related similar stories.

Informal Sector Employment

Most of Diepsloot's informal retail enterprises use unpaid family labor, which can be drawn in very flexibly at point of need, so they hardly employ regular staff. Some better-off informal businesses in the production or services sectors may employ staff with special skills in construction, welding, car repair, or similar fields. In addition to the security guards hired informally by South African-owned larger businesses, the foreign trading community employs a significant number of informal shop assistants as regular staff.

None of the people in the qualitative sample was employed in the informal small-business sector, but Richard S. (selling at a snacks table owned by his aunt's taxi-driver boyfriend at the taxi rank) and Jubane G. (assisting in an informal swimming-pool installation business) had been employed in the sector in the past. Richard S. used his informal employment to pay for his search for formal work until he found a call center job, which he was then able to use to complete his university degree. It is not clear how Jubane G. came to leave his informal laboring job, but it was not used to support the search for formal work and it does not appear to have lasted long. He and his brother currently live on successive serial temporary engagements, with unpredictable income levels backed up by family assistance.

Local Casual Labor

The "casual labor" category includes "odd jobs" that are ad hoc, neighborhood-level day jobs. Casual work around the neighborhood, such as child care, fetching water, cleaning, or similar unskilled tasks appeared in the qualitative case sample as a support option used by many women and some men in economically precarious households. The situation of heavy physical labor for very low pay faced by casual workers likely was far less favorable than that faced by serial temporary workers.

Volunteer Work

Different kinds of social agencies and nongovernmental organizations (NGOs) that operate in Diepsloot offer "volunteer" work opportunities without formal-sector contracts or full labor protection. However, in many cases, workers receive a small stipend (R 500–1,000 per month) to defray living expenses. Several respondents noted having done "paid" volunteer work of this kind, consistent with the significant presence of social agencies in the township.

Mangaliso C. narrates how his unemployed single mother did regular volunteer work at an orphanage to secure a stream of working capital for her street-located fast-food business; he himself has fallen back several times on volunteering. During the fieldwork period, he gave up part-time work in South Africa's CWP[11] to take up supporting himself, his girlfriend, and his child on the stipend from a new full-time volunteer position as a crossing guard and caretaker for a suburban school at Fourways. He argues that this "volunteer" slot represents a wage-work position equivalent to employment: "I am working, I am not unemployed."

Volunteering seems to be viewed in the communities both as a stepping stone into formal work and as a fallback option for household support in the face of unemployment. Focus group participants noted the value of volunteer work in providing unemployed youth with labor market experience as a route into formal sector employment.

The Foreign Trading Sector

It may well look poor, but Diepsloot has vast business opportunities open to all nations. Our businesses are running very well in this place, and we always pray that the xenophobia shouldn't come again.

The advantage of doing business here in Diepsloot is that one is likely to pick up customers very quickly and become a prominent businessman. However, the disadvantage is that one is also likely to be robbed and killed by criminals.

I'm likely to be better off here than I was at home, because what is important is whether I have money or not. Here, we have new customers every day, who are coming to our businesses as complete strangers.

—Foreign traders in Diepsloot, from interviews and
focus group discussions. 2012

Focus group discussions and interviews revealed significant differences in the perceptions of citizen residents relative to how the foreign nationals saw their own situation. The citizen-resident community often felt that foreign-born residents were favored over citizens for access to housing, in the labor market, and in competition for scarce resources because they offered bribes. For their part, the foreign traders see their own business community as being marginalized and exploited, at constant risk of violence, and facing regular demands for "donations" from the Diepsloot administrative authorities—experiences that sometimes curdled their attitudes toward the indigenous population.[12]

Zimbabwean restaurant owner Nokuthemba J. remarked that the police were slow to respond to calls from foreign migrants and that the foreign-born population had less access to the job market than the South African citizens. Her perceptions of the police and the labor market were exactly opposite to the views of the South African focus group participants.

Diepsloot "Welcomes Foreigners"

Although foreign traders frequently commented that Diepsloot "welcomes foreigners," the actual situation appears to be more complicated: ease of access at an administrative level risks popular resentment or violent backlash from the community level, in direct proportion. As the share of foreign nationals in the overall Diepsloot population rises, the clash of interests risks becoming more salient and pervasive, creating a potentially deadly fault line between the two communities.

The southern focus group members (see endnote 8) presented their shared reasoning for coming to South Africa in terms of a desperate need at home combined with the opportunities of coming to a richer country. As one of them expressed,

> Our reason to come to South Africa is that it is the richest country on the continent and that its Constitution allows friendly relations with its neighboring states—that's why we chose to come here. Our home countries are destroyed by civil wars, so that the state can no longer provide anything for its people. The plight of starvation is forcing families to disperse. Because there is no employment locally in our countries and most people have only a little education obtained in poor schools, they cannot compete well in the labor market. So our people opt for business when we come here.

Sudanese trader Aliya J. argued in her interview that Diepsloot functioned as a beacon destination, drawing network-driven in-migration directly from source areas in Africa to the north:

> Diepsloot is well known even in our mother countries, through our social networks. So when we leave home to migrate to South Africa, we leave knowing that the journey will end up in Diepsloot.

But she was not convinced that Diepsloot welcomed foreigners like her:

> I don't see people here as welcoming to us, because it looks to me like there is a time-bomb waiting for us. This is because each time the Diepsloot community residents hold a demonstration, they would want the foreign people to donate with food, and we don't dare refuse, we are frightened. I have a cousin who lived here before, and she is now running her business at Ezithobeni Township in Bronkhorstspruit—she hates Diepsloot now, because the father of her two kids was killed here during the xenophobia attacks in March 2008.

Concerns about Public Order and Crime

Concern about public order in Diepsloot surfaced often in the group participants' comments, in different forms:

> The main thing about Diepsloot is that its residents have a history of fighting with the government for service delivery, and they are no longer afraid of the police.

> Diepsloot is a good place to do business and its customer market is vast. However, the local people are too violent when dealing with problems or trying to solve anything.

> I think I'll be better off if the resentment by the locals doesn't run as high as before, when we lost our belongings, our money, and our businesses through being looted by the community.

Workshop participants seemed resigned to the impacts of Diepsloot's high crime rate, appearing to discount them as routine business expenses usually covered by their insurance. Not much was expected from the police. As one southern group member commented,

> Yes, we have cousins and brothers who are afraid of doing business here in Diepsloot, so they opted for the townships of Pretoria and the East Rand instead of here. And yes, most businesses here in the Diepsloot area have been robbed.

For the northern African and South Asian group (see endnote 8), reactions from the Diepsloot population were perceived as ambivalent. While they commented that many people were afraid of doing business in Diepsloot because they had been shocked by the xenophobic attacks of 2008, and had therefore chosen to try Tembisa or Soweto instead, many of the Diepsloot residents had been kind in welcoming foreigners. Still, they felt other residents were resentful because they saw foreign-owned businesses succeeding when they themselves were still unemployed, which contributed to the crime rate—which, as some described, is a constant concern:

> The most popular kinds of businesses here are supermarkets and spaza shops, and their challenge is that they are being robbed at any time.

> The police are not doing enough to protect businesses; they don't respond immediately to the scene. It is of course necessary to consult them anyway, even if you know that they will not be helpful—they need to be called just to get the documentary proof that a case has been opened, for insurance purposes.

Further comments also linked poor police response to crime to a climate of compromised institutions and to a demand for ad hoc money contributions, even from civil society:

> The advantage of my business is that it is located on the main road of Extension 2, and that it therefore has many customers. However, the disadvantage is being forced to make illegal donations to whichever local group is protesting against the government, and we are even expected to donate to local NGOs that are no longer in operation. Here, it all happens at the same time.

Lines of Business

There also noticeable differences in types of business run by the foreign group and citizen respondents. Foreign owned businesses seem to come in more varieties and are also typically of much larger scale. Specialized enterprises like linen dealerships don't seem to occur among the citizen community. The statement quoted below is from a foreign business owner who appears to be trying to refute popular perceptions that the foreign business community was taking market share away from local-owned businesses,

> Foreign business owners run different kinds of businesses, including spazas and community supermarkets, taverns, butcheries, salons, home furnishings, and cell phone businesses. The locals also run such businesses. The most popular ones are the supermarkets, spazas and taverns. Most of the locals and some foreigners are succeeding, especially those who are owning supermarkets or taverns, or letting rooms.

Business Credit and Role of Property Ownership

The role of housing as a platform for business emerges as critical in determining the kind of enterprise that gets started. The southern focus group participants noted that the first concern for people arriving in South Africa was to find a place to stay and to conduct the business, and only after that were they able to thoroughly assess the area, adapt their strategy, and settle on their lines of business:

> Most people have start-up capital when they come here, but do not know where to find premises. Rent for business here is too expensive—some local people can charge R 700 for a foreign business person to run a spaza shop in their yard. So people choose to run their businesses on the street and at the taxi rank.

> People here run businesses from home, but it is not easy to get a stand and build a shop, as the government is still looking for vacant land to relocate the people in Extension 1. Knowing the right people to connect you with the locals is also an added advantage in finding a place to rent or to buy.

> We normally get rented RDP houses, or rent an extended double garage from the landlords. But there are other foreigners who have managed to buy RDP houses and turned them into community supermarkets.

> I am running my salon here in Extension 7, and I have many customers, especially over the weekends, so my business can easily be expanded. The disadvantage is that the landlord keeps on increasing the rent on a regular basis whenever he sees customers coming to my enterprise.

Acknowledging the role of conflicts over housing and the prevailing resentment of foreigners, southern group members commented,

> As foreigners we are renting here—you can't build a house because there is no space left, and housing is being allocated only when the person has a South African ID. So we only have the right to rent and the right to buy. But many South Africans sell their RDP houses, for various reasons—some charge R 25,000 while others charge R 30,000 or more depending on extensions to the house. So then we are able to obtain housing by buying it—that's all that it is.

> Yes, there are people who are staying in clusters of households together, but we as foreigners don't stay in that fashion. We could easily be attacked by either the robbers or the locals when they are marching and protesting. We had that experience during the xenophobia uprising, when many foreigners lost their lives.

In his interview, the Congolese trader Jethro A. noted that people in the foreign community put great importance on having a legal right to their bought houses: since RDP houses cannot be legally sold for a term of years after they are allocated, it is not easy to obtain clear formal title to RDP housing, and the foreign buyers use lawyers to have their titles registered. Whether extralegal payments are involved is not indicated.

Mustafa B. notes that once a base of operation is in place, capital will be made available, and then it is possible to contact the business suppliers. Peter M. confirms,

> To start a business here, we identify a place first, then go through our social networks to get start-up capital and business contacts.

Housing therefore appears as the factor in short supply, while capital is not normally a problem for the foreign community. Accordingly, access to business credit through the formal banking sector for start-up or working capital does not appear to be common practice for the African traders' workshop group, despite the scale of some of their businesses. One group member noted,

> It is difficult for us as foreigners to obtain bank loans because they want an ID document which we don't have, and some of the banks don't want passports. So we have to make compromises to satisfy our customers and sustain our businesses. As foreigners coming from Africa, we obtain credit through our own social networks—that's also the method used by the Muslim people here to support their brothers and friends who are trading in foreign countries.

Business Costs, Supplies, and Transport

Obtaining business stock and arranging transport was also not seen as a challenge; many of the Muslim grouping from northeast Africa and South Asia have preferential access to supply chains including wholesale operations, and the rest of the foreign community appears to use the large formal wholesalers located within a feasible distance in Randburg, Johannesburg, and Pretoria. Smaller foreign business often use the same suppliers as the citizen household sector businesses—at Pretoria's Marabastad market—with vehicle transport at around the same price. Congolese trader Savant K. notes,

> There are no problems in obtaining stock. I need to travel regularly to Marabastad to buy my stock—it costs me R 300 for a return trip, because I normally hire a car or *bakkie*, and I go there twice a week. As foreigners we are not given credit to buy supplies, but we do extend credit to our daily customers.

However, the other Congolese trader, Jethro A., observed that he had no transport costs himself because the large wholesalers were willing to provide free delivery and also to run accounts for substantial customers who order in reliable quantities; this appears to be a common arrangement for the larger business operators. Ethnic or religious business organizations also seem to play an important role in transport of supplies as well as in providing capital and credit. Mustafa B. commented,

> As Muslim people, we have our business association operating in Gauteng that provides free transport to its members to bring our stock from the suppliers to our business operations.

A lower transport-cost burden seems to give a decisive competitive advantage of scale to the larger foreign-owned businesses over the smaller (local- and foreign-owned) businesses, where free delivery services were not reported.

Competition vs. Collaboration between Foreign- and Locally Owned Businesses

Within the foreign trading community, there were few comments indicating concern over competition from businesses owned by local citizens. One workshop participant noted,

> South Africans are good people mostly, but what generates anger among them against foreigners in general is the influence of those locals who are competing with us in business. So our competitors persuade the local residents not to buy from foreign business people by telling the people here that we don't pay tax.

Referring to the foreign community itself, a member of the southern group noted,

> Competition is very high here, because people have different methods of finding stock, and that allows some to set their prices cheaper as compared to their business neighbors. However, most business people who come here are skilled enough to compete with other big businesses.

In these remarks, competitive prices involved in sourcing stock appear as the key factor in determining the prices that business owners can offer customers to capture business.

However, the citizen sphere sees foreign competition as pervasive. It believes that the South African small-business sector is shrinking in proportion to the foreign commercial sector, and feels aggrieved by that. In the citizen focus groups, there was an acute perception of inadequate business skills relative to the foreign communities as well as fears of predatory pricing on the part of the foreign traders. Economic desperation on both sides only sharpens potential conflict.

The focus group discussions and the household interviews uncovered little or no evident willingness to transfer business skills to the South African citizen population, or to help directly with capital mobilization. Foreign traders who were asked about ways in which they could assist the citizen community often pointed to their role as employers of local labor and their ad hoc donations to various local interests, indicating that they were already contributing adequately. In a climate soured by the threat of violence, the reported continual demands for "donations" were seen as akin to extortion, and widened the gap between the parties.

In response to queries, foreign business people identified business development in Diepsloot as needing cooperatives, supported by government interventions including the promised housing delivery, with attention to use of subsidies and to youth training. However, respondents were unanimous in indicating that the citizen community and the government should work out options for themselves, as the outcomes were their own responsibility.

Development and Service Delivery Institutions

Member of the southern group felt that the government was letting down its own population by not providing housing and health care. They worried that as a knock-on this was creating more desperation which could spill into anger against foreigners who were earning money from the local population and could afford a better standard of living. They further argued that the area was large enough to deserve full hospital services, not just a clinic that operated until 4 p.m. and identified the main obstacle as inefficient or compromised government structures:

> The main problem in achieving the development goals here is that municipal officials are not living up to their promises, because they offer development programmes under the municipal IDP [Integrated Development Plan] every year but then do not deliver anything—except for short construction projects, and those are always in Extension 2. They are very welcoming to foreigners, and quickly turn out to promise permanent residential documents including an ID in return for a consideration, but nothing happens except requests for donations.

Perhaps tellingly for group relations, one southern workshop group member remarked,

> It's because most South Africans are destitute, without shelter or employment—they must be given houses as a matter of urgency.

Peter M. from Ethiopia added,

> No, the people who have authority over Diepsloot are not working on the right things—mostly they are self-serving leaders with many businesses in Diepsloot, including rental premises, leaving the majority of people destitute without food or shelter. However, the authorities do welcome foreigners here, and they are trying to encourage a sense of social cohesion between the residents and the foreigners. What should be done is that the government in partnership with companies should encourage small businesses to become sustainable, and should also push the communities to start cooperatives. Both the community and government are responsible for this goal. Most of the foreign businesses here have employed local people, and that is how we are helping the community while staying here in Diepsloot.

Integration into the Destination Communities

In his interview, Mustafa B. describes the Diepsloot community involvement of the South Asian traders—and perhaps of the foreign traders in general—as shallow-rooted, limited, and readily footloose if their security situation deteriorates. From the northern discussion group, a Somali trader adds,

> Yes, it's all right to have a business where the income is up and down—that's better, because as foreigners we can leave here anytime.

Finally, in the same workshop, a trader from the Indian subcontinent referred to the institutional issue, as they perceive it, in a forthright way:

> The authorities are the ones encouraging the people in communities to take in the foreigners—they do that because the officials know that they will be able to access bribery from them.

The tense community situation goes together with what may be perceived as a rent-seeking attitude from some officials and perhaps some citizen groups in the area, implying the possibility of misusing foreign migrants for personal gain after accepting them into the area in large numbers as potential golden geese.

This kind of weak or ambivalent insertion into the local society and institutions is unexceptional worldwide regarding unintegrated foreign trading communities in overseas contexts. The risk of violence boils under the surface wherever there are persisting differentials in income and employment levels. In Diepsloot, the dynamics appear repetitive and consistent, and the perceived risk of violence risk appears genuine.

Conclusions

With limited resources available to them, the types of business models open to Diepsloot's low-income households are intensely localized, with small client bases, low turnover, and high markups. At the same time, there is the growing pressure of new competition, especially in the basic-necessities lines and especially for Diepsloot's microenterprises. It is not clear how far the spreading competition in these lines—now being targeted by both the household-sector businesses and the foreign-owned operations—will trigger intensified movement by Diepsloot's locally owned businesses out of the basic-needs lines and into more substantial operations.

Moreover, the more viable, semiformal businesses in Diepsloot seem anchored in their proprietor-owners' past employment experience, which provided not only some prior business skills but also, perhaps even more importantly, contacts and capital. This route to entrepreneurship, therefore, is constricted by Diepsloot's (indeed, the country's) unusually high formal unemployment, which to a limited extent is offset by heavy reliance on recurrent temporary work, government grants, casual work, and small-business activity. The formal job market is difficult for Diepsloot residents to penetrate because they lack affordable public transport and need further skills and contacts to be hired in a saturated labor market.

These barriers to business also have elements that more deeply affect women, youth, and foreign nationals. This qualitative assessment highlighted some key challenges regarding these groups that should be addressed to expand economic opportunities in Diepsloot.

Ensuring public safety for women. Women entrepreneurs with experience of the formal economy outside Diepsloot most commonly get the exposure through employment as domestic helpers. This kind of preparation leads directly to the household-sector business specialization, which prioritizes small continuing income streams and stability without necessarily supporting expansion—making a low-level equilibrium trap for the household small business sector in the township.

Although women entrepreneurs operating near the profitable taxi stand and other high-traffic areas seem to be doing relatively well, women wanting to run businesses in Diepsloot told of feeling effectively trapped inside their neighborhoods because of poor public safety in the face of Diepsloot's extreme levels of unemployment-driven violent crime. Women's vulnerability to violence as a limit on their economic opportunities would suggest that much more vigorous action is required on the part of the government and the community to ensure public safety.

Removing entry barriers for youth. In the interviews and focus groups, Diepsloot's youth were anxious to avoid the household sector low-equilibrium trap and therefore keen to join the formal economy—the pathways to which appear to be very limited. In response to the extremely limited formal employment opportunities, a number of Diepsloot youth would like to open larger semiformal businesses. Favored lines for these attempts are most often in tech work, building and training services, or personal services: particularly, computer schools and cell phone-related services are reported in growing numbers as part of the informal business scene, and informal house construction is a significant Diepsloot industry. At the same time, lack of support, red tape, and barriers to certification appear to work against the youth who want formal registration of their businesses and access to outside capital, difficult as it is without a regular salary.

In addition, many of the personal and social services that youth seem to want to provide require paper qualifications and approvals from technical qualifications bureaucracy, which can be slow. Obtaining necessary permits was repeatedly reported to depend on extralegal payments to certifiers, inspectors, and staff at institutions offering training courses. Youth who wanted to provide training such as computer literacy, or to start child-minding or preschool child-care facilities, often reported facing expenses, structural requirements, and time costs that they could not sustain in impoverished family situations without wage income.

Likewise, the lack of business practice exposure, experience and contacts represents a serious barrier for youth. Government training programs, which seem relatively ineffective in this context, might benefit from taking another look at how business internships might be focused on providing youth with the kind of experience that seems necessary for starting successful semi-formal businesses on a scale that can hire employees.

Finding ways to benefit from the entrepreneurial zeal of foreign nationals. The fault line between the South African- and foreign-owned businesses has become deeply etched into the township's consciousness. Emotions around it are real, raw, and run high, and the political and social dynamics around the issue are going to shape the township's economic future to a large extent.

Immigrating foreign-born business people seem increasingly well aware of the Diepsloot market's characteristics, and usually arrive with a kit of resources well adapted to bottom-of-the-pyramid business models. Such businesses are embedded in perfectly legal and legitimate network associations—resources that are largely missing among the local people—and can often use high-turnover, low-margin strategies to grow to significant size, developing large client bases. However, their growth is often viewed by the local population as an encroachment into their own business space and an important reason for their lack of business growth. A proactive public-citizen stance that allows the township to fully benefit from the entrepreneurial zeal of its diverse residents, while finding ways to more broadly disseminate lessons for effectively running small businesses and growing them in a competitive township environment, will prove crucial to Diepsloot's long-term economic viability.

Notes

1. The Mogale/Tshwane Highway (N14), William Nicol Drive (R511), and the Ben Schoeman Highway (N1) are to the north, east, and west of Diepsloot, respectively.

2. For example, the extensive network of minibus taxis connecting Diepsloot to the economic centers nearby remains too expensive and time-consuming a means of transport to bridge the geographical divide in a meaningful way. No train or bus service exists that would offer a less expensive alternative.

3. An extension is a type of spatial division, or neighborhood, that often represents an expansion from an area's original boundaries.

4. Diepsloot is so densely occupied that sources' estimates vary widely, ranging between 150,000 and 350,000.

5. The noninterference principle goes far back into the precolonial history of South Africa's indigenous settlement systems (cf. testimony to Barry Commission, 1888, on newcomers not permitted to interfere with the undertakings of established families). In this light, the indigenous basic settlement system tends to see a new business as a hostile, socially disruptive act, which can lead to aggressive responses in the form of witchcraft or occasionally violence.

6. A *bakkie* is a pickup truck, a light motor vehicle with an open-top rear cargo area.

7. The most substantial businesses usually can operate only if they are able to buy and convert an RDP-subsidized property, at a cost of R 30,000–40,000 or more.

8. *Stokvels* (originating from the term "stock fairs") are a local name (more generally known as rotating savings and credit associations, or ROSCAs) for a traditional form of banking whereby a group of people agree to contribute at defined intervals to a fund that distributes the contributions to group members on a rotating basis.

9. Melanie N., who had once been a merchandiser in a large metropolitan store, and Lily M, who had once been a factory worker, were the only women in the interview group who had held a formal job outside the domestic and farm spheres.

10. Matric is equivalent to a high school diploma.

11. The CWP is a part-time paid work program operating in Diepsloot and more than 150 other sites around South Africa.

12. The two focus group workshops with foreign traders included (a) (on the northern Africa and South Asia side) one Ethiopian, two Pakistanis, and two Somalis; and (b) (on the central and southern African side) two Angolan participants and one each

from Mozambique, Tanzania, and Zimbabwe. The all-male members of the northern group included two owners of community supermarkets, a cell phone dealer, a linens retailer, and a large spaza shop owner. The southern African group seemed to operate somewhat smaller businesses, and included a shoemaker, a spaza owner, a beauty salon owner, a public phones operator, and a retail food business operator selling cooked cattle heads and tripe. This latter group included four men and one woman. In addition, seven individual interviews were conducted separately with foreign business operators.

References

Harber, A. 2011. *Diepsloot: A Place at the Side of the Road.* Johannesburg, South Africa: Jonathan Ball Publishers.

Philip, K. 2010. "Inequality and Economic Marginalisation: How the Structure of the Economy Impacts on Opportunities on the Margins." *Law, Democracy & Development* 14 (2010): 105–32.

Stats SA (Statistics South Africa). 2012. *The South Africa I Know, the Home I Understand.* Pretoria, South Africa: Stats SA. http://www.statssa.gov.za/Census2011/Products /Census_2011_Pictorial.pdf.

World Bank. 2013. "South Africa Economic Update: Focus on Financial Inclusion." South Africa Economic Update, Issue 4, World Bank, Washington, DC.

CHAPTER 6

Diepsloot's Investment Climate

Taye Mengistae

Amid Constraints, Growth Potential

This chapter is about the growth and job-creation potential of business enterprises in the township of Diepsloot. It evaluates several widely held views about the prospects of private enterprise across South Africa's townships and informal settlements. The most important of the prevalent views is that there is little room for township enterprises to profitably engage in manufacturing and thereby to be connected through supply-chain linkages with the production networks of the formal advanced economy. The reasoning is that domestic markets for their products have been saturated by imports and domestic mass production, against which they are not competitive enough (for example, see Financial Mail 2011). There is an additional concern that even the traditional informal economy, comprising mostly survivalist activity in the form of micro retail trading in townships, may also be at risk, faced with growing competition from large formal retailers operating on scale as well as foreign traders operating on smaller margins and stronger business networks (Financial Mail 2011).

The conventional wisdom also is based on some widely reported investment climate constraints specific to townships and informal settlements that impede enterprise development: inadequate access to credit, lack of specific business skills, underdeveloped entrepreneurial business networks among South Africans, widespread violent crime, inadequate access to basic public infrastructure and services, and an overbearing and burdensome regulatory environment.

This chapter empirically examines this conventional view of business and its potential in townships by analyzing a firm-level survey conducted for this report in Diepsloot—by a group of Diepsloot youth who, at the time of the survey, were armed with matric degrees but not with jobs. The group, which reported to a survey manager from the World Bank Group, carried out the survey in two stages in 2012: The first stage involved a census of all businesses in the township, registering the identity, location, activity line, and scale of each of them.

This generated a list of 2,509 distinct businesses, from which a stratified random sample of 450 firms was drawn for the second stage, which collected data on a wide range of economic and institutional variables. The survey instrument was a written questionnaire administered to business owners in face-to-face interviews. The questionnaire drew on items and modules that have been previously tested in similar business surveys by the World Bank in scores of countries, including South Africa.

The rest of the chapter describes the main characteristics of businesses in Diepsloot and assesses their performance and potential for growth and job creation. It also benchmarks its findings for Diepsloot against results from the FinScope South Africa Small Business Survey 2010 (FinMark Trust 2011). The FinScope survey covered a nationally representative sample of 5,676 micro and small businesses drawn from four types of settlements: urban formal settlements, urban informal settlements, settlements in tribal areas, and rural formal settlements. The survey results and discussion are presented as follows:

- *Diepsloot's Entrepreneurs* profiles the self-employed of Diepsloot and their businesses in terms of their social and family background, skill sets, line and scale of activities, business motives, and how they got started.
- *Potential for Enterprise Development* reveals the survey data about the potential for a viable formal sector to evolve in Diepsloot and whether any of this potential could lead to the development of processing industries in the township beyond retail trade.
- *Constraints to Enterprise Development* then discusses the survey results regarding the main impediments to enterprise development: inadequate access to credit, electricity, transport, serviced business sites, and storage space; crime; and relatively weak informal entrepreneurial networks.
- *Conclusions* summarizes the survey findings and specifies the structural and perceptual issues that a policy framework must address, even beyond the immediate constraints.

Diepsloot's Entrepreneurs

Who They Are: Ethnicity, Age, and Gender

The business census carried out for this report in Diepsloot produced a listing of 2,509 enterprises. Figure 6.1 and tables 6.1–6.3 collectively describe the business owners in terms of gender, age, ethnicity, and nationality. Regarding ethnicity, tables 6.1 and 6.2 show that some 90 percent of business owners in Diepsloot were Africans, of whom a little over 50 percent were South Africans and the rest recent migrants from other African countries, the vast majority from Mozambique and Zimbabwe. This is a striking result; given that foreign nationals make up only about 19 percent of Diepsloot's population, as chapter 7 further discusses. All the Asians save one were from Pakistan or Bangladesh. The full breakdown by nationality is shown in table 6.2.

Figure 6.1 Number of Diepsloot Business Owners, by Nationality Category, 2012

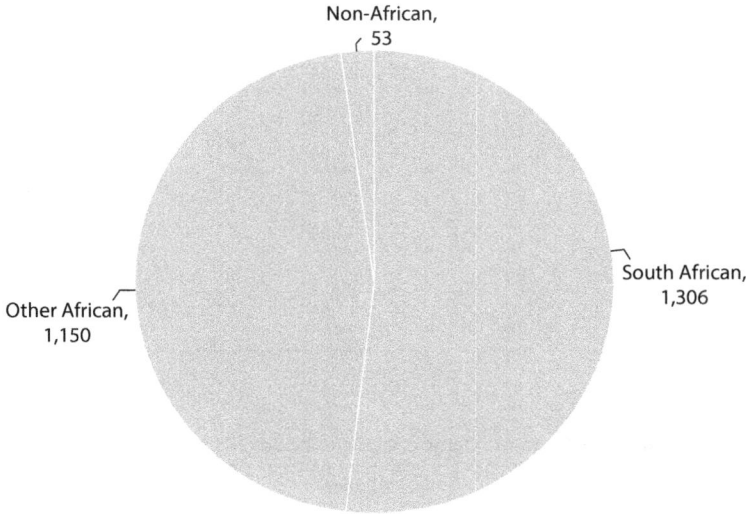

Non-African, 53

Other African, 1,150

South African, 1,306

Table 6.1 Diepsloot Business Owners, by Nationality Category, 2012

Nationality	Number	Percentage
Sample survey[a]		
South African	208	47.06
Other African	192	43.44
Non-African	42	9.50
Total	442	100
Census[b]		
South African	1,306	52.05
Other African	1,150	45.83
Non-African	53	2.11
Total	2,509	100

a. The sample survey collected data on a wide range of economic and institutional variables from a stratified random sample of 450 firms, drawn from the 2,509 businesses identified in the census.
b. The census registered the identity, location, activity line, and scale of all 2,509 businesses in the township.

Because the number of non-African migrants was small (53, or 2.1 percent of the total sample), the authors decided to include all non-African respondents in the postcensus survey sample, which was otherwise allocated proportionately among six strata defined by two employment-size categories (1–2 employees and 3+ employees) and three broad categories of nationality (South Africans, other Africans, and non-Africans). Therefore, the full sample

Table 6.2 Diepsloot Business Owners, by Nationality, 2012

Nationality	Number	Percentage
South Africa	1,306	52.1
Zimbabwe	478	19.0
Mozambique	476	19.0
Ethiopia	111	4.4
Somalia	43	1.7
Pakistan	40	1.6
Nigeria	13	0.5
Malawi	12	0.5
Bangladesh	6	0.2
Other	24	1.0
Total	2,509	100

Table 6.3 Diepsloot Business Owners, by Age Group, 2012

Age group	Number	Percentage
Sample survey[a]		
15–19	2	0.44
20–24	21	4.67
25–29	116	25.78
30–34	105	23.33
35–39	83	18.44
40–44	46	10.22
45 or older	77	17.11
Total	450	100
Census[b]		
14 or younger	1	0.04
15–19	37	1.47
20–24	282	11.24
25–29	534	21.28
30–34	531	21.16
35–39	452	18.02
40–44	279	11.12
45 or older	393	15.66
Total	2,509	100

a. The sample survey collected data on a wide range of economic and institutional variables from a stratified random sample of 450 firms, drawn from the 2,509 businesses identified in the census.
b. The census registered the identity, location, activity line, and scale of all 2,509 businesses in the township.

represents the census distribution on most dimensions as closely as possible. For example, 32 percent of business owners in the sample are female, compared with 35 percent in the census count (table 6.4). Likewise, in both the sample and the census count, close to 54 percent of business owners are aged 20–34 years, and another third are 35–44.

What They Do: Business Lines, Formality, and Scale
Business Lines

Table 6.5 shows that nearly 78 percent of all businesses in the township are engaged in retail trading. This level of retail activity is about 50 percent higher than the comparable share in other similar urban settlements in South Africa, as shown in table 6A.1.

Among Diepsloot's 1,910 retailers, over 60 percent deal exclusively in food items. Of the 529 nonretail businesses, about 60 percent provide personal and household services such as hairdressing, child care, and so forth. That leaves about 207 businesses that make or process things and provide repair services. In the "making things" category, about 80 businesses engaged in construction, welding, furniture making, and tailoring. Among the 105 repair services were appliance repairs, vehicle services, and shoe services.

Table 6.4 Diepsloot Business Owners, by Gender, 2012

Gender	Number	Percentage
Sample survey[a]		
Male	306	68.00
Female	144	32.00
Total	450	100
Census[b]		
Female	896	35.71
Male	1,613	64.29
Total	2,509	100

a. The sample survey collected data on a wide range of economic and institutional variables from a stratified random sample of 450 firms, drawn from the 2,509 businesses identified in the census.
b. The census registered the identity, location, activity line, and scale of all 2,509 businesses in the township.

Table 6.5 Distribution of Diepsloot Businesses, by Activity, 2012

Activity	Number	Percentage
Retail trade: food	1,191	48.83
Other retail trade	587	24.07
Hairdressing	273	11.19
Taverns	132	5.41
Personal or household services	49	2.01
Shoe repair	40	1.64
Appliance repair	39	1.60
Tailoring	31	1.27
Vehicle services	26	1.07
Business or finance services	21	0.86
Welding	20	0.82
Construction	15	0.62
Furniture making	15	0.62
Total	2,439	100

Note: Excluded from the total are 70 businesses for which no activity type was reported.

Economics of South African Townships • http://dx.doi.org/10.1596/978-1-4648-0301-7

The share of services as a whole in the total number of businesses (about 18 percent) is comparable to what the 2010 FinScope Small Business Survey found for informal urban settlements throughout South Africa, although lower than its finding for formal urban settlements, as shown in table 6A.1 (FinMark Trust 2011).

Formality and Scale

How do Diepsloot entrepreneurs conduct business? The short answer to this question is "as a rule, informally and mostly on a micro scale." (A business owner who exemplifies this rule is profiled in box 6.1.) Few enterprises operate from regular business (that is, nonresidential) premises: about 41 percent of the surveyed businesses were run from the business owners' homes and 35 percent from another person's residence. Only about one in five operated from fixed locations on nonresidential premises, as table 6.6 shows.

Box 6.1 The Exemplar: A Home-Based Spaza Shop

Mashudu Nemakhayhani owns and runs a micro convenience grocery store—popularly called a spaza shop in South Africa. Born and raised in Thohoyandou, a town in the Limpopo province, Nemakhayhani moved into Diepsloot's reception, or temporary relocation, area in 1996 in search of better job and economic opportunities. She was then relocated from the reception area into formal Reconstruction and Development Program (RDP) housing in 1997.[a]

Established in 2009, the shop is being run from home, an RDP house with title deeds. Besides herself, the business has no employees because it is such a small enterprise, and this has been the case since its establishment. In fact, the business remains very much a family-based one: the husband uses his car for any business-related freight and transport needs. It sells mainly groceries such as bread, cool drinks, sweets, and cigarettes. It trades seven days a week and operates from around 8 a.m. until about 8 p.m. She appreciates the flexibility, in terms of working hours, that owning a business brings into her life, and for this reason would prefer running her own business even if a job with the same returns were offered to her. She and her husband send money back to relatives in Limpopo, sending an average of around R 500 per month.

Nemakhayhani has studied up to grade 12, and her favorite pastime is shopping. Growing up, her dream was to be a policewoman, a dream she gave up because of financial difficulties. Her dream for her children is that they become medical doctors. She has three children, aged 3, 10, and 16 years.

Nemakhayhani is pessimistic about the future of Diepsloot. If not for financial constraints, she says, she would have moved to Cosmo City, a nearby township. She believes that aside from improved provision of affordable housing under the government's RDP, nothing much has improved in Diepsloot since she moved in. Her pessimism derives from the escalating levels of crime in Diepsloot, and, as a result, she is clear that if she could change anything about Diepsloot, it would to reduce crime. She attributes the rising crime rate partly to increased numbers of foreign nationals who are often unemployed and thus end up being forced into criminal activities. Her pessimism carries over to her views about the future of South Africa

box continues next page

Box 6.1 The Exemplar: A Home-Based Spaza Shop *(continued)*

Photo B6.1.1 Mashudu Nemakhayhani Runs Her Spaza Shop Seven Days a Week

© World Bank / Sandeep Mahajan. Used with permission. Further permission required for reuse.

as well: she will be optimistic about the country's future only if the government becomes more proactive and committed to fighting crime and corruption. It is unfair, she thinks, that Dainfern and Fourways residents live a life of opulence, in sharp contrast to her own life and that of her neighbors, and is bothered by how she feels they view Diepsloot—as a problem place of chaos, violence, and disorder.

a. Subsidized formal houses (built through the postapartheid Reconstruction and Development Program, thus called "RDP houses") are generally made of brick walls and iron-sheet roofing.

Table 6.6 Indicators of Diepsloot Business Formality, 2012

Indicator	Number	Percent
Business location		
Building other than owner's residence	160	35.6
Owner's residence	187	41.6
Fixed nonresidential site	97	21.6
No fixed location	6	1.3
Total[a]	450	100.0
Bookkeeping practices		
Keep formal financial records	159	35.3
Use professional accountants	17	3.8
Licensing and registration		
Registered for taxation	41	9.4
Hold business license	57	13.0

a. Totals are based on the number of businesses in the enterprise survey sample (450). Results considered are representative of the 2,509 Diepsloot businesses counted in the local enterprise census.

Most of these businesses were informal in other ways, too: Only a third of the sample kept any financial records, of which just 4 percent employed the services of a professional accountant for this purpose. Less than 10 percent are registered for tax purposes, and less than 15 percent are licensed by a national or local authority.

Diepsloot's business tax registration rate is slightly smaller than the 13 percent rate that the FinScope South Africa Small Business Survey 2010 reports for urban formal settlements but well above what the same survey finds for informal settlements and for settlements in tribal areas (FinMark Trust 2011). The proportion of businesses that professionally maintain financial records in Diepsloot is similar to what the FinScope survey reports for informal urban settlements and tribal areas but well below what is reported as the average for small and medium enterprises (SMEs) in urban settlements (table 6A.3).

As for business location, the proportion of businesses that are residence-based in Diepsloot is similar to what the 2010 FinScope Small Business Survey finds for other settlements (table 6A.2). It is somewhat striking that a much smaller proportion of microbusinesses in other settlements than in Diepsloot are run from their respective owners' residences, likely reflecting the peculiarities of housing allocation in Diepsloot.

Diepsloot's enterprises are also overwhelmingly micro (figure 6.2). A microenterprise here is defined as a business that has no more than five people working in it, including the owner. Of more than 2,500 Diepsloot businesses, the census found only 46 (less than 2 percent of the total) that engaged more than five persons, thereby meeting the scale threshold for being a "formal enterprise" by Statistics South Africa's definition. Twelve of these are in the survey sample and are analyzed as representatives of the formal businesses in the township.

Figure 6.2 Diepsloot Businesses, by Employment Size, 2012

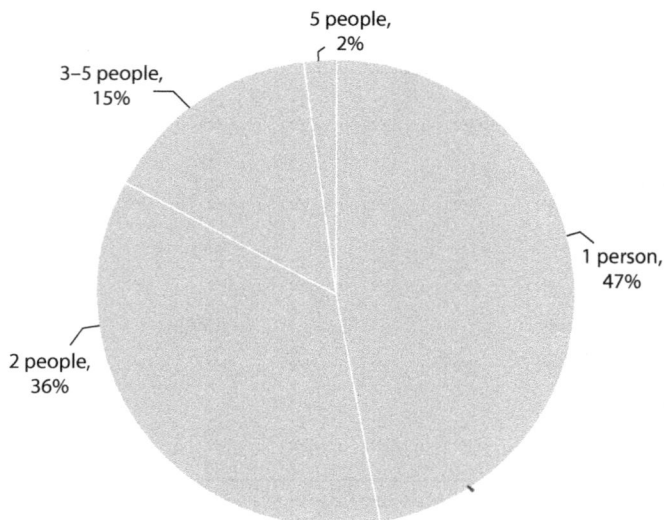

Almost half (1,200) of all businesses are one-person operations. Another 900 businesses (36 percent) engage two persons each, while 368 (15 percent) engage three to five people. The share of single-person businesses in Diepsloot is reasonably close to what the FinScope survey reports for formal urban settlements (FinMark Trust 2011).

When and How They Started
Start-Up Dates
More than half of all businesses in Diepsloot were started less than six years before the survey (that is, after 2006), as shown in figure 6.3. This is consistent with the age distributions of microenterprises reported in the 2010 FinScope Small Business Survey (FinMark Trust 2011) and is to be expected in any case given that Diepsloot is a relatively new settlement.

Start-Up Capital
Almost one in every three of the sampled business owners started up with a capital of R 500 or less (figure 6.4). Almost one in two started with a capital of R 1,000 or less. Three in every four of the sampled businesses started up with a capital of R 5,000 or less. And only 66 of the sampled businesses had a start-up capital of more than R 10,000. But this is by no means unique to Diepsloot. It is also the pattern across all four settlement types in South Africa, according to the FinScope Small Business Survey (table 6A.5).

Start-Up Scale
More than half of the sampled businesses started as one-person operations (figure 6.5). In about a quarter of the cases, the business started with an owner

Figure 6.3 Start-Ups of Diepsloot Businesses in Sample Survey, by Year, 1994–2012

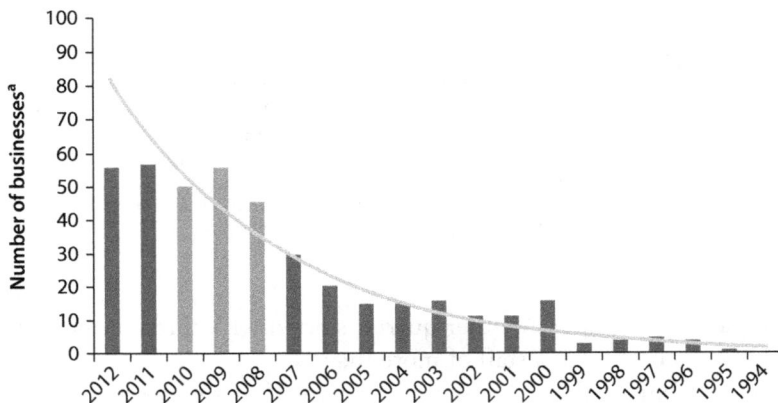

a. Based on 450 total businesses in the sample survey. Results considered representative of the 2,509 Diepsloot businesses counted in the local census.

Figure 6.4 Distribution of Diepsloot Businesses in Sample Survey, by Start-Up Capital, 2012

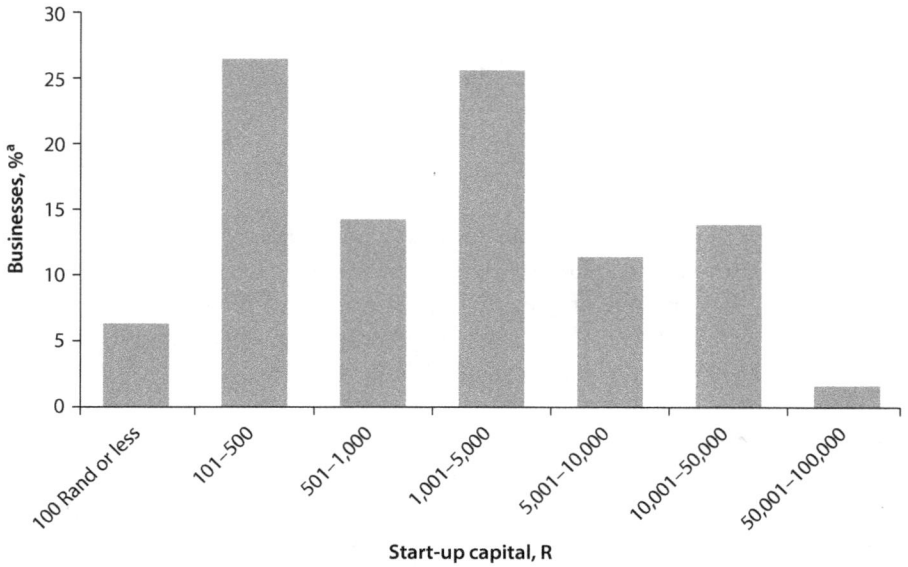

a. Based on 450 total businesses in the sample survey. Results considered representative of the 2,509 Diepsloot businesses counted in the local census.

Figure 6.5 Diepsloot Businesses in Sample Survey, by Employment Size at Start-Up, 2012

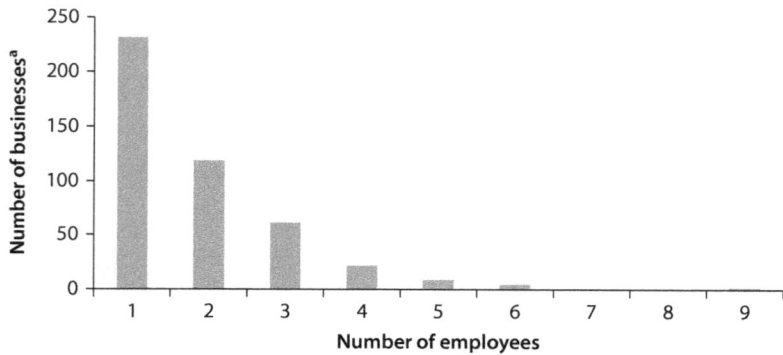

Note: None of the businesses employed either eight or nine workers at start-up.
a. Based on 450 total businesses in the sample survey. Results considered representative of the 2,509 Diepsloot businesses counted in the local census.

and one partner or helper. Another quarter started with three or more persons, and only two started with a staff of more than 10.

Ninety percent of the owners of the surveyed businesses are residents of Diepsloot—one in every five of them having come to live in the settlement within five years prior to the survey. Fifty-eight percent had arrived within the previous 10 years. Nearly one-third of respondents had started their enterprises within a year of their arrival in Diepsloot. More than half had done so within three years of their arrival. More than two in three had started the business within five years of arrival.

Prior Experience and Education
At the time of start-up, only one out of every five respondents had prior experience running their own business, while 36 percent had experience as paid employees (figure 6.6). Almost 30 percent of the sample responding to the enterprise survey had no work experience before opening their current business.

Few Diepsloot business owners (15 in all, or just 3 percent) had had vocational training (figure 6.7). Indeed, only a third had completed high school (including the hardware retailer profiled in box 6.2), while one in five had not even completed primary school. Diepsloot is very much average for South Africa in terms of the rate of high school completion by business owners, according to the FinScope survey (table 6A.6)—although it is somewhat of an outlier in that the share of those who had completed primary school is well above the average high for an urban setting.

Why They Started: "Survivalists" and "Active Entrepreneurs"
Nine times out of ten, the surveyed businesses were the full-time occupation of their owners. Moreover, 69 percent of the enterprises in the sample were the owners' main source of livelihood, amounting to over half their income.

Figure 6.6 Distribution of Diepsloot Business Owners' Work Experience Preceding Start-Up, 2012

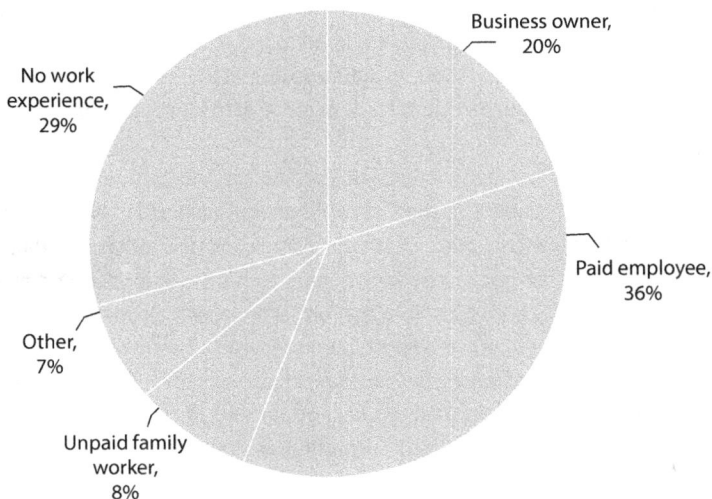

Note: Percentages based on 450 total businesses in the sample survey. Results considered representative of the 2,509 Diepsloot businesses counted in the local census.

Figure 6.7 Distribution of Diepsloot Business Owners in Sample Survey, by Educational Level, 2012

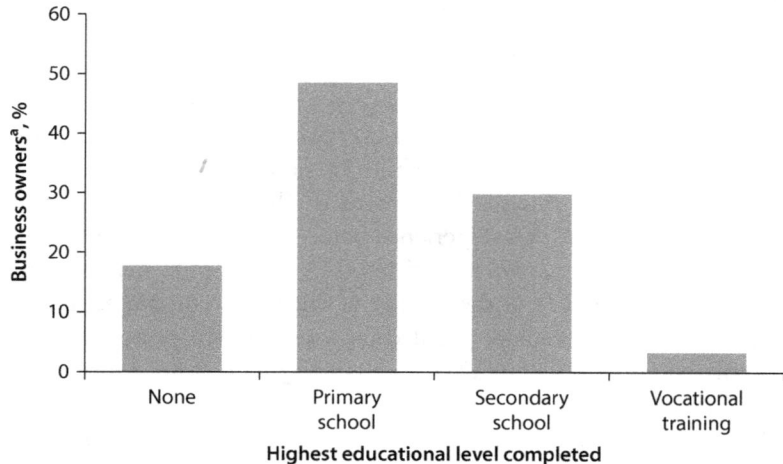

a. Percentages based on 450 total businesses in the sample survey. Results considered representative of the 2,509 Diepsloot businesses counted in the local census.

Box 6.2 The Salesman: A Larger Retail Enterprise

Mathew Lekhuana owns and runs the Mapulana Hardware Store in Extension 7, a relatively large business for Diepsloot; big enough for him to employ five people full time. Lekhuana was born and raised in the town of Bushback Ridge in Mpumalanga Province before moving to Diepsloot in 1998 in search of work and a place to live. He worked in the Kayasands Factory in Randburg (a neighboring area) before setting up his hardware store in Diepsloot in 2006 with two employees. Because business was good and he found the settlement too crime-ridden, he moved his residence to the neighboring, but more upscale, Cosmo City. His wife and three grown children (all now married) had chosen not to move with him and remained in Bushback Ridge.

Lekhuana likes the freedom that comes with running his own business—"I like being my own boss"—and also feels that that's where his skills are best suited. His business, open from 7 a.m. to 5 p.m. daily, stands on a piece of serviced land allocated to him to build his house on, a small deviation that has not caused him trouble with the authorities. Perhaps because of the size of his business, he is plugged into the formal financial system. He has banked with Standard Bank for quite some time, a relationship that allowed him to borrow from the bank to expand his business. He did not remember the interest rate on the loan, when asked.

He is pessimistic about the future, both of Diepsloot and of his country. At the broader level, he is fed up with the growing political corruption; at the local level, bad road conditions, frequent water leaks, the squalor of the squatter camps, and a constant stream of people moving into Diepsloot bother him. So much so that he doesn't think a single thing that has gotten

box continues next page

Box 6.2 The Salesman: A Larger Retail Enterprise *(continued)*

Photo B6.2.1 Mathew Lekhuana Found Opportunity as a Diepsloot Business Owner

better in Diepsloot in the 15 years since he arrived. He is quite open to the presence of foreigners, however, and didn't add any qualifications to that openness: they buy from him and are good for his business.

Like many other Diepsloot business owners, Lekhuana has a matric (high school) diploma. He wanted to be a farmer growing up and didn't feel the urge to study further. "Times were tough because of the freedom fight," he said, so he could not pursue his line of interest. He is most inspired by Nelson Mandela. Business keeps him occupied, and he doesn't feel close enough to anyone to call them his friend. "My wife is my only friend," he says, and he likes to travel to Mozambique with her whenever he finds the time. He feels that the neighboring affluent area of Dainfern is a whole different world, one that he has absolutely nothing to do with.

Nevertheless, as pointed out in chapter 5, not all of those who are self-employed indicated that that was their preferred occupation. The vast majority were working on their own account because they had no other means of earning a livelihood. In that sense, they were "survivalists," as illustrated by the case of Sipho Ndlovu (Harber 2011): "A Zimbabwean who came to Diepsloot in 2007, [Sipho] lives in Extension 5 but has been trading for only three months in clothes, socks, fabric and hats, and says: 'I came looking for a job, but I still have not found one, that's why you find me selling here.'"

Still, many were in business as a matter of active choice. These are people who had a real chance of making a living by working for others but who believed that they would earn even more by working on their own account by running their own business, or just had a strong personal preference for it. The sample survey results sort respondents between these two categories of microbusiness owner based on responses to a question about the business owners' motivation and reason for being self-employed.

In some of the analysis of the data reported below, we categorized as "active entrepreneurs" all those who said that they were in business because they could find a job but saw their comparative advantage in self-employment, much like the business owner profiled in box 6.3. By this rule, 24 percent of respondents would be active entrepreneurs as opposed to "survivalists"—a rate that is half of that implied by responses in formal urban settlements to the 2010 FinScope Small Business Survey (FinMark Trust 2011).

Box 6.3 The Entrepreneur: Success through a Diversified Portfolio

Mzolisi Mbikwana (Mzo) is a man of many interests, talents, and responsibilities: The successful Diepsloot businessman owns a tavern, a day-care center, and a recruitment agency that he has run from home since 2006. He is also the manager of the Diepsloot Mall, chairperson of the South African Communist Party in Diepsloot, and president of the Noweto (north-west townships) Chamber of Commerce and Industry.

Born in Burgersdorp in the Eastern Cape Province Mbikwana's entrepreneurship began in the ninth grade, selling ice cream to his school mates from a bicycle given by his grandfather. The business grew, and after a few years he acquired a mobile ice-cream van. The ice cream proceeds helped to pay for his education through high school and some tertiary level.

After obtaining a diploma in financial accounting from the Free State Technikon, Mbikwana moved to Diepsloot in 1999 in search of affordable housing and a job. He found a series of them: in the Edcon Group as call center supervisor, in the property marketing division of the Yakani Group in Diepsloot, and in the Fidentia Group. After moving to Diepsloot, he also identified the need for a preschool and opened a one-room-shack preschool in 2002 for 80 children. Success also brought with it an acute fear of failure, motivating him to diversify his business interests: in 2006 he opened a recruitment company, and in 2008 a tavern business, Slender Palace.

Mbikwana attributes his success to being driven and to accessing finance in unconventional ways: he raised the start-up capital for his preschool and the recruitment business by approaching individual business people as well as companies. He has never approached a commercial bank for a loan to start a business. He belongs to the Diepsloot Jazz *stokvel* with 19 others (mostly businessmen). Members meet every fortnight to listen to jazz music and carry out *stokvel* business: each member contributes R 1,250, with the full pot going to one member in each meeting, which is mostly used in business.

Mbikwana has moved on to live in a three-bedroom house in nearby Cosmo City with his wife and their three children (aged 4, 10, and 15 years). A bigger house and greater safety were their motivation. His move was triggered by a physical attack on his family while he

---

box continues next page

Box 6.3 The Entrepreneur: Success through a Diversified Portfolio *(continued)*

Photo B6.3.1 Among Many Business Pursuits, Mzolisi Mbikwana Manages Diepsloot Mall

was the chairperson of the local ANC party in Diepsloot. Mbikwana wasn't home, and his attackers destroyed his neighbors' houses by mistake. Out of fear, his wife jumped the fence of their backyard with their children to escape. But he is still quite positive about the future of Diepsloot: "Very much so! Diepsloot is a growing community with a lot of young people. They are the future. They will surely find a way to take Diepsloot forward." Houses and roads have improved while crime has worsened since he moved to Diepsloot. Asked about South Africa's future, he gets a bit ambivalent. He feels there is too much corruption and nepotism; without these the country's future would be bright. Very high rates of unemployment in South Africa and the "crime that results from it" also worry him a lot.

He is quite open to the presence of foreigners in Diepsloot as long as they are there legally. "We are all part of a global community and have so much to learn from each other." He likes the fact that foreigners come and open business in Diepsloot because "they bring opportunities," but he would also like to see them more tightly regulated and wants them to hire more South Africans. He also strongly opposes those foreigners who introduce crime into the community.

The person who most inspires him is former President Thabo Mbeki: "He's a thinker who portrays discipline and sounds educated when he talks." The latter part perhaps attracts him the most. He himself wanted to study economics after high school, "being the only kid to do higher-grade economics in my high school," an ambition he still hasn't given up on. Reality, alas, was too demanding to allow that and required him to give up studies after matric and start earning his living. His ambitions extend to his children's lives: to that of his oldest child (a daughter), whom he'd like to become a successful businesswoman, and to that of his son, who could become a professional rugby player because he's really good at the game. In his free time, Mzo like to read business books, listen to jazz music, and go out with friends.

It turns out that the more-educated respondents are more likely to be active entrepreneurs and less likely to be survivalists. For example, a high school graduate is 15 percent more likely to be an active entrepreneur than someone who had only completed primary school if we do not control for anything else.

Controlling for other demographic characteristics, women are about 8 percent less likely to say that they are in business by active choice, and high school graduates are 17 percent more likely to say the same. Similarly those in the 30–39 age group are 8–14 percent more likely than other age groups to report self-employment by active choice.

When we do not control for other demographic characteristics, the proportion of those reporting to have actively chosen self-employment is lower among South Africans than among Asians but a little higher than among Africans who are not South African. However, once we do control for differences in educational attainment, age group, and gender, no significant difference is evident between South Africans and foreign nationals in the proportion of those who have actively chosen to be self-employed. These demographic variables are all important factors in occupational choice and business motivation as well as in attitudes toward self-employment as opposed to working for others.

Those who were self-employed by active choice invest four to five times more in start-up capital than those who are self-employed for lack of a paid job. They are also far more likely to start out with at least one more helper and put in more hours into the business. But, surprisingly, the proportion of active entrepreneurs among the self-employed does not vary much by the scale of their current business. Similarly, there is no statistically significant association between the age of a business and whether its owner is self-employed as a matter of active choice.

The Potential for Enterprise Development

Business Growth

The rather steep downward direction of the bars in figure 6.3 that plot the number of Diepsloot firms by the year they started reflects both the recentness of migration into Diepsloot as well as the short life-spans of firms that had been recently started but no longer existed by the time the enterprise census for this report was conducted. At the same time, it is clear from the data that a sizable number of firms that do survive also managed to expand and thrive over the years—as seen in figure 6.8 and the transition matrix of table 6.7, which show the number of employees at start-up against the number of employees at the time of the survey. Of the surveyed businesses, 40 percent operated on a larger scale than what they started out with. Among them is the restaurant owned by Andries Magoro, profiled in box 6.4.

Productivity and Growth Prospects of Processing Activities

Many of the businesses in the sample that expanded after starting up are into making things and processing activity as opposed to retail trading and personal services. This is pertinent to one of the key hypotheses raised earlier in the

Figure 6.8 Change in Employment Levels among Diepsloot Businesses, 2012

Number of responses

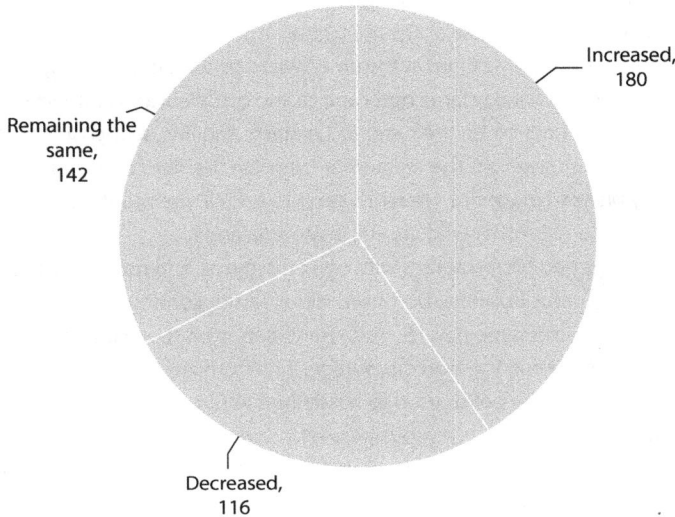

Note: Results based on responses from 438 of the 450 total businesses in the sample survey. (Twelve respondents did not answer this particular survey question.) Results considered representative of the 2,509 Diepsloot businesses counted in the local census.

Table 6.7 Change in Employment Size of Diepsloot Businesses in Sample Survey between Start-Up and 2012

Number employed at start-up	Number employed at time of 2012 survey					
	1	2	3	4	5 or more	Total
1	94	68	39	18	12	231
2	39	37	21	15	6	118
3	29	16	10	3	3	61
4	12	7	1	1	1	22
5 or more	5	10	2	0	1	18
Total	179	138	73	37	23	450

Note: Results based on responses from 450 total businesses in the sample survey. Results considered representative of the 2,509 Diepsloot businesses counted in the local census. Bold values represent decrease from start-up to 2012; italics represent increase from start-up to 2012.

chapter relating to the growth prospects of manufacturing activities in the township: that, according to one prevalent view, such enterprises will find it difficult to become profitable because they are not competitive enough with the imports and mass-produced goods that have saturated local markets.

To the contrary, our sample survey shows that processing activities in particular appear to have far larger scope for expansion than do retail trade and household services. Specifically, table 6.8 shows that net income (or value added) per worker is much higher in activities involving making things (including construction, welding, furniture making, tailoring, and food processing) and

Box 6.4 The Steady Operator: A Thriving Restaurant

Andries Magoro owns and runs the Dipetseng Tshekgolo restaurant on Ubuntu Road. A native of the Graskop village in the province of Mpumalanga, he moved to Diepsloot in 2001 when he was 21 years old. Diepsloot, he thought at the time, would be a ticket to employment because of the neighboring Montecasino (a large hotel and casino complex) and Fourways commercial center. That did not turn out to be the case, so he started selling seat covers and blankets, before successfully venturing into the restaurant business. He likes being in Diepsloot and does not have any plans to move out. He sends close to R 1,500 per month out of his earnings to support his mother and brother who are still in Mpumalanga.

In 2011, at 31, he started his restaurant with two employees, and now he has three. Having succeeded in the restaurant business, he would much rather continue in that than work for somebody else even for the same pay. His restaurant stands on municipal land, and he feels hampered by that. Not owning the land discourages him from improving the structure under which the restaurant runs. The police used to hassle him about squatting on public land, but they stopped some time ago. He has few business-related transport expenses because his suppliers have enough scale in Diepsloot to bring supplies to him without charge. Magoro belongs to an informal savings club because it periodically gives him lump-sum amounts that come in handy in running his business. He otherwise has not felt the need to borrow for his business.

Magoro, who is optimistic about Diepsloot's future, is impressed by the expansion of schools and roads in Diepsloot over the past decade, though not by the droves of people who have moved (and continue to move) into the township. He also worries about the lack of jobs for the young—the one thing he would want to change about Diepsloot if given the powers.

Photo B6.4.1 Busy Restaurateur Andries Magoro Achieves Slow but Steady Growth

© World Bank / Sandeep Mahajan. Used with permission. Further permission required for reuse.

box continues next page

Box 6.4 The Steady Operator: A Thriving Restaurant (*continued*)

His worry about the lack of employment opportunities for the youth extends to the rest of his country as well, But he remains hopeful about South Africa's future: "We will find a solution for the young people with government support," he asserts.

Magoro is inspired by Richard Branson—the magnate who founded Virgin Group, owner of the telecommunications company Virgin Mobile and more than 400 other companies— because "he started from nothing before becoming big. It gives hope." Magoro and his wife have a six-year-old son, whom he would like to see become an entrepreneur, although "he will support him in whatever he chooses to become." He himself wanted to become a chartered accountant as a child, but lack of funds put an end to that.

Magoro is extremely busy running his restaurant, which remains open from 8 a.m. to 8 p.m. (or until the food runs out, which comes first), leaving him with little time for relaxation. For the moment, he doesn't seem to mind that, though. He is also quite positive about the presence of foreigners in Diepsloot "because some bring skills that are needed." As for the wealthy neighboring suburb of Dainfern, it is a world apart, he feels. Its big houses are emblematic of the extreme inequality in South Africa, and he gets angered by that.

Table 6.8 Selected Financial Indicators of Diepsloot Businesses in Sample Survey, by Industry Group, 2012

Activity classification (1)	log, net income per person (R) (2)	log, fixed assets per person (R) (3)	log, value added per unit of fixed assets (R) (4)	Ratio of annual profits to fixed assets (5)	Ratio of fixed investment to fixed assets (6)
Making things	9.96	8.86	1.92	0.03	—
Repairing or servicing things	9.47	7.83	0.86	0.00	0.20
Personal or household services	9.36	7.96	1.38	0.00	0.04
Retail trade in food items	9.52	8.23	1.07	0.07	0.48
Other retail trade	9.10	7.30	1.63	0.14	0.36
Other	—	11.00	—	0.00	0.00

Note: Results based on responses from 450 total businesses in the sample survey, representing 2,509 Diepsloot businesses counted in the local census. R = rand; — = not available.

in modern services (notably, business services and finance) than in retail trade and personal and household services. This difference is partly explained by the fact that manufacturing and processing activities involve larger outlays in equipment and other fixed assets than do retail trade and household services, and the higher past investment thus increases the value added per unit of labor input. One such firm, a pipeline installer serving the construction industry, is profiled in box 6.5.

But, based again on the survey, processing activities and business services have two other important advantages and sources of higher productivity and growth over retail trading and personal and household services: First, these activities have attracted more skilled workers and entrepreneurs than the others, which is indicated by the fact that productivity would still be higher in those activities than it

Box 6.5   The Risk Taker: A Diepsloot-Based Construction Firm with Widespread Clientele

Enock Mmande is in the civic construction industry: the co-owner of a pipeline installation company that installs water reticulation pipes, air pipes, and even plastic water tanks. Based in Diepsloot, it was formed in 2006 and became fully operational in 2009. Mmande holds a N-5 certificate in electrical engineering from the FET College in Polokwane, while his partner Peter has an N-5 in civil engineering. Mmande was previously employed as a pipeline inspector by another company before undertaking this business venture.

Pipeline installation is a highly specialized and capital-intensive industry, facilitating the supply of air to either the cooling systems or production line machines in the manufacturing and mining industries. Mmande's clientele is spread throughout various parts of the country, including Pretoria and Olivenhoutbosch in Gauteng, Rustenburg in North West, Thabazimbi in Limpopo, and even in Northern Cape.

To raise capital for their business, Mmande and his partner individually took out loans with commercial banks, using their (mortgaged) homes as collateral. Not many would-be entrepreneurs would be able to do that. Taking such a risk was an incentive to work hard to ensure that the company succeeds. In addition, they put in a system of checks and balances using company policies and contracts that are legally binding and enforceable. The presence of institutional and financial management systems creates transparency and therefore an environment for trust to flourish, reducing the risk of moral hazard between the partners.

Photo B6.5.1   Enock Mmande Credits Success to Transparency, Efficiency, and Calculated Risk

© World Bank / Phindile Ngwenya. Used with permission. Further permission required for reuse.

box continues next page

Box 6.5 The Risk Taker: A Diepsloot-Based Construction Firm with Widespread Clientele (*continued*)

Mmande does not feel that they have benefited from the Black Economic Empowerment (BEE) policy. Much of the company's work is generated by referrals, including the companies that the partners used to work for. Some is also generated by bidding for tenders. Currently the business operations are based in Mmande's garage, which limits the machinery storage space and the ability to assemble equipment. He identified lack of access to land or industrial space close to Diepsloot as a binding constraint on the growth of his business.

The partners have about eight employees, all from Diepsloot, which reduces operating costs by reducing absenteeism and improving the response time to the sites that may have an emergency air pipe system failure. Other reasons he cites for the business's current success are its central location with respect to most of the work sites and its proximity to the main travel routes to those sites.

---

is in the retail trade and personal and household services even if we had set aside greater use of equipment and fixed assets of the manufacturing and processing activities, as shown in column (2) of table 6.8. Second, processing activities have higher rates of return to capital, which would make them more likely to attract further investment than retail trade and personal and household services. This is indicated by the higher average productivity of capital in those activities, as shown in column (3) of table 6.8, assuming that the differences in value added persist over time.

Table 6.8 also suggests that there is significant scope for the expansion of retail trade itself in the township, albeit with lower growth potential than the firms that are making things. In fact, at the time of the survey, retail trade appeared to be more profitable than making things (as shown in column [4]), which perhaps also explains why retail trade has managed to attract more fixed investment and more entrepreneurs than making things (as shown in column [5]). However, this relative performance of retail trade is not likely to persist given that the marginal productivity of capital is much lower in retail trading than in making things.

Constraints to Enterprise Development

A number of investment climate constraints emerge from the analysis of the survey carried out in Diepsloot for this report (figure 6.9). These are discussed below.

Access to Finance
Access to credit is cited as a major constraint by one-fifth to one-third of any group of business owners in Diepsloot (figure 6.9 and table 6.9). However, there

Figure 6.9 Business Constraints Cited by Diepsloot Business Owners, 2012

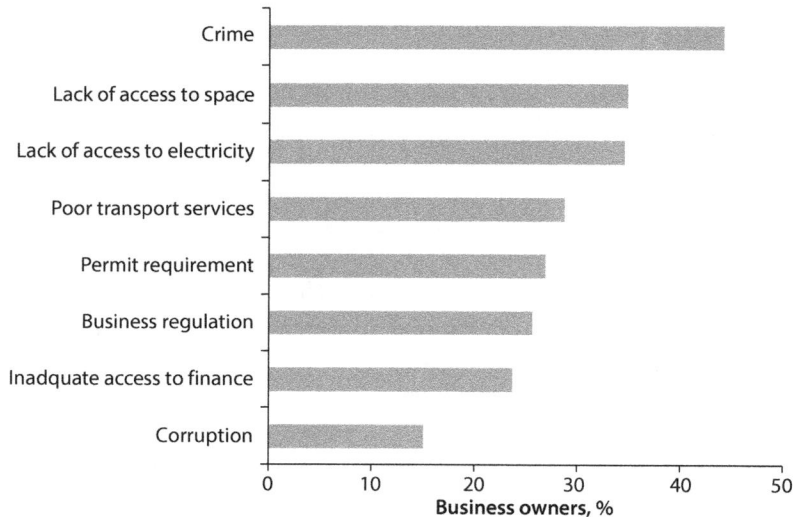

Note: Results based on responses from 450 total businesses in the sample survey, representing 2,509 Diepsloot businesses counted in the local census.

is no evidence that South African business owners face stronger credit constraints than foreign nationals in Diepsloot. Indeed, the most credit-constrained group are the Asians, who are 15 percent more likely to report being credit-constrained than indigenous South African business owners or migrants from other African countries (table 6A.7). This is controlling for the line and scale of the business, the time it has been in operation, business motives, and other demographic attributes of the owner, namely gender and age.

Results further indicate that solo operators are the most severely constrained, especially relative to those employing three to five people. Once we control for scale of operation and time in business, active entrepreneurs are less likely to be constrained than survivalists. There is no gender effect, but the owner's age does seem to matter: the most constrained tend to concentrate in the 20–39 age group.

It is important to stress that the reason that ethnicity and nationality do not seem to be a factor in complaint rates against lack of credit in table 6.9 is that their effect on credit access is mediated largely through their influence on the business line or scale. Larger businesses are less likely to report being credit-constrained, while solo operators (that is, one-person businesses) are the most likely to complain of the problem. A local business leader further describes the effect on small businesses in the profile in box 6.6. When we do control for size, Asian businesses are shown to be more likely to report being credit-constrained than South African business owners or migrant business owners from other African countries. This could be because they have greater demand for credit in

**Table 6.9 Distribution of Diepsloot Business Owners Citing Access
to Credit as a Business Constraint, 2012**

Business owners, by variable	Proportion reporting being credit-constrained	Standard error of proportion	Number of responses
All	0.238	0.020	450
Business motive			
Survivalist[a]	0.253	0.024	340
Active entrepreneur[b]	0.191	0.038	110
Gender			
Male	0.252	0.025	306
Female	0.208	0.034	144
National origin			
South African	0.240	0.030	208
Other African	0.208	0.029	192
Asian	0.333	0.074	42
Educational level			
None	0.235	0.047	81
Primary school	0.228	0.028	219
Secondary school	0.237	0.037	135
Vocational training	0.400	0.131	15
Line of industry			
Making things	0.182	0.059	44
Repairing or servicing things	0.167	0.069	30
Personal or household services	0.268	0.070	41
Retail trade in food items	0.247	0.026	287
Other retail trade	0.244	0.065	45
Number of persons engaged			
1	0.307	0.035	179
2	0.232	0.036	138
3–5	0.140	0.032	121
More than 5	0.250	0.131	12
Number of years in business (of the enterprise)			
Less than 5	0.236	0.025	284
5–10	0.279	0.049	86
More than 10	0.203	0.046	79

Note: Results based on responses from 450 total businesses in the sample survey. Results considered representative of the 2,509 Diepsloot businesses counted in the local census.
a. "Survivalist" = Business owner not by active choice but in lieu of preference for a formal sector job.
b. "Active entrepreneur" = Business owner as a matter of active choice, either in the belief one would earn more on one's own or from personal preference.

Box 6.6 The Survivor: An Array of Services Firms

Clifford Dube has lived in Diepsloot since 1998. He currently serves as secretary to the Noweto Chamber of Commerce and Industry; as chairperson of the local small-business community group, the Diepsloot Business Chamber; and as a businessman with a diversified portfolio. His office is attached to the double-storied house he lives in. His business ventures include personal security services to expatriates and celebrities as well as shuttle services, with a special focus on the Gautrain. He is an accredited assessor and moderator for the South African Safety and Security Sector Education and Training Authority (SASSETA); therefore he provides training and benchmarking services to training academies. Before setting up a business, Dube was part of the security personnel in the hospitality industry. He was laid off in 2000 and used his severance package to start his security company in 2002.

Dube knows firsthand how difficult the retail industry can be. He once sold beds for cash in Diepsloot, but beds are durable goods, his "cash"-based clientele became saturated. Then he began to supply beds on credit, which did not go well and he eventually had to close down the business. He then tried his hand in the telecommunications industry, operating public phones, but he couldn't compete successfully against bigger providers such as Vodacom, Cell-C, and MTN. Still, Dube did not give up on retailing. He went on to open a spaza shop at home, but once again he lost too much business to competitors. He closed down the spaza shop and

Photo B6.6.1 Hard-Won Experience Prepared Clifford Dube for Small-Business Leadership

© World Bank / Phindile Ngwenya. Used with permission. Further permission required for reuse.

box continues next page

Box 6.6 The Survivor: An Array of Services Firms (*continued*)

rented out the space to someone else to operate the shop. When the rental did not cover the operating costs of the shop, he terminated that arrangement.

The challenges that Dube outlines as facing small businesses in Diepsloot are similar to those also highlighted by entrepreneur Mzolisi Mbikwana (box 6.3): access to finance, low social cohesion, and regulatory constraints. Small businesses cannot access finance from commercial banks because they lack collateral. For example, in Tanganani settlement where he lives, the houses, though formal, were built without building certification. As a result, they cannot be evaluated and do not qualify to be used as collateral as the "bonded" homes can be. Local small-business competitors, who are mainly foreign nationals, have been able to overcome the finance challenge by "clubbing" together to get supplies, taking advantage of economies of scale—reducing their purchasing cost and enabling them to undercut the competition. Another source of handicap to accessing finance is that the kinds of contracts small firms get for their services are of a short-term nature, making it difficult to acquire finance. *Stokvels* are not common in Diepsloot, and the failure of the one that members of the Business Chamber tried left a bad taste.[a] It is difficult to start a *stokvel* in Diepsloot because of the lack of trust in the community. With respect to the regulatory environment, government processes are often misaligned, making it difficult for small businesses to comply. For example, many are not CIPRO-compliant because the registration processes is complicated.[b] As a result, they cannot be cleared for tax purposes.

Other challenges that erode the competitiveness of businesses in Diepsloot include the high cost of information technology and communications, particularly at Internet cafés (which are few), and many people lack the skills to even use the technology; reputable tertiary institutions are not near. Even though some level of skills training is available in Diepsloot, these facilities are not fully utilized because they are not perceived as credible. For example, the Skills Development Center offers subsidized computer courses as well as other skills such as welding and sewing.

Still, Dube is optimistic about the prospects for Diepsloot. He feels the crime perception is overrated, saying it is a relatively safe place. He is also optimistic about the planned mixed-use development in Diepsloot East, spearheaded by the Development Bank of Southern Africa.

a. *Stokvels* (originating from the term "stock fairs") are a local name (more generally known as rotating credit and savings associations, or ROSCAs) for a traditional form of banking whereby a group of people agree to contribute at defined intervals to a fund that distributes the contributions to group members on a rotating basis.
b. CIPRO, the Companies and Intellectual Property Registration Office, has since merged with the Office of Companies and Intellectual Property Enforcement (OCIPE) to form the current Companies and Intellectual Property Commission (CIPC).

absolute terms than other ethnic groups of business owners because they tend to grow faster. Alternatively, it could mean that they have less access to credit than the other groups, though results from the qualitative assessment in chapter 5 suggest this not to be the case.

The access to finance problem is primarily one of investment finance rather than the financing of working capital or trade credit. The survey suggests that all of the self-employed of Diepsloot rely heavily on various forms of trade credit which, on average, finance about 42 percent of their working capital (table 6A.8). That is true of South Africans as it is of recent migrants from other African countries and South Asia. There is also little variation in the utilization of trade credit by line of activity, business characteristics, or the demographic attributes of the business owners.

At the same time, only a small fraction of fixed investment taking place in the settlement is financed by borrowing (table 6A.9). The average reported share of borrowed funds in business capital expenditures is less than 5 percent. However, there is significant variation of the same indicator between business types and demographic groups of owners. In particular, controlling for lines and scale of activity and business experience, Asian businesses finance a larger percentage of their investment expenditures by borrowing than do indigenous South Africans and migrants from other African countries.

Although the share of external financing in fixed investment increases with the scale of the business and the number of years it has been operating, it does not seem to vary with the line of business. Controlling for all these three business characteristics also reveals significant association between the owners' ethnicity (and national origin) and external financing of business investment. Specifically, the share of external financing is typically higher for Asian-owned businesses than for those of indigenous South Africans and migrants from other African countries.

Access to Electricity

Approximately one in three business owners complain that inadequate access to electricity holds them back (figure 6.9). The rate rises to as high as 50 percent among those involved in processing or making things, as opposed to traders and those in services. The complaint is primarily that lack of access to Eskom's grid is hindering business activities (table 6.10), and it comes more often from South African business owners than from Asians or owners from other African countries, when we control for a wide range of other characteristics of the business and the owner.[1] The controls again include the business motives, age, and lines, which are both important covariates of complaints about access to infrastructure. Survivalist entrepreneurs are 16 percent more likely to complain of lack of access to the public grid than active entrepreneurs, and those in processing and making things as opposed to retail trading are more likely to do likewise. Younger business owners are also more likely to complain than older one.

Turning to objective indicators of access to infrastructure, as opposed to perceptions of it, less than half (46 percent) of the enterprises in the sample survey are directly connected to the Eskom power grid. The connection rate also varies more by business motivation, standing at about 37 percent for businesses owned by survivalists but twice that for those owned by active entrepreneurs. However, there is no evidence that either registration for taxes or licensing correlates with connection to the power grid, although

Table 6.10 Indicators of Access to Infrastructure and Business Space, by Diepsloot Business Owners, 2012

Business owner, by variable	Respondents connected to Eskom[a] power grid (%) (1)	Respondents with Internet access (%) (2)	Respondents lacking storage space (%) (3)	Shipments made using own transport (avg. %) (4)	Standard error of col. (4) (5)
All	0.46	0.05	0.17	10.03	1.31
Business motive					
Survivalist[b]	0.37	0.04	0.17	7.03	1.32
Active entrepreneur[c]	0.73	0.08	0.17	19.19	3.35
Gender					
Male	0.52	0.06	0.17	12.01	1.76
Female	0.33	0.03	0.16	5.89	1.67
National origin					
South African	0.50	0.05	0.16	9.60	1.94
Other African	0.39	0.05	0.17	6.36	1.52
Asian	0.55	0.07	0.21	27.81	6.54
Educational level					
None	0.40	0.02	0.16	2.04	1.41
Primary school	0.40	0.03	0.18	7.04	1.63
Secondary school	0.59	0.08	0.13	18.06	3.03
Vocational training	0.47	0.27	0.33	24.71	10.87
Line of industry					
Making things	0.34	0.16	0.27	16.90	5.07
Repairing or servicing things	0.37	0.07	0.27	18.21	7.35
Personal or household services	0.56	0.05	0.10	—	—
Retail trade in food items	0.47	0.03	0.16	9.26	1.58
Other retail trade	0.42	0.02	0.13	13.11	4.71
Number of persons engaged					
1	0.45	0.03	0.17	13.59	2.36
2	0.47	0.07	0.17	8.48	2.31
3–5	0.45	0.07	0.17	6.94	2.06
More than 5	0.50	0.00	0.08	4.17	4.17
Number of years in business (of the enterprise)					
Less than 5	0.48	0.06	0.16	7.33	1.37
5–10	0.38	0.02	0.17	17.02	3.95
More than 10	0.46	0.05	0.20	12.18	3.52

Note: Results based on responses from 450 total businesses in the sample survey, representing 2,509 Diepsloot businesses counted in the local census. — = not available.

a. Eskom is a South African electricity public utility that generates about 95 percent of the country's electricity.

b. "Survivalist" = Business owner not by active choice but in lieu of preference for a formal sector job.

c. "Active entrepreneur" = Business owner as a matter of active choice, either in the belief one would earn more on one's own or from personal preference.

gender and ethnicity do seem to matter a great deal. Female-owned businesses are less likely to be connected to the public grid, as are businesses owned by people from other African countries. Asian-owned businesses are the best connected, even though connection is far from universal even for that group.

Businesses of the better-educated and younger owners are also more likely to be connected. In terms of business characteristics, larger and younger businesses are more likely to be connected to the public grid. Surprisingly, the connection rate is lower (about one-third) for those making or processing things or in repair businesses than it is for those in other activities.

Access to Serviced Sites

About one-third of the sample also complained about lack of access to serviced business sites. In this case, however, there is relatively little variation by business motive or owner characteristics. The main differences here are by line of activity—those who make or process things being more likely than retail traders to cite lack of access to land. Partly for this reason, vocationally trained business owners are also more likely than others to complain about this issue. There is also a significant difference by nationality: business owners who have migrated from other African countries are 10 percentage points more likely to complain than are either South African business owners or those from Asia.

Access to Transport and the Internet

About 30 percent of all respondents complained about the lack or high cost of transport services, but again the complaint rate here is far higher among those engaged in making things than among those in trade or services. Unlike problems involving access to the power grid and access to space, those involving transport services affect smaller operators more than larger ones. Recent migrants from other African countries also complain more about this problem than do the South Africans and the Asians.

In Diepsloot, businesses need to rely more and more on their own vehicles for making shipments to customers as they grow and become more successful. Over the full sample, only about 10 percent of shipments are reported to involve the use of own transport, but the rate is twice that for active entrepreneurs than for survivalists, as well as for businesses that are better organized and more formal—such as those that keep business records and those with special business bank accounts. Complaints about high transport costs are also much higher for businesses that make, process, or repair things and those whose owners are better educated.

With under 5 percent of the respondents reporting regular use, Internet connectivity is also very low indeed (table 6.10). The key factor in Internet use seems to be education: the rate is three times higher for the vocationally trained relative to those who have no such training. Looking at the same thing a different way, businesses that make, process, or repair things are three times as likely to be connected to the Internet as those in services. Use is also significantly higher among active entrepreneurs than among survivalists, in larger business than smaller ones, in younger businesses than older ones, and among men than among women.

Access to Serviced Sites

About one-third of the sample also complained about lack of access to serviced business sites. In this case, however, there is relatively little variation by business motive or owner characteristics. The main differences here are by line of activity—those who make or process things being more likely than retail traders to cite lack of access to land. Partly for this reason, vocationally trained business owners are also more likely than others to complain about this issue. There is also a significant difference by nationality: business owners who have migrated from other African countries are 10 percentage points more likely to complain than are either South African business owners or those from Asia.

Access to Business Space for Storage Facilities

Some 17 percent of respondents reported that they were unable to build up as much inventory as they would like to for lack of storage space. The gravity of the problem did not differ much by business motive but was much higher for those who make, process, or repair things (27 percent of whom report shortage of space) than those in retail trade or personal services. Registered and licensed businesses were also more likely to report a space shortage, as were Asian enterprises.

Governance Issues: Crime and Regulations

Although reported losses due to theft and robbery as a share of sales revenue are not high by the standards of a developing country, some 45 percent of respondents thought of crime as an obstacle to their business activities (table 6A.10). Here also there were substantial differences between ethnic groups and along lines of activity. Asian business owners were more likely to complain of the problem, and they reported higher revenue losses from crime than did business owners of other national origins, as did those who make or process things relative to traders.

Respondents complained less about regulatory requirements than about crime (figure 6.9). Still, regulatory and compliance issues concerned a significant number of them. About 15 percent of business owners thought that excessive regulation of business transactions and trade was getting in their way. This is not high by the standard of surveys in similar situations in other countries, although the complaint rate against permit and licensing requirements (about one in five respondents) was about average by regional (Sub-Saharan Africa) standards.

Here are some of the differences that stand out within the sample: First, better-educated business owners and those who make or process things were more likely than other business owners to complain of excessive regulation and were more likely to report being required by ward councilors to obtain business permits. Second, businesses were also more likely to report having needed permits from government agencies or local councilors as they grew and became more established. Third, African business owners—indigenous as well as migrants from other African countries—were more likely than Asian business owners to report having needed permits from ward councilors and civic organizations, but they were also less likely to complain of excessive regulation.

Underdevelopment of Indigenous Business Networks

Informal entrepreneurial networks are often considered to be a critical component of the business environment of micro and small enterprises in that they can help mitigate some of the investment climate problems. It is therefore interesting that the Diepsloot sample survey results suggest that these networks are not as well developed among South Africans as they are for those from other countries.

Specifically, compared with migrants from Asia and other African countries, self-employed South Africans in Diepsloot are significantly less likely to have close relatives and close friends working in the same or some other line of business, either within Diepsloot or anywhere elsewhere in South Africa (figure 6.10). Eighty percent of self-employed migrants from Asia and 72 percent of those from other African countries have at least one other relative in business within South Africa. By contrast, only 55 percent of self-employed South Africans have relatives who are also in business in the country. The percentage of Asian business owners in Diepsloot who have relatives in business within Diepsloot itself is 71 percent, compared with 62 percent of self-employed migrants from other African countries and 46 percent of indigenous South African business owners.

Moreover, among the self-employed who do have relatives in business, the number of such relatives is higher for Asians and African migrants than for South Africans. The median number of relatives working in business within Diepsloot is zero for South Africans, one for other Africans, and three for Asians. The median number of relatives in businesses in South Africa as a whole is one for South Africans, three for other Africans, and six for Asians.

A second measure of the extent of business networking in Diepsloot is that less than one in five of the self-employed in the settlement belong to *stokvels*.[2] Half of those who are members of a *stokvel* have used that association to finance working capital or fixed investment. In addition, South Africans do not seem to have relationships with their primary suppliers that are as durable as those among the other two ethnic groups. South Africans are also less likely than Asians, although more likely than other Africans, to belong to a bulk-buying group.

Figure 6.10 Indicators of Business Networking by the Self-Employed in Diepsloot, 2012

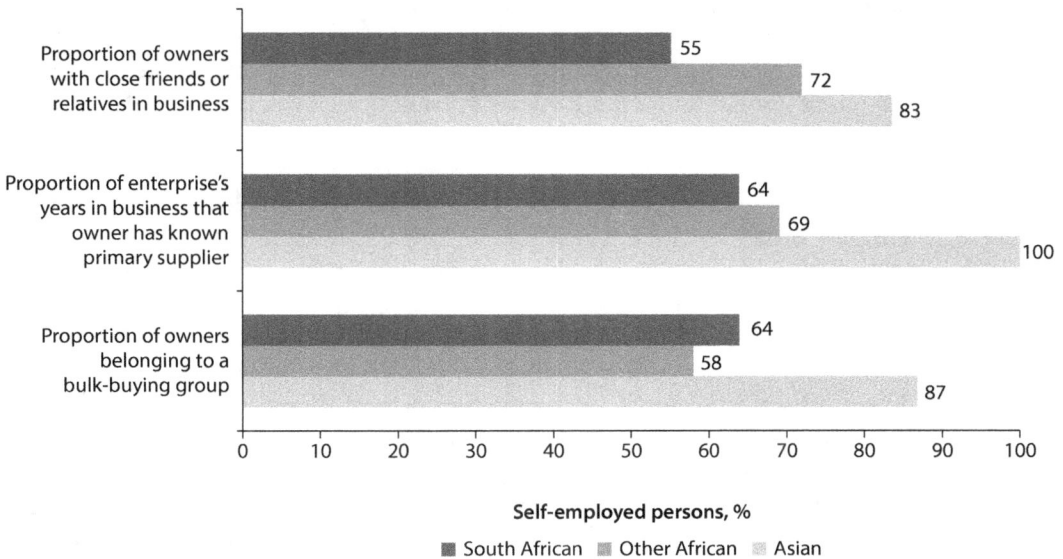

Self-employed persons, %

■ South African ■ Other African ■ Asian

Note: Results based on responses from 450 total businesses in the sample survey. Results considered representative of the 2,509 Diepsloot businesses counted in the local census.

Conclusions

This chapter described the main characteristics of business enterprises in the township of Diepsloot and assessed the growth and job creation potential of these enterprises. A firm-level survey conducted for this report was used for the purpose.

Survey results confirmed that the vast majority of the self-employed in the township are "survivalists": people who run businesses from residential premises but not by active choice, as they would much rather have formal sector jobs.[3] Diepsloot firms are also mostly informal, new, and micro-size— with only 10 percent of the firms registered for tax purposes, more than half coming into being after 2006, almost half being run by only the owner with no employee, and over three-quarters requiring less than R 5,000 as start-up capital. Therefore, most Diepsloot firms belong to the informal traditional economy described in chapter 2. Foreign nationals have an over-sized presence: while making up just 19 percent of the township's population (as further discussed in chapter 7), they own and run almost half of Diepsloot's businesses.

At the same time, the chapter also found evidence of a rising class of active entrepreneurs who are profitably running growth-oriented, employment-generating businesses, with the potential of doing so on an even larger scale. A high proportion of these are in processing activities or in construction, welding, and furniture making. These growth-oriented firms—that are in the mold of the informal modernizing economy mentioned in chapter 2—exhibit relatively high rates of return to fixed capital and attract more technically skilled entrepreneurs relative to retail trade and household services firms, suggesting their potential for future growth under more favorable conditions involving lower risk perceptions of townships by outsiders and fewer and less binding investment climate constraints.

The most widely reported investment climate constraints among Diepsloot business owners include fear of crime, lack of access to Eskom's power grid, shortage of space and serviced business sites, high transport costs, and lack of access to formal finance. Concerns around excessive licensing requirements and other regulatory burdens also seem to preoccupy many township business owners, although the numbers here are within the conventional ranges. The levels of educational attainment and past work experience also appear to shape success among business owners in Diepsloot. Membership in informal entrepreneurial networks is an important part of businesses' coping mechanisms against these constraints. The firm-level survey, however, found business connections among South Africans to be less dense than those among foreign migrants.

It is important to emphasize that this assessment of the investment climate constraints is based on existing business owners' perceptions. Perhaps more relevant are the set of issues that prevent people from successfully starting a business in the first place. That analysis, important as it is, cannot be deduced from the results of this report and will require deeper research work.

The existing situation—of townships functioning largely as dormitories—cannot be an optimal one, especially where unemployment and economic exclusion levels are so high. Policy makers would do well to focus attention on the identified business-climate constraints faced by township residents. The policy framework would need to extend beyond these immediate constraints, however, to also tackle the following issues:

- *Near absence of supply-chain linkages* between the township firms and the formal-economy firms that operate on significantly larger scales.
- *Low effective demand in the townships*, a function partly of their high unemployment and relatively low income levels and partly of general demand preferences that are skewed toward goods produced and sold in the formal economy.
- *Adverse perceptions of risks and security issues* that seem to keep outsiders from viewing townships as a places for commerce.

Turning the situation around is a tall order. It will require a major push on a broad range of policy areas inside and outside the township, a better understanding of consumer preferences, and an understanding of whether there are specific areas where strengthening of supply chains within the township makes economic sense.

Annex 6A: Detailed Data on Diepsloot's Investment Climate

Table 6A.1 Distribution of South African SMEs, by Business Activity and Settlement Type, 2010

SME activity	Distribution by settlement type (%)				
	Urban formal	Urban informal	Tribal area	Rural formal	All
Making or processing things	21.5	23.5	31.2	31.2	24.8
Retail trade	42.6	55.9	51.2	58.9	47.1
Services	35.9	20.6	17.5	9.9	28.2
Total	100	100	100	100	100
Number of enterprises	3,389	472	1,370	445	5,676

Source: FinMark Trust 2011.
Note: SMEs = small and medium enterprises (5–100 employees).

Table 6A.2 Distribution of South African SMEs, by Business Activity Site and Settlement Type, 2010

Business activity site	Distribution by settlement type (%)				
	Urban formal	Urban informal	Tribal area	Rural formal	All
Nonresidential building	8.4	1.9	2.0	2.9	5.9
Residence or farmstead	72.7	70.6	73.1	81.0	73.3
Fixed nonresidential site	2.4	1.7	2.2	2.0	2.2
No fixed site	16.5	25.7	22.7	14.0	18.6
Total	100	100	100	100	100
Number of enterprises	3,367	470	1,342	443	5,622

Source: FinMark Trust 2011.
Note: SMEs = small and medium enterprises.

Table 6A.3 Distribution of South African SMEs, by Financial Record Maintenance and Settlement Type, 2010

Percent

Settlement type	Maintain financial records	Use professionals for the purpose
Urban formal	54.0	15.9
Urban informal	37.5	1.2
Tribal area	37.8	2.3
Rural formal	36.4	9.9
Total	47.3	11.9

Source: FinMark Trust 2011.
Note: SMEs = small and medium enterprises.

Table 6A.4 Distribution of South African SMEs, by Number of Employees and Settlement Type, 2010

Percent

| Number of employees | Distribution by settlement type | | | | |
	Urban formal	Urban informal	Tribal area	Rural formal	All
1	58.5	71.6	78.7	71.5	65.5
2	15.0	12.7	13.4	11.7	14.2
3–5	19.7	14.8	6.3	12.4	15.5
More than 5	6.9	0.9	1.6	4.5	4.9
Total	100	100	100	100	100
Number of enterprises	3,389	472	1,370	445	5,676

Source: FinMark Trust 2011.
Note: SMEs = small and medium enterprises.

Table 6A.5 Distribution South African SMEs, by Amount of Start-Up Capital and Settlement Type, 2010

Percent

| Start-up capital (R) | Distribution by settlement type | | | | |
	Urban formal	Urban informal	Tribal area	Rural formal	All types
100 or less	22.8	22.4	27.0	30.8	24.5
101–500	16.6	28.9	23.8	20.8	19.8
501–1,000	10.8	13.1	13.6	13.3	11.9
1,001–2,000	7.9	12.6	9.2	6.4	8.5
2,001–5,000	11.7	9.5	10.4	9.2	11.0
5,001–10,000	9.5	5.2	7.0	6.1	8.2
10,001–20,000	6.1	3.1	3.7	4.4	5.1
20,001–50,000	6.6	4.4	3.5	4.7	5.5
50,001–100,000	3.9	0.5	1.2	2.2	2.8
More than 100,001	4.2	0.3	0.5	1.9	2.7
Total	100	100	100	100	100

Source: FinMark Trust 2011.
Note: SMEs = small and medium enterprises; R = rand.

Table 6A.6 Distribution of South African SMEs, by Owner's Educational Level and Settlement Type, 2010

Percent

| Owner's completed education | Distribution by settlement type | | | | |
	Urban formal	Urban informal	Tribal area	Rural formal	All
None	4.8	9.3	18.1	19.3	9.6
Primary school	42.3	62.1	56.4	52.6	48.2
Secondary school	33.4	25.4	21.8	22.2	29.1
Apprenticeship	2.6	0.0	0.6	0.4	1.7
Tertiary education	16.8	3.2	3.1	5.4	11.5
Total	100	100	100	100	100
Number of enterprises	3,389	472	1,372	445	5,676

Source: FinMark Trust 2011.
Note: SMEs = small and medium enterprises.

Table 6A.7 Marginal Effects of a Probit Model of a Diepsloot Business Reported by Owner to Be Credit-Constrained

	(1)	(2)	(3)	(4)
Line of industry or activity				
Repair services	n.a.	n.a.	−0.078 (0.90)	−0.072 (0.81)
Personal or household services	n.a.	n.a.	0.117 (1.03)	0.134 (1.15)
Retail trade in food items	n.a.	n.a.	0.066 (0.98)	0.070 (1.07)
Other retail trade	n.a.	n.a.	0.017 (0.19)	0.025 (0.28)
Scale = Number of persons engaged				
2	n.a.	n.a.	−0.082 (2.26)*	−0.091 (2.59)**
3–5	n.a.	n.a.	−0.158 (5.21)**	−0.162 (5.58)**
More than 5	n.a.	n.a.	−0.029 (0.23)	−0.041 (0.34)
Years in business (for the enterprise)				
Young = 5–10 years in business	n.a.	n.a.	n.a.	0.074 (1.23)
Established = 10 years or more in business	n.a.	n.a.	n.a.	−0.039 (0.68)
Business motive				
Active entrepreneur[a]	n.a.	−0.070 (1.59)	−0.070 (1.51)	−0.073 (1.61)
Owner's demographic characteristics				
Female	−0.037 (0.84)	−0.042 (0.94)	−0.052 (1.09)	−0.046 (0.98)
Schooling				
Primary school completed	−0.010 (283.88)**	−0.010 (271.99)**	−0.012 (360.78)**	−0.021 (0.33)
Secondary school completed	−0.018 (495.66)**	−0.005 (107.96)**	0.001 (265.27)**	−0.001 (0.02)
Vocational school trainee	0.140 (244.76)**	0.146 (246.64)**	0.141 (294.32)**	0.124 (0.83)
National origin				
Non-South African African	−0.031 (121.72)**	−0.031 (125.83)**	−0.025 (1367.24)**	−0.021 (298.43)**
Asian	0.092 (509.37)**	0.090 (539.32)**	0.128 (145.96)**	0.141 (258.77)**
Observations	442	442	439	438
Log likelihood	−236.9	−235.77	−225.5	223.79
LR chi2(k)	8.45	10.76	27.31	30.21
Pseudo R^2	0.02	0.02	0.057	0.06

Note: Dependent variable: the owner of the business considers access to credit to be a constraint to its growth. Omitted values of dummy variables: industry = "making things"; number of persons employed = one person; years in business = less than 5; business motive = "survivalist"; schooling = no schooling grade completed; owner's age = under 20 years; national origin: South African. Absolute value of z-statistics in parentheses. Results based on responses from 450 total businesses in the sample survey, representing 2,509 Diepsloot businesses counted in the local census.
a. "Active entrepreneur" = Business owner as a matter of active choice. "Survivalist" = Business owner not by active choice. n.a. = not applicable.
Significance level: * = 5 percent, ** = 1 percent.

Table 6A.8 Reported Share of Credit in Working Capital of Diepsloot Business Owners, 2012

Business owner, by variable	Share of credit in working capital (%)	Standard error	Number of responses
All	41.56	2.07	450
Business motive			
Survivalist[a]	42.86	2.39	340
Active entrepreneur[b]	37.54	4.08	110
Gender			
Male	40.77	2.47	306
Female	43.24	3.78	144
National origin			
South African	44.35	3.17	208
Other African	38.38	3.04	192
Asian	40.71	6.46	42
Educational level			
None	40.19	4.85	81
Primary school	45.92	3.04	219
Secondary school	36.79	3.63	135
Vocational training	28.33	9.83	15
Line of industry			
Making things	39.11	6.64	44
Repairing or servicing things	39.83	8.10	30
Personal or household services	47.56	6.86	41
Retail trade in food items	40.26	2.62	287
Other retail trade	46.24	6.03	45
Number of persons engaged			
1	40.49	3.26	179
2	45.58	3.73	138
3–5	36.41	3.97	121
More than 5	63.33	12.45	12
Number of years in business (of the enterprise)			
Less than 5	40.57	2.59	284
5–10	44.80	4.71	86
More than 10	40.87	5.06	79

Note: Results based on responses from 450 total businesses in the sample survey, representing 2,509 Diepsloot businesses counted in the local census.

a. "Survivalist" = Business owner not by active choice but in lieu of preference for a formal sector job.

b. "Active entrepreneur" = Business owner as a matter of active choice, either in the belief one would earn more on one's own or from personal preference.

**Table 6A.9 Reported Share of Fixed Investment Financed by Borrowing from
Formal Sources, by Diepsloot Business Owners, 2012**

Business owners, by variable	Share of borrowing in capital expenditure (%)	Standard error	Number of responses
All	4.22	0.87	450
Business motive			
Survivalist[a]	4.62	1.06	340
Active entrepreneur[b]	3.00	1.41	110
Gender			
Male	4.71	1.15	306
Female	3.18	1.22	144
National origin			
South African	3.64	1.21	208
Other African	4.17	1.29	192
Asian	5.79	3.45	42
Educational level			
None	0.62	0.48	81
Primary school	7.11	1.63	219
Secondary school	1.28	0.83	135
Vocational training	8.00	6.70	15
Line of industry			
Making things	4.55	3.18	44
Repairing or servicing things	1.23	1.23	30
Personal or household services	5.41	3.15	41
Retail trade in food items	4.32	1.09	287
Other retail trade	4.44	3.11	45
Number of persons engaged			
1	0.22	0.16	179
2	4.34	1.66	138
3–5	9.60	2.42	121
More than 5	8.33	8.33	12
Number of years in business (of the enterprise)			
Less than 5	3.08	0.96	284
5–10	7.17	2.55	86
More than 10	3.89	1.88	79

Note: Results based on responses from 450 total businesses in the sample survey, representing 2,509 Diepsloot businesses counted in the local census.
a. "Survivalist" = Business owner not by active choice but in lieu of preference for a formal sector job.
b. "Active entrepreneur" = Business owner as a matter of active choice, either in the belief one would earn more on one's own or from personal preference.

Table 6A.10 Indicators of the Incidence and Perception of Crime among Diepsloot Business Owners, 2012

Business owner, by variable	Respondents identifying crime as a business obstacle (%)	Reported instances of theft at business premises (avg. no.)	Standard error of col. (2)	Loss of revenue due to theft and robbery (avg. no. with revenue loss)	Standard error of col. (4)
	(1)	(2)	(3)	(4)	(5)
All	0.44	0.70	0.13	0.24	0.10
Business motive					
Survivalist[a]	0.46	0.74	0.17	0.11	0.03
Active entrepreneur[b]	0.40	0.60	0.16	0.64	0.41
Gender					
Male	0.45	0.89	0.19	0.12	0.04
Female	0.43	0.31	0.08	0.47	0.31
National origin					
South African	0.41	0.35	0.07	0.35	0.22
Other African	0.46	0.90	0.29	0.09	0.04
Asian	0.55	1.50	0.41	0.33	0.13
Educational level					
None	0.46	0.99	0.58	0.56	0.47
Primary school	0.48	0.67	0.15	0.11	0.04
Secondary school	0.39	0.66	0.15	0.28	0.19
Vocational training	0.40	0.13	0.09	0.02	0.01
Line of industry					
Making things	0.68	0.51	0.20	0.02	0.01
Repairing or servicing things	0.43	1.17	0.80	0.38	0.27
Personal or household services	0.46	0.39	0.16	0.03	0.02
Retail trade in food items	0.42	0.71	0.18	0.30	0.16
Other retail trade	0.38	0.84	0.27	0.07	0.03
Number of persons engaged					
1	0.40	0.39	0.08	0.18	0.14
2	0.49	1.09	0.37	0.38	0.28
3–5	0.44	0.78	0.24	0.12	0.07
More than 5	0.55	0.33	0.14	0.54	0.37
Number of years in business (of the enterprise)					
Less than 5	0.43	0.65	0.18	0.16	0.09
5–10	0.51	0.65	0.15	0.16	0.06
More than 10	0.43	0.96	0.37	0.60	0.49

Note: Results based on responses from 450 total businesses in the sample survey. Results considered representative of the 2,509 Diepsloot businesses counted in the local census.

a. "Survivalist" = Business owner not by active choice but in lieu of preference for a formal sector job.

b. "Active entrepreneur" = Business owner as a matter of active choice, either in the belief one would earn more on one's own or from personal preference.

Table 6A.11 Indicators of the State of Business and Trade Regulation Cited by Diepsloot Business Owners, 2012

Percent

Business owner, by variable	Respondents complaining of excessive regulation	Respondents complaining of licensing requirement	Respondents complaining of permit requirement from local officials
All	0.15	0.21	0.22
Business motive			
Survivalist[a]	0.13	0.22	0.22
Active entrepreneur[b]	0.24	0.16	0.22
Gender			
Male	0.17	0.20	0.21
Female	0.13	0.23	0.22
National origin			
South African	0.13	0.18	0.23
Other African	0.17	0.23	0.23
Asian	0.21	0.26	0.10
Educational level			
None	0.14	0.23	0.19
Primary school	0.14	0.22	0.24
Secondary school	0.17	0.16	0.17
Vocational training	0.33	0.33	0.46
Line of industry			
Making things	0.34	0.32	0.14
Repairing or servicing things	0.13	0.20	0.24
Personal or household services	0.12	0.32	0.18
Retail trade in food items	0.13	0.17	0.23
Other retail trade	0.18	0.23	0.23
Number of persons engaged			
1	0.20	0.23	0.17
2	0.15	0.25	0.22
3–5	0.10	0.13	0.28
More than 5	0.08	0.17	0.33
Number of years in business (of the enterprise)			
Less than 5	0.16	0.20	0.21
5–10	0.19	0.17	0.27
More than 10	0.09	0.25	0.16

Note: Results based on responses from 450 total businesses in the sample survey. Results considered representative of the 2,509 Diepsloot businesses counted in the local census.

a. "Survivalist" = Business owner not by active choice but in lieu of preference for a formal sector job.

b. "Active entrepreneur" = Business owner as a matter of active choice, either in the belief one would earn more on one's own or from personal preference.

Notes

1. Eskom, a South African electricity public utility, generates about 95 percent of the electricity used in South Africa and is the largest producer of electricity in Africa as a whole.

2. *Stokvels* (originating from the term "stock fairs") are a local name (more generally known as ROSCAs) for a traditional form of banking whereby a group of people agree to contribute at defined intervals to a fund that distributes the contributions to group members on a rotating basis.

3. It should be stressed that entry into "survivalist" entrepreneurship is by no means cost-less and is likely to occur against significant barriers (such as lack of finance for start-up capital) that could be prohibitive to some members of the labor force who would remain unemployed as a result. Indeed, the household survey described in chapter 7 shows that about 30 percent of Diepsloot's labor force is unemployed. Although it is quite possible that not all the unemployed would want to start a business even if they could, it is more likely that at least some of them are deterred from self-employment by factors that are beyond their control. The distinction between survivalists and those who are active entrepreneurs as a matter of positive choice can nonetheless be useful in certain settings.

References

Financial Mail. 2011. "Spaza Shops: Battered from All Sides." November 11.

FinMark Trust. 2011. *FinScope South Africa Small Business Survey 2010*. Survey report, Johannesburg. http://www.finmark.org.za/publication/finscope-south-africa-small-business-survey-2010-report.

CHAPTER 7

Income and Expenditure Patterns in Diepsloot

Phindile Ngwenya and Precious Zikhali

Household-Level View of a Township Economy

Tapping into the full economic potential of townships and informal settlements (T&IS) requires a systematic understanding of their socioeconomic dynamics. This chapter contributes to such an understanding using socioeconomic indicators from a representative household survey from the township of Diepsloot, which box 7.1 discusses in detail. The survey investigated the demographic profile, income composition, income sources, and consumption and expenditure patterns of Diepsloot residents. These indicators situate Diepsloot within the broader national context explored in the chapter 3 analysis of national-level household surveys. It also adds a quantitative dimension to the qualitative assessment in chapter 5.

The chapter seeks to inform the policy debate aimed at stimulating the economies of T&IS by promoting an informal modernizing economy (IME) (as defined in the analytical framework discussed in chapter 2). In part, development of the township economy relies on the strength of the demand for township-produced goods and services. Demand will naturally be determined by not only the purchasing power of the township households and other urban consumers but also by their preferences for goods and services produced in townships over those from outside. To deepen the understanding of these facets, this chapter measures consumer preferences in Diepsloot to examine how growing income levels in the township are likely to affect the demand for goods and services in Diepsloot.

The rest of the chapter is organized as follows: The next section profiles the demographic and social characteristics of Diepsloot households and compares those characteristics with those of other T&IS in South Africa. After that, we describe Diepsloot households' sources of income, household expenditure patterns, and how these differ between income groups. Our subsequent estimate of expenditure elasticities for different commodity types (goods, services, and expenditures grouped by whether they were produced or bought within or

Box 7.1 Survey Sampling Methodology and Data Collection

The household survey was the third phase of surveys to quantify the contours of Diepsloot's population and economy. (The first phase was a business census to generate a database of businesses, which became the sampling frame for the second-phase enterprise survey, both of which are covered in chapter 6.)

The survey team selected a representative sample of 800 households across Diepsloot through the following multistage, simple random sampling framework:

1. Based on aerial photographs and on-site observations, the total area of Diepsloot was subdivided into 16 zones of approximately the same number of dwellings to take housing densities into account.
2. Two random starting points were selected within each of the 16 zones.
3. Specific routes were then delineated from each of the 32 starting points to make sure that the routes did not intersect with one another.
4. Fieldworkers selected every 10th household for the survey along the delineated routes, with a total of 25 households interviewed along each of the 32 routes. (If any dwelling unit on a particular lot was identified as part of the main household on that lot, it was disregarded and counted as a separate household for counting to the next "10th" household.)

In all, 30 enumerators participated in the three phases of primary data collection, 15 of whom conducted the household survey, using a survey instrument adapted from the those of the national Income and Expenditure Surveys. The enumerators conducted personal interviews of household heads and recorded the responses on personal digital assistants (PDAs) into which the questionnaire was loaded. This method made data entry, cleaning, and editing easier and faster.

outside Diepsloot) can then establish the likely secondary impacts of household income growth on Diepsloot's economic activity. The concluding section summarizes the main findings and discusses policy implications.

Demographic and Social Profile of Diepsloot Households

Demographics

One of Diepsloot's most distinctive traits—its relative proximity to economic hubs—creates an undeniable reality: it's a magnet for work seekers. It is not surprising therefore that the townships has attracted a population whose working-age component (70 percent) is almost three percentage points higher than the working-age percentage of the overall T&IS population in national surveys (further discussed in chapter 3). Like the rest of South Africa, Diepsloot's population is young, with an average age of around 25 years. With young and old dependency ratios of 38.7 percent and 1.3 percent, respectively, the burden of Diepsloot's productive population is more on raising children than on caring for the elderly. Also consistent with the national statistics, the gender composition of the Diepsloot population is fairly balanced. And, as is typical for T&IS in South Africa, Diepsloot lacks racial diversity, with about 97 percent of residents being black, as shown along with other summary statistics in table 7.1.

Unfortunately, formal education and training are lacking among Diepsloot's population, as table 7.1 shows. Although an estimated 62 percent of its residents attained some postprimary education, 13 percent have no formal education,

Table 7.1 Summary Demographic Statistics for Diepsloot, 2012

Variable	Description	Proportion of Diepsloot residents (%)
Household-based businesses		
Dwelling unit as business	No. using household dwelling unit as a business	11.42
Gender		
Male	=1 if male	49.24
Male adults	=1 if male over 15 years of age	34.69
Female adults	=1 if female over 15 years of age	35.58
Age structure		
Working age	=1 if 14–65 years of age	70.47
Youth	=1 if 15–24 years of age, inclusive	19.08
Young dependents	=1 if younger than 15 years of age	27.24
Old dependents	=1 if older than 64 years of age	0.93
Black	=1 if African/black	96.95
Other race	=1 if nonblack	3.05
Education		
No education	=1 if no formal education	13.02
Primary school not completed	=1 if started but did not complete primary school	16.61
Primary school completed	=1 if completed primary school	5.41
Secondary school not completed	=1 if started but did not complete secondary school	32.25
Secondary school completed	=1 if completed secondary school	23.37
Tertiary education	=1 if started but did not complete OR completed university or tertiary training	1.31
Vocational training	=1 if vocational training and other	4.69
Do not know	=1 if education level not known	3.34
Education of those 7–25 years of age		
No education	=1 if no formal education	2.04
Primary school not completed	=1 if started but did not complete primary school	26.24
Primary school completed	=1 if completed primary school	5.39
Secondary school not completed	=1 if started but did not complete secondary school	36.30
Secondary school completed	=1 if completed secondary school	21.28
Tertiary education	=1 if started but did not complete OR completed university or tertiary training	2.04
Vocational training	=1 if vocational training and other	4.37
Do not know	=1 if education level not known	2.34

Note: Results based on a representative sample of 800 households, stratified by geographical zone across Diepsloot. The survey instrument was adapted from the instruments used in the national Income and Expenditure Survey.

16 percent started but did not complete primary school, about 5 percent completed primary school but did not study further, about a third started but did not finish secondary school, and only about a quarter completed secondary school. Only about 6 percent had some form of tertiary education or vocational training. Educational outcomes are improving gradually but unevenly with the current school-age generation (aged 7–25). Only 2 percent of this cohort has not had any formal education, although a large share (26 percent) started but did not complete primary education.

In line with narratives in chapter 5 that suggested that business operations in Diepsloot are closely integrated into the household ecosystems, the survey found that 11 percent of Diepsloot's residents operate some form of business from the household dwelling unit. Females made up an estimated 49.6 percent of those operating home-based businesses.

Labor Market Indicators

Diepsloot's employment rate is 44.1 percent—higher than the rates for the whole country (40.9 percent) and other townships (42.1 percent) but lower than those of the informal settlements (45.6 percent) and other urban settlements (54.7 percent), as shown in table 7.2.[1] Diepsloot's relative proximity to economic hubs implies more and better job and business opportunities than in other townships. This geographical advantage is further reflected in Diepsloot's narrow unemployment rate, which, at 30.2 percent, is lower than that of other T&IS (33.4 percent and 32.6 percent, respectively).[2]

Though still a major concern, youth labor market outcomes are slightly more favorable. The youth unemployment rate in Diepsloot (43.2 percent) is lower than either the national averages or those of T&IS as a whole (50.4 percent and about 61 percent, respectively).[3]

At the same time, the data also reveal a gender bias in labor markets. For one thing, the unemployment rate for males is 15.7 percentage points lower than that of females. For another, the participation rate of males (70 percent) is also

Table 7.2 Labor Market Indicators in Diepsloot (2012) versus National Indicators, by Settlement Type (2011)
Percent

| Indicator | Diepsloot | | | | National | | | |
	Total	Youth (15–24 years)	Male	Female	Total	Urban TS	Urban IS	Other urban
Not economically active	36.9	54.3	30.0	43.4	38.7	31.9	28.1	31.9
Unemployment rate, narrow	30.2	43.2	23.1	38.8	25.0	33.4	32.6	16.0
Labor force participation rate	63.1	45.7	70.0	56.6	54.6	63.2	67.6	65.2
Employment rate	44.1	25.9	53.9	34.6	40.9	42.1	45.6	54.7

Source: National data from Stats SA 2011.
Note: TS = townships; IS = informal settlements. The "narrow" unemployment rate excludes "discouraged workers": working-age people (aged 15–64 years) who were unemployed, wanted to work, and were available for work but who had stopped actively seeking work in the belief that no jobs would be available. The "broad" unemployment rate includes discouraged workers, but data challenges prevented calculation of that indicator.

much higher than that of women (56.6 percent), although this difference partially reflects the fact that some females stay at home to look after their families.

The Diepsloot survey results suggest that completing secondary school is associated with a slightly higher likelihood of employment. As shown in figure 7.1, 44 percent of the employed have completed secondary school compared with the 39 percent of the unemployed.

For those who do work and must pay for transport to work, high transport costs use up substantial percentages of their earnings. The most common

Figure 7.1 Educational Profiles of Diepsloot Adult Population, by Employment Status, 2012
Percent

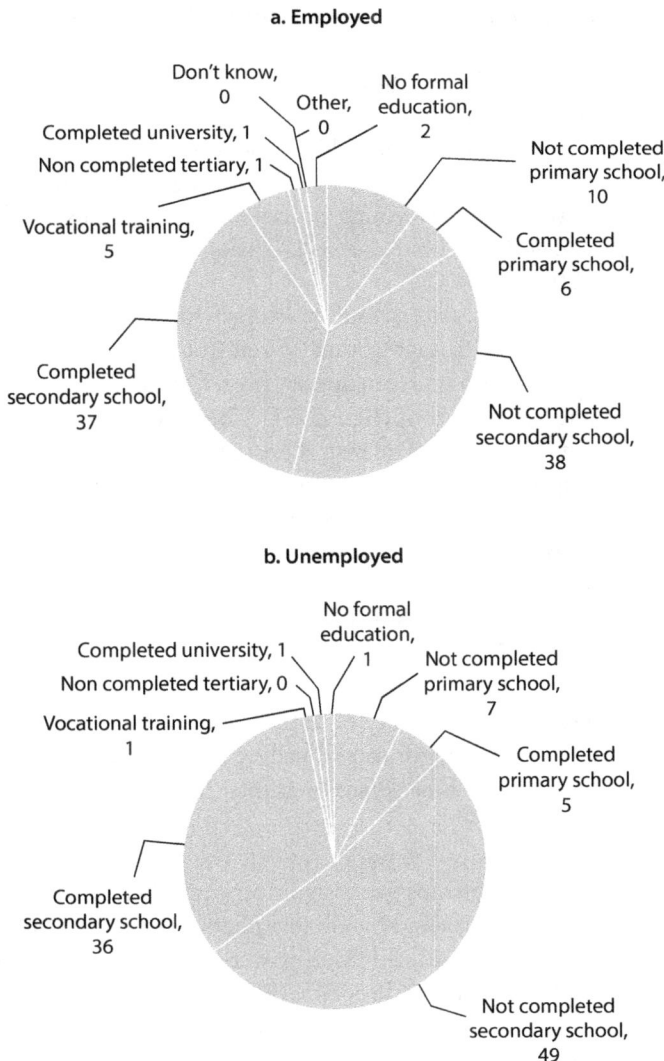

mode of transport to work is the minibus taxi, an expensive option. (No train or bus service exists that would offer a less expensive alternative.) About 57 percent of the employed respondents indicated they had transport costs of R 251–500 per month, while 28 percent spent R 501–1,000 on transport to work (figure 7.2c).

These are high costs, considering that about 38 percent of Diepsloot's employed residents earn less than R 2,500 per month (table 7.3). Moreover, the average total monthly expenditure on transport to work is close to R 507, which is about 17 percent of the average total monthly salary of R 2,938. Because of Diepsloot's relative proximity to places of employment, travel time to work is relatively less onerous for Diepsloot residents than for people in other townships: 57 percent need 30 minutes or less to get to work.

Heads of Households and Support to Nonhousehold Members

An estimated 81 percent of household heads in Diepsloot are of South African nationality. Most households with heads of foreign nationality are Zimbabwean, followed by Mozambicans (figure 7.3).

Overall, 60 percent of the household heads are male, consistent with the national average of 60.6 percent in 2011. The average household size of 2.96 is reasonable given the relatively young household heads, whose average age is 36.8 years. The average household size in Diepsloot is lower than the national average of 3.65 in 2011.

Around 31 percent of Diepsloot households provide full or partial support to nonhousehold members. A disaggregation of remittances by destination shows that 64 percent of those who receive support from Diepsloot households live in South Africa but outside Diepsloot (figure 7.4). This is followed by people living in other countries, at 28 percent. The rest, 8 percent, goes to Diepsloot residents. The presence of support to other countries is in tandem with the fact that 19 percent of household heads are of foreign origin, which means they might be sending remittances back to their countries of origin. In fact, close to 70 percent of persons who live in other countries and receive support from Diepsloot households get this support from households headed by foreign nationals.

Housing

Diepsloot is characterized by a variety of both formal and informal accommodation. At a combined 47 percent, informal dwelling units—loosely termed "shacks" and consisting of both shacks in backyards and those not in backyards—dominate housing in Diepsloot (table 7.4).

The prevalence of shacks in Diepsloot reflects the broader housing dynamics in South African T&IS. Townships get a significant number of in-migrants from mainly rural areas who are attracted by job prospects in economic hubs as well as the possibility of receiving subsidized housing mainly through the government's Reconstruction and Development Program (RDP). More often than not, new households live in informal housing (shacks) while waiting for an RDP house or a lot with a title deed.

Figure 7.2 Transport Mode, Work Travel Time, and Travel Expense of Diepsloot Residents, 2012

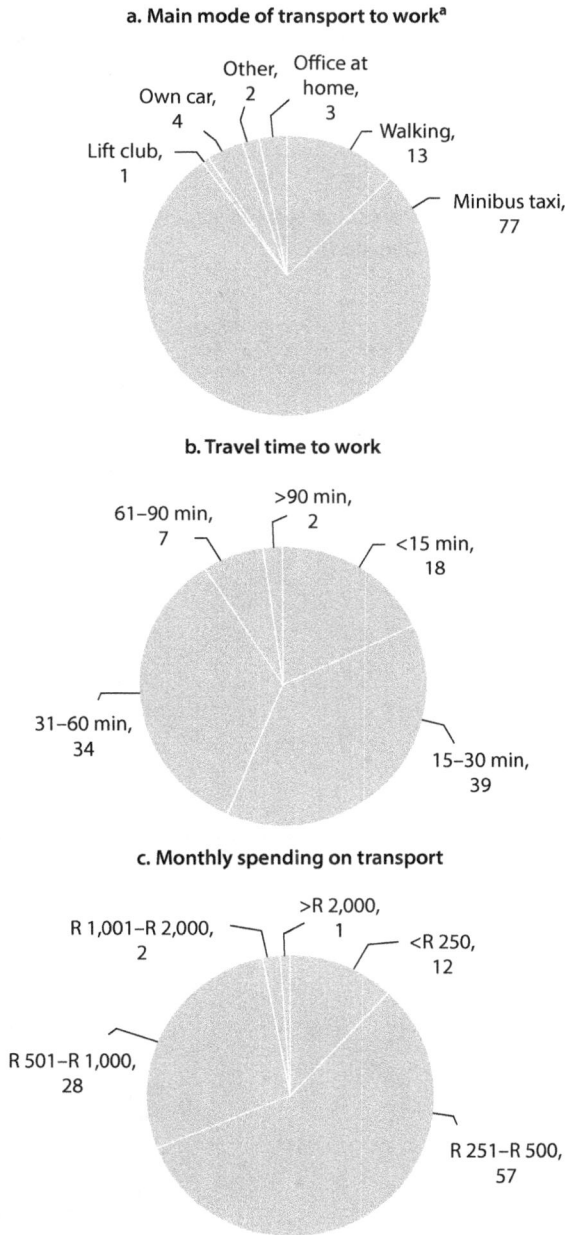

Percent

a. Main mode of transport to work[a]

Other, 2

Own car, 4

Office at home, 3

Lift club, 1

Walking, 13

Minibus taxi, 77

b. Travel time to work

>90 min, 2

61–90 min, 7

<15 min, 18

31–60 min, 34

15–30 min, 39

c. Monthly spending on transport

R 1,001–R 2,000, 2

>R 2,000, 1

<R 250, 12

R 501–R 1,000, 28

R 251–R 500, 57

a. A "lift club" is an informal ride-sharing arrangement that enables commuters to share rides and costs with others who live in the same general area and are traveling to and from the same destination. "Other" modes of transport include bicycle or motorcycle, bus, and train (the latter two often in combination with a minibus taxi to reach the bus or train station).

Table 7.3 Monthly Wages and Salaries of Diepsloot Residents, 2012

Monthly wage or salary (R)	Percentage of Diepsloot residents
<1,000	5.9
1,000–2,499	32.4
2,500–5,000	50.4
>5,000	11.3

Note: R = rand.

Figure 7.3 Nationality of Foreign Household Heads in Diepsloot, 2012

Percent

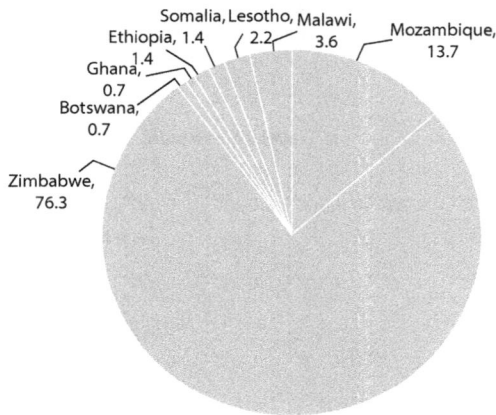

Figure 7.4 Location of People Receiving Support from Diepsloot Households, 2012

Percent

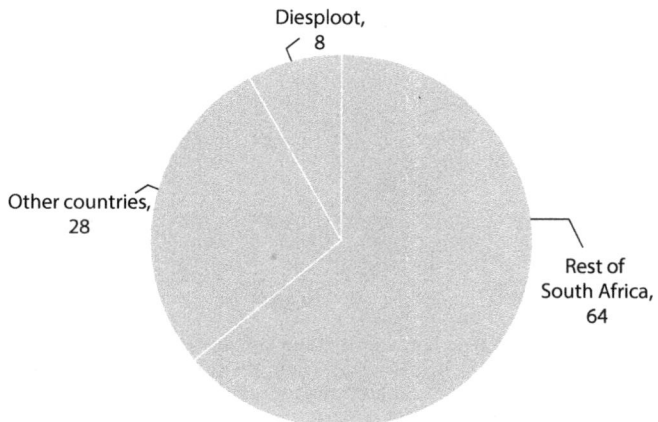

Table 7.4 Main Dwelling Units, by Type, and Connection to Main Electricity Supply in Diepsloot, 2012

Percent

Main dwelling type	Share of all main dwelling units	Share of all main dwelling units connected to mains electricity supply
Dwelling or brick structure on a separate lot or yard	34.97	48.96
Informal dwelling or shack in a backyard	24.15	1.04
Informal dwelling or shack not in a backyard, such as in an informal or squatter settlement	22.64	8.59
Townhouse, cluster house, or semidetached house	4.91	5.99
Traditional dwelling, hut, or structure made of traditional material	4.65	18.49
Dwelling, flat, or room in a backyard	3.40	2.86
Room or flatlet, servants' quarters, or granny flat	1.64	0.01
Caravan or tent	0.13	5.99
Other	3.52	8.07

Access to Electricity

Significant gaps exist in access to services such as electricity: only 48 percent of households have a connection to the mains electricity supply (table 7.4). This is comparable to 51.7 percent for informal settlements but significantly lower than the national estimate of 82 percent and the 80.6 percent for townships. As expected, almost half of the households connected to the electricity supply mains live in brick structures, and only about 10 percent of them live in shacks—the latter often with illegal connections to a nearby house.

Dwelling Ownership

Most households (62 percent) indicated that they "own" their main dwelling unit (figure 7.5). Of these, 98 percent have paid off their main dwelling units. The statistics seem exaggerated, however, and need to be interpreted with caution. In particular, the households living in backyard shacks (shacks built on the same property as an RDP house or other type of brick structure) might not have formal ownership rights or control over the land on which their shacks stand. Of those households that rent their units, 75 percent indicated that the property owners live in Diepsloot.

Disaggregating dwelling ownership by the household head's nationality, most of the households (65 percent) headed by a South African national own their dwelling unit, which is significantly higher than the 50 percent of households headed by a foreign national. Put another way, households headed by foreign nationals are more likely to rent than those headed by South African nationals. These patterns might point to insecurity of ownership on the part of foreign nationals, who may fear potential dispossession. They may

Figure 7.5 Dwelling Ownership Status of Diepsloot Households, 2012

Percent

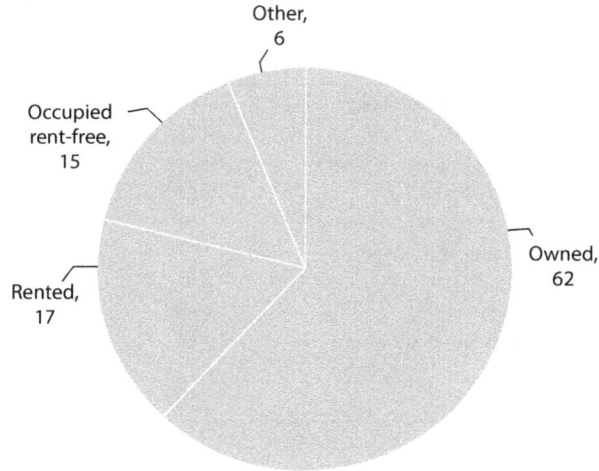

also reflect foreign-born residents' disinclination to invest in housing given their uncertain residency status.

That the household head's nationality matters in terms of dwelling ownership status is also borne out statistically: the Pearson χ^2 (3) and likelihood-ratio χ^2 (3) statistics from the data both reject the null hypothesis of independence between the two variables, as the survey results shown in figure 7.6 reflect.

Gender-related distinctions regarding dwelling ownership are harder to detect (figure 7.7). Intragroup comparisons show that 64 percent of female-headed households own their dwelling units, 11 percent rent, and 19 percent live rent-free. Of the male-headed households, 61 percent own their dwelling units. However, the share of households that rent is significantly larger—and the share living rent-free in someone else's dwelling significantly lower—for men than women.

Sources of Income for Diepsloot Households

A large portion of Diepsloot households' aggregate income comes from salaries and wages (80.7 percent), followed by business expenses (8.3 percent) and social grants and pensions (6.2 percent), as shown in figure 7.8.

Although salaries and wages constitute the largest source of income for all groups, the importance of other income sources varies by income quintile (table 7.5). In general, the contribution of salaries and wages to total regular income increases as total income increases. Notably, social grants and pensions are an important source of income for the bottom 20 percent, accounting for almost 22 percent of all regularly received income.

Figure 7.6 Dwelling Ownership Status by Nationality of Household Head in Diepsloot, 2012

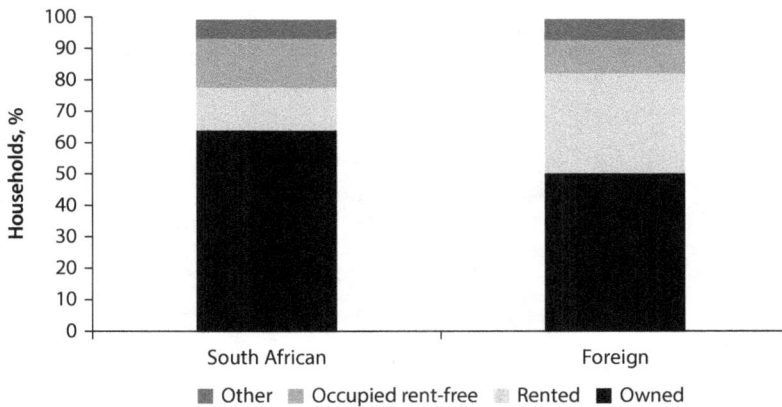

Note: Pearson chi²(3) = 31.4725, Pr = 0.000. Likelihood-ratio chi²(3) = 27.8289, Pr = 0.000. Cramér's V = 0.1985.

Figure 7.7 Dwelling Ownership Status by Gender of Household Head in Diepsloot, 2012

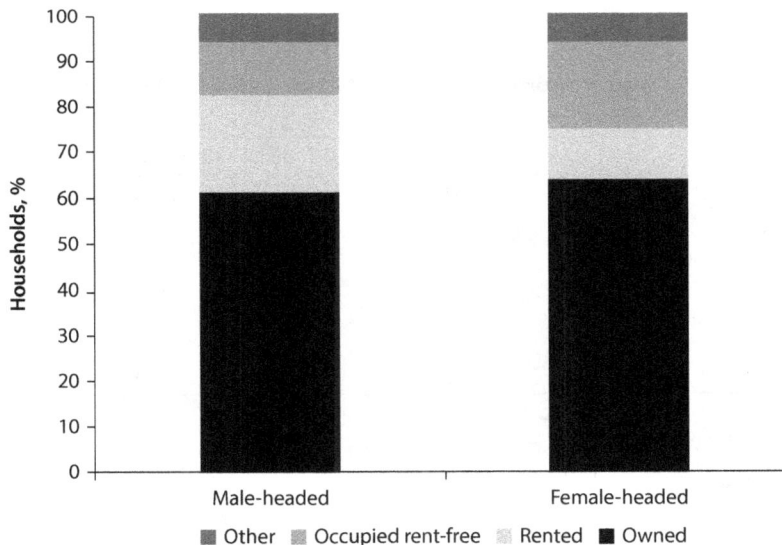

Household Expenditure Patterns for Diepsloot

Broad Overview
Household consumption patterns were analyzed on three dimensions: the type of commodities purchased, the total value of expenditures, and the proportion of this value spent within Diepsloot.

Figure 7.8 Sources of Regular Household Income in Diepsloot, 2012

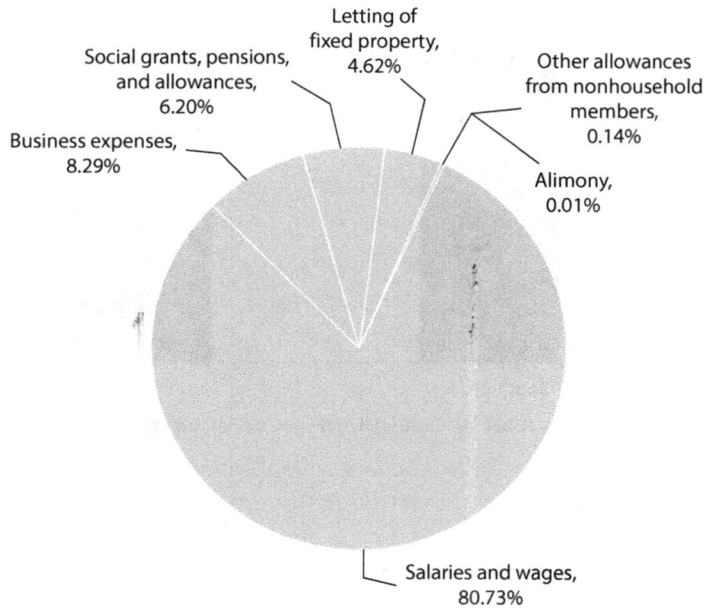

Letting of
fixed property,
4.62%

Social grants, pensions,
and allowances,
6.20%

Other allowances
from nonhousehold
members,
0.14%

Business expenses,
8.29%

Alimony,
0.01%

Salaries and wages,
80.73%

Table 7.5 Proportion of Sources of Regular Income, by Household Income Quintile in Diepsloot, 2012

Percent

Income source	Lower quintile	Second quintile	Third quintile	Fourth quintile	Upper quintile
Salaries and wages	61.92	67.24	64.99	85.48	87.30
Business profits	8.07	7.73	10.75	4.99	6.00
Social grants, pensions, and allowances	21.71	16.13	15.78	5.71	2.52
Letting of fixed property	2.22	4.23	5.38	3.04	2.83
Other allowances from nonhousehold members	0.18	0.32	1.29	0.01	0.00
Alimony	0.00	0.00	0.03	0.00	0.02

Total Spending

Diepsloot households' total spending is shown in table 7.6. Household expenditure was led by groceries; followed by housing-related items; then clothing and footwear; and finance charges, income tax and investment items. On average, a typical household spends about 66 percent of its total household spending within Diepsloot.

Poorer households in Diepsloot spend, on average, a greater proportion of their total expenditure on groceries than wealthier households (table 7.7). In the bottom 20 percent of households, around 80 percent of spending goes toward groceries, while the richest households spend the largest share (close to 35 percent) of their spending on housing.

Table 7.6 Total Annual Household Spending, by Category in Diepsloot, 2011/12

	Proportion of households paying for item (%)	Share of total annual spending (%)	Avg. spent (R)	Avg. spent in Diepsloot (R)	Proportion spent in Diepsloot (%)	Avg. per capita spending (R)
Groceries	99.50	58.19	1,254	1,117	85.51	6,658
Clothing and footwear	79.63	7.37	196	54	38.13	1,009
Household textiles	35.00	0.68	21	10	54.00	97
Furniture	13.38	0.73	30	10	45.95	125
Appliances	51.88	1.92	58	18	63.85	289
Musical instruments	24.38	0.59	22	9	60.51	124
Other household equipment, misc. goods	25.63	0.28	8	3	56.95	42
Recreation, entertainment, sport	9.25	0.11	4	1	49.51	17
Computer and telecommunication equipment	56.00	2.38	70	38	67.66	398
Expenditures away from home	26.50	1.43	44	8	21.55	207
Domestic workers	0.38	0.01	0	0	50.88	1
Education: public and private institutions	19.88	1.03	45	13	15.95	203
Reading material	15.13	0.12	29	23	90.46	25
Health: public and private sector	9.88	0.22	7	2	27.92	29
Transport	36.88	2.59	96	59	73.04	486
Housing	58.88	15.68	671	206	33.11	3,790
Finance charges, income taxes, investments	46.00	6.67	302	109	42.16	1,522
Total expenditure		100.00	33,899	19,135	66.43	15,022

Note: R = rand. The 2011/12 survey period covered the 12 months preceding the survey, comprising part of both years.

Table 7.7 Household Expenditures, by Consumption Quintile in Diepsloot, 2011/12

Percent

	Lower quintile	Second quintile	Third quintile	Fourth quintile	Upper quintile
Groceries	79.69	70.32	60.71	50.13	30.10
Clothing and footwear	6.24	7.85	7.91	8.42	6.44
Household contents and services	2.73	3.97	3.44	5.57	5.35
Housing and utilities	3.65	8.56	14.10	17.25	34.83
Finance charges, income taxes, investments	2.99	3.49	5.89	8.39	12.59
Communication	1.70	2.37	2.56	2.81	2.45
Transport	1.28	1.84	2.72	3.28	3.84
Recreation and culture	1.07	1.13	1.94	2.32	1.85
Education	0.39	0.40	0.54	1.61	2.23
Health	0.27	0.07	0.21	0.23	0.32

Note: The 2011/12 survey period covered the 12 months preceding the survey, comprising part of both years.

Grocery Spending

Groceries constitute, by far, the largest household spending category in Diepsloot—almost 60 percent of households' annual expenditures (table 7.6). Table 7.6 reveals that, on average, a household spends around R 1,254 (R 558 per household member) every month on groceries, almost 90 percent (R 1,117) of which is spent within Diepsloot. Broken down by product type meat consumption accounts for the biggest share of total grocery expenditures by an average household (16.6 percent), followed by grain (14.2 percent), and personal care items (9.2 percent), as shown in table 7.8.

The grocery items in table 7.8 may be further classified into three broad groups: food, alcoholic beverages and tobacco, and "other," which includes the remaining expenditures (cleaning materials, other household items, medicine, personal care items, and restaurants). The proportion of total grocery spending on each of these groups is illustrated in figure 7.9b. Food accounts for 70 percent of all grocery spending. These are bought mostly within Diepsloot—85 percent of all food expenditures were made in Diepsloot. Similarly, 87 percent of all alcoholic beverage and tobacco expenditures were made in Diepsloot.

Poorer households in Diepsloot spend, on average, a greater proportion of their total monthly grocery expenditure on food and nonalcoholic beverages

Table 7.8 Monthly Household Spending on Groceries, by Product Type in Diepsloot, 2011/12

Product type	Share of households buying product (%)	Share of grocery spending (%)	Avg. spent (R)	Avg. spent in Diepsloot (R)	Proportion spent in Diepsloot (%)	Avg. per capita spending (R)
Grain	98.75	14.21	168	159	95.11	70
Meat	97.75	16.58	217	187	88.58	93
Fish	76.63	3.73	64	54	87.37	29
Milk, cheese, eggs	92.25	5.46	75	66	89.83	34
Fats and oils	94.75	4.23	57	49	89.48	26
Fruit	88.50	3.86	53	49	93.36	23
Nuts	49.00	1.17	30	27	90.49	14
Vegetables	93.38	6.23	77	73	94.26	34
Sugar, sweets, desserts	89.13	3.80	54	47	89.91	24
Other food products	60.13	3.31	75	62	83.25	36
Coffee, tea, cocoa	89.50	3.32	48	42	90.05	22
Nonalcoholic beverages	73.50	4.95	84	75	91.76	38
Sorghum beer	2.13	0.13	69	71	68.42	21
Alcoholic beverages	20.25	3.33	199	182	86.80	94
Cigarettes, cigars, tobacco	21.50	2.39	132	124	85.88	63
Cleaning materials	83.00	5.59	85	74	88.85	37
Other household items	46.13	2.67	73	63	86.95	35
Medicine	47.63	3.45	96	81	84.18	41
Personal care items	84.63	9.23	137	118	89.31	61
Restaurants	33.00	2.34	91	78	84.98	46
			1,254	1,117	90.27	558

Note: R = rand. The 2011/12 survey period covered the 12 months preceding the survey, comprising part of both years.

Economics of South African Townships • http://dx.doi.org/10.1596/978-1-4648-0301-7

Figure 7.9 Monthly Household Grocery Expenditures in Diepsloot, 2011/12

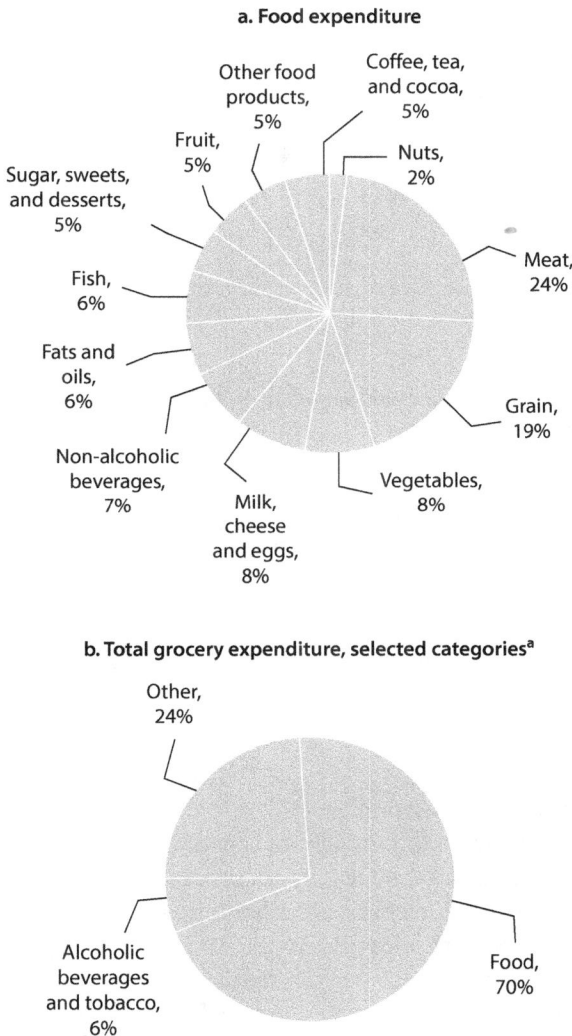

a. Food expenditure

b. Total grocery expenditure, selected categories[a]

a. "Other" includes cleaning materials, other household items, medicine, personal care items, and restaurants. The 2011/12 survey period covered the 12 months preceding the survey, comprising part of both years.

than wealthier households (table 7.9). The bottom 20 percent of households spent around 81 percent of their monthly grocery spending on food and nonalcoholic beverages, 1.5 percent on alcoholic beverages and tobacco, and 17 percent on "other" grocery items. Households in the wealthier quintiles, on the other hand, spend more on alcoholic beverages and tobacco as well as on other grocery items than poorer ones: the top 20 percent of households spent 68 percent on food and nonalcoholic beverages, 13 percentage points lower than the bottom 20 percent of households.

Table 7.9 Monthly Household Spending on Groceries, by Income Quintile in Diepsloot, 2011/12

Percent

Income quintile	Food and nonalcoholic beverages	Alcoholic beverages and tobacco	Other
Lower quintile	81.24	1.49	17.27
Second quintile	73.18	3.18	23.64
Third quintile	73.34	4.44	22.22
Fourth quintile	68.61	6.80	24.60
Upper quintile	68.26	6.84	24.90

Note: "Other" includes cleaning materials, other household items, medicine, personal care items, and restaurants. The 2011/12 survey period covered the 12 months preceding the survey, comprising part of both years.

Table 7.10 Monthly Household Spending on Transport to Work, by Income Quintile in Diepsloot, 2011/12

Household income quintile	Average spent (R)	Household size	Share spent on transport to work (% of all expenditure)
Lower quintile	9,086	2.35	48.65
Second quintile	17,221	2.65	39.98
Third quintile	25,555	2.97	25.96
Fourth quintile	37,294	3.21	15.33
Upper quintile	80,337	3.55	8.16

Note: R = rand. Calculations are based on households that actually spent something on transport to work. The 2011/12 survey period covered the 12 months preceding the survey, comprising part of both years.

Spending on Transport to Work

As highlighted in table 7.10, the share of spending on transport to work declines with income. Taking into account only those households that paid for transport to work, the bottom 20 percent of households by income spent almost half of all expenditures (49 percent) on transport to work. Even though Diepsloot is near places of employment, evidence suggests that transport costs to work pose a sizable burden on households and, as a result, hinder job search and economic integration.

Expenditures Made Within versus Outside Diepsloot

This subsection focuses on whether the spending occurred within or outside Diepsloot. Such an analysis helps to assess the likely impact that income growth in Diepsloot will have on households' expenditure patterns, location of their purchases of goods and services, and on overall economic activity within the township.

To get a broad understanding of expenditure types by location, the analysis starts by categorizing expenditures into two main groups: one for expenditures on goods and services within Diepsloot and the other for expenditures outside Diepsloot. Among those households from which the survey gathered expenditure data, about 99 percent had purchased at least one commodity or service from within Diepsloot within the previous year—13 percentage points more than the 86 percent of households that had purchased at least one commodity or service from outside Diepsloot. Table 7.11 shows that Diepsloot residents spent approximately R 1.5 billion inside Diepsloot in a year, almost twice the R 784 million they spent outside Diepsloot.

Expenditures were then classified into seven commodity groups, by location of both production and purchase (either inside or outside Diepsloot) and by commodity type (good versus service). The objective was to distinguish how economic activity in different categories translated into incomes for Diepsloot residents. In addition, this classification makes it possible to examine how the variation in consumer preferences across commodity types influences expenditure patterns, particularly regarding spending inside versus outside Diepsloot. These classifications, along with examples of goods and services for each category, are presented in table 7.12. (The data analysis shows that only 0.01 percent of households produced and consumed any category 1 goods. This category was therefore dropped from the subsequent analysis.)

Figure 7.10 shows the percentage of Diepsloot households that bought at least one item per commodity group. Consistent with the aggregate patterns for purchases inside and outside Diepsloot, most households buy their goods within Diepsloot, and most households (98 percent) buy at least one good in

Table 7.11 Overview of Annual Household Spending, Inside versus Outside Diepsloot, 2011/12

Rand

	Inside Diepsloot	*Outside Diepsloot*
Total spending	1,507,753,706	783,586,696
Total average spending per household	23,584	12,257
Average per capita expenditure	7,981	4,148

Note: The 2011/12 survey period covered a continuous 12 months comprising part of both years.

Table 7.12 Definition of Commodity Groups for Consumer Demand Estimation, in Diepsloot, 2012

Commodity group	Location of production and purchase	Income accruing to Diepsloot residents	Examples
1	Goods produced and consumed inside Diepsloot	Value added	Maize, vegetables, eggs, sorghum beer
2	Goods produced outside and purchased inside Diepsloot	Trading margin	Food grains, consumer durables
3	Goods produced and purchased outside Diepsloot	None	Food grains, consumer durables
4	Services purchased inside Diepsloot	Value added	Personal care, repair services
5	Services purchased outside Diepsloot	None	Personal care, repair services
6	Other expenditures to insiders	Mostly income	Remittances to Diepsloot residents
7	Other expenditures to outsiders	None	Taxes, banking fees, bribes, remittances to residents outside Diepsloot

Note: Category 1 was dropped from the subsequent analysis because only 0.01 percent of households produced and consumed any category 1 goods.

Figure 7.10 Share of Diepsloot Households Making at Least One Purchase in Defined Commodity Groups, 2011/12

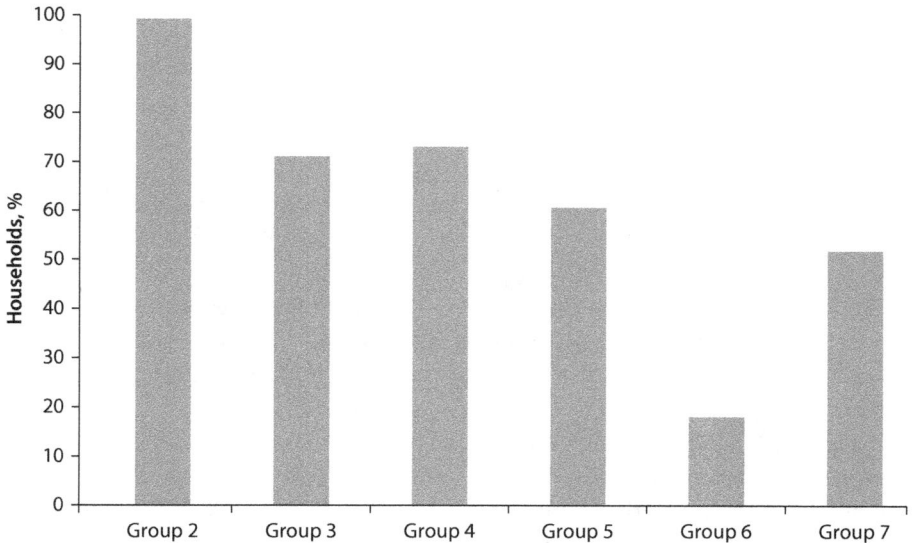

Note: Group 2: goods purchased in Diepsloot. Group 3: goods purchased outside Diepsloot. Group 4: services purchased in Diepsloot. Group 5: services purchased outside Diepsloot. Group 6: other expenditures to Diepsloot residents. Group 7: other expenditures to non-Diepsloot residents. The 2011/12 survey period covered the 12 months preceding the survey, comprising part of both years.

Table 7.13 Overview of Annual Household Spending Patterns, by Commodity Group, in Diepsloot, 2011/12

Commodity group	Total spent in Diepsloot (R, millions)	Total spent per household (R)	Avg. per capita expenditure (R)
2	1,138	17,807	6,026
3	260	4,063	1,375
4	333	5,213	1,764
5	233	3,641	1,232
6	36	564	191
7	291	4,551	1,540

Note: Group 2: goods purchased in Diepsloot. Group 3: goods purchased outside Diepsloot. Group 4: services purchased in Diepsloot. Group 5: services purchased outside Diepsloot. Group 6: other expenditures to Diepsloot residents. Group 7: other expenditures to non-Diepsloot residents. The 2011/12 survey period covered the 12 months preceding the survey, comprising part of both years.

Group 2 (comprising foodstuffs and essential household supplies). At the same time, only about 72 percent of households buy some form of service within the township.

Table 7.13 shows that the highest expenditure levels, in terms of monetary values, went to goods purchased in Diepsloot (Group 2), which amounted to around R 1.1 billion. This was followed by services purchased in Diepsloot and "other" expenditures to non-Diepsloot residents, which includes mainly transfers and finance charges. The highest level of spending in this latter group was for housing-related transfers such as levies, assessment rates, and taxes; water and electricity rates; and gas supplied by public networks, which altogether accounted for around 53 percent of total spending in Group 7, followed by finance charges, which accounted for 46 percent. These patterns are consistent with the patterns on total spending per household: nearly R 18,000 per year on Group 2, followed by R 4,551 on Group 7. The average per capita spending by each household was around R 6,026 for Group 2 and R 1,540 for Group 7.

Implications of Income Growth for Economic Activity in Diepsloot

Next we estimate the elasticity of spending within Diepsloot with respect to changes in total expenditure (as a proxy for income). Because the expenditure data are disaggregated by commodity, we can further estimate a system of demand equations across the six commodity groups (Groups 2–7) as outlined in table 7.12 and calculate income elasticities for each commodity group. The elasticity estimates are expected to indicate the likely impacts that income growth in Diepsloot would have on expenditure patterns and the location of purchase of goods and services. For instance, if income or expenditure elasticities for goods or services purchased in Diepsloot are high, then growth of income in Diepsloot would have a strong secondary impact on economic growth in Diepsloot.

Table 7.14 presents the elasticities at different expenditure levels, measured as a proportion of mean total expenditure (see annex 7A for details on the estimation procedure). Overall, elasticities for purchases inside Diepsloot decline with income. Elasticities for expenditures outside Diepsloot, on the other hand, increase with income. Only at very low income and expenditure levels (where the expenditure to mean ratio is 0.15) do elasticities for purchases inside Diepsloot tend to be higher than those for expenditures for purchases outside Diepsloot. This gets reversed at higher expenditure levels. Overall, results show that a

Table 7.14 Expenditure Elasticities at Different Expenditure Levels in Diepsloot, 2012

Expenditure level as proportion of mean	Average annual household expenditure (R)	Inside Diepsloot	Outside Diepsloot
0.15	4,156	1.03	0.90
0.25	6,927	0.97	1.09
0.50	13,854	0.89	1.33
0.75	20,780	0.84	1.48
1.00	27,707	0.80	1.58
1.25	34,634	0.78	1.66
1.50	41,561	0.75	1.73
1.75	48,488	0.74	1.78
2.00	55,415	0.72	1.83

Note: R = rand.

Table 7.15 Expenditure Elasticities at Different Expenditure Levels by Commodity Group in Diepsloot, 2012

Expenditure level as proportion of mean	Average annual household expenditure (R)	Expenditure elasticities at predicted means					
		Group 2	Group 3	Group 4	Group 5	Group 6	Group 7
0.15	4,156	1.12	0.97	0.99	0.99	0.94	0.32
0.25	6,927	0.98	0.99	1.02	1.01	0.96	1.10
0.50	13,854	0.82	1.02	1.05	1.04	0.99	2.15
0.75	20,781	0.73	1.04	1.07	1.06	1.01	2.77
1.00	27,707	0.66	1.05	1.08	1.08	1.02	3.21
1.25	34,634	0.61	1.06	1.09	1.09	1.03	3.55
1.50	41,561	0.57	1.06	1.10	1.09	1.04	3.82
1.75	48,488	0.53	1.07	1.11	1.10	1.05	4.06
2.00	55,415	0.50	1.07	1.11	1.11	1.05	4.26

Note: R = rand. Group 2: goods purchased in Diepsloot. Group 3: goods purchased outside Diepsloot. Group 4: services purchased in Diepsloot. Group 5: services purchased outside Diepsloot. Group 6: other expenditures to Diepsloot residents. Group 7: other expenditures to non-Diepsloot residents.

significant portion of increases in income (derived by proxy from expenditure levels) leak out of the Diepsloot economy and get spent outside the township.

For a more detailed understanding of these dynamics, table 7.15 presents, for each of the six commodity groups, elasticities at different expenditure levels as a proportion of mean total expenditure. The table shows that the broad picture for spending inside Diepsloot (shown in table 7.14) is influenced mainly by consumption patterns for Group 2, which includes goods produced outside but bought within Diepsloot. Specifically, of all the groups involving expenditure inside Diepsloot, only Group 2 sees expenditure elasticities fall with income levels.

That goods purchased in Diepsloot (Group 2) have sharply declining income elasticity across expenditure levels means that rising incomes in the township are not likely to contribute much to demand for those goods in Diepsloot. In contrast, demand for goods produced and purchased outside the township (Group 3) would increase as income and expenditure levels rise in the township.

In a positive sign for the township, the elasticities for Group 4 (services purchased inside Diepsloot) increase with overall income and expenditure levels, suggesting that the demand for these economic activities would increase as income levels rise. This group includes hair and beauty salons, computer training schools, repairing and servicing of household equipment, upholstery, and other services. Elasticities for Group 4 and Group 5 (services purchased outside Diepsloot) are strikingly similar.

Conclusions

The foregoing analysis uses Diepsloot as a case study to better understand the demographics, income and expenditure patterns, and other socioeconomic characteristics of a large urban South African township.

In terms of demographics, the population of Diepsloot is almost entirely (97 percent) black, young (average age 25 years), and mostly migrant—the latter reflecting Diepsloot's development as a postapartheid phenomenon and its location relatively close to economic opportunities. A significant proportion (almost 20 percent) of the population is foreign-born. Formal education and training are lacking among Diepsloot's population, and educational outcomes are improving gradually but unevenly with the current school-age generation.

Diepsloot's relative proximity to wealthier urban economic centers plays out in a number of ways:

- *Its labor market outcomes are somewhat more favorable relative to other townships.* The narrow unemployment rate (excluding discouraged workers) in Diepsloot, is an estimated 30 percent, which is in the range of the unemployment rates for townships as a group and informal settlements (both close to 33 percent). The youth unemployment rate is also noticeably lower: 43 percent in Diepsloot compared with about 50 percent nationwide in 2011 and an average of about 61 percent for T&IS. At 63 percent, Diepsloot's labor force participation rate exceeds the 55 percent national rate. It is, however, lower than that for informal settlements (67.6 percent) and other urban settlements (65 percent) and at par with townships as a group.

- *While its commuters' travel time to work is less onerous than it is in most other townships, travel costs to work are still significant.* For almost 60 percent of the population, it takes 30 minutes or less to get to work. Even so, the related costs constitute a significant proportion (20 percent, on average) of the wages of those who work outside Diepsloot. Among the households in the bottom income quintile, those who must pay for some form of transport (as opposed to walking) to work spend an average of almost half of all household expenditures on transport to work; for those in the second quintile, the average is 40 percent.

- *Salaries and wages are by far the most important source of income.* Overall, 80 percent of Diepsloot households' total income comes from salaries and wages. The relative significance of income sources varies by income groups, however. While the contribution of salaries and wages to total income is greatest for those in the higher income quintiles, social grants and pensions constitute a higher share for those in the lower income quintiles, accounting for just over a fifth of the income of the bottom quintile.

- *Its household purchases from inside the township are relatively high, although the goods purchased are mostly produced outside.* The survey results show that a significant proportion of spending by Diepsloot residents goes to purchases inside the township—especially for groceries and other essentials. Total spending on purchases inside the township is estimated to be twice as large as spending on outside purchases. Three-quarters of the spending within the township goes to the purchase of goods (rather than services) that are produced outside but retailed through a web of formal or informal supply chains within the township. The bulk (40 percent) of spending outside Diepsloot goes toward transfers and financial charges, suggesting that either limited use of financial services in Diepsloot, low accessibility to such services, and the high cost of financial services within Diepsloot.

However, the results also show that the scope for Diepsloot's income to leak out of the township increases as income levels rise. The income elasticity of expenditures made inside Diepsloot declines with income, while the one for purchases outside Diepsloot increases with income. The former trend is explained entirely by the declining propensity of residents to buy goods (as opposed to services) within Diepsloot as their incomes rise. Preference for nontradable services that are purchased within Diepsloot—such as personal care, training schools, and repairs—would increase with income levels. This analysis some sheds light on the kinds of growth-oriented activity that can be expected to mushroom in Diepsloot and other similarly large townships.

Annex 7A: Estimation Procedure

A translog expenditure system (Swamy and Binswanger 1983) is estimated, in which the share of total expenditure a household i spends on commodity group j (s_j) is assumed to be related to its total expenditure (Y_i) as follows:

$$s_{ij} = \alpha_j + \beta_{1j} \ln(Y_i) + \beta_{2j} \ln(Y_i)^2 + e_{ij}, \qquad (7A.1)$$

for $i = 1,....,n$ households and $j = 1,....,m-1$ commodity groups. s_j is defined as $S_j = \dfrac{E_j}{\sum\limits_{j=1}^{m} E_j}$, with E_{ij} being expenditures of household i on item j. By definition, the expenditure shares add up to one, meaning only $m-1$ expenditure shares are

independent. The parameters to be estimated in the system are α_j, β_{1j}, and β_{2j}. The error terms are denoted by e_{ij}.

Based on (7A.1), the expenditure elasticities with respect to actual expenditure per commodity groups are calculated as follows:

$$\mu_j = \frac{\beta_{1j} + 2\beta_{2j} \ln(Y_i)}{s_j} + 1 \qquad (7A.2)$$

Estimating the system of equations in (7A.1) using ordinary least squares (OLS), in which an equation for each commodity group is estimated separately, poses the challenge arising from possible interdependency among expenditures across all the groups. First of all, any income shocks would affect all commodity shares. Second, the shares add up to one, which means that if one share goes up, then at least another one has to go down. Therefore any change in an unobserved error in one equation must give rise to a change in an unobserved error in another equation. In technical terms, this means that the error terms for each of the equations might be correlated. Disregarding this interdependency and estimating equations in (7A.1) using OLS would result in inefficient estimates.

Accordingly, the econometric strategy is to estimate (7A.1) using a seemingly unrelated regression (SUR) framework. It was developed by Zellner (1962) as an extension of the OLS model to specifically facilitate efficient estimation of a system of multiple equations with cross-equation parameter restrictions and correlated error terms. The SUR model allows for nonzero covariance between the error terms for a given household between the six equations, while assuming zero covariance between different households. As a result, using SUR presents efficiency gains in estimation compared with single equation estimation methods such as OLS by using information on different equations and specifically accounting for the systematic correlation in the error terms (Zellner 1962; Wooldridge 2002). Further, the SUR framework makes it possible to impose or test restrictions that involve parameters in different equations embedded in (7A.1).

The analysis uses a classical linear SUR model which assumes that for each equation in (7A.1) the vector of independent variables is of full rank and that conditional on the independent variables, the error terms are identical and independently distributed (*iid*) with zero mean and homoskedastic variance. The variance matrix is further assumed to be positive definite (Zellner 1962; Wooldridge 2002). The Breusch-Pagan test of independence of error is conducted to check whether the SUR framework is appropriate given the data.

In sum, the estimation strategy is such that for each household, separate equations for each of the 6 commodity groups are specified and estimated simultaneously using Zellner's SUR. By definition, the expenditure shares add up to one, meaning that only five out of six equations are linearly independent. To be able to estimate the system, one equation is dropped (which happens to be the equation for commodity Group 7 in this case). The adding-up constraint for the shares is thus a maintained hypothesis. The elasticities for the five commodity groups are computed based on equation (7A.1). The elasticity for the commodity group for which the equation was dropped from the estimation (Group 7) is computed residually as follows:

$$\mu_m = \frac{1 - \sum_{j=1}^{m-1} S_j \mu_j}{S_m}. \tag{7A.3}$$

Annex 7B: Estimation Results and Discussion

Before running estimations per commodity group, we estimate the expenditure shares for two broad categories: one for goods and/or services purchased in Diepsloot and another for goods and/or services purchased outside Diepsloot. Given the adding-up constraint discussed earlier, only the equation for "inside" Diepsloot purchases were estimated via OLS. The results are reported in table 7B.1. It is notable that the coefficients are precisely estimated.

Table 7B.2 reports the expenditure elasticities computed from the estimates obtained in table 7B.1. The computation uses mean household expenditure

Table 7B.1 OLS Regressions of Expenditure Shares Spent in Diepsloot

Variable	Coefficient	Std. error
Log of total expenditure	0.779***	0.088
Square of log of expenditure	−0.045***	0.005
Constant	−2.492***	0.422
Observations	799	
Adjusted R^2	0.183	

Note: OLS = ordinary least squares. Standard errors in parentheses.
Significance level: *** = 1 percent.

Table 7B.2 Expenditure Elasticities at Predicted Means

Group	Expenditure elasticities at predicted means	Std. error	t-statistic	95% confidence interval	
Diepsloot: goods and services purchased inside Diepsloot	0.80	0.01	53.83	0.77	0.83
Non-Diepsloot: goods and services purchased outside Diepsloot	1.58	n.a.	n.a.	n.a.	n.a.

Note: n.a. = not applicable.

shares predicted by mean values of total household expenditure. The mean predicted share was 0.75 for the share spent in Diepsloot, and the mean total expenditure used is R 27,707.26.

The expenditure elasticity for goods and services purchased outside Diepsloot (1.5832) is almost twice that for goods and services purchased inside Diepsloot (0.8029).

To gain a more detailed understanding of these dynamics, the subsequent analysis estimates elasticities by commodity group previously outlined in table 7.12. The results from seemingly unrelated regression (SUR) estimation are presented in table 7B.3 and the mean shares presented in table 7B.4. A mean total expenditure of R 27,707.26 was used. Although an OLS estimation of the system gave estimates that were fairly similar to the SUR estimates in table 7B.3, in terms of both coefficients and standard errors, the SUR results were used in the analysis because of the significance of the Breusch-Pagan test of independence, which suggests the error terms of the five equations are not independent (p-value = 0.0000).

The coefficients and the intercepts are estimated with high precision, and the R^2 range from 2.8 percent to 30 percent, with the most important group, Group 2, having the highest R^2. Group 2 has a positive term for the log of income and a negative term for the square of the log of income, while for all of the other groups the signs are the opposite. This suggests that Group 2 is the commodity group that determines the declining income elasticities for purchases from inside Diepsloot, while for all other groups they are likely to increase.

Table 7B.5 reports the expenditure elasticity for each of the six commodity groups. These, too, are estimated with high precision. All groups except Group 2 are found to have elasticities that are higher than one. This means that although an increase in income will lead to a rise in expenditures on all commodity groups,

Table 7B.3 SURs of Expenditure Shares, by Commodity Group

Variable	Group 2	Group 3	Group 4	Group 5	Group 6
Log of total expenditure	1.28*** (0.10)	−0.227*** (0.055)	−0.23*** (0.06)	−0.25*** (0.047)	−0.28*** (0.020)
Square of log of total expenditure	−0.07*** (0.01)	0.013*** (0.003)	0.01*** (0.003)	0.014*** (0.002)	0.014*** (0.001)
Constant	−4.84*** (0.46)	1.110*** (0.263)	1.01*** (0.30)	1.08*** (0.23)	1.34*** (0.09)
χ^2	338.81	22.96	42.97	64.72	197.01
R^2	0.30	0.03	0.05	0.08	0.20
Breusch-Pagan test of independence: χ^2 (10)	484.19				

Note: SURs = seemingly unrelated regressions. Standard errors in parentheses. This system was also estimated via ordinary least squares (OLS), and the resultant estimates were fairly similar to the SUR estimates, in terms of both coefficients and standard errors. Significance level: *** = 1 percent.

Table 7B.4 Mean Shares per Commodity Group and Mean Total Expenditure

Commodity group	Predicted shares
Group 2: goods purchased inside Diepsloot	0.63
Group 3: goods purchased outside Diepsloot	0.10
Group 4: services purchased inside Diepsloot	0.11
Group 5: services purchased outside Diepsloot	0.07
Group 6: other expenditures to Diepsloot residents	0.01
Group 7: other expenditures to non-Diepsloot residents	0.09

Table 7B.5 Expenditure Elasticities at Predicted Means

Commodity group	Expenditure elasticities at predicted means	Std. error	Z-statistic	95% confidence interval	
Group 2: goods purchased inside Diepsloot	0.66	0.02	34.57	0.62	0.70
Group 3: goods purchased outside Diepsloot	1.05	0.01	94.53	1.02	1.07
Group 4: services purchased inside Diepsloot	1.08	0.01	87.08	1.06	1.11
Group 5: services purchased outside Diepsloot	1.08	0.01	112.80	1.06	1.09
Group 6: other expenditures to Diepsloot residents	1.02	0.004	257.45	1.01	1.03
Group 7: other expenditures to non-Diepsloot residents	3.21	n.a.	n.a.	n.a.	n.a.

Note: n.a. = not applicable.

the increase in demand for Group 2 will be less than proportionate. Group 2 goods can be considered necessities for which there is a limited need to consume additional quantities as incomes rise. The rest of the commodity groups, on the other hand, could be broadly classified as luxury commodities, meaning that demand rises more than proportionate to a change in income. Consumers can manage to do without these commodities at low income levels.

The highest elasticity is reported to be 3.21 for Group 7, which is the reference group and includes mainly financial transfers to non-Diepsloot residents. This is followed by the elasticity for services purchased inside Diepsloot (Group 4), which was found to be 1.08. This group includes, for example, repairs to clothing;

furniture; musical instruments; household wares; recreational equipment; and computers and communication equipment, as well as expenditures when away from home, payment to domestic workers, expenditures on public and hired transport, housing repairs, and so on. The least elasticity—for goods purchased within Diepsloot (Group 2)—is reported to be 0.66, which includes mainly foodstuffs and essential household supplies. Looking at it from an "inside versus outside Diepsloot" perspective shows that, with the exception of purchases of services (Groups 4 and 5), elasticities for "outside Diepsloot" purchases are higher than elasticities for "inside Diepsloot" purchases: Group 3 elasticity is higher than that of Group 2, while Group 7 elasticity is higher than that of Group 6.

Notes

1. The employment rate is calculated as the proportion of the employed in the working-age population. The employed are defined as those who, during the reference week, either (a) did any work or business for at least one hour, or (b) had a job or business but were not at work (temporarily absent).

2. The narrow unemployment rate is calculated as: unemployed/(unemployed + employed). The unemployed includes individuals aged 15–64 years who were not employed in the reference week and who met one of the following conditions: (a) actively looked for work or tried to start a business in the week prior to the survey and were available for work or business; or (b) had not actively looked for work in the four weeks preceding the survey but had a job or business to start at a definite date in the future and were available. Data challenges prevented calculation of the broad unemployment rate, which includes "discouraged workers," defined as follows: a working-age person who was not employed during the reference period, wanted to work, and was available to work or to start a business but who took no active steps to find work during the previous four weeks and gave one of the following main reasons for not seeking work: no jobs available in the area, unable to find work requiring his/her skills, or lost hope of finding any kind of work.

3. The national and T&IS youth unemployment rates are drawn from the Statistics South Africa data presented in chapter 3, table 3B.4.

References

Stats SA (Statistics South Africa). 2011. "Quarterly Labor Force Survey: Quarter 3, 2011." Statistical Release P0211, Stats SA, Pretoria.

Swamy, G., and H. P. Binswanger. 1983. "Flexible Consumer Demand Systems and Linear Estimation: Food in India." *American Journal of Agricultural Economics* 65 (4): 675–84.

Wooldridge, J. M. 2002. *Econometric Analysis of Cross Section and Panel Data*. Cambridge, MA: MIT Press.

Zellner, A. 1962. "An Efficient Method of Estimating Seemingly Unrelated Regressions and Tests for Aggregation Bias." *Journal of the American Statistical Association* 57 (298): 348–68.

CHAPTER 8

A Social Accounting Matrix for the Economy of Diepsloot

Rob Davies and Dirk van Seventer

Modeling a Township as an Economic Entity

This chapter presents a Social Accounting Matrix (SAM) for the township of Diepsloot to study how robust Diepsloot's internal economy may be. We particularly want to answer these questions: How extensive are the economic transactions within Diepsloot compared with those between Diepsloot and the rest of South Africa? Does a multiplier magnify any initial income-creating impulse in Diepsloot? Could such an internal economy provide an engine for driving growth there?

Understanding how each part of the Diepsloot economy works, taken on its own, provides important insights for policy makers. We can learn a great deal from careful analysis of household or employment surveys. But such insights are confined to particular aspects of residents' economic lives. The surveys tell us how people earn their incomes, or how they spend them, but they do not give us an overall picture of how these two activities interact. In other words, they give us a snapshot of Diepsloot's residents but no panoramic view of Diepsloot as an economic entity. The SAM for Diepsloot in this chapter provides such a view.

National SAMs, and the models based on them, have been widely used over the past four decades to investigate policy impacts at the countrywide level, particularly regarding trade and poverty alleviation. Regional SAMs also have a long history in developed countries as tools to examine policy and other impacts such as external shocks at the subnational level. The same techniques have been used for developing countries to throw light on development processes and the structures and institutions that condition how policy and other exogenous shocks spread through economies. Some of those applications have examined villages in agricultural settings.

Although constructing the SAM for Diepsloot, a large township in the Johannesburg metropolitan area, involves many issues similar to those involved in SAMs for agricultural villages, it also presents some different ones. For example, any subnational region, rural or urban, will be much more open than most national economies. Its borders will be more porous for both goods and people, and its markets more integrated with the larger economy in which it is situated. There are generally no explicit policy-based or legal barriers to the movement of goods or people, although locational inertia might act rather like nontariff barriers. This porousness is probably similar for any kind of subnational region. In practice, however, Diepsloot's proximity to major metropolitan and commercial centers probably makes its more porous than a rural village. Put differently, the costs of transacting business between Diepsloot and Johannesburg or Tshwane are much lower than between, say, rural KwaZulu-Natal and Durban.

At one level, we might even question the legitimacy of identifying a particular subregion as an economic entity. Certainly there are administrative boundaries, but in what sense do these constitute economic boundaries? A province or metropolitan area has some self-governance and budgetary powers that might distinguish it from other parts of the same national economy: They are likely to have production specializations that constitute poles of economic activity at the core of a provincial or metropolitan economy. Were we able to measure the full network of economic linkages, we would find that these areas have significant internal linkages that permit us to speak of a subregional economy.

For its part, Diepsloot is a subregion of a subregion of a subregion. Its governance structure and budgetary powers are subsumed under the City of Johannesburg. It is a region that is defined on other, noneconomic criteria: It is not only an administrative unit within Johannesburg—a focal entity as far as city policy is concerned—but also an icon, with its own trope that differentiates it from its surroundings. When we enter or leave Diepsloot, we know it. When its citizens interact in the community, it is with a cohesive identity as "residents of Diepsloot." However, for many South Africans, including policy makers, Diepsloot—along with Khayelitsha, Mitchell's Plains, Umlazi, and other iconic South African townships—is the "other": "sprawling." "teeming," "informal," "crime-ridden," "unemployed," "ill-educated," "foreign." The townships represent problems, to be acted on. They are rarely, if ever, seen as opportunities for growth and job creation.

And yet these settlement areas do have a vibrant internal life: people live there and go about their daily lives—making money or looking to make money, spending money, saving money, and investing money; caring for their children and older family members, some living with them, some back home wherever that might be; working and playing in perpetual motion and frequent commotion, which give life in these townships their meaning. Communities, neighborhoods, and organizations work to make them better. Preschools, primary schools, and high schools strive to develop the children's promise. In Diepsloot, myriad grassroots organizations as well as individuals contribute to building better lives for themselves and their fellow residents: WASSUP,[1] the Diepsloot Youth Project, the Diepsloot Arts and Culture Network, MaJacky,[2] the supporters of Diepsloot's official website (www.diepsloot.com), Zizanani,[3] and countless others all exemplify this vibrancy and commitment.

The next section defines the SAM, addresses basic conceptual and design issues, summarizes the practical issues faced in its empirical construction, and presents the SAM and some related analysis. The "Multipliers for Diepsloot" section constructs multipliers to measure the impact of exogenous inflows on incomes in Diepsloot, then analyzes those results to assess the strength or weakness of the township's internal economic links. "Policy Implications" applies the multiplier analysis to assess potential interventions to strengthen Diepsloot's economy, including a proposal for nearby industrial parks or special economic zones. The chapter concludes with a discussion of the lessons learned from the SAM and multiplier analysis as well as the potential gains from further study.

A Diepsloot SAM: Conceptual and Design Issues

Economies have long been depicted as a circular flow of goods and services between different types of agents: producers, for example, buy factor services from households, which use the income to buy goods from producers, and so on. A SAM represents this circular flow in a matrix format (in this case, spreadsheet with rows and columns) (see box 8.1). Conventionally, each type of actor (more generally, "account") appears both as a row and as a column in the matrix. In the columns we record all spending transactions for that account; in the row we record all receipts. Any particular cell of the matrix thus records payments from the column account to the row account.

The structure of SAMs is not as standardized as national accounting has become over the decades. A wide variety of SAMs have been constructed, with differing account structures depending on the focus of the SAM and the constraints of data availability. For example, an agricultural analysis might suggest a SAM with a lot of agricultural but little industrial or service detail; a project on income distribution might require substantial household and less production detail. However, for a SAM to be useful, it must record *all* transactions in the economy: it has to be exhaustive. Because any particular account cannot use resources it does not have ("borrowing" is negative saving) and must use all resources at its disposal ("nonuse" is saving), the total of any account column must equal the total of that account's row. It is this property that gives SAMs their power as a means of organizing data: any imbalance highlights an error, and imbalances can often be used to infer data that we do not have direct access to.

A typical SAM includes six main types of accounts. Four of them are fairly obvious:

- *Activity (or sector) accounts*, which record transactions related to production and supply of goods.
- *Institutional accounts* (for households, government, and so on), which record incomes received from production and the transfers and uses of those incomes.
- *Rest of the world accounts*, which record all transactions with the outside world (imports, exports, various transfers, and income flows).

Box 8.1 What Is a Social Accounting Matrix?

A SAM is primarily a way of organizing data to provide a comprehensive and consistent picture of the circular flow of income within a particular area over a certain period of time. It identifies a number of accounts that represent exhaustively the main "agents" in the economy we wish to describe: production activities, goods and services, various primary factors of production, institutions such as households and enterprises, government, and so on. It then records all incomings (incomes, receipts, resources) and outgoings (expenditures, payments, uses) for each account. Because the set of accounts covers the whole economy, expenditure by one account represents an income for another, and the total incomings must equal the total out-goings for each and every account because it covers all resources and uses. A SAM thus records all transactions in the economy consistently, providing a picture of it over the given period.

The self-balancing requirement of a SAM makes it a useful data tool for situations in which the primary data are incomplete or inconsistent. Internal imbalances suggest where data problems and gaps might exist. Where we cannot get data, residual balancing items might be the best first approximation for these gaps.

Once constructed the SAM can also be used, in conjunction with other data and assump-tions about how the various agents behave, to create a model of the economy. Such mod-els have been useful in helping us understand the economywide impacts of various policies and other factors. Many policies have wider impacts than those on the targeted groups they are designed to affect. When these unintended consequences are negative, they reduce the economywide benefits of the policy. When they are positive, they reinforce the argument in favor of the policy. Policy makers need to know what the wider impacts may be if they are to weigh the pros and cons of the policy. Economywide models built on SAMs provide a tool for measuring the possibilities.

- *Accumulation accounts*, which (to make sure the SAM exhaustively covers all transactions in the economy) record all use of goods for investment (including changes in stocks) and all savings from households, government, and the rest of the world.

These four types of accounts would be sufficient to record all transactions exhaustively. But it has been useful, for many purposes, to include two seemingly fictional accounts as well:

- *Factor accounts*, which enable a richer exploration of income distribution by adding an additional circuit of income: the receipt of incomes from the produc-tion process (say, labor costs) and their distribution (through labor accounts) to various institutional (household) accounts, including the rest of the world accounts.
- *Product accounts*, which can record aggregated production activities and more easily incorporate imported goods by distinguishing between activities (say,

farming) and the products they produce (wheat, maize, cattle, and so on), treating such activities as supplying goods to the product accounts (which also receive imports and in turn supply users) rather than as direct selling of outputs to users.

These six broad account types are disaggregated into specific accounts according to the intended use of the SAM and data availability. The rest of this section discusses the structure we have used in this study.

We constructed two prototype SAMs for Diepsloot: The first is a *macro SAM* with little detail (as is common in all SAM-based studies, to show the main flows in the economy). The second is a *disaggregated SAM* that provides some detail on the structure of the Diepsloot economy, although this is still not highly disaggregated. The data we use do not support fine distinctions, and therefore a fairly aggregated SAM is more robust than a highly detailed one would be. At this stage we want to get the broad contours of the economy right, and adding too much detail can complicate this process.

This section outlines some of the considerations we took into account in designing the prototype macro and disaggregated SAMs. Our main concerns were over how various accounts are disaggregated, where Diepsloot's borders are; and how to map Diepsloot's connections with rest of South Africa.

Disaggregation of Accounts

Given our primary intention to construct a picture of Diepsloot's internal economy, we would like to depict a fair amount of detail about its structure. At the same time, our interest in the links between Diepsloot and the external South African economy suggests we should set up our disaggregation in ways that permit a mapping between the two economies. These considerations lead us to adopt activity, factor, and institutional accounts.

Production/Supply Accounts

The linkages between producers, through their sales to and purchases from one another, are one of the primary determinants of multipliers in any economy. Our SAM therefore includes a number of activity accounts as well as production accounts. We could categorize activities according to the standard industrial classification used in the broader South African economy, but most Diepsloot activity would fall into one or two such categories. We need a finer distinction than that, to capture more structure in the internal economy. We therefore use an extended classification of activities, as shown in table 8.1.

We distinguish between production activities undertaken and the products produced and traded because our prior belief is that Diepsloot is primarily a trading economy: most of the goods and services used will be imported from outside. Focusing on products makes it easier to account for imports. The data sources at our disposal allow for such a distinction, and we have tried to incorporate this. However, because of the high level of aggregation, we ended up with a

Table 8.1 Aggregated Industrial Structure for Diepsloot SAM, 2012

Sector	Activities
Agriculture, mining, and electricity	• Agriculture • Mining • Electricity, gas, and water supply
Diepsloot manufacturing	• Parts of food processing • Fabricated metals • Furniture • Other manufacturing nec
Non-Diepsloot manufacturing	• All manufacturing outside of Diepsloot
Construction	• Construction
Retail	• Retail trade
Hotels and restaurants	• Boarding and lodging • Beer taverns
Post and telecommunication	• Post and telecommunications
Public administration	• Public administration
Education	• Education
Health	• Health and social work
Nonprofit institutions	• Other community, social, and personal services activities • Activities of membership organizations • Recreational, cultural, and sporting activities • Other service activities
Other services	• Wholesale trade • Transport services • Financial intermediation, insurance, real estate, and business services • Other services nec

Note: SAM = Social Accounting Matrix; nec = not elsewhere classified.

supply structure that resembles one assuming that each activity produces a single product and each product is produced by only one activity.

Most activities in Diepsloot could be regarded as informal. If we define as formal any firm that is registered or licensed, then the enterprise survey (ES) underlying the SAM data (detailed in chapter 6 and further discussed later in this chapter) suggests that 84 percent of respondents ran informal businesses. It might therefore be appropriate to identify them explicitly in the SAM. We do not do so for our prototype SAM.

Factor Accounts
In our initial construction, we disaggregate factors simply into labor and capital. For some purposes it may be useful to disaggregate labor by skill levels. We have data on educational levels that would allow some further disaggregation, but this is better done after constructing the prototype with a single labor category.

Institutional Accounts
The institutional structure is important for considering policy analysis. SAMs typically include four kinds of institutional accounts: households, enterprises, government, and rest of the world. Below we discuss our treatment of the first

three, treating the rest-of-the-world account in subsequent subsection, "Relations with the Rest of South Africa."

These broad institutional categories can be disaggregated in various ways, depending on the issue at hand and the availability of data. In constructing a SAM, the disaggregation often occurs after constructing a balanced SAM with single accounts for each institution.

Households and Enterprises. Among the disaggregation-related issues, the data used to split households into rich and poor (based as they are on information from surveys) are often fragile. Furthermore, different policy issues might require different disaggregations. For example, it would be useful for some purposes to split Diepsloot households not only along income lines but also according to whether the household heads are South African or foreign-born. A SAM with a single household sector allows researchers to bring other information to bear in making these splits. We therefore follow this practice regarding households in the prototype SAMs. This precludes investigation of issues related to size distribution of income at this stage. We also have a single enterprise account that receives capital income and distributes it to households, both inside and outside Diepsloot. It may be useful in the future to split the enterprise account into formal and informal enterprises.

Households and enterprises are clearly domestic institutions, in the sense that there is no doubt that they reside in Diepsloot. It is therefore appropriate that they are accounted for in the same way as in any normal SAM. This is not so clear for most other institutions, and it is important to distinguish between resident and nonresident institutions. Although some are obviously resident, such as churches, most other economically significant institutions can be treated as nonresident. They have a presence in Diepsloot, but their income is largely generated outside, where their governance and decision-making structures reside. There are charitable organizations and government departments that operate in Diepsloot but are not resident. A City of Johannesburg or a Randburg Church outreach program visiting Diepsloot schools on a regular but infrequent basis provides a service that is essentially an import. We could therefore treat, say, government departments as nonresident and account for their connection to Diepsloot through inflows and outflows on Diepsloot's balance of payments. This would apply equally to most nonprofit institutions (NPIs).

We could thus treat all institutions whose head offices are outside Diepsloot as nonresident. However, we believe that it is useful (and more proper) to follow a similar approach to national income accounting and treat some institutions as resident. Our criterion is that there be an office in Diepsloot that operates at least normal business hours.

Any institution is typically represented in a SAM both by an institutional account and by activity accounts. The activity accounts show the institution as a producer—assembling inputs, including labor, and producing an output (often a service). The institutional account shows the organization's revenues and outlays. One of the outlays is for the purchase of the output of the activity.

Government. Government is treated differently in a small regional model than in a national SAM. It would be of interest in some situations to treat Diepsloot as a self-contained area for government purposes and to construct a budget of expenditures in Diepsloot balanced against revenue raised in Diepsloot, with an implied Diepsloot budget balance (most likely a deficit). In a full picture of the economy, it might be useful for policy makers to know the net flow of fiscal resources into or out of areas like Diepsloot, giving some insight into the spatial equity of the fiscus.

We do not do this in this study, primarily because deficiencies in the data would not warrant any conclusions being drawn about a rather sensitive political issue. Rather, we assume that all tax revenues are transferred out of Diepsloot and that all government expenditure within Diepsloot is paid for by transfers from outside. (One can still estimate the net flow of these transfers, but we do not emphasize it.)

It would be useful to disaggregate government as an institution into the three levels of national, provincial, and local. For Diepsloot, local government is probably a more important institution than either provincial or national government, but we do not have sufficient detail to make this distinction. We therefore treat the government as a single institution. However, as is common, education and health are treated as separate activities, so that "government" produces essentially public administration (including law and order).

Nonprofit Institutions. Nonprofit institutions (NPIs) are defined as self-governing institutions, largely independent of government, that do not generate profits so that they may distribute proceeds among specific persons or owners and whose membership and support are not mandatory.[4]

It is useful to think about how these institutions fit into the Diepsloot economy. In principle, such institutions might connect through eight channels, as table 8.2 sets out. To fully identify the channel, the source of the institution's income should also be considered. Because, in principle, these could be from inside or outside Diepsloot, the eight categories expand to 16 pure channels. Any institution might have a combination of any or all of these connections.

Typically NPIs are aggregated with households. However, for many applications of a Diepsloot model it may be useful to keep NPIs separately. We have therefore tried to separate them from households in the prototype SAMs. Although table 8.1 showed education, health, and NPIs as separate sectors, the SAMs treat them as a single institutional account.

Definition of Borders
Many SAMs and models built on them at this level of regional detail conceive of the focus area as a city or village surrounded by a hinterland, a natural economic penumbra that surrounds the core area. For example, in their study of 30 rural towns in five European countries, van Leeuwen and Nijkamp (2009) construct SAMs for the towns, including the area within a 7-kilometer radius. Similarly, in their study of a village in Kenya, Lewis and Thorbecke (1992) take the area to

Table 8.2 Channels of Impact of Nonprofit Institutions on the Diepsloot Economy

Impact type		Direct	Secondary
As an employer	1	Of Diepsloot residents	
	2	Of foreign nationals	2a: Who spend money in Diepsloot
			2b: Who do not spend money in Diepsloot
As a supplier	1	Free	
	2	For a fee	2a: To Diepsloot residents
			2b: To foreign nationals
As a purchaser	1	From Diepsloot suppliers	
	2	From foreign suppliers	

Note: "Foreign" = non-Diepsloot residents.

be the village and the area within a 7-kilometer radius. This definition not only expands the study area to internalize more transactions but also creates a large border area around the core town, creating a clearer separation between the town and the larger economy.

We considered applying a similar border definition to Diepsloot, but it seemed incorrect. Although we expect a greater density of flows between Diepsloot and its nearer external areas than its farther ones, these nearer areas cannot be regarded as a hinterland of Diepsloot; they are areas pressing hard against its borders. Diepsloot is not yet a growth pole that provides an impetus to growth in these contiguous areas. Rather, its growth will be driven *by* them. We thus take the boundary of Diepsloot as being the administrative region.

One difference between constructing a SAM for Diepsloot and building one for similar areas elsewhere is that less preexisting data are available for Diepsloot. Studies in developed countries appear to have access to better administrative data—in part because of different governance and reporting norms, and in part because of Diepsloot's rapid growth. The rate of in-migration means that data become outdated even during collection. Estimates of population and population growth vary enormously. And the informality of much of Diepsloot's housing means that any measure of its stock rapidly becomes an understatement.

For many research purposes, this rapidly changing character does not pose a problem. To the extent that growth represents more of the same, a sample survey can provide the basis for statistical estimation of relationships that may be stable despite the expansion. One concern of this chapter, however, is with the size of the economy. Unable to do a complete enumeration, we use representative enterprise and household surveys (HSs) to say something about both the structure and the size.

Relations with the Rest of South Africa

The Diepsloot SAM has two objectives: to describe the internal economy of Diepsloot and to identify the ways it is linked to and affected by the rest of South Africa. We initially proposed constructing a biregional SAM, showing both

Diepsloot and South Africa in a single format. This has been done for countries (van Seventer and Schade 2008) and also for regions within countries, where, for example, a provincial SAM may be embedded in a national SAM. This approach has two advantages: First, at the construction level, the consistency requirements of the overall SAM can be helpful in estimating some flows. Second, significant feedback effects may operate in both directions. For example, an increase in motor production in the Eastern Cape will increase its demand for inputs sourced from other provinces, raising incomes there, which may in turn increase the demand for agricultural produce in the Eastern Cape.

Although it may still be possible to construct such a matrix showing Diepsloot embedded in, say, the broader Gauteng economy, we have not done so in our prototype for several reasons:

- Matching the flows across the two economies would, in practice, lead to a loss of information about the Diepsloot economy, which we wanted the initial prototype to focus on.
- The data suggest that the Diepsloot economy is small enough that the feedback effects involving the rest of the country that a biregional SAM might capture are likely to be insignificant.
- The data do not enable us to capture the structure of the linkages, as opposed to their size. For example, the HS asked respondents whether they worked outside Diepsloot but not which sector they worked in.
- No SAM for either Gauteng Province or South Africa was publicly available in the reference year.

Our SAM therefore captures Diepsloot's economic linkages with the rest of South Africa through a single institutional account, which acts in the same way as the rest-of-the-world account does in a national SAM, capturing all transactions between residents and foreigners (defined as non-Diepsloot residents). Thus, for example, wages earned by Diepsloot residents outside Diepsloot are depicted as factor payments from abroad. In that way, we capture the level of transactions between the two economies, and some broad structure in the nature of the flows, but not a lot of detailed structure. It is debatable whether such detailed structure would make much difference.

We do not have a separate rest-of-the-world account, effectively assuming that Diepsloot does not deal directly with the world outside South Africa; all such transactions are mediated through South Africa. This seems reasonable as far as most flows are concerned, but, given the high proportion of foreign immigrants living in Diepsloot, remittances might constitute a significant direct flow. We do not capture that.

Not constructing the biregional SAM means we have not been able to take advantage of the consistency requirements referred to above. However, as explained in the separate report on data, we have drawn on the 2011 South African Supply and Use Tables in an ad hoc manner to develop some of the required data.

Construction of the SAM

The data used to build the SAM come from a number of sources—the primary sources being the Diepsloot enterprise census (EC), the ES based on the EC, and the HS conducted for this report, whose findings are presented in chapters 6 and 7.

The EC aimed to compile a list of all enterprises in Diepsloot, with a minimal amount of descriptive data to classify the sector of operation (based on the main product sold or the main service offered). Each enterprise was also classified into one of six strata, based on a combination of the owner's nationality (South African, Other African, or Non-African) and the number of employees ("two or less" or "three or more").

The EC identified 2,557 Diepsloot enterprises. It is not possible to assess how complete the EC coverage was. However, because the process involved identifying enterprises by walking the streets, it certainly missed many operations not visible from the street. In addition, the HS asked whether any businesses were run from the house and, if so, whether they were visible from the street. Less than 10 percent (74 out of the 800-household sample) indicated they did run home-based businesses, and, of those, fewer than half (30 out of 74) indicated they were not visible from the street. Without investigating whether these businesses were associated with particular household characteristics, this finding would suggest that the EC may have missed a total of 2,500 such enterprises. These are likely to be small, family-based informal enterprises.

From the strata derived in the EC, we generated a stratified sample of 454 enterprises, which the ES then investigated in depth through interviews with business owners. Because the ES sampling strategy missed some activities identified in the EC and deemed to be important for constructing the SAM, we selected a supplementary set of 10 enterprises from the EC for further data collection.

The HS comprised 800 households. As detailed in chapter 7, we allocate the expenditures recorded in the HS to the relevant SAM commodity groups (goods, services, and expenditures grouped by whether they were produced or bought within or outside Diepsloot). Other outlays comprise transfers and income tax payments, and savings completes the expenditures. On the income side, we use labor and capital income earned locally, and we assume that the residual to match household expenditures is earned outside Diepsloot from labor.

In addition to these primary instruments, interviews with a nonrandom sample of 15 institutions obtained data from important institutions. The responses were disappointing, and thus the data on institutions were supplemented with data gathered from various reports and the Internet. In particular, this effort allowed us to complete the expenditures of the public sector, education, health, and NPIs.

A Prototype SAM for Diepsloot
A Macro SAM

A prototype SAM for Diepsloot is shown in macro format below in table 8.3 as well as in a relatively disaggregated format in table 8.5.

Table 8.3 A Prototype Macro SAM for Diepsloot, 2012

R, thousands, 2012 current prices

	Activities	Commodities	Trade margins	Labor	Enterprises	Rent	Enterprises	Households	Government	Nonprofit institutions	Tax	Saving = Inv	Rest of SA	Total
Activities		662,809	182,491	n.a.	n.a.	n.a.	n.a.	n.a.	n.a.	n.a.	n.a.	n.a.	n.a.	845,300
Commodities	188,142	n.a.	n.a.	n.a.	n.a.	n.a.	n.a.	2,265,624	170,412	188,556	n.a.	2,746	n.a.	2,815,479
Trade margins	n.a.	182,491	n.a.	n.a.	n.a.	n.a.	n.a.	n.a.	n.a.	n.a.	n.a.	n.a.	n.a.	182,491
Labor	275,318	n.a.	n.a.	n.a.	n.a.	n.a.	n.a.	n.a.	n.a.	n.a.	n.a.	n.a.	1,555,563	1,830,881
Enterprises	152,355	n.a.	n.a.	n.a.	n.a.	n.a.	n.a.	n.a.	n.a.	n.a.	n.a.	n.a.	227,686	380,041
Rent	227,478	n.a.	n.a.	n.a.	n.a.	n.a.	n.a.	n.a.	n.a.	n.a.	n.a.	n.a.	n.a.	227,478
Enterprises	n.a.	n.a.	n.a.	n.a.	355,523	n.a.	n.a.	n.a.	n.a.	n.a.	n.a.	n.a.	15,731	371,254
Households	n.a.	n.a.	n.a.	1,693,342	n.a.	227,478	386,097	33,594	n.a.	n.a.	n.a.	n.a.	67,582	2,408,092
Government	n.a.	n.a.	n.a.	n.a.	n.a.	n.a.	n.a.	n.a.	n.a.	n.a.	54,767	n.a.	170,412	225,179
Nonprofit institutions	n.a.	n.a.	n.a.	n.a.	n.a.	n.a.	n.a.	n.a.	n.a.	n.a.	n.a.	n.a.	188,556	188,556
Tax	2,008	13,822	n.a.	n.a.	n.a.	n.a.	1,844	37,093	n.a.	n.a.	n.a.	n.a.	n.a.	54,767
Saving = Inv	n.a.	n.a.	n.a.	n.a.	n.a.	n.a.	−16,688	71,782	n.a.	n.a.	n.a.	n.a.	−52,348	2,746
Rest of SA	n.a.	1,956,356	n.a.	137,539	24,518	n.a.	n.a.	n.a.	54,767	n.a.	n.a.	n.a.	n.a.	2,173,181
Total	**845,300**	**2,815,479**	**182,491**	**1,830,881**	**380,041**	**227,478**	**371,254**	**2,408,092**	**225,179**	**188,556**	**54,767**	**2,746**	**2,173,181**	

Note: SAM = Social Accounting Matrix; R = rand; SA = South Africa; Inv = investment; n.a. = not applicable.

Only aggregate economic flows are shown. A "macro" SAM shows the main flows in the economy as the aggregate activity of each type of account (or actor) in both a row (the account's receipts) and a column (the account's spending transactions).

The prototype macro SAM tells us that the equivalent of gross domestic product (GDP) at market prices for Diepsloot is estimated at R 671 million. It includes R 2.3 billion in household expenditure, R 170 million in government expenditure, R 189 million by NPIs, R 3 million in investment, and a trade balance of about –R 2 billion. The latter is equivalent to total imports of goods and services since there are no exports.

On the income side, the SAM includes R 275 million in factor payments to labor, R 152 million in payments to capital (gross operating surplus), R 227 million in payments to capital as housing rents, R 2 million in activity taxes, and R 14 million in sales taxes.[5]

If we factor in the net factor payments to and from the rest of world (in this case, South Africa), we arrive at the equivalent of gross national product (GNP) for Diepsloot. Net factor payments are estimated at R 1,621 million so that the GNP equivalent can be estimated at R 2,292 million. A small correction for net indirect taxes allows us to calculate gross national income (GNI) at R 2,278 million.

In addition, with a number of other payments to and receipts from the rest of South Africa, we can construct a balance on the current account. The trade balance of Diepsloot, as noted above, is estimated to be –R 1,958 million (total imports of goods and services), while net transfer receipts are R 2,008 million. The balance on current account is then R 52 million.

What does it tell us about the economy? Predictably, most income available to residents of Diepsloot is earned outside the township. Of R 1.83 billion in total household wage income in Diepsloot, about R 1.55 billion, or 85 percent, is earned outside the township.

A Disaggregated SAM

Next, we seek to extract more detail about the Diepsloot economy from another prototype SAM that, relative to the macro SAM, is somewhat disaggregated, as seen in table 8.5. Among the activities in the Diepsloot economy (columns 1–3 of table 8.4), the four main ones are retail, other services, education, and public administration. The distribution of income between factors (labor and capital) differs across industries (as shown in columns 2–3). As expected (and mainly because of the underlying assumptions), large shares are recorded for capital income in retail, accommodation, and "other services"—the latter mainly due to housing rents. However, labor gets a relatively large share of income from manufacturing (although the activity is small), public administration, and education.

The commodity information (columns 4 and 5 of table 8.4) shows that the highest shares of household expenditure on various commodities (column 4) are recorded for manufacturing goods produced outside Diepsloot (47.1 percent) and "other services" (32.6 percent), with much of the latter associated with

Table 8.4 Selected Structural Features of the Diepsloot Economy, 2012
Percent

	1	2	3	4	5
	GDP share	*Wages and salaries share of GDP*	*Gross operating surplus share of GDP*	*HH exp share*	*Import ratio[a]*
Description	*Activities*	*Activities*	*Activities*	*Commodities*	*Commodities*
Agr/Min/Electr	0.0			5.7	100.0
Diepsloot manufacturing	0.5	64.2	35.8	5.5	91.5
Non-Diepsloot manufacturing	0.0			47.1	100.0
Construction	0.1	100.0	0.0	0.1	59.5
Ratail	22.8	15.5	84.5		0.0
Hotels and restaurants	4.6	13.4	86.6	6.3	61.4
Post and telecommunication	0.0	100.0	0.0	1.3	98.9
Public administration	14.4	89.4	10.6	0.2	14.2
Education	19.4	99.9	0.1	1.0	7.1
Health	0.02			0.4	23.6
Other services[b]	32.7	1.7	98.3	32.6	71.0

Note: GDP = gross domestic product; GOS = gross operating surplus; HH exp = household expenditure. "Activities" designate income-generating activities. "Commodities" designate expenditures on goods/services.

a. "Import ratio" = percentage of expenditures on commodities not produced in Diepsloot (at basic prices, excluding margins and sales taxes).

b. "Other services" include wholesale trade; transport services; housing rents; and financial intermediation, insurance, real estate, and business services.

housing rents, transport, and financial intermediation services. Column 5 shows import ratios (at basic prices, that is, excluding margins and sales taxes)—the shares of expenditures on commodities not produced in Diepsloot. By assumption, there are no imports of retail services. Note the relatively low import share for education, public administration, and health services.

Multipliers for Diepsloot

A standard use of SAMs is to construct various multipliers for the economy concerned. Many sources explain the technicalities of SAM multipliers (for example, Pyatt and Round 1979; Round 2003), so we give only an intuitive account here. Some flows in the SAM emanate primarily from outside Diepsloot's circular flow of income. For example, the income flowing into Diepsloot from the rest of South Africa is driven by the South African economy, not Diepsloot's. These exogenous inflows, or injections, add to incomes in Diepsloot. Furthermore, the recipients of these incomes spend them, creating additional incomes. Thus an injection raises incomes in Diepsloot both directly and indirectly. Multiplier analysis measures this impact by measuring the ratio of the overall rise in income to the initial rise in the injection.

SAM multipliers differ from standard macroeconomic multipliers because they work not only through aggregate injections into and leakages from the circular flow of final goods but also through flows of intermediate goods between activities. The rise in demand for one good creates a rise in demand for goods used in its production and so on. So the size of the multiplier depends in part upon these internal linkages. We will see later that we can decompose the multipliers to gain more insight into what determines them.

Multiplier Calculations

A preliminary sense of Diepsloot's multipliers can be gleaned from table 8.5. The second column shows the impact on value added (at factor costs) for a R 1 million increase in exogenous final demand for the commodities listed in the leftmost column. Multipliers from a South Africa-wide SAM (derived from a 2009 SAM used at the National Treasury) are presented in the last two columns for comparison purposes.

Table 8.6 shows that a R 1 million increase in the demand for agriculture, mining, and electricity has no impact on value added and household income in Diepsloot directly or indirectly, because the township produces no such goods. The same result might be expected for non-Diepsloot manufacturing (so labeled to specify production outside the township), but those results (in the third row) do show some impact. The reason is that some of these goods are locally purchased, as the HS shows. Although not produced locally, the trading of such products in the township generates a margin that contributes to value added and hence household income. Interestingly, a similar increase in demand for locally produced, but also imported, manufacturing (shown in the second row), shows only a slightly higher impact.

Significant impacts can be expected from the exogenous demand for construction goods and government services (public administration, health, and education), although the former is based on only a few ES observations. Government services do employ a relatively large number of workers, so one can expect some impact there, even if most of those workers do not necessarily live in the township. The multiplier estimate of "other services" and accommodation is relatively large and can be associated with the rental activities (regular, imputed, and boarding). Still, comparable multipliers for construction and government services from a South African SAM suggest much higher impacts, as can be seen in the last two columns.

In the last two rows, we show the impact of a R 1 million increase in labor payments and household income. These impacts can be thought of as originating from employment or wage growth in the rest of South Africa, through a public works program (labor) or transfers. In the case of labor, net output in Diepsloot rises by R 1.2 million, but household income rises by only R 1.1 million. In the case of a transfer to households of R 1 million, net output goes up by only R 0.2 million, while household income goes up by R 1.18 million. Still, relative to South Africa as a whole, the Diepsloot multipliers are smaller by a magnitude of several units.

Multiplier Analysis

The lack of significant multipliers in Diepsloot can easily be understood from figure 8.1, a simplified depiction of the circular income flow in Diepsloot.

Table 8.5 A Prototype Disaggregated SAM for Diepsloot, 2012

R, millions

		1	2	3	4	5	6	7	8	9
		A01_AMEW	A02_DMAN	A03_NMAN	A04_CONS	A05_RETL	A06_ACCM	A07_TCOM	A08_GOVT	A09_EDUC
1	A01_AMEW	–	–	–	–	–	–	–	–	–
2	A02_DMAN	–	–	–	–	–	–	–	–	–
3	A03_NMAN	–	–	–	–	–	–	–	–	–
4	A04_CONS	–	–	–	–	–	–	–	–	–
5	A05_RETL	–	–	–	–	–	–	–	–	–
6	A06_ACCM	–	–	–	–	–	–	–	–	–
7	A07_TCOM	–	–	–	–	–	–	–	–	–
8	A08_GOVT	–	–	–	–	–	–	–	–	–
9	A09_EDUC	–	–	–	–	–	–	–	–	–
10	A10_HLTH	–	–	–	–	–	–	–	–	–
11	A11_NPRF	–	–	–	–	–	–	–	–	–
12	A12_OSRV	–	–	–	–	–	–	–	–	–
13	C01_AMEW	–	270	–	12	4,289	629	65	1,183	1,321
14	C02_DMAN	–	1,178	–	–	239	242	–	1,309	1,152
15	C03_NMAN	–	3,745	–	456	8,674	22,810	115	14,924	6,112
16	C04_CONS	–	–	–	–	–	–	–	748	312
17	C05_RETL	–	–	–	–	–	–	–	–	–
18	C06_ACCM	–	–	–	–	–	–	–	472	208
19	C07_TCOM	–	394	–	15	2,956	166	113	7,657	1,087
20	C08_GOVT	–	–	–	–	–	–	–	22,096	–
21	C09_EDUC	–	–	–	–	–	–	–	–	50
22	C10_HLTH	–	–	–	–	–	–	–	3,672	3,382
23	C11_NPRF	–	–	–	–	–	–	–	–	–
24	C12_OSRV	–	519	–	205	16,406	698	77	23,020	4,651
25	C12_MARG	–	–	–	–	–	–	–	–	–
26	F1_DLAB	–	2,108	–	395	23,198	4,032	76	84,266	127,275
27	F3_DGOS	–	1,173	–	–	126,373	6,823	–	9,992	119
28	F5_RENT	–	–	–	–	–	19,137	–	–	–
29	I4_ENTP	–	–	–	–	–	–	–	–	–
30	I1_HHLD	–	–	–	–	–	–	–	–	–
31	I2_GOVT	–	–	–	–	–	–	–	–	–
32	I3_NPRF	–	–	–	–	–	–	–	–	–
33	T1_ITAX	–	–	–	–	–	–	–	–	–
34	T2_LTAX	–	78	–	2	356	135	–	1,075	16
35	T3_CTAX	–	–	–	–	–	–	–	–	–
36	SAVINV	–	–	–	–	–	–	–	–	–
37	ROSAFR	–	–	–	–	–	–	–	–	–
38	TOTAL	–	9,466	–	1,084	182,491	54,671	447	170,412	145,686

10	11	12	13	14	15	16	17	18	19
A10_HLTH	A11_NPRF	A12_OSRV	C01_AMEW	C02_DMAN	C03_NMAN	C04_CONS	C05_RETL	C06_ACCM	C07_TCOM
–	–	–	–	–	–	–	–	–	–
–	–	–	–	9,207	258	–	–	–	–
–	–	–	–	–	–	–	–	–	–
–	–	–	–	–	–	1,084	–	–	–
–	–	–	–	–	–	–	–	–	–
–	–	–	–	–	–	–	–	54,671	–
–	–	–	–	–	–	–	–	–	447
–	–	–	–	–	–	–	–	–	–
–	–	–	–	–	–	–	–	–	–
–	–	–	–	–	–	–	–	–	–
–	–	–	–	–	–	–	–	–	–
–	–	–	–	–	–	–	–	–	–
731	126	409	–	–	–	–	–	–	–
834	33	30	–	–	–	–	–	–	–
4,462	816	13,503	–	–	–	–	–	–	–
149	39	–	–	–	–	–	–	–	–
–	–	–	–	–	–	–	–	–	–
46	21	–	–	–	–	–	–	–	–
755	131	162	–	–	–	–	–	–	–
2,128	2	–	–	–	–	–	–	–	–
11	7	–	–	–	–	–	–	–	–
85	49	–	–	–	–	–	–	–	–
–	–	–	–	–	–	–	–	–	–
3,839	1,041	1,103	–	–	–	–	–	–	–
–	–	–	9	18,842	163,640	–	–	–	–
7,934	22,317	3,717	–	–	–	–	–	–	–
5,945	–	1,931	–	–	–	–	–	–	–
–	–	208,341	–	–	–	–	–	–	–
–	–	–	–	–	–	–	–	–	–
–	–	–	–	–	–	–	–	–	–
–	–	–	–	–	–	–	–	–	–
–	–	–	–	–	–	–	–	–	–
–	–	–	–	–	–	–	–	–	–
275	–	71	–	–	–	–	–	–	–
–	–	–	–	890	40	20	–	1,374	7
–	–	–	–	–	–	–	–	–	–
–	–	–	137,696	99,667	980,840	1,593	0	86,835	41,935
27,194	24,583	229,267	137,706	128,607	1,144,778	2,697	0	142,879	42,388

table continues next page

Table 8.5 **A Prototype Disaggregated SAM for Diepsloot, 2012** *(continued)*

R, millions

		20	21	22	23	24	25	26	27	28
		C08_GOVT	C09_EDUC	C10_HLTH	C11_NPRF	C12_OSRV	C12_MARG	F1_DLAB	F3_DGOS	F5_RENT
1	A01_AMEW	–	–	–	–	–	–	–	–	–
2	A02_DMAN	–	–	–	–	–	–	–	–	–
3	A03_NMAN	–	–	–	–	–	–	–	–	–
4	A04_CONS	–	–	–	–	–	–	–	–	–
5	A05_RETL	–	–	–	–	–	182,491	–	–	–
6	A06_ACCM	–	–	–	–	–	–	–	–	–
7	A07_TCOM	–	–	–	–	–	–	–	–	–
8	A08_GOVT	170,412	–	–	–	–	–	–	–	–
9	A09_EDUC	–	145,686	–	–	–	–	–	–	–
10	A10_HLTH	–	–	27,194	–	–	–	–	–	–
11	A11_NPRF	–	–	–	24,583	–	–	–	–	–
12	A12_OSRV	–	–	–	–	229,267	–	–	–	–
13	C01_AMEW	–	–	–	–	–	–	–	–	–
14	C02_DMAN	–	–	–	–	–	–	–	–	–
15	C03_NMAN	–	–	–	–	–	–	–	–	–
16	C04_CONS	–	–	–	–	–	–	–	–	–
17	C05_RETL	–	–	–	–	–	–	–	–	–
18	C06_ACCM	–	–	–	–	–	–	–	–	–
19	C07_TCOM	–	–	–	–	–	–	–	–	–
20	C08_GOVT	–	–	–	–	–	–	–	–	–
21	C09_EDUC	–	–	–	–	–	–	–	–	–
22	C10_HLTH	–	–	–	–	–	–	–	–	–
23	C11_NPRF	–	–	–	–	–	–	–	–	–
24	C12_OSRV	–	–	–	–	–	–	–	–	–
25	C12_MARG	–	–	–	–	–	–	–	–	–
26	F1_DLAB	–	–	–	–	–	–	–	–	–
27	F3_DGOS	–	–	–	–	–	–	–	–	–
28	F5_RENT	–	–	–	–	–	–	–	–	–
29	I4_ENTP	–	–	–	–	–	–	–	355,523	–
30	I1_HHLD	–	–	–	–	–	–	1,693,342	–	227,478
31	I2_GOVT	–	–	–	–	–	–	–	–	–
32	I3_NPRF	–	–	–	–	–	–	–	–	–
33	T1_ITAX	–	–	–	–	–	–	–	–	–
34	T2_LTAX	–	–	–	–	–	–	–	–	–
35	T3_CTAX	599	9,329	1,032	–	531	–	–	–	–
36	SAVINV	–	–	–	–	–	–	–	–	–
37	ROSAFR	28,127	11,079	8,421	0	560,163	–	137,539	24,518	–
38	TOTAL	199,139	166,095	36,647	24,583	789,961	182,491	1,830,881	380,041	227,478

Note: SAM = Social Accounting Matrix; - = no value. See the key for other definitions of codes used in the table.
AMEW = Agr/Min/Electr; DMAN = Diepsloot manufacturing; NMAN = Non-Diepsloot manufacturing; CONS = Construction; RETL = Retail;
ACCM = Hotels and restaurants; TCOM = Post and telecommunication; GOVT = Public Administration; EDUC = Education; HLTH = Health;
NPRF = Non-Profit Institutions; OSRV = Other Services; F1_DLAB = Wages; F3_DGOS = Gross Operating Surplus; F5_RENT = Rent;
I4_ENTP = Enterprise; I1_HHLD = Households; I2_GOVT = Public Administration; I3_NPRF = Non-Profit Institutions; T1_ITAX = Direct taxes;
T2_LTAX = Local taxes; T3_CTAX = Indirect taxes; SAVINV = Accumulation; ROSAFR = Rest of South Africa.

29	30	31	32	33	34	35	36	37	38
I4_ENTP	I1_HHLD	I2_GOVT	I3_NPRF	T1_ITAX	T2_LTAX	T3_CTAX	SAVINV	ROSAFR	TOTAL
–	–	–	–	–	–	–	–	0	0
–	–	–	–	–	–	–	–	0	9,466
–	–	–	–	–	–	–	–	0	0
–	–	–	–	–	–	–	–	0	1,084
–	–	–	–	–	–	–	–	0	182,491
–	–	–	–	–	–	–	–	0	54,671
–	–	–	–	–	–	–	–	0	447
–	–	–	–	–	–	–	–	0	170,412
–	–	–	–	–	–	–	–	0	145,686
–	–	–	–	–	–	–	–	0	27,194
–	–	–	–	–	–	–	–	0	24,583
–	–	–	–	–	–	–	–	0	229,267
–	128,671	–	–	–	–	–	–	0	137,706
–	123,591	–	–	–	–	–	–	0	128,607
–	1,066,728	–	–	–	–	–	2,434	0	1,144,778
–	1,137	–	–	–	–	–	312	0	2,697
–	–	–	–	–	–	–	–	0	0
–	142,132	–	–	–	–	–	–	0	142,879
–	28,952	–	–	–	–	–	–	0	42,388
–	4,500	170,412	–	–	–	–	–	0	199,139
–	23,389	–	142,637	–	–	–	–	0	166,095
–	8,122	–	21,337	–	–	–	–	0	36,647
–	–	–	24,583	–	–	–	–	0	24,583
–	738,402	–	–	–	–	–	–	0	789,961
–	–	–	–	–	–	–	–	0	182,491
–	–	–	–	–	–	–	–	1,555,563	1,830,881
–	–	–	–	–	–	–	–	227,686	380,041
–	–	–	–	–	–	–	–	0	227,478
–	–	–	–	–	–	–	–	15,731	371,254
386,097	33,594	–	–	–	–	–	–	67,582	2,408,092
–	–	–	–	38,937	2,008	13,822	–	170,412	225,179
–	–	–	–	–	–	–	–	188,556	188,556
1,844	37,093	–	–	–	–	–	–	0	38,937
–	–	–	–	–	–	–	–	0	2,008
–	–	–	–	–	–	–	–	0	13,822
−16,688	71,782	–	–	–	–	–	–	−52,348	2,746
–	–	54,767	–	–	–	–	–	–	2,173,181
371,254	2,408,092	225,179	188,556	38,937	2,008	13,822	2,746	2,173,181	

Table 8.6 Selected Multipliers, by Commodity Type, for Diepsloot (2012) and South Africa (2009) SAMs
Impact (in R, millions) from a R 1 million rise in exogenous demand

	Diepsloot			South Africa	
	Comm output multiplier[a]	VA multiplier[b]	HH income multiplier[c]	VA multiplier	HH income multiplier
Agr/Min/Electr	0.000	0.000	0.000	1.253	0.995
Dipsloot manufacturing	1.264	0.186	0.182	1.052	0.861
Non-Diepsloot manufacturing	0.000	0.146	0.143	0.956	0.781
Construction	1.271	0.224	0.215	1.292	1.045
Retail	1.242	0.000	0.000	1.441	1.184
Hotels and restaurants	1.281	0.278	0.277	1.121	0.893
Post and telecommunication	1.182	0.003	0.003	1.296	1.033
Public administration	1.357	0.705	0.674	1.639	1.443
Education	1.215	0.942	0.893	1.404	1.142
Health	1.314	0.553	0.535	1.398	1.140
Non-Profit institutions	1.199	1.103	1.046	1.372	1.099
Other services[d]	1.281	0.330	0.333	1.429	1.169
Diepsloot labor[e]	1.185	1.192	1.129	1.942	1.811
Households[f]	1.281	0.207	1.220	0.944	1.815

Source: South Africa data from National Treasury 2009.
Note: SAM = Social Accounting Matrix; VA = value added; HH = household; R = rand.
a. The commodity output multiplier shows the increase (in R, millions) in net output from a R 1 million increase in exogenous demand for the specified product or activity type.
b. The VA multipliers show the increase in value added (in R, millions, at factor costs) from a R 1 million increase in exogenous demand for the specified activity type.
c. The HH income multipliers show the rise (in R, millions) in household income from a R 1 million increase in exogenous demand for the specified activity type.
d. "Other services" include wholesale trade; transport services; housing rents; and financial intermediation, insurance, real estate, and business services.
e. The "Labor payment" multipliers show the impacts of employment or wage growth in the rest of South Africa—for instance, through the national public works program.
f. The "Households" multipliers show the increases from a R 1 million rise in exogenous transfers—for example, through public transfers or (in the case of the South Africa household multipliers) remittances.

Suppose that wages rise for Diepsloot residents who work outside the township. That increase will inject income into Diepsloot households, which will spend it in three different ways:

- Much of it will simply go toward purchases of goods from outside Diepsloot—a direct leakage that curtails the size of the multiplier directly.
- Part of it may be "transferred" to other Diepsloot households—for example, as direct transfers to other households or as additional rents.[6] Insofar as these transfers continue to circulate within the household economy of Diepsloot, they contribute to the overall multiplier. But in practice this circulation, shown on the left of figure 8.1, is small.
- Part of it will go toward purchases from inside Diepsloot. This spending affects the township's enterprises, raising their income, the bulk of which flows out of Diepsloot to pay for goods and services sourced outside. A small part circulates around the enterprise economy of Diepsloot, creating a multiplier circuit like

Figure 8.1 Stylized Diagram of Diepsloot's Circular Economic Flows

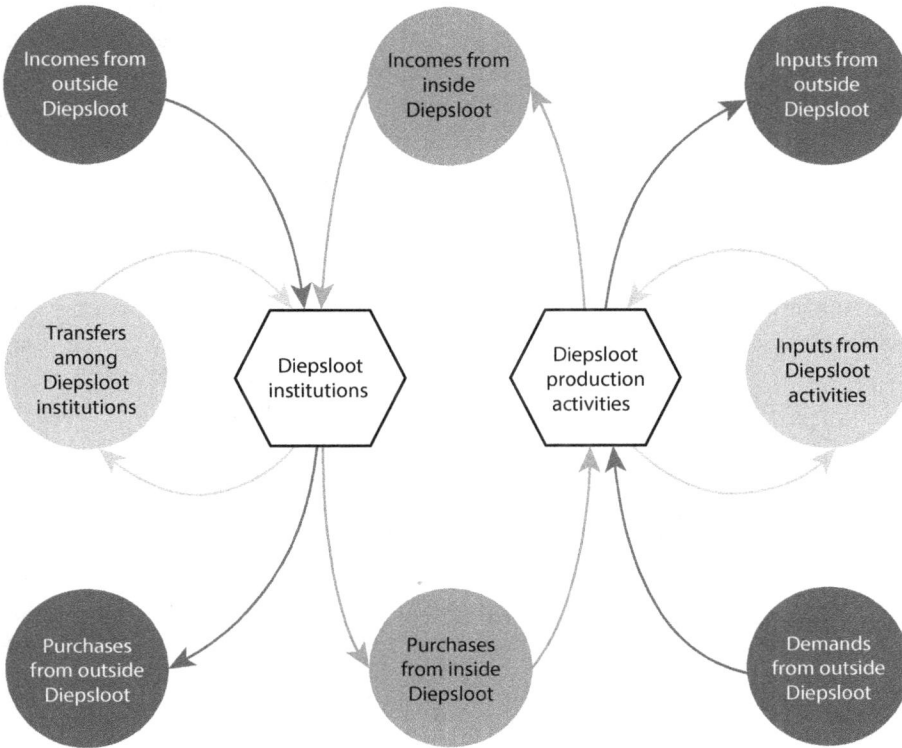

that of the household economy and shown on the right of figure 8.1. Again, this effect is small because firms in Diepsloot tend not to source inputs from other firms in Diepsloot. Some of the firms' income might flow back to households in the form of factor incomes—another small effect.

So the small multipliers arise essentially because of the weak linkages within Diepsloot. This is the outcome that was expected at the start of this project. Unfortunately, our process of data collection and analysis has not uncovered some strong but hidden linkages that we had overlooked in forming our prior expectations.

Policy Implications

We can put some flesh on the bones of the previous section by applying the multiplier analysis to specific interventions. To illustrate, we consider South Africa's Community Works Program (CWP) and a proposal for special economic zones. We emphasize (and will do so repeatedly in what follows) that this discussion aims simply to show what the SAM multipliers suggest, not to evaluate either of these interventions.

Economics of South African Townships • http://dx.doi.org/10.1596/978-1-4648-0301-7

Application: Community Works Program

The CWP is a national pilot program to provide minimum guaranteed employment. By 2011, the CWP operated at some 154 sites around South Africa, including Diepsloot.[7] It has provided a guaranteed two days per week of paid work to well over 100,000 participants. The CWP aims, in part, to provide the qualitative benefits of work experience. At the same time, the guaranteed income not only assists the direct recipients but also injects income into their communities, with potential multiplier effects. To illustrate the use of the Diepsloot multiplier, we consider the impact of a tenfold increase in the current CWP expenditure in Diepsloot. We emphasize that the multiplier analysis at best captures the quantitative impact on the economy and does not address the qualitative aspects that may, in the long run, be more important.[8] We also emphasize that this is not intended as an assessment of CWP but is merely as an illustration of how multiplier analysis might be used.

In 2011 the CWP expenditure on the Diepsloot site was approximately R 3.2 million, of which R 2.1 million was on wages and R 1.1 million on various nonlabor inputs. According to the project records, all of the latter were purchased outside Diepsloot, so only the wage component was an injection into the economy. We scale this up tenfold and exogenously inject just over R 20.7 million into Diepsloot's labor income account from the rest of South Africa. Assuming the nonlabor expenditures rise in proportion, the total CWP expenditure on the Diepsloot site would increase to some R 32 million.

This R 20.7 million increase in labor income directly increases total labor income, as estimated in the SAM, by 1.1 percent. The multiplier effects add a further 0.1 percent of indirect income, so that the total direct and indirect impact on labor income constitutes 1.2 percent of current labor income or just over R 21 million. The total direct and indirect impact on Diepsloot's GDP (at factor cost) is just under R 25 million, or 1 percent, while the impact on household income is of similar relative magnitude (1 percent) or R 23.5 million. Thus, the modeled intervention has a secondary impact beyond the initial injection of around R 2 million on labor income, R 2.5 million on GDP, and R 2.3 million on household incomes.

Activities in Diepsloot that can be expected to benefit most are those that are relatively well represented in the township (such as manufacturing, retail, and "other services"), all of which report impacts of just under 1 percent. Other sectors that are active in the township (such as construction, education, government, and health) report a negligible impact following this intervention.

These impacts can be regarded as modest, given that they arise from an increase in CWP expenditure of R 32 million. Of course, the R 10 million spent on nonwage components produced outside Diepsloot has an impact on other parts of the South African economy. This low impact arises from Diepsloot's lack of internal linkages as discussed in the previous section. One impact of the CWP may be to change those linkages over time, as the CWP participants use the pay received and experience gained to establish their own businesses. But it is not clear that the types of businesses established will create such internal linkages, since they tend toward trading activities, which have high and immediate leakages out of the economy.

The CWP can try to contribute to this process of structural change by sourcing nonwage components from within Diepsloot. However, under the township's current structure, these sources will probably themselves buy supplies from outside Diepsloot. Thus local procurement injects only the trading margin or markup on the goods into the Diepsloot economy. The CWP does promote some productive activities, such as vegetable growing, but we do not have any information on how the outputs are distributed.

These conclusions apply to any similar schemes in Diepsloot operated by charities and faith-based organizations. They have important direct impacts on the lives of recipients, but their multiplier incomes are low.

These conclusions, being specific to Diepsloot as depicted in the SAM we have constructed, may not apply to other CWP sites. For example, it is possible that local economy production linkages may be stronger in rural areas or in older, more established urban settlements.

Application: Industrial Parks or Special Economic Zones

One proposal to stimulate development in Diepsloot is to locate industrial parks or possibly special economic zones close by. Indeed, the Gauteng Provincial Government is partnering with Century Property Development to establish a R 1.6 billion industrial park in the Diepsloot area (City of Johannesburg 2013). This park is reportedly expected to create 15,000 sustainable jobs on completion,[9] injecting R 1.8 billion per year into Diepsloot if all these jobs were filled by Diepsloot residents paid an average of R 10,000 per month. Clearly this represents a massive injection of income—possibly bigger than a similar increase of income for Diepsloot residents who working farther afield because the reduction in transport costs would leave people more income to spend on nontransport consumption. Some additional incomes could also be created if Diepsloot residents become entrepreneurs earning profits in the industrial park.

However, given the current structure of Diepsloot's economy, the multiplier effects of this substantial initiative will be small: total income in Diepsloot will rise by little more than the direct injection of incomes. Even if the boundaries of Diepsloot were changed to incorporate the industrial park, the multipliers would not change significantly unless the firms in the park had significant linkages to each other.

One of the main drivers of the Diepsloot multipliers, such as they are, is income generated through household rents, either explicit or imputed to owner-occupied housing. One effect that an industrial park or special economic zone might have is to speed up the influx of people into Diepsloot, as it becomes known that there are jobs nearby. To the extent that housing supplies do not keep up, this could raise rents and thus incomes of house owners. Our analysis has not taken that explicitly into account.

Conclusions

We constructed a SAM for Diepsloot and then used it to undertake some simple multiplier analysis of the Diepsloot economy. Our intention was to explore the extent to which the Diepsloot economy has some internal dynamism that enhances any external attempts to raise the incomes of Diepsloot residents. The analysis suggests that multipliers are very small, largely because the bulk of goods and services used by both households and enterprises in Diepsloot are sourced from outside.

At one level, this is disappointing; it would be gratifying to know that this area, home to a large number of people, is expanding rapidly and seems on the surface to have some local economic activity. On another level, one could ask why we should expect anything different from what is essentially a residential area. Had we carried out the same exercise on wealthier areas of Johannesburg, such as Observatory or Parkview, we would almost certainly have found even lower multipliers. So why should we expect Diepsloot to be different?

Expectations and Perceptions

In part we do have different expectations because of a perception that poor areas should have a more integrated local economy than rich ones. Poverty should make areas more inward-looking, more reliant on local (that is, "informal") activities than the rich are, since the latter can better access goods and services from afar, made more costly by high transport and retail costs.

From our study, this perception does not appear to play out in reality. Although there are local activities, these are largely services, with high "import" dependence. This highlights an economic conundrum of South African townships: whether such dependence stems from penetration of Diepsloot by large suppliers against whom the small local suppliers cannot compete, or from the preferences of relatively poor South Africans for the same quality of goods that their richer compatriots buy. There is evidence for both these hypotheses, but our study does not answer them.

Our perception that Diepsloot should be different is also because we know that the various mechanisms of apartheid forced townships to be more self-contained than they might otherwise have been. From this perspective, the relative youthfulness of Diepsloot may mean that its local economy has not had sufficient time to develop, and that we would find something different in other longer-established former townships. This is probably true, but could only be examined by undertaking similar studies elsewhere.

Further Study

How applicable are the findings of the present study to other similar areas of South Africa? If it is desirable for such areas to have more vibrant local economies, could appropriate policy interventions speed up their development? Our study has not directly addressed such issues. Moreover, the analysis undertaken here has not exhausted the potential of this SAM-based study. The data collected can be analyzed further in a number of ways. The household sector could be disaggregated further, possibly into those headed by South Africans and by non-South Africans, if not in other ways. The data on nonenterprise activities, particularly those of government and NPIs, could be improved. Some further disaggregation of the activities might also be possible. Taking the work further in these directions would deepen our insight into the economy, although we do not think those pursuits would change our principal conclusion that Diepsloot's multipliers are low.

The foregoing questions do raise the broader issue of whether studies similar to the present one might be useful in other areas. Our applications have only scratched the surface of what might be drawn from such studies for policy purposes. Local, provincial, and national governments benefit from greater knowledge about the nature of the areas under their jurisdictions. SAMs have the merit of providing a consistent and comprehensive framework of assembling such information, which can help inform the design of consistent policies based on viewing areas in a holistic rather than compartmentalized way. But SAMs are only one way of approaching these issues, and the cost of undertaking similar studies across the whole economy would be prohibitively high.

Nonetheless, it may be useful to develop this approach further, both theoretically and empirically, to better understand South Africa's township economies. They are home to many South Africans and to many of the poorest. If the ideal of inclusive growth is ever to be achieved, surely the townships are where significant development and policy efforts will have to be focused.

Notes

1. The Water Amenities Sanitation Services Upgrading Program (WASSUP) is a community organization that maintains and repairs public toilet facilities. Its mission: "When you go into the toilet, you go in with dignity; When you come out of the toilet, you come out with dignity." For more information, see the WASSUP website at http://www.stickysituations.org/wassup-diepsloot/.

2. MaJacky is Jacqueline Makhubele, who has cared for and sheltered homeless children since she moved to Diepsloot in 1996. To read more about her, see "MaJacky Cares for Diepsloot Kids" on the City of Johannesburg's website: http://www.joburg.org.za/index.php?option=com_content&id=6892:majacky-cares-for-diepsloot-kids&Itemid=210.

3. Zizanani (derived from Zulu, "helping each other") aims "to improve the lives of at-risk women and children through empowerment." The founder, artist Glenys van Halter, was drawn to Diepsloot in the mid-1990s following her experience teaching art to some of the township's children. Zizanani has established, among its many programs, a birthing center and other health services; several day-care centers and schools; an orphanage; three "houses of safety" (government-registered shelters for abused or abandoned children); and numerous counseling services, including support for those affected by HIV/AIDS (human immunodeficiency virus and acquired immune deficiency syndrome). For more information, see the Zizanani website at http://www.zizanani.co.za.

4. "Nonprofit institutions" is a rather cold term for many of the organizations we want to capture. Diepsloot has numerous organizations, both local and from outside, that do important community work. They are often initiatives started by impressive individuals who show initiative and commitment.

5. The taxes were mostly on educational services given the collection rate observed in the South Africa Supply and Use Tables.

6. In our SAM, we follow the standard practice of having rents paid to a real estate sector, which distributes gross operating surpluses to households. For purposes of the illustration, however, we ignore this intermediate circuit.

7. The CWP was initiated by TIPS, which managed the program's pilot phase before it was transferred to the Department of Cooperative Governance and Traditional Affairs in April 2010.

8. In this sense, our analysis does not capture the specificity of CWP, but applies *mutatis mutandis* to any scheme injecting wages into Diepsloot.

9. In addition, the park's development will temporarily boost construction sector jobs.

References

City of Johannesburg. 2013. "Diepsloot to Get a R 1,6 Billion Industrial Park." *News update*, City of Johannesburg website, February 27. http://www.joburg.org.za/index .php?option=com_content&id=8528:diepsloot-to-get-a-r16-billion-industrial-park &Itemid=266.

Lewis, B. D., and E. Thorbecke. 1992. "District-Level Economic Linkages in Kenya: Evidence Based on a Small Regional Social Accounting Matrix." *World Development* 20 (6): 881–97.

National Treasury. 2009. *Social Accounting Matrix*. Republic of South Africa, Pretoria.

Pyatt, G., and J. Round. 1979. "Accounting and Fixed Price Multipliers in a Social Accounting Matrix Framework." *Economic Journal* 89 (356): 850–73.

Round, J. I. 2003. "Constructing SAMs for Development Policy Analysis: Lessons Learned and Challenges Ahead." *Economic Systems Research* 15 (2): 161–83.

van Leeuwen, E. S., and P. Nijkamp. 2009. "Social Accounting Matrices: The Development and Application of SAMs at the Local Level." Serie Research Memoranda 0045, Faculty of Economics, Business Administration and Econometrics, VU University, Amsterdam.

van Seventer, D., and K. Schade. 2008. "Linking a South African and Namibian Social Accounting Matrix: An Attempt to Quantify Spillover Effects in a Comparative Static Fixed Coefficient Impact Analysis Framework." Namibian Economic Policy Research Unit, Windhoek, Namibia.

green
press
INITIATIVE